Mastering Bash

Automate daily tasks with Ba[sh]

Giorgio Zarrelli

BIRMINGHAM - MUMBAI

Mastering Bash

Copyright © 2017 Packt Publishing

All rights reserved. No part of this book may be reproduced, stored in a retrieval system, or transmitted in any form or by any means, without the prior written permission of the publisher, except in the case of brief quotations embedded in critical articles or reviews.

Every effort has been made in the preparation of this book to ensure the accuracy of the information presented. However, the information contained in this book is sold without warranty, either express or implied. Neither the author, nor Packt Publishing, and its dealers and distributors will be held liable for any damages caused or alleged to be caused directly or indirectly by this book.

Packt Publishing has endeavored to provide trademark information about all of the companies and products mentioned in this book by the appropriate use of capitals. However, Packt Publishing cannot guarantee the accuracy of this information.

First published: June 2017

Production reference: 1190617

Published by Packt Publishing Ltd.
Livery Place
35 Livery Street
Birmingham
B3 2PB, UK.
ISBN 978-1-78439-687-9

www.packtpub.com

Credits

Author
Giorgio Zarrelli

Reviewer
Sebastian F. Colomar

Commissioning Editor
Kartikey Pandey

Acquisition Editor
Rahul Nair

Content Development Editor
Abhishek Jadhav

Technical Editor
Aditya Khadye

Copy Editors
Dipti Mankame
Yesha Gangani

Project Coordinator
Judie Jose

Proofreader
Safis Editing

Indexer
Rekha Nair

Graphics
Kirk D'Penha

Production Coordinator
Melwyn Dsa

About the Author

Giorgio Zarrelli is a passionate GNU/Linux system administrator and Debian user, but has worked over the years with Windows, Mac, and OpenBSD, writing scripts, programming, installing and configuring services--whatever is required from an IT guy. He started tinkering seriously with servers back in his university days, when he took part in the Computational Philosophy Laboratory and was introduced to the Prolog language. As a young guy, he had fun being paid for playing games and write about them in video game magazines. Then he grew up and worked as an IT journalist and Nagios architect, and recently moved over to the threat intelligence field, where a lot of interesting stuff is happening nowadays.

Over the years, he has worked for start-ups and well-established companies, among them In3 incubator and Onebip as a database and systems administrator, IBM as QRadar support, and Anomali as CSO, trying to find the best ways to help companies make the best out of IT.

Giorgio has written several books in Italian on different topics related to IT, from Windows security to Linux system administration, covering MySQL DB administration and Bash scripting.

> *At last, some acknowledgments since we cannot do much without the help of the people who make our lives better. Firstly, Ilaria, who had to go through all the weekends and the mornings I spent writing instead of strolling downtown. Then, mum and dad and my brother, Maurizio. Being Italian, my mum would kill me if I did not acknowledge her--and, by the way, they are such an important part of my life. Let's keep it short, since I cannot thank all the people who enrich my life and have put some flourishes into this book. So let me thank my bosses at Anomali, Gabe and Mitul, for supporting me and letting me use a Mac (I do whatever needed to write a book, even if it is crazy) when my laptop broke and the replacement was stuck somewhere around the globe. Thanks to my editor, Abhishek, for being supportive, professional, and patient during the writing of this book. Finally, thank you, dear reader, for having a look at this book--sometimes IT can be boring; I've tried to make it fun.*

About the Reviewer

Sebastian F. Colomar is a GNU/Linux system engineer specializing in the scripting, installation, configuration, and maintenance of Linux servers for better security and performance.

He is currently an infrastructure architect at Hanscan, having been a consultant for scripting and Linux administration for many companies, such as IBM, Indra, Thales, Accelya, Accenture, AXA, Cetelem, RTVCM, EMT, and ESA.

www.PacktPub.com

For support files and downloads related to your book, please visit `www.PacktPub.com`.

Did you know that Packt offers eBook versions of every book published, with PDF and ePub files available? You can upgrade to the eBook version at `www.PacktPub.com` and as a print book customer, you are entitled to a discount on the eBook copy. Get in touch with us at `service@packtpub.com` for more details.

At `www.PacktPub.com`, you can also read a collection of free technical articles, sign up for a range of free newsletters and receive exclusive discounts and offers on Packt books and eBooks.

`https://www.packtpub.com/mapt`

Get the most in-demand software skills with Mapt. Mapt gives you full access to all Packt books and video courses, as well as industry-leading tools to help you plan your personal development and advance your career.

Why subscribe?

- Fully searchable across every book published by Packt
- Copy and paste, print, and bookmark content
- On demand and accessible via a web browser

Customer Feedback

Thanks for purchasing this Packt book. At Packt, quality is at the heart of our editorial process. To help us improve, please leave us an honest review on this book's Amazon page at https://www.amazon.com/dp/1784396877.

If you'd like to join our team of regular reviewers, you can e-mail us at customerreviews@packtpub.com. We award our regular reviewers with free eBooks and videos in exchange for their valuable feedback. Help us be relentless in improving our products!

Table of Contents

Preface	1
Chapter 1: Let's Start Programming	9
I/O redirection	13
Messing around with stdin, stdout, and stderr	18
Time for the interpreter: the sha-bang	21
Calling your script	23
Something went wrong, let's trace it	29
Variables	32
Assigning a variable	33
Keep the variable name safe	34
Variables with limited scope	35
Environment variables	37
Variable expansion	45
Pattern matching against variables	50
Special variables	55
Summary	60
Chapter 2: Operators	61
Arithmetic operators	61
The + operator	62
The - operator	63
The * operator	63
The / operator	63
The % operator	63
The ** operator	64
Assignment operators	64
The += operator	64
The -= operator	65
The *= operator	65
The /= operator	66
The %= operator	66
The ++ or -- operators	67
Bitwise operators	68
Left shift (<>)	70
Bitwise AND (&)	71

Bitwise OR (|)	72
Bitwise XOR (^)	72
Bitwise NOT (~)	72
Logical operators	74
Logical NOT (!)	74
Logical AND (&&)	75
Logical OR (||)	76
Comma operator (,)	77
Operators evaluation order and precedence in decreasing relevance	78
Exit codes	78
Exiting a script	81
Summary	84

Chapter 3: Testing — 85

What if...else	85
Test command recap	93
Testing files	94
Testing integers	112
Testing strings	119
More on tests	125
Summary	127

Chapter 4: Quoting and Escaping — 129

Special characters	130
The hash character (#)	130
The semicolon character (;)	131
The double semicolon character (;;)	132
The case terminator (;;&) and (;&))	133
The dot character (.)	133
The double quotes (	139
The single quotes ('...')	139
The comma character (,)	139
The ,, and , () case modificators	140
The ^^ and ^ () case modificators	140
The backslash (\\)	142
The forward slash (/)	142
'...'	142
The colon character (:)	142
The exclamation (!)	143
Keywords	143

The asterisk (*)	144
The double asterisk (**)	146
Test operators (?)	146
The substitution ($)	148
The parameter substitution (${})	149
The quoted string expansion ($'...')	149
The exit status ($?)	150
The process ID ($$)	150
Grouping the command (command1 ; command2 ; commandn)	150
Braces ({})	153
The full path ({} \;)	153
Expression ([])	153
Expression ([[]])	154
The array index ([])	154
Characters range ([])	154
Integer expansion ($[…])	155
Integer expansion (((..)))	155
>, &>, >&, >>, < and <>	155
The here document (<)	157
The pipe character (|)	157
The force redirection (>|)	158
The logical OR (||)	159
&	159
Logical AND (&&)	160
The dash character (-)	160
The double dash (--)	161
Operator =	161
Operator +	162
The modulo operator (%)	162
Operator ~	162
Operator ~+	162
Operator ~-	163
Operator ~=	163
Operator ^	163
The control characters (^ and ^^)	163
Quoting and escaping	**165**
The backslash (\)	165
Double quotes (	166
Single quotes (')	167

Summary	168
Chapter 5: Menus, Arrays, and Functions	**169**
The case statement	169
Arrays	185
Functions	200
Summary	208
Chapter 6: Iterations	**209**
The for loop	209
Let's do something while, until…	214
Exiting the loop with break and continue	216
Time to give our client a menu	218
CLI, passing the arguments to the command line	223
Summary	235
Chapter 7: Plug into the Real World	**237**
What is Nagios?	237
Active and passive checks	238
Active checks	238
Passive checks	238
Returning code and thresholds	241
Command and service definitions	243
Our first Nagios plugin	261
Summary	285
Chapter 8: We Want to Chat	**287**
The Slack messaging service	287
Slack WebHooks	290
What is a JSON?	293
Do you like cURLing?	294
Formatting our messages	297
Message attachments	306
Our wee chatty script for Slack	310
Summary	326
Chapter 9: Subshells, Signals, and Job Controls	**327**
What is a subshell?	328
Background processes	328
Signals	329
Job controls	331
Subshells and parallel processing	335

Summary	342
Chapter 10: Let's Make a Process Chat	**343**
Pipes	343
Redirection to a file	346
The command substitution	347
The process substitution	348
Environment variables	350
Coprocesses	352
/dev/tcp and /dev/udp	355
Netcat	357
Summary	365
Chapter 11: Living as a Daemon	**367**
What is a daemon?	367
nohup and &	368
nohup	372
disown	374
Double fork and setsid	375
Becoming a daemon	378
Trapping a daemon	378
Going dark with the daemon	384
Summary	388
Chapter 12: Remote Connections over SSH	**389**
What is SSH?	389
Configuration files	392
The sshd_config file	396
ssh_config	402
Passwordless connections	409
Configuring the server	409
Preparing the remote account	416
Configuring the client	418
Proxies and tunnels	423
Summary	428
Chapter 13: It's Time for a Timer	**429**
One shot at it	429
The cron scheduler	439
cron	440
Summary	451

Chapter 14: Time for Safety — 453
The restricted shell — 453
Restricted shells for OpenSSH — 458
Restricted sftp sessions with OpenSSH — 464
Summary — 482
Index — 483

Preface

Bash is a common tool for everyday tasks that almost every Linux user relies on. Whatever you want to do, you have to log in to a shell, and most of the time, it will be Bash. This book aims to explain how to use this tool to get the most out of it, whether it be programming a plugin or network client or simply explaining why a double dot means what it means, we will dig a bit deeper than usual to become fully confident with our shell. Starting from the basics but with a different point of view, we will climb up step by step, focusing on the programming side of our environment, looking at how to prevent any issues in setting up our recurring tasks and ensure that everything works fine. Make it once, take your time, debug, improve, and then fire and forget; as in old Linux saying states, "If it works, why change it?" So, since we are dealing with sayings, we could stick to the other two cornerstones: "KISS: Keep it simple, stupid" and "Do only one thing, but do it well." These are three principles around which Linux revolves: making something, not everything, and making it simple and reliable and taking your time to make it work well so you do not have to modify it too often over time. When something is focused and simple, it is easy to understand, well maintained, and safe. And that is our approach, since Bash is not only a tool but also the environment we spend a lot of time in, and so understanding it, making the best use of it, and keeping everything clean and tidy should be our daily aim.

What this book covers

Chapter 1, *Let's Start Programming*, is our first brush with the magic of Bash. We will use basic shell programming bits to write easy code that will forecast all the benefits of more advanced scripts.

Chapter 2, *Operators*, is where we perform some simple operations, such as checking whether something is greater, equal to, or less than something else and how to add, subtract, and fiddle with numbers. This is the first step toward imposing conditions on events dealt with in our scripts.

Chapter 3, *Testing*, explains how checking whether something fits into boundaries and certain conditions are met or not is fundamental to making our scripts able to react to events and to decide what to do based on real-time indicators coming from the system or from other programs.

Chapter 4, *Quoting and Escaping*, tells you how the shell has its own reserved words, which cannot be used without knowing exactly what they do. Furthermore, the variables hold values that must be preserved while we are working on them. This is where we'll learn to be cautions about what we are going to write.

Chapter 5, *Menus, Arrays, and Functions*, explores how to make the script interact with the user, for example, giving the user the chance to answer some questions and deal with the options highlighted. This involves the ability to create a command-line interface for the program itself and a way to store the data in a structure that will make it easy to retrieve that data. And that is what arrays are all about.

Chapter 6, *Iterations*, explains how iterations are fundamental to going over data and extracting and processing them based on some conditions while they last, for instance, or for some values we use as counters. We will learn how to use while and for loops.

Chapter 7, *Plug into the Real World*, introduces one of the most famous open source monitoring system, Nagios, which is all about plugins. You can write complex programs in any language to perform whichever checks you want on your sites and applications. But some of the most tricky plugins I have used have been written using Bash, and nothing else.

Chapter 8, *We Want to Chat*, is about Slack, currently one of the most widely used messaging systems. Why not write a small fragment of code to send our thoughts over a Slack channel and, maybe, make a communication plugin out of it, enabling other scripts to send messages through the messaging system?

Chapter 9, *Subshells, Signals, and Job Controls*, discusses how sometimes a single process is not enough. Our script has to do many things at once, using a sort of raw parallelism to get to the desired outcome. Well, it's time to see what we can spawn inside a shell, how to control our jobs, and send signals.

Chapter 10, *Let's Make a Process Chat*, explores the topic of processes talking to each other, feeding each other data and sharing the burden of data elaboration. Pipes, redirections, process substitution, and a bit of netcat--this could open up new scenarios, and we'll see how.

Chapter 11, *Living as a Daemon*, explains how sometimes sending a script into the background is not enough. It will not survive long, but you can use some tricks such as double forking, setsid, and disowning to make it a bit devilish and survive until process death. Make it a daemon and let it wait for your orders.

Chapter 12, *Remote Connections over SSH*, tells you how scripts can be run locally, but they can do much more for you. They can log in remotely over a secure channel and issue commands on your behalf without you inputting any further instructions. Everything is stored in a key, which unlocks a whole bunch of new possibilities.

Chapter 13, *It's Time for a Timer*, discusses how to fully automate routine tasks. We have to have a method to run our scripts based on some conditions. The most common is based on time, such as hourly, daily, weekly, or monthly repetitions. Just think about a simple log rotation triggered on certain conditions, the most common being on a daily schedule.

Chapter 14, *Time for Safety*, explains how safety is a must in your working environment. Scripting often means access to remote servers and interacting with them, so learning some tricks to keep your server more secure will help you prevent intrusions and keep your job away from unwanted eyes.

What you need for this book

This book assumes a good level of experience with Linux operating systems and an intermediate knowledge of the Bash shell, and since there will be some chapters dealing with Nagios monitoring and Slack messaging, basic understanding of networking concepts is required.

A simple Linux installation is required with really low specifications, as even the Nagios plugin can be tested without requiring the actual installation of the monitoring system. So, this is the minimum configuration required:

- CPU: single-core
- Memory: 2 GB
- Disk space: 20 GB

For this book, you will need the following software:

- Linux operating system: Debian 8
- Nagios Core 3.5.1
- OpenSSH 6.7p1
- rssh 2.3.4

Internet connectivity is required to install the necessary service packages and to try out some of the examples.

Who this book is for

This book is intended for advanced users who are engaged in complex daily tasks. Starting from the basics, this book aims to serve as a reference manual where one can find handy solutions and advice to make their scripts flexible and powerful.

Conventions

In this book, you will find a number of text styles that distinguish between different kinds of information. Here are some examples of these styles and an explanation of their meaning.

Code words in text, database table names, folder names, filenames, file extensions, pathnames, dummy URLs, user input, and Twitter handles are shown as follows: "What is interesting here is that the value of real is slightly different between the two commands."

A block of code is set as follows:

```
#!/bin/bash
set -x
echo "The total disk allocation for this system is: "
echo -e "\n"
df -h
echo -e "\n"
set +x
df -h | grep /dm-0 | awk '{print "Space left on root partition: " $4}'
```

Any command-line input or output is written as follows:

```
gzarrelli:~$ time echo $0
/bin/bash
real  0m0.000s
user  0m0.000s
sys 0m0.000s
gzarrelli:~$
```

New terms and **important words** are shown in bold.

Warnings or important notes appear in a box like this.

Tips and tricks appear like this.

Reader feedback

Feedback from our readers is always welcome. Let us know what you think about this book-what you liked or disliked. Reader feedback is important for us as it helps us develop titles that you will really get the most out of.

To send us general feedback, simply e-mail feedback@packtpub.com, and mention the book's title in the subject of your message.

If there is a topic that you have expertise in and you are interested in either writing or contributing to a book, see our author guide at www.packtpub.com/authors.

Customer support

Now that you are the proud owner of a Packt book, we have a number of things to help you to get the most from your purchase.

Downloading the example code

You can download the example code files for this book from your account at http://www.packtpub.com. If you purchased this book elsewhere, you can visit http://www.packtpub.com/support and register to have the files e-mailed directly to you.

You can download the code files by following these steps:

1. Log in or register to our website using your e-mail address and password.
2. Hover the mouse pointer on the **SUPPORT** tab at the top.
3. Click on **Code Downloads & Errata**.
4. Enter the name of the book in the **Search** box.
5. Select the book for which you're looking to download the code files.
6. Choose from the drop-down menu where you purchased this book from.
7. Click on **Code Download**.

Once the file is downloaded, please make sure that you unzip or extract the folder using the latest version of:

- WinRAR / 7-Zip for Windows
- Zipeg / iZip / UnRarX for Mac
- 7-Zip / PeaZip for Linux

The code bundle for the book is also hosted on GitHub at https://github.com/PacktPublishing/Mastering-Bash. We also have other code bundles from our rich catalog of books and videos available at https://github.com/PacktPublishing/. Check them out!

Downloading the color images of this book

We also provide you with a PDF file that has color images of the screenshots/diagrams used in this book. The color images will help you better understand the changes in the output. You can download this file from https://www.packtpub.com/sites/default/files/downloads/MasteringBash_ColorImages.pdf.

Errata

Although we have taken every care to ensure the accuracy of our content, mistakes do happen. If you find a mistake in one of our books-maybe a mistake in the text or the code-we would be grateful if you could report this to us. By doing so, you can save other readers from frustration and help us improve subsequent versions of this book. If you find any errata, please report them by visiting http://www.packtpub.com/submit-errata, selecting your book, clicking on the **Errata Submission Form** link, and entering the details of your errata. Once your errata are verified, your submission will be accepted and the errata will be uploaded to our website or added to any list of existing errata under the Errata section of that title.

To view the previously submitted errata, go to https://www.packtpub.com/books/content/support and enter the name of the book in the search field. The required information will appear under the **Errata** section.

Piracy

Piracy of copyrighted material on the Internet is an ongoing problem across all media. At Packt, we take the protection of our copyright and licenses very seriously. If you come across any illegal copies of our works in any form on the Internet, please provide us with the location address or website name immediately so that we can pursue a remedy.

Please contact us at `copyright@packtpub.com` with a link to the suspected pirated material.

We appreciate your help in protecting our authors and our ability to bring you valuable content.

Questions

If you have a problem with any aspect of this book, you can contact us at `questions@packtpub.com`, and we will do our best to address the problem.

1
Let's Start Programming

Mastering Bash is the art of taking advantage of your environment to make the best out of it. It is not just a matter of dealing with boring routine tasks that can be automated. It is crafting your working space so that it becomes more efficient for your goals. Thus, even though Bash scripting is not as expressive as other more complex languages, such as Python or JavaScript, it is simple enough to be grabbed in a short time, and so flexible that it will suffice for most of your everyday tasks, even the trickiest ones.

But is Bash so plain and easy? Let's have a look at our first lines in Bash. Let's begin with something easy:

```
gzarrelli:~$ time echo $0
/bin/bash
real 0m0.000s
user 0m0.000s
sys 0m0.000s
gzarrelli:~$
```

Now, let us do it again in a slightly different way:

```
gzarrelli:~$ time /bin/echo $0/bin/bash
real 0m0.001s
user 0m0.000s
sys 0m0.000s
```

What is interesting here is that the value of `real` is slightly different between the two commands. OK, but why? Let's dig a bit further with the following commands:

```
gzarrelli:~$ type echo
echo is a shell builtin
gzarrelli:~$ type /bin/echo
/bin/echo is /bin/echo
```

Let's Start Programming

Interestingly enough, the first seems to be a `shell builtin`, the second simply a system program, an external utility, and it is here that lies the difference. `builtin` is a command that is built into the shell, the opposite of a system program, which is invoked by the shell. An internal command, the opposite to an external command.

To understand the difference between internal and external shell commands that lead to such different timing, we have to understand how an external program is invoked by the shell. When an external program is to be executed, Bash creates a copy of itself with the same environment of the parent shell, giving birth to a new process with a different process ID number. So to speak, we just saw how forking is carried out. Inside the new address space, a system exec is called to load the new process data.

For the `builtin` commands, it is a different story, Bash executes them without any forks, and this leads to a couple of the following interesting outcomes:

- The `builtin` execution is faster because there are no copies and no executables invoked. One side note is that this advantage is more evident with short-running programs because the overhead is before any executable is called: once the external program is invoked, the difference in the pure execution time between the `builtin` command and the program is negligible.
- Being internal to Bash, the `builtin` commands can affect its internal state, and this is not possible with the external program. Let's take into account a classic example using `builtincd`. If `cd` were an external program, once invoked from shell as:

    `cd /this_dir`

    - The first operation would be our shell forking a process for `cd`, and this latter would change the current directory for its own process, not for the one we are inside and that was forked to give birth to the `cd` process. The parent shell would remain unaffected. So, we would not go anywhere.

Curious about which `bulitins` are available? You have some options, to either execute the following `builtin`:

`compgen -b`

Or this other `builtin`:

`enable -a | awk '{ print $2 }'`

To better understand why there is a difference between the execution of a `builtin` and an external program, we must see what happens when we invoke a command.

- First, remember that the shell works from left to right and takes all the variable assignments and redirections and saves them in order to process later.
- If nothing else is left, the shell takes the first word from the command line as the name of the command itself, while all the rest is considered as its arguments.
- The next step is dealing with the required input and output redirection.
- Finally, before being assigned to a variable, all the text following the sign = is subject to tilde expansion, parameter expansion, command substitution, arithmetic expansion, and quote removal.
- If no command name comes out as a result of the last operation, the variable can then affect the environment. If an assignment fails, an error is raised and the command invoked exits with a non-zero status.
- If no command name is the outcome of the operation seen before, all the redirections are applied, but differently from variables, they do not affect the current environment. Again, if any error occurs, there is a non-zero status exit.

Once the preceding operations are performed, the command is then executed and exited with a status, depending on whether one or more expansions contain command substitutions. The overall exit status will be the one from the last command substitution, and if no command substitution were performed, the exit status will be zero.

At this point, we are finally left with a command name and some optional arguments. It is at this point the roads of `builtins` and external programs divert.

- At first, the shell looks at the command name, and if there are no slashes, it searches for its location
- If there are no slashes, the shell tries to see if there is a function with that name and executes it
- If no functions are found, the shell tries to hit `builtin`, and if there is anyone with that name, it is executed

OK, now if there is any `builtin`, it already got invoked. What about an external program?

- Our Bash goes on, and if it finds no `builtins` by that name on the command line, there are three chances:
    - The full path of the command to execute is already contained into its internal hash table, which is a structure used to speed up the search

- If the full path is not in the hash, the shell looks for it into the content of the environmental `PATH` variable, and if it finds it, it is added to the hash table
- The full path is not available in the `PATH` variable, so the shell returns with an exit status of 127

Hash can even be invoked as follows:

```
gzarrelli:~$ hash
hits command
1    /usr/bin/which
1    /usr/bin/ld
24   /bin/sh
1    /bin/ps
1    /usr/bin/who
1    /usr/bin/man
1    /bin/ls
1    /usr/bin/top
```

The second column will then tell you not only which commands have been hashed, but also how many times each of them has been executed during the current session (hits).

Let's say that the search found the full path to the command we want to execute; now we have a full path, and we are in the same situation as if the Bash found one or more slashes into the command name. In either case, the shell thinks that it has a good path to invoke a command and executes the latter in a forked environment.

This is when we are lucky, but it can happen that the file invoked is not an executable, and in this case, given that our path does not point to a directory instead of a file, the Bash makes an educated guess and thinks to run a shell script. In this case, the script is executed in a subshell that is at all a new environment, which inherits the content of the hash table of the parent shell.

Before doing anything else, the shell looks at the first line of the script for an optional `sha-bang` (we will see later what this is) - after the `sha-bang`, there is the path to the interpreter used to manage the script and some optional arguments.

At this point, and only at this point, your external command, if it is a script, is executed. If it is an executable, it is invoked a bit before, but way after any `builtin`.

During these first paragraphs, we saw some commands and concepts that should sound familiar to you. The next paragraphs of this chapter will quickly deal with some basic elements of Bash, such as variables, expansions, and redirections. If you already know them, you will be able to use the next pages as a reference while working on your scripts. If, on the contrary, you are not so familiar with them, have a look at what comes next because all you will read will be fundamental in understanding what you can do in and with the shell.

I/O redirection

As we saw in the previous pages, redirection is one of the last operations undertaken by Bash to parse and prepare the command line that will lead to the execution of a command. But what is a redirection? You can easily guess from your everyday experience. It means taking a stream that goes from one point to another and making it go somewhere else, like changing the flow of a river and making it go somewhere else. In Linux and Unix, it is quite the same, just keep in mind the following two principles:

- In Unix, each process, except for daemons, is supposed to be connected to a standard input, standard output, and standard error device
- Every device in Unix is represented by a file

You can also think of these devices as streams:

- Standard input, named `stdin`, is the intaking stream from which the process receives input data
- Standard output, named `stdout`, is the outbound stream where the process writes its output data
- Standard error, named `stderr`, is the stream where the process writes its error messages

These streams are also identified by a standard POSIX file descriptor, which is an integer used by the kernel as a handler to refer to them, as you can see in the following table:

Device	Mode	File descriptor
`stdin`	read	0
`stdout`	write	1
`stderr`	write	2

So, tinkering with the file descriptors for the three main streams means that we can redirect the flows between `stdin` and `stdout`, but also `stderr`, from one process to the other. So, we can make different processes communicate with each other, and this is actually a form of IPC, inter-process communication, which we will look at it in more detail later in this book.

How do we redirect the **Input/Output (I/O)**, from one process to another? We can get to this goal making use of some special characters:

>

Let's start stating that the default output of a process, usually, is the `stdout`. Whatever it returns is returned on the `stdout` which, again usually, is the monitor or the terminal. Using the > character, we can divert this flow and make it go to a file. If the file does not exist, it is created, and if it exists, it is flattened and its content is overwritten with the output stream of the process.

A simple example will clarify how the redirection to a file works:

```
gzarrelli:~$ echo "This is some content"
This is some content
```

We used the command `echo` to print a message on the `stdout`, and so we see the message written, in our case, to the text terminal that is usually connected to the shell:

```
gzarrelli:~$ ls -lah
total 0
drwxr-xr-x   2 zarrelli  gzarrelli    68B 20 Jan 07:43 .
drwxr-xr-x+ 47 zarrelli  gzarrelli   1.6K 20 Jan 07:43 ..
```

There is nothing on the filesystem, so the output went straight to the terminal, but the underlying directory was not affected. Now, time for a redirection:

```
gzarrelli:~$ echo "This is some content" > output_file.txt
```

Well, nothing to the screen; no output at all:

```
gzarrelli:~$ ls -lah
total 8
drwxr-xr-x   3 gzarrelli  gzarrelli   102B 20 Jan 07:44 .
drwxr-xr-x+ 47 gzarrelli  gzarrelli   1.6K 20 Jan 07:43 ..
-rw-r--r--   1 gzarrelli  gzarrelli    21B 20 Jan 07:44 output_file.txt
```

Actually, as you can see, the output did not vanish; it was simply redirected to a file on the current directory which got created and filled in:

```
gzarrelli:~$ cat output_file.txt
This is some content
```

Here we have something interesting. The `cat` command takes the content of the `output_file.txt` and sends it on the `stdout`. What we can see is that the output from the former command was redirected from the terminal and written to a file.

>>

This double mark answers a requirement we often face: *How can we add more content coming from a process to a file without overwriting anything?* Using this double character, which means no file is already in place, create a new one; if it already exists, just append the new data. Let's take the previous file and add some content to it:

```
gzarrelli:~$ echo "This is some other content" >> output_file.txt
gzarrelli:~$ cat output_file.txt
This is some content
This is some other content
```

Bingo, the file was not overwritten and the new content from the `echo` command was added to the old. Now, we know how to write to a file, but what about reading from somewhere else other than the `stdin`?

<

If the text terminal is the `stdin`, the keyboard is the standard input for a process, where it expects some data from. Again, we can divert the flow or data reading and get the process read from a file. For our example, we start creating a file containing a set of unordered numbers:

```
gzarrelli:~$ echo -e '5\n9\n4\n1\n0\n6\n2' > to_sort
```

And let us verify its content, as follows:

```
gzarrelli:~$ cat to_sort
5
9
4
1
0
6
2
```

Let's Start Programming

Now we can have the sort command read this file into its stdin, as follows:

```
gzarrelli:~$ sort < to_sort
0
1
2
4
5
6
9
```

Nice, our numbers are now in sequence, but we can do something more interesting:

```
gzarrelli:~$ sort < to_sort > sorted
```

What did we do? We simply gave the file to_sort to the command sort into its standard input, and at the same time, we concatenated a second redirection so that the output of sort is written into the file sorted:

```
gzarrelli:~$ cat sorted
0
1
2
4
5
6
9
```

So, we can concatenate multiple redirections and have some interesting results, but we can do something even trickier, that is, chaining together inputs and outputs, not on files but on processes, as we will see now.

|

The pipe character does exactly what its name suggests, *pipes* the stream; could be the stdout or stderr, from one process to another, creating a simple interprocess communication facility:

```
gzarrelli:~$
ps aux | awk '{print $2, $3, $4}' | grep -v [A-Z] | sort -r -k 2 -g | head -n 3
95 0.0 0.0
94 0.0 0.0
93 0.0 0.0
```

In this example, we had a bit of fun, first getting a list of processes, then piping the output to the `awk` utility, which printed only the first, eleventh, and twelfth fields of the output of the first command, giving us the process ID, CPU percentage, and memory percentage columns. Then, we got rid of the heading `PID %CPU %MEM`, piping the `awk` output to the input of `grep`, which performed a reverse pattern matching on any strings containing a character, not a number. In the next stage, we piped the output to the `sort` command, which reverse-ordered the data based on the values in the second column. Finally, we wanted only the three lines, and so we got the `PID` of the first three heaviest processes relying on CPU occupation.

Redirection can also be used for some kind of fun or useful stuff, as you can see in the following screenshot:

```
13:11:57-root:/tmp$ who
gzarrelli  console  Jan 20 06:49
gzarrelli  ttys000  Jan 20 06:49
gzarrelli  ttys002  Jan 20 06:49
gzarrelli  ttys003  Jan 20 13:10
13:12:00-root:/tmp$ echo "Hello, how are you doing?" > /dev/ttys003
13:12:03-root:/tmp$ Fine, thanks
```

```
x bash
▶13:11:53-gzarrelli:~$ Hello, how are you doing?

▶13:12:06-gzarrelli:~$ echo "Fine, thanks" > /dev/ttys002
▶13:12:08-gzarrelli:~$
```

Let's Start Programming

As you can see, there are two users on the same machine on different terminals, and remember that each user has to be connected to a terminal. To be able to write to any user's terminal, you must be root or, as in this example, the same user on two different terminals. With the `who` command we can identify which terminal (`ttys`) the user is connected to, also known as *reads from*, and we simply redirect the output from an `echo` command to his terminal. Because its session is connected to the terminal, he will read what we send to the `stdin` of his terminal device (hence, `/dev/ttysxxx`).

Everything in Unix is represented by a file, be it a device, a terminal, or anything we need access to. We also have some special files, such as `/dev/null`, which is a sinkhole - whatever you send to it gets lost:

```
gzarrelli:~$ echo "Hello" > /dev/null
gzarrelli:~$
```

And have a look at the following example too:

```
root:~$ ls
output_file.txtsortedto_sort
root:~$ mv output_file.txt /dev/null
root:~$ ls
to_sort
```

Great, there is enough to have fun, but it is just the beginning. There is a whole lot more to do with the file descriptors.

Messing around with stdin, stdout, and stderr

Well, if we tinker a little bit with the file descriptors and special characters we can have some nice, really nice, outcomes; let's see what we can do.

- `x < filename`: This opens a file in read mode and assigns the descriptor named a, whose value falls between 3 and 9. We can choose any name by the means of which we can easily access the file content through the `stdin`.
- `1 > filename`: This redirects the standard output to filename. If it does not exist, it gets created; if it exists, the pre-existing data is overwritten.
- `1 >> filename`: This redirects the standard output to filename. If it does not exist, it is created; otherwise, the contents get appended to the pre-existing data.

- `2 > filename`: This redirects the standard error to filename. If it does not exist, it gets created; if it exists, the pre-existing data is overwritten.
- `2 >> filename`: This redirects the standard error to filename. If it does not exist, it is created; otherwise, the contents get appended to the pre-existing data.
- `&> filename`: This redirects both the `stdout` and the `stderr` to filename. This redirects the standard error to filename. If it does not exist, it gets created; if it exists, the pre-existing data is overwritten.
- `2>&1`: This redirects the `stderr` to the `stdout`. If you use this with a program, its error messages will be redirected to the `stdout`, that is, usually, the monitor.
- `y>&x`: This redirects the file descriptor for y to x so that the output from the file pointed by descriptor y will be redirected to the file pointed by descriptor x.
- `>&x`: This redirects the file descriptor 1 that is associated with the `stdout` to the file pointed by the descriptor x, so whatever hits the standard output will be written in the file pointed by x.
- `x<> filename`: This opens a file in read/write mode and assigns the descriptor x to it. If the file does not exist, it is created, and if the descriptor is omitted, it defaults to 0, the `stdin`.
- `x<&-`: This closes the file opened in read mode and associated with the descriptor x.
- `0<&-` or `<&-`: This closes the file opened in read mode and associated with the descriptor 0, the `stdin`, which is then closed.
- `x>&-`: This closes the file opened in write mode and associated with the descriptor x.
- `1>&-` or `>&-`: This closes the file opened in write mode and associated with the descriptor 1, the `stdout`, which is then closed.

If you want to see which file descriptors are associated with a process, you can explore the `/proc` directory and point to the following:

/proc/pid/fd

Under that path, change `PID` with the ID of the process you want to explore; you will find all the file descriptors associated with it, as in the following example:

```
gzarrelli:~$ ls -lah /proc/15820/fd
total 0
dr-x------ 2 postgres postgres  0 Jan 20 17:59 .
dr-xr-xr-x 9 postgres postgres  0 Jan 20 09:59 ..
lr-x------ 1 postgres postgres 64 Jan 20 17:59 0 -> /dev/null
(deleted)
```

```
l-wx------ 1 postgres postgres 64 Jan 20 17:59 1 ->
/var/log/postgresql/postgresql-9.4-main.log
lrwx------ 1 postgres postgres 64 Jan 20 17:59 10 ->
/var/lib/postgresql/9.4/main/base/16385/16587
lrwx------ 1 postgres postgres 64 Jan 20 17:59 11 -> socket:[13135]
lrwx------ 1 postgres postgres 64 Jan 20 17:59 12 -> socket:[1502010]
lrwx------ 1 postgres postgres 64 Jan 20 17:59 13 ->
/var/lib/postgresql/9.4/main/base/16385/16591
lrwx------ 1 postgres postgres 64 Jan 20 17:59 14 ->
/var/lib/postgresql/9.4/main/base/16385/16593
lrwx------ 1 postgres postgres 64 Jan 20 17:59 15 ->
/var/lib/postgresql/9.4/main/base/16385/16634
lrwx------ 1 postgres postgres 64 Jan 20 17:59 16 ->
/var/lib/postgresql/9.4/main/base/16385/16399
lrwx------ 1 postgres postgres 64 Jan 20 17:59 17 ->
/var/lib/postgresql/9.4/main/base/16385/16406
lrwx------ 1 postgres postgres 64 Jan 20 17:59 18 ->
/var/lib/postgresql/9.4/main/base/16385/16408
l-wx------ 1 postgres postgres 64 Jan 20 17:59 2 ->
/var/log/postgresql/postgresql-9.4-main.log
lr-x------ 1 postgres postgres 64 Jan 20 17:59 3 -> /dev/urandom
l-wx------ 1 postgres postgres 64 Jan 20 17:59 4 -> /dev/null
(deleted)
l-wx------ 1 postgres postgres 64 Jan 20 17:59 5 -> /dev/null
(deleted)
lr-x------ 1 postgres postgres 64 Jan 20 17:59 6 -> pipe:[1502013]
l-wx------ 1 postgres postgres 64 Jan 20 17:59 7 -> pipe:[1502013]
lrwx------ 1 postgres postgres 64 Jan 20 17:59 8 ->
/var/lib/postgresql/9.4/main/base/16385/11943
lr-x------ 1 postgres postgres 64 Jan 20 17:59 9 -> pipe:[13125]
```

Nice, isn't it? So, let us do something that is absolute fun:

First, let's open a socket in read/write mode to the web server of a virtual machine created for this book and assign the descriptor 9:

```
gzarrelli:~$ exec 9<> /dev/tcp/172.16.210.128/80 || exit 1
```

Then, let us write something to it; nothing complex:

```
gzarrelli:~$ printf 'GET /index2.html HTTP/1.1\nHost:
172.16.210.128\nConnection: close\n\n' >&9
```

We just requested a simple HTML file created for this example.

And now let us read the file descriptor 9:

```
gzarrelli:~$ cat <&9
HTTP/1.1 200 OK
Date: Sat, 21 Jan 2017 17:57:33 GMT
Server: Apache/2.4.10 (Debian)
Last-Modified: Sat, 21 Jan 2017 17:57:12 GMT
ETag: "f3-5469e7ef9e35f"
Accept-Ranges: bytes
Content-Length: 243
Vary: Accept-Encoding
Connection: close
Content-Type: text/html
<!DOCTYPE HTML PUBLIC "-//W3C//DTD HTML 4.01//EN"
    "http://www.w3.org/TR/html4/strict.dtd">
<HTML>
    <HEAD>
        <TITLE>This is a test file</TITLE>
    </HEAD>
    <BODY>
        <P>And we grabbed it through our descriptor!
    </BODY>
</HTML>
```

That's it! We connected the file descriptor to a remote server through a socket, we could write to it and read the response, redirecting the streams over the network.

For dealing just with the command line, we have done a lot so far, but if we want to go further, we have to see how to script all these commands and make the most out of them. It is time for our first script!

Time for the interpreter: the sha-bang

When the game gets tougher, a few concatenations on the command line cannot be enough to perform the tasks we are meant to accomplish. Too many bits on single lines are too messy, and we lack clarity, so better to store our commands or `builtins` in a file and have it executed.

When a script is executed, the system loader parses the first line looking for what is named the `sha-bang` or shebang, a sequence of characters.

```
#!
```

Let's Start Programming

This will force the loader to treat the following characters as a path to the interpreter and its optional arguments to be used to further parse the script, which will then be passed as another argument to the interpreter itself. So, at the end, the interpreter will parse the script and, this time, we will ignore the `sha-bang`, since its first character is a hash, usually indicating a comment inside a script and comments do not get executed. To go a little further, the `sha-bang` is what we call a 2-bit magic number, a constant sequence of numbers or text values used in Unix to identify file or protocol types. So, `0x23 0x21` is actually the ASCII representation of `#!`.

So, let's make a little experiment and create a tiny one line script:

```
gzarrelli:~$ echo "echo \"This should go under the sha-bang\"" > test.sh
```

Just one line. Let's have a look:

```
gzarrelli:~$ cat test.sh
echo "This should go under the sha-bang"
```

Nice, everything is as we expected. Has Linux something to say about our script? Let's ask:

```
gzarrelli:~$ file test.sh
test.sh: ASCII text
```

Well, the file utility says that it is a plain file, and this is a simple text file indeed. Time for a nice trick:

```
gzarrelli:~$ sed -i '1s/^/#!\/bin\/sh\n/' test.sh
```

Nothing special; we just added a `sha-bang` pointing to `/bin/sh`:

```
gzarrelli:~$ cat test.sh
#!/bin/sh
echo "This should go under the sha-bang"
```

As expected, the `sha-bang` is there at the beginning of our file:

```
gzarrelli:~$ file test.sh
test.sh: POSIX shell script, ASCII text executable
```

No way, now it is a script! The file utility makes three different tests to identify the type of file it is dealing with. In order: file system tests, magic number tests, and language tests. In our case, it identified the magic numbers that represent the `sha-bang`, and thus a script, and this is what it told us: it is a script.

Now, a couple of final notes before moving on.

- You can omit the `sha-bang` if your script is not using a shell `builtins` or shell internals
  - Pay attention to `/bin/sh`, not everything that looks like an innocent executable is what it seems:

```
gzarrelli:~$ ls -lah /bin/sh
lrwxrwxrwx 1 root root 4 Nov  8  2014 /bin/sh -> dash
```

In some systems, `/bin/sh` is a symbolic link to a different kind of interpreter, and if you are using some internals or `builtins` of Bash, your script could have unwanted or unexpected outcomes.

Calling your script

Well, we have our two-line script; time to see if it really does what we want it to do:

```
gzarrelli:~$ ./test.sh
-bash: ./test.sh: Permission denied
```

No way! It is not executing, and from the error message, it seems related to the file permissions:

```
gzarrelli:~$ ls -lah test.sh
-rw-r--r-- 1 gzarrelli gzarrelli 41 Jan 21 18:56 test.sh
```

Interesting. Let us recap what the file permissions are. As you can see, the line describing the properties of a file starts with a series of letters and lines.

Type	User	Group	Others
-	rw-	r--	r--

For type, we can have two main values, d - this is actually a directory, or - and means this is a regular file. Then, we can see what permissions are set for the user owning the file, for the group owning the file, and for all other users. As you may guess, r stands for permission to read; w stands for being able to write; x stands for permission to execute; and - means no right. These are all in the same order, first r, then w, then x. So wherever you see a - instead of an r, w, or x, it means that particular right is not granted.

Let's Start Programming

The same works for directory permission, except that x means you can traverse the directory; r means that you can enumerate the content of it; w means that you can modify the attributes of the directory and removes the entries that are eventually in it.

Indicator	File type
-	Regular file
b	Block file (disk or partition)
c	Character file, like the terminal under /dev
d	Directory
l	Symbolic link
p	Named pipe (FIFO)
s	Socket

So, going back to our file, we do not see any execution bit set. Why? Here, a shell `builtin` can help us:

```
gzarrelli:~$ umask
0022
```

Does it make any sense to you? Well, it should, once we see how the permissions on files can be represented in numeric form. Think of permissions as bits of metadata pertaining to a file, one bit for each grant; no grant is 0:

```
r-- = 100
-w- = 010
--x = 001
```

Now, let's convert from binary to decimal:

Permission	Binary	Decimal
r	100	4
w	010	2
x	001	1

Now, just combine the decimal values to obtain the final permission, but remember that you have to calculate read, write, and execution grants in triplets - one set for the user owning the file, one for the group, and one for the others.

Back again to our file, we can change its permissions in a couple of ways. Let's say we want it to be readable, writable, and executable by the user; readable and writable by the group; and only readable by the others. We can use the command `chmod` to accomplish this goal:

```
chmod u+rwx filename
chmod g+wfilename
```

So, + or – add or subtract the permissions to the file or directory pointed and u, g, w to define which of the three sets of attributes we are referring to.

But we can speed things up using the numeric values:

```
User - rwx: 4+2+1 =7
Group - rw: 4+2 = 6
Other - r = 4
```

So, the following command should do the trick in one line:

```
chmod   764 test.sh
```

Time to verify:

```
gzarrelli:~$ ls -lah test.sh
-rwxrw-r-- 1 gzarrelli gzarrelli 41 Jan 21 18:56 test.sh
```

Here we are. So we just need to see whether our user can execute the file, as the permissions granted suggest:

```
gzarrelli:~$ ./test.sh
```

This should go under the `sha-bang`.

Great, it works. Well, the script is not that complex, but served our purposes. But we left one question behind: *Why was the file created with that set of permissions?* As a preliminary explanation, I ran the command `umask`, and the result was `0022` but did not go further.

Count the digits in `umask`, and those in the numeric modes for `chmod`. Four against three. What does that leading digit means? We have to introduce some special permission modes that enable some interesting features:

- Sticky bit. Think of it as a user right assertion on a file or directory. If a sticky bit is set on a directory, the files inside it can be deleted or renamed only by the file owner, the owner of the directory the file is in, or by root. Really useful in a shared directory to prevent one user from deleting or renaming some other user's file. The sticky bit is represented by the t letter at the end of the of the list of permissions or by the octal digit 1 at the beginning. Let's see how it works:

    ```
    gzarrelli:~$ chmod +t test.sh
    gzarrelli:~$ ls -lah test.sh
    -rwxrw-r-T 1 gzarrelli gzarrelli 41 Jan 22 09:05 test.sh
    ```

- Interestingly, the t is capital, not lower, as we were talking about. Maybe this sequence of commands will make everything clearer:

    ```
    gzarrelli:~$ chmod +t test.sh
    gzarrelli:~$ ls -lah test.sh
    -rwxrw-r-T 1 gzarrelli gzarrelli 41 Jan 22 09:05 test.sh
    gzarrelli:~$ chmod o+x test.sh
    gzarrelli:~$ ls -lah test.sh
    -rwxrw-r-t 1 gzarrelli gzarrelli 41 Jan 22 09:05 test.sh
    ```

- You probably got it: the t attribute is a capital when, on the file or directory, the execution bix (x) is not set for the others (o).
- And now, back to the origins:

    ```
    gzarrelli:~$ chmod 0764 test.sh
    gzarrelli:~$ ls -lah test.sh
    -rwxrw-r-- 1 gzarrelli gzarrelli 41 Jan 22 09:05 test.sh
    ```

- We used the four-digit notations, and the leading 0 cleared out the 1 which referred to the sticky bit. Obviously, we could also use `chmod -t` to accomplish the same goal. One final note, if sticky bit and GUID are in conflicts, the sticky bit prevails in granting permissions.

- **Set UID**: The **Set User ID** (**SUID** upon execution) marks an executable, so that when it runs, it will do so as the file owner, with his privileges, and not as the user invoking it. Another tricky use is that, if assigned to a directory, all the files created or moved to that directory will have the ownership changed to the owner of the directory and not to the user actually performing the operation. Visually, it is represented by an s in the position of the user execution rights. The octal number referring to it is 4:

    ```
    gzarrelli:~$ chmod u+s test.sh
    gzarrelli:~$ ls -lah test.sh
    -rwsrw-r-- 1 gzarrelli gzarrelli 41 Jan 22 09:05 test.sh
    ```

- **Set GID**: The **SGID** (**Set Group ID** upon execution) marks an executable, so that when it is run, it does as the user invoking it was in the group that owns the file. If applied to a directory, every file created or moved to the directory will have the group set to the group owning the directory rather than the one the user performing the operation belongs to. Visually, it is represented by an s in the position of the group execution rights. The octal number referring to it is 2.
- Let's reset the permissions on our `test` file:

    ```
    gzarrelli:~$ chmod 0764 test.sh
    gzarrelli:~$ ls -lah test.sh
    -rwxrw-r-- 1 gzarrelli gzarrelli 41 Jan 22 09:05 test.sh
    ```

- Now we apply SGID using the octal digit referring to it:

    ```
    gzarrelli:~$ chmod 2764 test.sh
    gzarrelli:~$ ls -lah test.sh
    -rwxrwSr-- 1 gzarrelli gzarrelli 41 Jan 22 09:05 test.sh
    ```

In this example, the s is capital because we do not have the execution permission granted on the group; the same applies for SUID.

So, now we can go back again to our umask, and at this point you probably already know what is the meaning of the four-digit notation is. It is a command that modifies the permissions on a file creation, denying the permission bits. Taking our default creation mask for directory:

0777

Let's Start Programming

We can think of `umask` of `0022` as:

```
0777 -
0022
------
0755
```

Do not pay attention to the first `0`; it is the sticky bit and simply subtracts from the default grant mask for a directory, `rwx` for user, group, and others, the value of the `umask`. The remaining value is the current permission mask for file creation. If you are not comfortable with the numeric notation, you can see the `umask` values in the familiar `rwx` notation using:

```
gzarrelli:~$ umask -S
u=rwx,g=rx,o=rx
```

For the files, the default mask is `666`, so:

```
0666 -
0022
--------
0644
```

It is actually a tad more complicated than this, but this rule of thumb will let you calculate the masks quickly. Let us try to create a new `umask`. First, let's reset the `umask` value:

```
gzarrelli:~$ umask
0000
gzarrelli:~$ umask -S
u=rwx,g=rwx,o=rwx
```

As we can see, nothing gets subtracted:

```
zarrelli:~$ touch test-file
gzarrelli:~$ mkdir test-dir
gzarrelli:~$ ls -lah test-*
-rw-rw-rw- 1 gzarrelli gzarrelli     0 Jan 22 18:01 test-file

test-dir:
total 8.0K
drwxrwxrwx 2 gzarrelli gzarrelli 4.0K Jan 22 18:01 .
drwxr-xr-x 4 gzarrelli gzarrelli 4.0K Jan 22 18:01 ..
```

The `test` file has `666` access rights and the directory `777`. This is really way too much:

```
zarrelli:~$ umask o-rwx,g-w
gzarrelli:~$ umask -S
u=rwx,g=rx,o=
```

```
gzarrelli:~$ touch 2-test-file
gzarrelli:~$ mkdir 2-test-dir
gzarrelli:~$ ls -lah 2-test-*
-rw-r----- 1 gzarrelli gzarrelli    0 Jan 22 18:03 2-test-file

2-test-dir:
total 8.0K
drwxr-x--- 2 gzarrelli gzarrelli 4.0K Jan 22 18:03 .
drwxr-xr-x 5 gzarrelli gzarrelli 4.0K Jan 22 18:03 ..
```

As you can see, the permissions are 750 for directories and 640 for files. A bit of math will help:

```
0777 -
0750
--------
0027
```

You would get the same result from the `umask` command:

```
gzarrelli:~$ umask
0027
```

All these settings last as long as you are logged in to the session, so if you want to make them permanent, just add the `umask` call with the appropriate argument to `/etc/bash.bashrc`, or `/etc/profile` for a system-wide effect or, for a single user mask, add it to the `.bashrc` file inside the user home directory.

Something went wrong, let's trace it

So, we have a new tiny script named `disk.sh`:

```
gzarrelli:~$ cat disk.sh
#!/bin/bash
echo "The total disk allocation for this system is: "
echo -e "\n"
df -h
echo -e "\n
df -h | grep /$ | awk '{print "Space left on root partition: " $4}'
```

Nothing special, a shebang, a couple of echoes on a new line just to have some vertical spacing, the output of `df -h` and the same command but parsed by `awk` to give us a meaningful message. Let's run it:

```
zarrelli:~$ ./disk.sh
```

Let's Start Programming

The total disk allocation for this system is:

```
Filesystem         Size  Used Avail Use% Mounted on
/dev/dm-0          19G   15G  3.0G  84%  /
udev               10M   0    10M   0%   /dev
tmpfs              99M   9.1M 90M   10%  /run
tmpfs              248M  80K  248M  1%   /dev/shm
tmpfs              5.0M  4.0K 5.0M  1%   /run/lock
tmpfs              248M  0    248M  0%   /sys/fs/cgroup
/dev/sda1          236M  33M  191M  15%  /boot
tmpfs              50M   12K  50M   1%   /run/user/1000
tmpfs              50M   0    50M   0%   /run/user/0
Space left on root partition: 3.0G
```

Nothing too complicated, a bunch of easy commands, which in case of failure print an error message on the standard output. However, let's think for a moment that we have a more flexible script, more lines, some variable assignments, loops, and other constructs, and something goes wrong, but the output does not tell us anything. In this case, be handy to see a method that is actually running inside our script so that we can see the output of the commands, the variable assignments, and so forth. In Bash, this is possible; thanks to the `set` command associated with the `-x` argument, which shows all the commands and arguments in the script printed to the `stdout`, after the commands have been expanded and before they are actually invoked. The same behavior can be obtained running a subshell with the `-x` argument. Let's see what would happen if it was used with our script:

```
gzarrelli:~$ bash -x disk.sh
+ echo 'The total disk allocation for this system is: '
The total disk allocation for this system is:
+ echo -e '\n'

+ df -h
Filesystem         Size  Used Avail Use% Mounted on
/dev/dm-0          19G   15G  3.0G  84%  /
udev               10M   0    10M   0%   /dev
tmpfs              99M   9.1M 90M   10%  /run
tmpfs              248M  80K  248M  1%   /dev/shm
tmpfs              5.0M  4.0K 5.0M  1%   /run/lock
tmpfs              248M  0    248M  0%   /sys/fs/cgroup
/dev/sda1          236M  33M  191M  15%  /boot
tmpfs              50M   12K  50M   1%   /run/user/1000
tmpfs              50M   0    50M   0%   /run/user/0
+ echo -e '\n'
+ awk '{print "Space left on root partition: " $4}'
+ grep /dm-0
+ df -h
Space left on root partition: 3.0G
```

Now it is quite easy to understand how the stream of data flows inside the script: all the lines beginning with a + sign are commands, and the following lines are outputs.

Let's think for a moment that we have longer scripts; for most parts, we are sure that things work fine. For some lines, we are not completely sure of the outcome. Debugging everything would be *noisy*. In this case, we can use set-x to enable the logging only for those lines we need to inspect, turning it off with set+x when it is no longer needed. Time to modify the script, as follows:

```
#!/bin/bash
set -x
echo "The total disk allocation for this system is: "
echo -e "\n"
df -h
echo -e "\n"
set +x
df -h | grep /dm-0 | awk '{print "Space left on root partition: " $4}'
```

And now, time to run it again, as follows:

```
gzarrelli:~$ ./disk.sh
+ echo 'The total disk allocation for this system is: '
The total disk allocation for this system is:
+ echo -e '\n'

+ df -h
Filesystem      Size  Used Avail Use% Mounted on
/dev/dm-0       19G   15G  3.0G  84%  /
udev            10M   0    10M   0%   /dev
tmpfs           99M   9.1M 90M   10%  /run
tmpfs           248M  80K  248M  1%   /dev/shm
tmpfs           5.0M  4.0K 5.0M  1%   /run/lock
tmpfs           248M  0    248M  0%   /sys/fs/cgroup
/dev/sda1       236M  33M  191M  15%  /boot
tmpfs           50M   12K  50M   1%   /run/user/1000
tmpfs           50M   0    50M   0%   /run/user/0
+ echo -e '\n'

+ set +x
Space left on root partition: 3.0G
```

As you can see, we see the instructions given in the block marked by set-x, and we also see the set+x instruction given, but then, after this, the line with awk disappears and we see only its output, filtering out what was not so interesting for us and leaving only the part we want to focus on.

This is not a powerful debugging system typical of more complex programming languages, but it can be really helpful in scripts of hundreds of lines where we can lose track of sophisticated structures, such as evaluations, cycles, or variable assignments, which make the scripts more expressive but even more difficult to get hold of and master. So, now that we are clear on how to debug a file, which permissions are needed to make it safely executable, and how to shell parse the command line, we are ready to spice things up looking at how we can use variables to add more flexibility to our hand-crafted tools.

Variables

What is a variable? We could answer that it is something not constant; nice joke, but it would not help us so much. Better to think of it as a bucket where we can store some information for later processing: at a certain point of your script you get a value, a piece of info that you do not want to process at that very moment, so you fit it into a variable that you will recall later in the script. This is, in an intuitive way, the use of a variable, a way to allocate a part of the system memory to hold your data.

So far, we have seen that our scripts could retrieve some pieces of information from the system and had to process them straight away, since, without the use of a variable, we had no way to further process the information except for concatenating or redirecting the output to another program. This forced us to have a linear execution, no flexibility, no complexity: once you get some data, you process it straight away redirecting the file descriptors, one link in the chain after the other.

A variable is nothing really new; a lot of programming languages use them to store different types of data, integers, floating, strings, and you can see many different kinds of variables related to different kinds of data they hold. So, you have probably heard about casting a variable, which means, roughly, changing its type: you get a value as a string of numbers and you want to use it as an integer, so you cast it as an `int` and proceed processing it using some math functions.

Our shell is not so sophisticated, and it has only one type of variable or, better, it has none: whatever you store in it can be later processed without any casting. This can be nice because you do not have to pay attention to what type of data you are holding; you get a number as a string and can process it straight away as an integer. Nice and easy, but we must remember that restrictions are in place not just to prevent us from doing something, but also to help us not do something that would be unhealthy for our code, and this is exactly the risk in having flat variables, to write some piece of code that simply does not work, cannot work.

Assigning a variable

As we just saw, a variable is a way to store a value: we get a value, assign it to a variable and refer to the latter to access the former. The operation of retrieving the content of a variable is named **variable substitution**. A bit like, if you think about descriptors, the way that you use them to access files. The way you assign a variable is quite straightforward:

```
LABEL=value
```

`LABEL` can be any string, can have upper and lowercase, start with or contain numbers and underscores, and it is case sensitive.

The assignment is performed by the = character, which, be wary, is not the same as the *equal to* == sign; they are two different things and are used in different contexts. Finally, whatever you put at the right of the assignment operator becomes the value of the variable. So, let's assign some value to our first variable:

```
gzarrelli:~$ FIRST_VARIABLE=amazing
```

Now we can try to access the value trying to perform an action on the variable itself:

```
gzarrelli:~$ echo FIRST_VARIABLE
FIRST_VARIABLE
```

Not exactly what we expected. We want the content, not the name of the variable. Have a look at this:

```
gzarrelli:~$ echo $FIRST_VARIABLE
amazing
```

This is better. Using the $ character at the beginning of the variable name identified this as a variable and not a plain string, so we had access to the content. This means that, from now on, we can just use the variable with any commands instead of referring to the whole content of it. So, let us try again:

```
gzarrelli:~$ echo $first_variable
gzarrelli:~$
```

The output is null, and not 0; we will see later on that zero is not the same as null, since null is no value but zero is indeed a value, an integer. What does the previous output mean? Simply that our labels are case sensitive, change one character from upper to lower or vice versa, and you will have a new variable which, since you did not assign any value to it, does not hold any value, hence the null you receive once you try to access it.

Keep the variable name safe

We just saw that $label is the way we reference the content of a variable, but if you have a look at some scripts, you can find another way of retrieving variable content:

```
${label}
```

The two ways of referencing the content of a variable are both valid, and you can use the first, more compact, in any case except when concatenating the variable name to any characters, which could change the variable name itself. In this case, it becomes mandatory to use the extended version of the variable substitution, as the following example will make clear.

Let's start printing our variable again:

```
gzarrelli:~$ echo $FIRST_VARIABLE
amazing
```

Now, let's do it again using the extended version of substitution:

```
gzarrelli:~$ echo ${FIRST_VARIABLE}
amazing
```

Exactly the same output since, as we said, these two methods are equivalent. Now, let us add a string to our variable name:

```
gzarrelli:~$ echo $FIRST_VARIABLEngly
gzarrelli:~$
```

Nothing, and we can understand why the name of the variable changed; so we have no content to access to. But now, let us try the extended way:

```
gzarrelli:~$ echo ${FIRST_VARIABLE}ly
amazingly
```

Bingo! The name of the variable has been preserved so that the shell was able to reference its value and then concatenated it to the `ly` string we added to the name.

Keep this difference in mind, because the graphs will be a handy way to concatenate strings to a variable to spice your scripts up and, as a good rule of thumb, refer to variables using the graphs. This will help you avoid unwanted hindrances.

Variables with limited scope

As we said before, variables have no type in shell, and this makes them somehow easy to use, but we must pay attention to some sorts of limits to their use.

- First, the content of a variable is accessible only after the value has been assigned
- An example will make everything clearer:

```
gzarrelli:~$ cat disk-space.sh
#!/bin/bash
echo -e "\n"
echo "The space left is ${disk_space}"
disk_space=`df -h | grep /$ | awk '{print $4}'`
echo "The space left is ${disk_space}
```

We used the variable disk space to store the result of the `df` command and try to reference its value on the preceding and following lines. Let us run it in debug mode:

```
gzarrelli:~$ sh -x disk-space.sh
+ echo -e \n
-e
+ echo The space left is
The space left is
+ awk {print $4}
+ grep /dm-0
+ df -h
+ disk_space=3.0G
+ echo The space left is 3.0G
The space left is 3.0G
```

As we can see, the flow of execution is sequential: you access the value of the variable only after it is instanced, not before. And bear in mind that the first line actually printed something: a null value. Well, now let us print the variable on the command line:

```
gzarrelli:~$ echo ${disk_space}
gzarrelli:~$
```

The variable is instanced inside the script, and it is confined there, inside the shell spawned to invoke the command and nothing passed to our main shell.

Let's Start Programming

We can ourselves impose some restrictions to a variable, as we will see with the next example. In this new case, we will introduce the use of a function, something that we are going to look at in more detail further in this book and the keyword local:

```
gzarrelli:~$ cat disk-space-function.sh
#!/bin/bash
echo -e "\n"
echo "The space left is ${disk_space}"
disk_space=`df -h | grep /dm-0 | awk '{print $4}'`
print () {
echo "The space left inside the function is ${disk_space}"
local available=yes
last=yes
echo "Is the available variable available inside the function?
${available}"
}
echo "Is the last variable available outside the function before it is
invoked? ${last}"
print
echo "The space left outside is ${disk_space}"
echo "Is the available variable available outside the function?
${available}"
echo "Is the last variable available outside the function after it is
invoked? ${last}"
```

Now let us run it:

```
gzarrelli:~$ cat di./pace-function.sh
The space left is
Is the last variable available outside the function before it is invoked?
The space left inside the function is 3.0G
Is the available variable available inside the function? yes
The space left outside is 3.0G
Is the available variable available outside the function?
Is the last variable available outside the function after it is invoked?
yes
```

What can we see here?

The content of variable `disk_space` is not available before the variable itself is instanced. We already knew this.

The content of a variable instanced inside a function is not available when it is defined in the function, but when the function itself is invoked.

[36]

A variable marked by the keyword local and defined inside a function is available only inside the function and only when the function is invoked. Outside the block of code defined by the function itself; the local variable is not visible to the rest of the script. So, using local variables can be handy to write recursive code, even though not recommended.

So, we just saw a few ways to make a variable really limited in its scope, and we also noted that its content is not available outside the script it was instanced in. Wouldn't it be nice to have some variables with a broader scope, capable of influencing the execution of each and every script, something at environment level? It would, and from now on we are going to explore the environment variables.

Environment variables

As we discussed earlier, the shell comes with an environment, which dictates what it can do and what not, so let's just have a look at what these variables are using the env command:

```
zarrelli:~$ env
...
LANG=en_GB.utf8
...
DISPLAY=:0.0
...
USER=zarrelli
...
DESKTOP_SESSION=xfce
...
PWD=/home/zarrelli/Documents
...
HOME=/home/zarrelli
...
SHELL=/bin/bash
...
LANGUAGE=en_GB:en
...
GDMSESSION=xfce
...
LOGNAME=zarrelli
...
PATH=/usr/local/bin:/usr/bin:/bin:/usr/local/games:/usr/games
_=/usr/bin/env
```

Let's Start Programming

Some of the variables have been omitted for the sake of clarity; otherwise, the output would have been too long, but still we can see something interesting. We can have a look at the PATH variable content, which influences where the shell will look for a program or script to execute. We can see which shell is being currently used, by which user, what the current directory is and the previous one.

But environment variables can not only be read; they can be instanced using the export command:

```
zarrelli:~$ export TEST_VAR=awesome
```

Now, let us read it:

```
zarrelli:~/$ echo ${TEST_VAR}
awesome
```

That is it, but since this was just a test, it is better to unset the variable so that we do not leave unwanted values around the shell environment:

```
zarrelli:~$ unset TEST_VAR
```

And now, let us try to get the content of the variable:

```
zarrelli:~/$ echo ${TEST_VAR}
zarrelli:~/$
```

No way! The variable content is no more, and as you will see now, the environment variables disappear once their shell is no more. Let's have a look at the following script:

```
zarrelli:~$ cat setting.sh
#!/bin/bash
export MYTEST=NOWAY
env | grep MYTEST
echo ${MYTEST}
```

We simply instance a new variable, grep for it in the environment and then print its content to the stdout. What happens once invoked?

```
zarrelli@:~$ ./setting.sh ; echo ${MYTEST}
MYTEST=NOWAY
NOWAY
zarrelli:~$
```

We can easily see that the variable was grepped on the env output, so this means that the variable is actually instanced at the environment level and we could access its content and print it. But then we executed the echo of the content of MYTEST outside the script again, and we could just print a blank line. If you remember, when we execute a script, the shell forks a new shell and passes to it its full environment, thus the command inside the program shell can manipulate the environment. But then, once the program is terminated, the related shell is terminated, and its environment variables are lost; the child shell inherits the environment from the parent, the parent does not inherit the environment from the child.

Now, let us go back to our shell, and let us see how we can manipulate the environment to our advantage. If you remember, when the shell has to invoke a program or a script, it looks inside the content of the PATH environment variable to see if it can find it in one of the paths listed. If it is not there, the executable or the script cannot be invoked just with their names, they have to be called passing the full path to it. But have a look at what this script is capable of doing:

```
#!/bin/bash
echo "We are into the directory"
pwd
```

We print our current user directory:

```
echo "What is our PATH?"
echo ${PATH}
```

And now we print the content of the environment PATH variable:

```
echo "Now we expand the path for all the shell"
export PATH=${PATH}:~/tmp
```

This is a little tricky. Using the graphs, we preserve the content of the variable and add a, which is the delimiter for each path inside the list held by PATH, plus the ~/tmp, which literally means the tmp directory inside the home directory of the current user:

```
echo "And now our PATH is..."
echo ${PATH}
echo "We are looking for the setting.sh script!"
which setting.sh
echo "Found it!"
```

Let's Start Programming

And we actually found it. Well, you could also add some evaluation to make the `echo` conditional, but we will see such a thing later on. Time for something funny:

```
echo "Time for magic!"
echo  "We are looking for the setting.sh script!"
env PATH=/usr/bin which setting.sh
echo "BOOOO, nothing!"
```

Pay attention to the line starting with `env`; this command is able to overrun the `PATH` environment variable and to pass its own variable and related value. The same behavior can be obtained using export instead of `env`:

```
echo "Second try..."
env PATH=/usr/sbin which setting.sh
echo "No way..."
```

This last try is even worse. We modified the content of the `$PATH` variable which now points to a directory where we cannot find the script. So, not being in the `$PATH`, the script cannot be invoked by just its name:

```
zarrelli:~$ ./setenv.sh
```

We are in the directory:

```
/home/zarrelli/Documents/My books/Mastering bash/Chapter 1/Scripts
```

What is our `PATH`?

```
/usr/local/bin:/usr/bin:/bin:/usr/local/games:/usr/games
```

Now we expand the path for all the shell.

And now our `PATH` is:

```
/usr/local/bin:/usr/bin:/bin:/usr/local/games:/usr/games:/home/zarrelli/tmp
```

We are looking for the `setting.sh` script!

```
/home/zarrelli/tmp/setting.sh
```

Found it!

Time for magic!

We are looking for the `setting.sh` script!

BOOOO, nothing!

Second try...

env: 'which': No such file or directory

No way...

Environment variable	Use
BASH_VERSION	The version of the current Bash session
HOME	The home directory of the current user
HOSTNAME	The name of the host
LANG	The locale used to manage the data
PATH	The search path for the shell
PS1	The prompt configuration
PWD	The path to the current directory
USER	The name of the currently logged in user
LOGNAME	Same as user

We can also use env with the -i argument to strip down all the environment variables and just pass to the process what we want, as we can see in the following examples. Let's start with something easy:

```
zarrelli:~$ cat env-test.sh
#!/bin/bash
env PATH=HELLO /usr/bin/env | grep -A1 -B1 ^PATH
```

Nothing too difficult, we modified the PATH variable passing a useless value because HELLO is not a searchable path, then we had to invoke env using the full path because PATH became useless. Finally, we piped everything to the input of grep, which will select all the rows (^) starting with the string PATH, printing that line and one line before and after:

```
zarrelli:~$ ./env-test.sh
2705-XDG_CONFIG_DIRS=/etc/xdg
2730:PATH=HELLO
2741-SESSION_MANAGER=local/moveaway:@/tmp/.ICE-
unix/888,unix/moveaway:/tmp/.ICE-unix/888
```

Let's Start Programming

Now, let's modify the script, adding `-i` to the first `env`:

```
zarrelli:~$ cat env-test.sh
#!/bin/bash
env -i PATH=HELLO /usr/bin/env | grep -A1 -B1 ^PATH
```

And now let us run it:

```
zarrelli:~/$ ./env-test.sh
PATH=HELLO
zarrelli:~/$
```

Can you guess what happened? Another change will make everything clearer:

```
env -i PATH=HELLO /usr/bin/env
```

No `grep`; we are able to see the complete output of the second `env` command:

```
zarrelli:~$ env -i PATH=HELLO /usr/bin/env
PATH=HELLO
zarrelli:~$
```

Just `PATH=HELLO` `env` with the argument `-i` passed to the second `env` process, a stripped down environment with only the variables specified on the command line:

```
zarrelli:~$ env -i PATH=HELLO LOGNAME=whoami/usr/bin/env
PATH=HELLO
LOGNAME=whoami/usr/bin/env
zarrelli:~$
```

Because we are engaged in stripping down, let us see how we can make a function disappear with the well-known `unset -f` command:

```
#!/bin/bash
echo -e "\n"
echo "The space left is ${disk_space}"
disk_space=`df -h | grep vg-root | awk '{print $4}'`
print () {
echo "The space left inside the function is ${disk_space}"
local available=yes
last=yes
echo "Is the available variable available inside the function? ${available}"
}
echo "Is the last variable available outside the function before it is invoked? ${last}"
print
echo "The space left outside is ${disk_space}"
```

```
echo "Is the available variable available outside the function?
${available}"
echo "Is the last variable available outside the function after it is
invoked? ${last}"
echo "What happens if we unset a variable, like last?"
unset last
echo "Has last a referrable value ${last}"
echo "And what happens if I try to unset a while print functions using
unset -f"
t
print
unset -f print
echo "Unset done, now let us invoke the function"
print
```

Time to verify what happens with the `unset` command:

```
zarrelli:~$ ./disk-space-function-unavailable.sh
```

The space left is:

```
Is the last variable available outside the function before it is invoked?
The space left inside the function is 202G
Is the available variable available inside the function? yes
The space left outside is 202G
Is the available variable available outside the function?
Is the last variable available outside the function after it is invoked?
yes
What happens if we unset a variable, like last?
Has last a referrable value
And what happens if I try to unset a while print functions using
unset -f
The space left inside the function is 202G
Is the available variable available inside the function? yes
```

Unset done, now let us invoke the function:

```
zarrelli:~$
```

The `print` function works well, as expected before we unset it, and also the variable content becomes no longer available. Speaking about variables, we can actually unset some of them on the same row using the following:

```
unset -v variable1 variable2 variablen
```

Let's Start Programming

We saw how to modify an environment variable, but what if we want to make it read-only so to protect its content from an unwanted modification?

```
zarrelli:~$ cat readonly.sh
#!/bin/bash
echo "What is our PATH?"
echo ${PATH}
echo "Now we make it readonly"
readonly PATH
echo "Now  we expand the path for all the shell"
export PATH=${PATH}:~/tmp
```

Look at the line `readonlyPATH`, and now let's see what the execution of this script leads us to:

```
zarrelli:~$ ./readonly.sh
What is our PATH?
/usr/local/bin:/usr/bin:/bin:/usr/local/games:/usr/games
Now we make it readonly
Now  we expand the path for all the shell
./readonly.sh: line 10: PATH: readonly variable
zarrelli:~$
```

What happened is that our script tried to modify the `PATH` variable that was just made `readonly` a few lines before and failed. This failure then led us out of the screen with a failure, and this is confirmed by printing the value of the `$?` variable, which holds the exit state of the last command invoked:

```
zarrelli:~$ echo $?
1
zarrelli:~$ echo $?
0
```

We will see the use of such a kind of variable later, but now what interests us is to know what that 0 and 1 mean: the first time we issued the `echo` command, right after invoking the script, it gave us the exit code 1, which means failure, and this makes sense because the script exited abruptly with an error. The second time we ran `echo`, it showed 0, which means that the last command executed, the previous `echo` went well, without any errors.

Variable expansion

The variable expansion is the method we have to access and actually change the content of a variable or parameter. The simplest way to access or reference the variable value is as in the following example:

```
x=1 ; echo $x
zarrelli:~$ x=1 ; echo $x
1
```

So, we assigned a value to the variable x and then referenced the value preceding the variable name with the dollar sign $. So, echo$x prints the content of x, 1, to the standard output. But we can do something even more subtle:

```
zarrelli:~$ x=1 ; y=$x; echo "x is $x" ; echo "y is $y"
x is 1
y is 1
```

So, we gave a value to the variable x, then we instanced the variable y referencing the content of the variable x. So, y got its assignment referencing the value of x through the $ character, not directly using a number after the = char. So far, we saw two different ways to reference a variable:

```
$x
${x}
```

The first one is terser, but it would be better to stick to the second way because it preserves the name of the variable and, as we saw a few pages before, it allows us to concatenate a string to the variable without losing the possibility of referencing it.

We just saw the simplest among different ways to manipulate the value held by a variable. What we are going to see now is how to thinker with a variable to have default values and messages, so we make the interaction with the variable more flexible. Before proceeding, just bear in mind that we can use two notations for our next example and they are equivalent:

```
${variable-default}
${variable:-default}
```

So, you could see either of the two in a script, and both are correct:

```
${variable:-default} ${variable-default}
```

Simply, if a variable is not set, return a default value, as we can see in the following example:

```
#!/bin/bash
echo "Setting the variable x"
x=10
echo "Printing the value of x using a default fallback value"
echo "${x:-20}"
echo "Unsetting x"
unset -v x
echo "Printing the value of x using a default fallback value"
echo "${x:-20}"
echo "Setting the value of x to null"
x=
echo "Printing the value of x with x to null"
echo "${x:-30}
```

Now, let's execute it:

```
zarrelli:~$ ./variables.sh
Setting the variable x
Printing the value of x using a default fallback value
10
Unsetting x
Printing the value of x using a default fallback value
20
Setting the value of x to null
Printing the value of x with x to null
30
```

As mentioned before, the two notations, with or without the colon, are quite the same. Let us see what happens if in the previous script we substitute ${x:-somenumber} with ${x-somenumber}.

Let's run the modified script:

```
Setting the variable x
Printing the value of x using a default fallback value
10
Unsetting x
Printing the value of x using a default fallback value
20
Setting the value of x to null
Printing the value of x with x to null
zarrelli:$
```

Everything is fine, but the last line. So what is the difference at play here? Simple:

- *${x-30}: The notation with a colon forces a check on the existence of a value for the variable and this value may well be null. In case you have a value, it does print the value of the variable, ignoring the fallback.
    - `unset -f x`: It unsets the variable, so it has no value and we have a fallback value
    - x=: It gives a null to x; so the fallback does not come in to play, and we get back the variable value, for example, null
- ${x:-30}: This forces a fallback value in case the value of a variable is null or nonexistent
    - `unset -f x`: It unsets the variable, so it has no value and we have a fallback value
    - x=: It gives a null to x, but the fallback comes in to play and we get a default value

Default values can be handy if you are writing a script which expects an input or the customer: if the customer does not provide a value, we can use a fallback default value and have our variable instanced with something meaningful:

```bash
#!/bin/bash
echo "Hello user, please give me a number: "
read user_input
echo "The number is: ${user_input:-99}"
```

We ask the user for an input. If he gives us a value, we print it; otherwise, we fallback the value of the variable to 99 and print it:

```
zarrelli:~$ ./userinput.sh
Hello user, please give me a number:
10
The number is: 10
zarrelli:~/$
zarrelli$ ./userinput.sh
Hello user, please give me a number:
The number is: 99
zarrelli:~/$
${variable:=default} ${variable=default}
```

Let's Start Programming

If the variable has a value, it is returned; otherwise, the variable has a default value assigned. In the previous case, we got back a value if the variable had no value; or null, here the variable is actually assigned a value. Better to see an example:

```
#!/bin/bash
#!/bin/bash
echo "Setting the variable x"
x=10
echo "Printing the value of x"
echo ${x}
echo "Unsetting x"
unset -v x
echo "Printing the value of x using a default fallback value"
echo "${x:-20}"
echo "Printing the value of x"
echo ${x}
echo "Setting the variable x with assignment"
echo "${x:=30}"
echo "Printing the value of x again"
echo ${x}
```

We set a variable and then print its value. Then, we unset it and print its value, but because it is unset, we get back a default value. So we try to print the value of x, but since the number we got in the preceding operation was not obtained by an assignment, x is still unset. Finally, we use `echo "${x:=30}"` and get the value 30 assigned to the variable x, and indeed, when we print the value of the variable, we get something. Let us see the script in action:

```
Setting the variable x
Printing the value of x
10
Unsetting x
Printing the value of x using a default fallback value
20
Printing the value of x
Setting the variable x with assignement
30
Printing the value of x again
30
```

Notice the blank line in the middle of the output: we just got a value from the preceding operation, not a real variable assignment:

```
${variable:+default} ${variable+default}
```

[48]

Force a check on the existence of a non null value for a variable. If it exists, it returns the default value; otherwise it returns null:

```
#!/bin/bash
#!/bin/bash
echo "Setting the variable x"
x=10
echo "Printing the value of x"
echo ${x}
echo "Printing the value of x with a default value on
assigned value"
echo "${x:+100}"
echo "Printing the value of x after default"
echo ${x}
echo "Unsetting x"
unset -v x
echo "Printing the value of x using a default fallback value"
echo "${x:+20}"
echo "Printing the value of x"
echo ${x}
echo "Setting the variable x with assignment"
echo "${x:+30}"
echo "Printing the value of x again"
echo ${x}
```

Now, let us run it and check, as follows:

```
Setting the variable x
Printing the value of x
10
Printing the value of x with a default value on assigned value
100
Printing the value of x after default
10
Unsetting x
Printing the value of x using a default fallback value
Printing the value of x
Setting the variable x with assignment
Printing the value of x again
zarrelli:~$
```

As you can see, when the variable is correctly instanced, instead of returning its value, it returns a default `100` and this is double-checked in the following rows where we print the value of `x` and it is still `10`: the `100` we saw was not a value assignment but just a default returned instead of the real value:

```
${variable:?message} ${variable?message}
#!/bin/bash
x=10
y=
unset -v z
echo ${x:?"Should work"}
echo ${y:?"No way"}
echo ${y:?"Well"}
```

The results are quite straightforward:

```
zarrelli:~$ ./set-message.sh
10
./set-message.sh: line 8: y: No way
```

As we tried to access a `void` variable, but for the unset would have been the same, the script exited with an error and the message we got from the variable expansion. All good with the first line, `x` has a value and we printed it but, as you can see, we cannot arrive to the third line, which remains unparsed: the script exited abruptly with a default message printed.

Nice stuff, isn't it? Well, there is a lot more, we have to look at the pattern matching against variables.

Pattern matching against variables

We have a few ways to fiddle with variables, and some of these have a really interesting use in scripts, as we will see later on in this book. Let's briefly recap what we can do with variables and how to do it, but remember we are dealing with values that are returned, not assigned back to the variable:

```
${#variable)
```

It gives us the length of the variable, or if it is an array, the length of the first element of an array. Here is an example:

```
zarrelli:~$ my_variable=thisisaverylongvalue
zarrelli:~$ echo ${#my_variable}
20
```

And indeed `thisisaverylongvalue` is made up of 20 characters. Now, let us see an example with arrays:

```
zarrelli:~$ fruit=(apple pear banana)
```

Here, we instantiated an array with three elements `apple`, `pear`, and `banana`. We will see later in this book how to work with arrays in detail:

```
zarrelli@moveaway:~$ echo ${fruit[2]}
banana
```

We printed the third element of the array. Arrays start with an index of 0, so the third element is at index 2, and it is banana, a 6 characters long word:

```
zarrelli@moveaway:~$ echo ${fruit[1]}
pear
```

We print the second element of the array: pear, a 4 characters long word:

```
zarrelli@moveaway:~$ echo ${fruit[0]}
apple
```

And now, the first element, that is, apple is 5 characters long. Now, if the example we saw is true, the following command should return 5.

```
zarrelli:~$ echo ${#fruit}
5
```

And indeed, the length of the word apple is 5 characters:

${variable#pattern)

If you need to tear out your variable, for a part of it you can use a pattern and remove the shortest occurrence of the pattern from the beginning of the variable and return the resulting value. It is not a variable assignment, not so easy to grasp, but an example will make it clear:

```
zarrelli:~$ shortest=1010201010
zarrelli:~$ echo ${shortest#10}
10201010
zarrelli:~$ echo ${shortest}
1010201010
```

${variable##pattern)

This form is like the preceding one but with a slight difference, the pattern is used to remove its largest occurrence in the variable:

```
zarrelli:~$ my_variable=10102010103
```

Let's Start Programming

We instanced the variable with a series of recurring digits:

```
zarrelli:~$ echo ${my_variable#1*1}
02010103
```

Then, we tried to match a pattern, which means any digit between a leading and ending 1, the shortest occurrence. So it took out 10102010103:

```
zarrelli:~$ echo ${my_variablet##1*1}
03
```

Now, we cut away the widest occurrence of the pattern, and so 10102010103, resulting in a meager 03 as the value returned:

`${variable%pattern}`

Here, we cut away the shortest occurrence of the pattern but now from the end of the variable value:

```
zarrelli:~$ ending=10102010103
zarrelli:~$ echo ${ending%1*3}
10102010
```

So, the shortest occurrence of the `1*3` pattern counted from the end of the file is `10102010103` so we get `10102010` back:

`${variable%%pattern}`

Similar to the previous example, with `##`, in this case, we cut away the longest occurrence of the pattern from the end of the variable value:

```
zarrelli:~$ ending=10102010103
zarrelli:~$ echo ${ending}
10102010103
zarrelli:~$ echo ${ending%1*3}
10102010
zarrelli:~$ echo ${ending%%1*3}
zarrelli:~$
```

Quite clear, isn't it? The longest occurrence is `1*3` is `10102010103`, so we tear away everything and we return nothing, as this example which makes use of the evaluation of `-z` (is empty) will show:

```
zarrelli:~$ my_var=${ending%1*3}
zarrelli:~$ [[ -z "$my_var" ]] && echo "Empty" || echo "Not empty"
Not empty
zarrelli:~$ my_var=${ending%%1*3}
zarrelli:~$ [[ -z "$my_var" ]] && echo "Empty" || echo "Not empty"
```

```
Empty
${variable/pattern/substitution}
```

The reader familiar with regular expressions probably already understood what the outcome is: replace the first occurrence of the pattern in the variable by substitution. If substitution does not exist, then delete the first occurrence of a pattern in variable:

```
zarrelli:~$ my_var="Give me a banana"
zarrelli:~$ echo ${my_var}
Give me a banana
zarrelli:~$ echo ${my_var/banana/pear}
Give me a pear
zarrelli:~$ fruit=${my_var/banana/pear}
zarrelli:~$ echo ${fruit}
Give me a pear
```

Not so nasty, and we were able to instance a variable with the output of our find and replace:

```
${variable//pattern/substitution}
```

Similar to the preceding, in this case, we are going to replace the occurrences of a pattern in the variable:

```
zarrelli@moveaway:~$ fruit="A pear is a pear and is not a banana"
zarrelli@moveaway:~$ echo ${fruit//pear/watermelon}
A watermelon is a watermelon and is not a banana
```

Like the preceding example, if substitution is omitted, a pattern is deleted from the variable:

```
${variable/#pattern/substitution}
```

If the prefix of the variable matches, then replace the pattern with substitution in variable, so this is similar to the preceding but matches only at the beginning of the variable:

```
zarrelli:~$ fruit="a pear is a pear and is not a banana"
zarrelli:~$ echo ${fruit/#"a pear"/}
 is a pear and is not a banana
zarrelli:~$ echo ${fruit/#"a pear"/"an apple"}
an apple is a pear and is not a banana
```

As usual, omitting means deleting the occurrence of the pattern from the variable.

```
${variable/%pattern/substitution}
```

Once again, a positional replacement, this time at the end of the variable value:

```
zarrelli:~$ fruit="a pear is not a banana even tough I would
like to eat a banana"
zarrelli:~$ echo ${fruit/%"a banana"/"an apple"}
a pear is not a banana even though I would like to eat an apple
```

A lot of nonsense, but it makes sense:

```
${!prefix_variable*}
${!prefix_variable@}
```

Match the name of the variable names starting with the highlighted prefix:

```
zarrelli:~$ firstvariable=1
zarrelli:~$ secondvariable=${!first*}
zarrelli@:~$ echo ${secondvariable}
firstvariable
zarrelli:~$ thirdvariable=${secondvariable}
zarrelli:~$ echo ${thirdvariable}
firstvariable
${variable:position}
```

We can decide from which position we want to start the variable expansion, so determining what part of its value we want to get back:

```
zarrelli:~$ picnic="Either I eat an apple or I eat a raspberry"
zarrelli:~$ echo ${picnic:25}
I eat a raspberry
```

So, we just took a part of the variable, and we decided the starting point, but we can also define for how long cherry-picking is done:

```
${variable:position:offset}
zarrelli:~$ wheretogo="I start here, I go there, no further"
zarrelli:~$ echo ${wheretogo:14:10}
I go there
```

So we do not go further, start at a position and stop at the offset; this way, we can extract whatever consecutive characters/digits we want from the value of a variable.

So far, we have seen many different ways to access and modify the content of a variable or, at least, of what we get from a variable. There is a class of very special variables left to look at, and these will be really handy when writing a script.

Special variables

Let's see now some variables which have some spacial uses that we can benefit from:

${1}, ${n}

The first interesting variables we want to explore have a special role in our scripts because they will let us capture more than an argument on our first command-line execution. Have a look at this bunch of lines:

```
!/bin/bash
fistvariable=${1}
secondvariable=${2}
thirdvariable=${3}
echo "The value of the first variable is ${1}, the second
is ${2}, the third is ${3}"
```

Pay attention to $1, $2, $3:

```
zarrelli:~$ ./positional.sh
The value of the first variable is , the second is , the third is
```

First try, no arguments on the command line, we see nothing printed for the variables:

```
zarrelli:~$ ./positional.sh 1 2 3
The value of the first variable is 1, the second is 2,
the third is 3
```

Second try, we invoke the script and add three digits separated by spaces and, actually, we can see them printed. The first on the command line corresponds to $1, the second to $2, and the third to $3:

```
zarrelli:~$ ./positional.sh Green Yellow Red
```

The value of the first variable is Green; the second is Yellow; and the third is Red.

Third try, we use words with the same results. But notice here:

```
zarrelli:~$ ./positional.sh "One sentence" "Another one"
A third one
The value of the first variable is One sentence, the second
is Another one, the third is A
```

Let's Start Programming

We used a double quote to prevent the space between one sentence and another being interpreted as a divider for the command-line bits, and in fact, the first and second sentences were added as a complete string to the variables, but the third came up just with an A because the subsequent spaces, not quoted, were considered to be separators and the following bits taken as $4, $5, and $n. Note that we could also mix the order of assignment, as follows:

```
thirdvariable=${3}
fistvariable=${1}
secondvariable=${2}
```

The result would be the same. What is important is not the position of the variable we declare, but what positional we associate with it.

As you saw, we used two different methods to represent a positional variable:

```
${1}
$1
```

Are they the same? Almost. Look here:

```
#!/bin/bash
fistvariable=${1}
secondvariable=${2}
thirdvariable=${3}
eleventhvariable=$11
echo "The value of the first variable is ${fistvariable},
the second is ${secondvriable}, the third is ${thirdvariable},
the eleventh is ${eleventhvariable}"
```

Now, let's execute the script:

```
zarrelli:~$ ./positional.sh "One sentence" "Another one" A
third one
The value of the first variable is One sentence, the second
is Another one, the third is A, the eleventh is One sentence1
```

Interesting, the `eleventhvariable` has been interpreted as it were the positional $1 and added a 1. Odd, let's rewrite the echo in the following way:

```
eleventhvariable=${11}
```

And run the script again:

```
zarrelli$ ./positional.sh "One sentence" "Another one" A third one
The value of the first variable is One sentence, the second is
Another one, the third is A, the eleventh is
```

Now we are correct. We did not pass an eleventh positional value on the command line, so the `eleventhvariable` has not been instantiated and we do not see anything printed to the video. Be cautious, always use `${}`; it will preserve the value of the variable in your complex scripts when having a grasp of every single detail would be really difficult:

`${0}`

This expands to the full path to the script; it gives you a way to handle it in your script. So, let's add the following line at the end of the script and execute it:

```
echo "The full path to the script is $0"
zarrelli:~$ ./positional.sh 1 2 3
The value of the first variable is 1, the second is 2, the
third is 3, the eleventh is
The full path to the script is ./positional.sh
```

In our case, the path is local, since we called the script from inside the directory that is holding it:

`${#}`

Expands into the number of the arguments passed to the script, showing us the number of arguments that have been passed on the command line to the script. So, let's add the following line to our script and let's see what comes out of it:

```
echo "We passed ${#} arguments to the script"
zarrelli:~$ ./positional.sh 1 2 3 4 5 6 7
The value of the first variable is 1, the second is 2, the
third is 3, the eleventh is
The full path to the script is ./positional.sh
We passed 7 arguments to the script
${@}
${*}
```

Gives us the list of arguments passed on the command line to the script, with one difference: `${@}` preserves the spaces, the second doesn't:

```
#!/bin/bash
fistvariable=${1}
secondvariable=${2}
thirdvariable=${3}
eleventhvariable=${11}
export IFS=*
echo "The value of the first variable is ${fistvariable},
the second is ${secondvariable}, the third is ${thirdvariable},
the eleventh is ${eleventhvariable}"
echo "The full path to the script is $0"
```

[57]

Let's Start Programming

```
echo "We passed ${#} arguments to the script"
echo "This is the list of the arguments ${@}"
echo "This too is the list of the arguments ${*}"
IFS=
echo "This too is the list of the arguments ${*}"
```

We changed the characters used by the shell as a delimiter to identify single words. Now, let us execute the script:

```
zarrelli:~$ ./positional.sh 1 2 3
The value of the first variable is 1, the second is 2,
the third is 3, the eleventh is
The full path to the script is ./positional.sh
We passed 3 arguments to the script
This is the list of the arguments 1 2 3
This too is the list of the arguments 1*2*3
This too is the list of the arguments 123
```

Here, you can see the difference at play:

- *: This expands to the positional parameters, starting from the first and when the expansion is within double quotes, it expands to a single word and separates each positional parameter using the first character of IFS. If the latter is null, a space is used, if it is null the words are concatenated without separators.
- @: This expands to the positional parameter, starting from the first, and if the expansion occurs within a double quote, each positional parameter is expanded to a word on its own:

    ${?}

This special variable expands to the exit value of the last command executed, as we have already seen:

```
zarrelli:~$ /bin/ls disk.sh ; echo ${?} ; tt ; echo ${?}
disk.sh
0
bash: tt: command not found
127
```

The first command was successful, so the exit code is 0 ; the second gave an error `127command not found`, since such a command as `tt` does not exist.

`${$}` expands to the process number of the current shell and for a script is the shell in which it is running. Let us add the following line to our `positional.sh` script:

```
echo "The process id of this script is ${$}"
```

Then let's run it:

```
zarrelli:~$ ./positional.sh 1 2 3
The value of the first variable is 1, the second is 2, the
third is 3, the eleventh is
The full path to the script is ./positional.sh
We passed 3 arguments to the script
This is the list of the arguments 1 2 3
This too is the list of the arguments 1*2*3
This too is the list of the arguments 123
The process id of this script is 13081
```

Step by step, our script is telling us more and more:

`${!}`

This is tricky; it expands to the process number of the last command executed in the background. Time to add some other lines to our script:

```
echo "The background process id of this script is ${!}"
echo "Executing a ps in background"
nohup ps &
echo "The background process id of this script is ${!}"
```

And now execute it:

```
zarrelli:~$ ./positional.sh 1 2 3
The value of the first variable is 1, the second is 2,
the third is 3, the eleventh is
The full path to the script is ./positional.sh
We passed 3 arguments to the script
This is the list of the arguments 1 2 3
This too is the list of the arguments 1*2*3
This too is the list of the arguments 123
The process id of this script is 13129
The background process id of this script is
Executing a ps in background
The background process id of this script is 13130
nohup: appending output to 'nohup.out'
```

We used `nohup ps &` to send the `ps` in the background (`&`) and detach it from the current terminal (`nohup`). We will see later, in more details the use of background commands; it suffices now to see how, before sending the process in to the background, we had no value to print for `${!}` ; it was instanced only after we sent `ps` in to the background.

Do you see that?

```
nohup: appending output to 'nohup.out'
```

Well, for our purposes, it has no value, so how can we redirect this useless output and get rid of it during the execution of our script? You know what? It is a tiny exercise for you to do before you start reading the next chapter, which will deal with the operators and much more fun.

Summary

In this chapter, we touched on some of the very basics of the shell, such as things that you should know how to deal with in the correct way. Failing to preserve variable names can, for instance, lead us to unwanted results and, on a different side, knowing how to access environment variables will help us create a better environment for our day-to-day tasks. As we said, basic but important things that a Bash master should know by heart, because unmasks, file descriptors, and fiddling with variables are what let you play awesome tricks and are the building blocks to becoming more advanced. So, do not just overlook them; they will help you.

2
Operators

What we have looked at so far is tinkering with values returned from variable expansions and descriptors used in a tricky way. So, something nice, but we could not do much more, since we do not have a way to actually relate values, compare or even modify at our will.

Here is where the operators come in to play, and we will see how to modify the value of a variable so that it will hold a value and, over time, modify to gather new information. So, let's start from something simple, from basic math then move on to something more complex.

One last thing we have to bear in mind before proceeding is that the operators follow an order of precedence:

- The compound logical operators `-a`, `-o`, and `&&` have a low precedence
- The arithmetic operators have the following precedence:
    - Multiply
    - Divide
    - Add
    - Subtract
- The evaluation of operators with equal precedence is from left to right

Arithmetic operators

Arithmetic operators do what you think they do, that is, add, subtract, divide, and so on. It is something we are familiar with even without specific programming knowledge. Let's see each of them and how they can be used to manipulate the value of variables.

Operators

Before proceeding, keep in mind that for a shell script, a number is a decimal unless you prefix that with a 0 for the octal, a 0x for a hexadecimal number, or a base#number for a number that evaluates on the base.

The + operator

This is like what we see at primary school; this operator allows us to add an integer to the value of the variable, as we can see in the following example:

```
#!/bin/bash
echo "Hello user, please give me a number: "
read user_input
echo "And now another one, please: "
read adding
addition=$((user_input+adding))
echo "The number is: ${user_input:-99}"
echo "The number added of ${adding} is: ${addition}"
```

Now time to invoke the script:

```
zarrelli:$ ./useraddition.sh
Hello user, please give me a number:
120
And now another one, please:
30
The number is: 120
The number added of 30 is: 150
```

As you have probably noted, we used a double parenthesis construct $(( )) to perform this arithmetic expansion and evaluation: in short, it is as we said, expand and evaluate, then return the value. It is a common notation in binary operators and also allows us to quote special characters as if we'd enclosed them into double quotes, so we are not compelled to escape that. The only exception is the double quote, which still must be escaped. Do not worry; we will read more about special characters and how to quote them later on.

Now, just try to run the script and give no numbers:

```
The number is: 99
The number added of is: 0
```

The number 99 is not an assignment, just a default value we were returned in case the variable held no usable values, but the first and second variables have no assignment so adding one value to the other leads us to 0.

[62]

The - operator

Well, in this case, we are going to subtract something from the value of the variable with a little caveat: this is a left-associative operation, with the evaluation order from left to right, and this means that we are subtracting the value at the right of the minus sign from the value on the left:

```
zarrelli:~$ a=20 ; b=5 ; c=$((a-b)) ; echo ${c}
15
```

The * operator

To multiply, we do not need to care about the order; one value is multiplied for another one, no matter which direction we take:

```
zarrelli:~$ a=20 ; b=5 ; c=$((${a}*${b})) ; echo ${c}
100
```

The / operator

Division is another operation left-associative, so we divide the number on the left of the division character by the number on the right:

```
zarrelli:~$ a=20 ; b=5 ; c=$((a/b)) ; echo ${c}
4
```

The % operator

The modulo operator gives us the remainder of the division between two integers:

```
zarrelli:~$ a=29 ; b=5 ; c=$((a/b)) ; echo ${c}
5
zarrelli:~$ a=29 ; b=5 ; c=$((a%b)) ; echo ${c}
4
```

The ** operator

As we saw at school, exponentiation is a number multiplied by itself as many times as imposed by the exponent:

```
zarrelli:~$ a=4 ; b=5 ; c=$((a**b)) ; echo ${c}
1024
zarrelli:~$ a=4 ; c=$((a*a*a*a*a)) ; echo ${c}
1024
```

In this case, we are facing a left-associative operation and the order matters. Be aware that, in any case, the variables are expanded before the evaluation takes place with all the operators we have seen so far. We are using both $a and ${a} to get you used to what you will face in real life, looking at the scripts you will find on the Internet.

Assignment operators

We have seen how to manipulate the value assigned to a variable and an integer so far, and then reassign this value to another variable or the same one. But why use two operations when you can alter the value of a variable and reassign it at the same time using the assignment operators?

The += operator

This operator adds a quantity to the value of the variable and assigns the outcome to the variable itself, but to clarify its use, let's rewrite one of the examples we've seen before:

```
#!/bin/bash
echo "Hello user, please give me a number: "
read user_input
echo "And now another one, please: "
```

Adding

```
echo "The user_input variable value is: ${user_input}"
echo "The adding variable value is: ${adding}"
echo "${user_input} added of ${adding} is: $((user_input+=adding))"
echo "And the user_input variable has now  the value of
${user_input}"
echo"But the adding variable has still the value of ${adding}"
```

And now, let's run it, as follows:

```
zarrelli:~$ ./userreassign.sh
Hello user, please give me a number:
150
And now another one, please:
50
The user_input variable value is: 150
The adding variable value is: 50
150 added of 50 is: 200
And the user_input variable has now the value of 200
But the adding variable has still the value of 50
```

Easy! And we did not have to reassign the value of 200 explicitly.

The -= operator

Actually, this is very similar to the the former operator, only in this case, we do a subtraction and reassign the value. Let's rewrite our last script with the operator and see what happens:

```
zarrelli:~$ ./userreassign-subtract.sh
Hello user, please give me a number:
200
And now another one, please:
50
The user_input variable value is: 200
The adding variable value is: 50
200 subtracted of 50 is: 150
And the user_input variable has now  the value of 150
But the adding variable has still the value of 50
```

The *= operator

In this case, we are multiplying the value of the variable for the given number and reassigning:

```
zarrelli:~$ ./userreassign-multiply.sh
Hello user, please give me a number:
-1
And now another one, please:
9223372036854775808
The user_input variable value is: -1
The adding variable value is: 9223372036854775808
```

```
-1 multiplied for   9223372036854775808 is:
-9223372036854775808
And the user_input variable has now the value of
-9223372036854775808
But the adding variable has still the value of
9223372036854775808
```

Nice! Indeed, we reached one of boundaries of the modern Bash: in the past, the value held by a variable could be represented by a 32-bit signed long, but from version 2.05b onward it switched to a 64-bit signed integer in the following range of:

`-9,223,372,036,854,775,808 to 9,223,372,036,854,775,807`

Remember that values containing a comma are interpreted as a character string.

The /= operator

In this case, we are dividing the value of the variable for a given number and reassigning the new value to it:

```
zarrelli@:~$ ./userreassign-division.sh
Hello user, please give me a number:
10
And now another one, please:
2
The user_input variable value is: 10
The adding variable value is: 2
10 divided for 2 is: 5
And the user_input variable has now the value of 5
But the adding variable has still the value of 2
```

The %= operator

With modulo assignment, we divide the value of the variable for a given number and reassign the remainder. Let's just modify a couple of lines in our script:

```
echo "The value of ${user_input} divided by ${adding} is:
$((user_input/=adding))"
echo "The remainder of ${user_input} divided by ${adding} is:
$((user_input%=adding))"
```

And execute it:

```
zarrelli@:~$ ./userreassign-modulo.sh
Hello user, please give me a number:
324
And now another one, please:
12
The user_input variable value is: 324
The adding variable value is: 12
The value of 324 divided by 12 is: 27
The remainder of 27 divided by 12 is: 3
And the user_input variable has now  the value of 3
But the adding variable has still the value of 12
```

The ++ or -- operators

This is the unary operator ++ (or --), which allows us to increase/decrease the value of a variable of 1 and reassign it, but be careful, the position of the operator matters:

```
zarrelli:~$ a=15 ; echo $((a++)) ; echo ${a}
15
16
zarrelli:~$ a=15 ; echo $((++a)) ; echo ${a}
16
16
```

Can you figure out what happened? Simply, in the first case, the first operator returned the value and, only after, added 1 to it; in the second case, first it added 1 to the value and then returned it. Pay attention to this operator because it is widely used inside loops to count the cycles and eventually break out from them:

```
zarrelli:~$ cat loop.sh
#!/bin/bash
counter=10
while [ $counter -gt 0 ];
do
echo"Loop number: $((counter--))"
done
```

We instance a variable named counter with a value of 10, then we define a loop, which while the counter value is greater than 0, it prints the value of the counter and decreases it, reassigning it. At each cycle, the variable value is printed and then lowered by 1. Once the counter reaches 0, the while condition is no longer valid and the loop stops:

```
zarrelli:~$ ./loop.sh
Loop number: 10
Loop number: 9
Loop number: 8
Loop number: 7
Loop number: 6
Loop number: 5
Loop number: 4
Loop number: 3
Loop number: 2
Loop number: 1
```

Bitwise operators

Bitwise operators are useful when dealing with bit masks, but in normal practice, they are not so easy to use, and so you will not encounter them very often. However, since they are available in Bash we are going to have a look at them with some examples.

Left shift (<<)

The bitwise left shift operators simply multiplies by 2 a value for each shift position; the following example will make everything more clear:

```
zarrelli:~$ x=10 ; echo $((x<<1))
20
zarrelli:~$ x=10 ; echo $((x<<2))
40
zarrelli:~$ x=10 ; echo $((x<<3))
80
zarrelli:~$ x=10 ; echo $((x<<4))
160
```

What happened? As we said before, the bitwise operators work on a bit mask, so let's start converting the integer 10 to its binary representation in 16-bit and using a power of 2 table to check the values.

In this case, a simple method to represent a decimal in a binary form is to use the power of two notations, starting with dividing our integer in a sum of power of two numbers. In our example, the highest power of two that fits into 10 is 2^3, which is 8, plus 2^1, that is, 2. So, among the powers of two we select only 23 and 21 and we can represent this in a table like the following:

2^7	2^6	2^5	2^4	2^3	2^2	2^1	2^0
128	64	32	16	8	4	2	1
0	0	0	0	1	0	1	0
				8		2	

If we mark with a 1 the powers of 2, we used to represent the number 10 and with 0 those unused, the result will be 1010, or 00001010 if we use 8-bit to represent the number.

What we are going to do now is to shift all the digits to the left by one position, but this gives us an issue with the right end digit, which has no digit on its right to take over its place. So, for the last right slot, we will use a 0:

10100

128	64	32	16	8	4	2	1
0	0	0	1	0	1	0	0
			16		4		

And this number, converted into decimal, is 20. So now, let's see what echo$((x<<2)) turns into:

128	64	32	16	8	4	2	1
0	0	1	0	1	0	0	0
		32		8			

So, we have 40. Now it is time to go over $((x<<3)), moving out the first one on the left, adding a trailing 0 and adding a sign bit at the beginning:

1010000

128	64	32	16	8	4	2	1
0	1	0	1	0	0	0	0
	64		16				

We reached 80; now, let's go for $((x<<4))$, same procedure:

10100000

128	64	32	16	8	4	2	1
1	0	1	0	0	0	0	0
128		32					

Well, 160 is the result, as you can imagine. So now we know a really fast method to multiply a number by the power of two, but what if we want to divide?

Right shift (>>)

The bitwise right shift is a great method to divide a number by 2 at each position, so division by power of 2, shifting the bit to the right. Note that this operation pads on the left with the most significant bit, that is the sign bit, so everything will be padded by one, but the following example will make everything easier:

```
zarrelli:~$ x=160 ; echo $((x>>1))
80
zarrelli:~$ x=160 ; echo $((x>>2))
40
zarrelli:~$ x=160 ; echo $((x>>3))
20
zarrelli:~$ x=160 ; echo $((x>>4))
10
```

So, let's start with 160:

10100000

128	64	32	16	8	4	2	1
1	0	1	0	0	0	0	0
128		32					

What we will do now is to shift one position to the right:

1010000

128	64	32	16	8	4	2	1
0	1	0	1	0	0	0	0
	64		1				

Now we have 80, but again, one position to the left:

128	64	32	16	8	4	2	1
0	0	1	0	1	0	0	0
		32		8			

Now, as an exercise, calculate by yourself the remaining values.

Bitwise AND (&)

This is the bitwise AND operator; it is similar to a logical AND but works on the bit mask on the binary representation of the integer. The binary bits are read from left to right and compared between the two numbers: if, in the same position of each number, we find a 1, the result will be 1, otherwise it will be 0:

```
zarrelli:~$ x=50 ; y=20; echo $((x&y))
16
```

How did we come to such a value? Let's create a matrix with the binary values of 50 and 20:

	128	64	32	16	8	4	2	1
50	0	0	1	1	0	0	1	0
20	0	0	0	1	0	1	0	0
&	0	0	0	1	0	0	0	0

The result is the binary 00010000, which in decimal is 16.

Bitwise OR (|)

The bitwise OR operator is similar to an inclusive OR and checks two integers using their binary representation: if there is at least a 1 on the same position for each number, the result will be 1:

```
zarrelli:~$ x=50 ; y=20; echo $((x|y))
54
```

As we can see from the following table:

	128	64	32	16	8	4	2	1
50	0	0	1	1	0	0	1	0
20	0	0	0	1	0	1	0	0
|	0	0	1	1	0	1	1	0

Bitwise XOR (^)

This is what we would call exclusive OR or XOR: the result will be 1 only if at the same slot, there is only a 1, and if there are two 1, the result will be 0:

```
zarrelli:~$ x=50 ; y=20; echo $((x^y))
38
```

So, let's check again with our matrix:

	128	64	32	16	8	4	2	1
50	0	0	1	1	0	0	1	0
20	0	0	0	1	0	1	0	0
^	0	0	1	0	0	1	1	0

And that is, 36.

Bitwise NOT (~)

The bitwise NOT is a unary operator, and this means it is used with just one operator, flipping the bit used to represent the integer in binary notation:

```
zarrelli:~$ x=50 ; echo $((~x))
-51
```

Have a look at the following table:

	128	64	32	16	8	4	2	1
50	0	0	1	1	0	0	1	0
~	1	1	0	0	1	1	0	1
	-128	64			8	4		1

We have to keep in mind that the most significant bit on the left for a signed integer (and this is a signed integer, even though we do not write +50 because Bash represents integer with a sign long at 64-bit) holds the sign value. So, flipping the first significant bit actually inverted the value. As the rule of thumb, the bitwise NOT leads to the same result as of a two's complement of the number minus 1:

```
zarrelli:~$ x=30 ; echo $((~x))
-31
```

	128	64	32	16	8	4	2	1
30	0	0	0	1	1	1	1	0
~	1	1	1	0	0	0	0	1
	-128	64	32					1

However, we can also calculate the bitwise by not first converting the integer in binary, inverting the digits and adding to the result a 1 in binary notation in a so-called two's complement:

50	0	0	1	1	0	0	1	0
invert	1	1	0	0	1	1	0	1
add 1	0	0	0	0	0	0	0	1
-51	1	1	0	0	1	1	0	1

So, as you can see, in the two's complement, binaries with the leftmost bit set to 1 have a negative value; those starting with 0 are positive integers.

Logical operators

Here, we come to something really useful for our scripts, a bunch of operators that will enable us to perform some tests and react as a consequence. So, we will be able to make our script react to a some change or user input and be more flexible. Let's see what is available.

Logical NOT (!)

The NOT operator is used to test whether an expression is true and holds true when the expression is false:

```
[! expression ]
```

Let's go back to one of our previous scripts and make it more user-friendly:

```
#!/bin/bash
echo "Hello user, please give me a number between 10 and 12: "
read user_input
if [ ! ${user_input} -eq11 ]
then
echo "The number ${user_input} is not what we are looking for..."
else
echo "Great! The number ${user_input} is what we were looking for!"
fi
```

What we are doing here is asking the user for a number between 10 and 12. We read the value from its input and evaluate it: if the user inputs a value that is not equal to 11, then we write a boo sentence; otherwise, we have found our number. Do not worry; we will have a look at if...then...else later in this book, just take if for what it is a simple conditional. Let's run the script and see what happens when we input the right answer and when we fail the input:

```
zarrelli:~$ ./userinput-not.sh
Hello user, please give me a number between 10 and 12:
11
Great! The number 11 is what we were looking for!
zarrelli:~$ ./userinput-not.sh
Hello user, please give me a number between 10 and 12:
12
The number 12 is not what we are looking for...
```

Great! The script became quite interactive, and its output changes based on the conditions we imposed and the input we gave.

Logical AND (&&)

The AND operator tests the success of two or more expressions and holds true if all the conditions are true. This comes in handy to make our script a bit more complex so that we must pass at least a couple of conditions to make something trigger:

```
#!/bin/bash
echo "Hello user, please give me a number between 10 and 20: "
read user_input
if [ ${user_input} -ge 10 ] && [ ${user_input} -le 20 ]
then
echo "Great! The number ${user_input} is what we were looking for!"
else
echo "The number ${user_input} is not what we are looking for..."
fi
```

In this case, we ask for a couple of conditions that must hold true at the same time: the number given by the user must be equal or greater than 10 and lesser or equal than 20. Let's see:

```
zarrelli:~$ ./userinput-and.sh
Hello user, please give me a number between 10 and 20:
9
The number 9 is not what we are looking for...
The number 9 is not a valid value: it is less than 20 but
not bigger than 10.
zarrelli:~$ ./userinput-and.sh
Hello user, please give me a number between 10 and 20:
10
Great! The number 10 is what we were looking for!
```

Yes, 10 is good, since it is equal to 10 and less than 20. Both conditions are true at the same time. We have the following code:

```
zarrelli:~$ ./userinput-and.sh
Hello user, please give me a number between 10 and 20:
11
Great! The number 11 is what we were looking for!
```

With 11, we are OK, because it is more than 10 but at the same time, less than 20:

```
zarrelli:~$ ./userinput-and.sh
Hello user, please give me a number between 10 and 20:
19
Great! The number 19 is what we were looking for!
```

Still a valid answer because it is more than 10 and less than 20:

```
zarrelli:~$ ./userinput-and.sh
Hello user, please give me a number between 10 and 20:
20
Great! The number 20 is what we were looking for!
```

This should be the last valid answer. The value is above 10 and equal to 20, but 20 is our upper limit, so one more and we are out of our boundaries:

```
zarrelli:~$ ./userinput-and.sh
Hello user, please give me a number between 10 and 20:
21
The number 21 is not what we are looking for..
```

Here we are: above 10 but also above 20, and our second condition holds true only if the value is less than or equal to 20. So, just one condition is true, the other is false, and 21 is not the number we were looking for.

Logical OR (||)

The OR operator tests the success of two or more expressions and holds true if at least one condition is true:

```
#!/bin/bash
echo "Hello user, please give me a number between 10 and 20
or between 50 and 10: "
read user_input
if [[ ${user_input} -ge 10 && ${user_input} -le 20 ]] ||
[[ ${user_input} -ge 50 && ${user_input} -le 100 ]]
then
echo "Great! The number ${user_input} is what we were looking
for!"
else
echo "The number ${user_input} is not what we are looking for..."
fi
```

What we see here are a few interesting things. First, we used a compound condition test so that we can now check between four different conditions, grouped by 2. Our test holds true if the user give us a number that is equal to or higher than 10 and at the same time, lower than or equal to 20, or if he types a number that is equal to or higher than 50, and at the same time lower or equal to 100.

Note that we had to use the test command with double brackets [[; this is a Bash improvement over the single bracket, and it should be preferred over this last one. To be true, the [is an actual binary, a command you can find into the operating system and [[is a keyword available only in Bash, **Zsh** and **Korn** shell.

There are quite a few interesting improvements with the double bracket. As an example, it does not suffer from word splitting or glob expansion, so deals better with spaces and empty strings and you do not have to quote your variables. Other advantages are that you do not have to escape any parenthesis inside the double brackets, and you can also use !, &&, and || inside them to combine different expressions. We used the [] test operator in our examples just to get used to them, but you will see in most of the scripts, you will encounter that the brackets are usually adopted for file or string test, whereas for testing numbers, you will prefer using the arithmetic operations $(()) because the first is deprecated for arithmetic operations.

Comma operator (,)

One last operator that actually does not fit into any other category is the comma operator, which is used to chain together arithmetic operations. All the operations are evaluated, but only the value from the last one is returned:

```
zarrelli:~$ echo $((x=1, 7-2))
5
zarrelli@moveaway:~$ echo ${x}
1
```

Operators evaluation order and precedence in decreasing relevance

Operators are evaluated in a precise order and we must keep this in mind when working with them. It is not so easy to remember what is evaluated before and what after, so the following table will help us to keep in mind the order and precedence of operators:

Operator	Evaluation order
++ --	Unary operators for incrementing/decrementing, evaluated from left to right
+- !~	Unary plus and minus, evaluated from right to left
* / %	Multiplication, division, modulo, are evaluated from left to right and are evaluated after
+ -	Addition and subtraction are evaluated from left to right
<<>>	Bitwise shift are evaluated from left to right
<= =><>	Comparison operators, from left to right
== !=	Equality operators, from left to right
&	Bitwise AND, from left to right
^	Bitwise XOR, from left to right
|	Bitwise OR, from left to right
&&	Logic AND, from left to right
||	Logic OR, from left to right
= += -+ */ /= %= &= ^= <<= =>> }=	Assignment operators, from left to right

Exit codes

We have already seen that when a program encounters issues it *exits*, usually with an error message. What does exits means? Simply that the code execution terminates and the program, or the script, returns an exit code that informs the system of what happened. This is very handy for us, since we can trap the exit code of a program and decide what to do based on its value.

0	Success
1	Failure
2	Misuse of builtin
126	Command not executable
127	Command not found
128	Invalid argument
128+x	Fatal error exit with signal x
130	Execution terminated by Ctrl +C
255	Exit state out of boundary (0-255)

So, maybe you already guessed, each execution terminates with an exit code, whether successful or not, with an error message or silently:

```
zarrelli:~$ date ; echo $?
Thu  2 Feb 19:17:48 GMT 2017
0
```

As you can see, the exit code is 0 because the command was executed without issues. Now, let's try this:

```
zarrelli:~$ asrw ; echo $?
bash: asrw: command not found
127
```

It is a `command not found` as we just typed a meaningless bunch of characters. Now a while cycle will not terminate until we press Ctrl + C.

```
while true ; do echo 1 ; done
```

You will see your screen filling up with a column of infinite 1. Press Ctrl + C and you will see:

```
^C
```

Now, let's check the exit code:

```
zarrelli:~$ echo $?
130
```

Operators

Now, let's create a never-ending script:

```
#!/bin/bash
while true; do
echo ${$}
done
```

Although true is a never-ending cycle, since the condition is always true, it will print to the stdout the PID of the shell, which the script is running in. Let's open a second terminal and launch the script from the first; you will see the same PID repeated indefinitely:

```
1764
1764
1764
1764
1764
```

Now, from the second terminal, using the same user or root user, issue:

```
zarrelli:~$ kill -9 1764
```

Go back to the first terminal, and you see your script terminated:

```
1764
1764
1764
1764
Killed
```

Time to check the exit status of the script:

```
zarrelli:~$ echo $?
137
```

Which is `128 + 9`, 9 being the signal we used to kill the process. Let's run the script again:

```
1778
1778
1778
1778
```

Now kill it from the second terminal with:

```
zarrelli:~$ kill -15 1778
1778
1778
1778
1778
Terminated
```

[80]

Back to the first terminal to check the exit code of the script:

```
zarrelli:~$ echo $?
143
```

And `143` is exactly `128 + 15`, as we expected.

Exiting a script

So far, we have seen how a script terminated with the exit status of the last command issued, and how a `$?` allows us to read the exit value. This is possible because every command returns an exit code, whether issued on the command line or from inside a script, and even functions that we can think of as a compound of commands return a value. Now we are going to see how a script can return an exit code on its own, despite of the result of the last command issued:

```
#!/bin/bash
counter=10
while [ $counter -gt 0 ];
do
echo "Loop number: $((counter--))"
done
exit 20
```

We took one of our previous scripts and added this:

```
exit 20
```

As you can see, we used the command `exit` followed by a positive number to give an exit code. Remember that you can use any code between:

```
0-255
```

With the exclusion of the reserved values, we saw in the previous chapter. Now, let's run the script:

```
zarrelli:~$ ./loop-exit.sh ; echo $?
Loop number: 10
Loop number: 9
Loop number: 8
Loop number: 7
Loop number: 6
Loop number: 5
Loop number: 4
Loop number: 3
Loop number: 2
```

Operators

```
Loop number: 1
20
```

Here we are. Instead of having a 0 as the script exit value, since the last instruction was successful, we have a 20, provided by the exit command.

Let's modify the script a bit so that the exit will be just above our `echo` command:

```
#!/bin/bash
counter=10
exit_at=5
while (( counter > 0 ));
do
echo "Loop number: $((counter--))"
if (( $counter <exit_at )); then
exit 18
fi
done
```

Note a couple of things:

- We are using both `$(())` and `(())`. The first is an arithmetic expansion and gives us a number, the second is a command that gives us an exit status so we can read *if it is true (0)* that the value of counter is less than value of `exit_at`.
- We used a condition to break out of this infinite loop. Once the value of counter is less than the value of `exit_at`, we exit the whole script with a code of 18, regardless of the fact that the last command, the evaluation of the `if` condition got a value of 1, so was a failure.

And now, execute the following script:

```
zarrelli:~$ /loop-premature-exit.sh ; echo $?
Loop number: 10
Loop number: 9
Loop number: 8
Loop number: 7
Loop number: 6
Loop number: 5
18
```

Here we are. The script exited once it passed the boundary of 5, so the remaining five `echo` commands were not executed at all and we got 18 as the exit value. So, now you have a handy loop that you can use to iterate over items and stop when a condition is reached.

We said that the `exit` command prevents the further execution of a script and the previous example gave us a glimpse of it, but let's modify our previous loop script moving the `exit 20` command to some lines earlier:

```
#!/bin/bash
counter=10
while [ $counter -gt 0 ];
do
exit 20
echo"Loop number: $((counter--))"
done
```

Now, let's execute it:

```
zarrelli:$ ./loop-upper-exit.sh ; echo $?
20
```

Well, no output and the exit value is 20. The script had no time to reach the echo line, it was forced to exit well before. Now, let's see how our `exit` command masquerades the exit code from a command not found:

```
#!/bin/bash
counter=10
while [ $counter -gt 0 ];
do
echo "Loop number: $((counter--))"
fsaapoiwe
done
exit 20
```

Have a loop at the line under `echo`, that is, a bunch of characters without any sense, so it will throw an error for sure:

```
zarrelli:~$ ./loop-error-exit.sh ; echo $?
Loop number: 10
./loop-error-exit.sh: line 8: fsaapoiwe: command not found
Loop number: 9
./loop-error-exit.sh: line 8: fsaapoiwe: command not found
Loop number: 8
./loop-error-exit.sh: line 8: fsaapoiwe: command not found
Loop number: 7
./loop-error-exit.sh: line 8: fsaapoiwe: command not found
Loop number: 6
./loop-error-exit.sh: line 8: fsaapoiwe: command not found
Loop number: 5
./loop-error-exit.sh: line 8: fsaapoiwe: command not found
Loop number: 4
```

Operators

```
./loop-error-exit.sh: line 8: fsaapoiwe: command not found
Loop number: 3
./loop-error-exit.sh: line 8: fsaapoiwe: command not found
Loop number: 2
./loop-error-exit.sh: line 8: fsaapoiwe: command not found
Loop number: 1
./loop-error-exit.sh: line 8: fsaapoiwe: command not found
20
```

It did, we had errors at each cycle, but the overall exit code is still `20`, since we forced this using the `exit` command.

What are the benefits we can get from the usage of the `exit` command? Well, we just saw a nice and easy counter that can be useful to iterate over numbers, items, arrays, lists, but in a broader way, we can use the exit codes to check the result of a function we created, of a command we invoked and based on the value we get, react accordingly. To do this, though, we need to a way to verify and react, to check whether a condition is met or not, and based on that, to do something or something else, we need to have a closer look at the `if...else` statement and at the tests operators.

Summary

In the previous chapter, we had a look at the variable; now we have just looked at how to correlate them. Assigning values and being able to perform some math or logic operations on them gives us more flexibility, since we do not just collect something, but transform it into something different and new. We also learned that exit codes can sometimes be pitfalls, trapping us with red herrings, and this tells us something important: never take anything as a given, always double-check what you are writing in your code, and always try to catch all the possible outcomes and exceptions. It seems like something obvious, but being such common sense, we tend to overlook this simple but effective code style advice.

3
Testing

We have stressed so far the importance of giving a structure to our scripts, to make them flexible, and to have them react to some conditions and situations so that they will help us automate some routine tasks making decisions and performing actions on our behalf. What we saw in the previous chapters enables us to assign variables, change their values in different ways, and also to preserve them; but from the examples shown, it is clear that we need some more and this is what this new chapter is all about. We will see how to test, make comparisons, and get to react accordingly to the results, and we will give our first structure to a script having to make a decision if something happens.

What if...else

Let's take one of our previous examples and examine it in more detail:

```
#!/bin/bash
echo "Hello user, please give me a number between 10 and 20: "
read user_input
if [ ${user_input} -ge 10 ] && [ ${user_input} -le 20 ]
then
echo "Great! The number ${user_input} is what we were looking for!"
else
echo "The number ${user_input} is not what we are looking for..."
fi
```

As an exercise to ease its comprehension, let's try to write it in natural language:

1. Print a greeting asking for a number between 10 and 20
2. Read the user input and save it in the `user_input` variable
3. If the value of `user_input` is greater or equal to `10` and the value of `user_input` is less or equal to `2`, then print an OK message to the user

4. Otherwise (else), if the conditions are not met, print a not OK message
5. `Fi`, end of condition

These are the basics of a conditional statement and it lets you explore on condition: if it succeeds, an instruction is executed, if it fails, another block of instructions is invoked. We can also make it a bit more flexible, introducing an alternative condition to check in case the first fails (`elif`):

- `if` the exit code of the condition tested is 0
- then
- do something
- `elif` the exit code of this other condition tested is 0
- do something
- `else if` any of the previous conditions returned 0
- do something
- `fi` we exit from the conditional statement

So in this more articulated shape, the condition offers more flexibility and keep in mind that you can have as many `elif` blocks as you want and even nest `if` into `if`, even though it is not recommended for clarity's sake. Now, let us make a real-life example with return codes, starting with the creation of three `test` files:

zarrelli:~$ touch test1 test2 test3

Now, let us create a small script that will check for the existence of these three files:

```
#!/bin/sh
echo "We are going to test for files test1 test2 test3"
if ls test1
then
echo "File test1 exists so the ls test1 execution returns $?"
elif ls test2
then
echo "File test2 exists so the ls test2 execution returns $?"
elif ls test3
then
echo "File tes3 exists so the ls test3 execution returns $?"
else
echo "Neither or test1 or test2 or test3 exist so the the exit
code is $?"
fi
echo "End of the script"
```

Now, let's run it and have a look at what happens:

```
zarrelli:~$ ./test-files.sh
We are going to test for files test1 test2 test3
test1
File test1 exists so the ls test1 execution returns 0
End of the script
```

What happened? The first `ls` on `test1` returned 0, so it was successful and the conditional did not proceed testing the other options end exited the statement executing the next instruction outside the conditional and this was:

```
echo "End of the script"
```

Now it is time to see what happens if the first condition encountered fails, so we are going to delete the `test1` file:

```
rm test1
```

And execute the script again:

```
zarrelli:~$ ./test-files.sh
We are going to test for files test1 test2 test3
ls: cannot access 'test1': No such file or directory
test2
File test2 exists so the ls test2 execution retuns 0
End of the script
```

Again, what happened? The first instruction, `ls test1`, failed since there is no `test1` file left to show with `ls` and so the instruction returned 1. The script then proceeded further into the conditional statement to the second condition, executing `ls test2`. In this case, since `file2` exists, the command returned 0 and the script exited the statement, executing the first instruction outside the conditional, again:

```
echo "End of the script"
```

Let us go on, deleting `test2`:

```
rm test1
```

And now invoke the script:

```
zarrelli:~$ ./test-files.sh
We are going to test for files test1 test2 test3
ls: cannot access 'test1': No such file or directory
ls: cannot access 'test2': No such file or directory
test3
```

```
File test3 exists so the ls test3 execution retuns 0
End of the script
```

Since `test1` and `test2` do not exist, the first two `ls` fail and so the first two conditions with them, but not the third `ls` since `test3` still exists. The third `ls` then is successful and returns 0, the script exits the conditional and executes the first instruction outside of it, again:

```
echo "End of the script"
```

Final test, time to remove `test3`:

```
rm test3
```

And execute the script:

```
zarrelli:$ ./test-files.sh
We are going to test for files test1 test2 test3
ls: cannot access 'test1': No such file or directory
ls: cannot access 'test2': No such file or directory
ls: cannot access 'test3': No such file or directory
Neither or test1 or test2 or test3 exist so the the exit code is 2
End of the script
```

It should be clear now what is going on. All the `if...then` conditions failed and so the last resort is the else sections, which report the exit code of the `lstest3`. Once this is done, the script exits the conditional and executes the first instruction outside of it, which is:

```
echo "End of the script"
```

Be aware that the overall exit status of a conditional statement is the one belonging to the last instruction executed and the overall exit code of the script is the one of the last instruction executed by the script itself:

```
zarrelli:~$ ./test-files.sh ; echo $?
We are going to test for files test1 test2 test3
ls: cannot access 'test1': No such file or directory
ls: cannot access 'test2': No such file or directory
ls: cannot access 'test3': No such file or directory
Neither or test1 or test2 or test3 exist so the the exit code is 2
End of the script
0
```

What we see here is the script returning a value of 0, and this is correct since the last instruction executed `echo End of the script` was successful. Let's now change the last instruction of the script with the following:

```
else
:
```

The colon actually means *do nothing*, so let's see:

```
zarrelli$ ./test-files.sh ; echo $?
We are going to test for files test1 test2 test3
ls: cannot access 'test1': No such file or directory
ls: cannot access 'test2': No such file or directory
ls: cannot access 'test3': No such file or directory
0
```

Again, 0. Now, let's do an inverse check, modifying the third condition adding an !.

```
elif !ls test3
then
echo "File test3 exists so the ls test3 execution retuns $?"
```

So, the check is successful if `ls test3` returns 1:

```
zarrelli:~./test-files-not.sh ; echo $?
We are going to test for files test1 test2 test3
ls: cannot access 'test1': No such file or directory
ls: cannot access 'test2': No such file or directory
ls: cannot access 'test3': No such file or directory
File test3 exists so the ls test3 execution retuns 0
0
```

Well, the message printed is a red herring since the execution of `ls test3` is not successful and cannot return 0:

```
zarrelli:~$ ls test3 ; echo $?
ls: cannot access 'test3': No such file or directory
2
```

What returns 0 is actually the check we made on the inverted condition:

```
elif !ls file3
```

It can be read as the `if` condition is verified if `ls file3` is not verified. So, since for us verified is successful and successful is represented by a return value of 0, the condition is verified (0) only if the `if ls file3` is not verified (`-ne 0`). So, be careful when using such conditions because you could incur in some unexpected results.

We just saw how to check a condition one at a time, but we can combine operators in a single case check so that we can achieve more interesting results. Have a look at the following script:

```
#!/bin/bash
echo "Hello user, please give me a number between 10 and 20,
it must be even: "
read user_input
if [[ ${user_input} -ge 10 && ${user_input} -le 20 &&
$(( $user_input % 2 )) -eq 0 ]]
then
echo "Great! The number ${user_input} is what we were looking for!"
else
echo "The number ${user_input} is not what we are looking for..."
fi
```

What we are doing here is testing three different conditions at the same time so the `if` will be verified only when the user inputs a number between `10` and `20` and it must be even. In other words, it must be divisible by 2 and we test it checking that the modulo of the value is `0`. Let's try some values:

```
zarrelli:~$ ./userinput-and.sh
Hello user, please give me a number between 10 and 20, it
must be even:
8
The number 8 is not what we are looking for...
```

This number satisfied both the third and second conditions since it is even and lower than 20 but it fails the first since it is not equal to or above 10. So, the `if` condition is not verified and `else` action is triggered:

```
zarrelli:~$ ./userinput-and.sh
Hello user, please give me a number between 10 and 20, it
must be even:
9
The number 9 is not what we are looking for...
```

Now the number fails the first and third conditions and satisfies the first, it is not equal or above `10`, it is not even but it is less than `20`, so the else action is triggered.

```
zarrelli:~$ ./userinput-and.sh
Hello user, please give me a number between 10 and 20, it
must be even:
10
Great! The number 10 is what we were looking for!
```

Number `10` is good. It satisfies the first and second conditions because it is equal to 10 and less than 20, and it satisfied the third condition because it is even, so the action in the `then` block is triggered.

```
zarrelli:~$ ./userinput-and.sh
Hello user, please give me a number between 10 and 20, it
must be even:
15
The number 15 is not what we are looking for...
```

In this case, the first and second conditions are verified, but the third is not. `15` is not even, so the `else` block action is triggered:

```
zarrelli:~$ ./userinput-and.sh
Hello user, please give me a number between 10 and 20, it
must be even:
20
Great! The number 20 is what we were looking for!
```

`20` is good, it is above `10`, equal to `20`, and we can divide it by `2`, so all three conditions are verified and the `if` block action is triggered:

```
zarrelli:~$ ./userinput-and.sh
Hello user, please give me a number between 10 and 20, it
must be even:
21
The number 21 is not what we are looking for...
```

This number satisfies the first condition, being above `10`, but fails the other two since it is not equal to or below `20` and it is not even. So the else block action is triggered:

```
zarrelli:~$ ./userinput-and.sh
Hello user, please give me a number between 10 and 20, it
must be even:
22
The number 22 is not what we are looking for...
```

Not even this number is good. It satisfies the first condition, being above `10`, but fails the second since it is not equal to or below `20`. The third condition is satisfied, but this is not enough. So the else block action is triggered.

Testing

As we can see, when dealing with multiple conditions, we have to be really careful about what we write and think about the outcome since sometimes we could get something we did not actually want. A rule of thumb, try to keep your conditions as simple as you can or take your time to check them thoroughly. Did we say simple? Look at this:

```
#!/bin/bash
echo "Hello user, please give me an even number: "
read user_input
if ! (( $user_input % 2 ))
then
    echo "Great! The number ${user_input} is what we were looking for!"
fi
```

We are using an arithmetic evaluation compound command and negate it to check whether a number is even: if it is not true that the modulo operation fails, then the condition is verified. But, look, we have no `else` block, we just evaluate the `if` condition and exit the conditional because we are not interested in reacting to any other cases. This is typical, for instance, counter exit conditions, as we saw before: we want to exit the loop if the counter reaches a specific value, otherwise we let the cycle run. Let's have a look at the results:

```
zarrelli:~$ ./userinput-and-simple.sh
Hello user, please give me an even number:
20
Great! The number 2 is what we were looking for!
The modulo of 20 by 2 is 0:
zarrelli:~$ a=$((20 % 2 )) ; echo ${a}
0
```

The modulo operation does not give a result. Have a look at the return code of this operation:

```
zarrelli:~/$ ((20 % 2 )) ; echo $?
1
```

And here we are, the return code is 1, which means it is not OK for us. So if a number passed through a modulo operation and gives 0, the return code is failure and this means that dividing the number by two has no reminder. All this means that if a number is divisible for 2; for example, it does not give us any reminder from the division, and it is even. Now, let us try an odd number:

```
zarrelli:~$ ./userinput-and-simple.shsimple.sh
Hello user, please give me an even number:
25
```

[92]

No `then` block action is triggered, since this is an odd number. Let us verify it:

```
zarrelli:~$ ((25 % 2 )) ; echo $?
0
```

The operation is successful so we have to get some remainder. Double check:

```
zarrelli:~$ a=25 ; b=2 ; c=$((a/b)) ; echo ${c}
12
```

We have 12 as a remainder of the division of 25 by 2. So now the condition we saw in the previous script is clearer:

```
if ! (( $user_input % 2 ))
```

The `if` statement is fulfilled if the modulo by two arithmetic operation fails. So, if a number is not divisible by 2 it is even, simple. Now it is time to take a look at how we can test our conditions.

Test command recap

As we have seen in some of our previous examples, we used the shell built-in test to perform some checks on variables and files along with the conditional `if...then` so that we could make our script react to conditions: if the test is successful it returns 0, if it is not, 1, and these are the values that triggered our reactions so far.

We can use a couple of different notations to execute a test and we already saw them:

```
[expression]
```

or

```
[[expression]]
```

We already spoke about the differences between the two, but let us quickly recap them before proceeding:

- The single bracket implements the standard POSIX compliant `test` command and it is available in all POSIX shells. `[` is actually a command whose argument is `]`, and this prevents the single brackets from receiving further arguments.
  - Some Linux versions still have a `/bin/[` command, but the built-in version has the precedence in execution.
- The double brackets is only available in Bash, `zsh`, and `korn` shells.

- The double brackets is a keyword, not a program, available from the 2.02 version of the Bash and offers some great features, as follows:
  - The =~ operator for regular expression matching
  - The = or == are available for pattern matching
  - You can use <> without having to escape the \> \<
  - You can use && instead of -a and || instead of -o
  - You do not need to escape the parenthesis \(\) to group expressions
  - Glob expansion so a *can expand to everything, and this comes handy in pattern matching
  - You do not have to quote variables to keep safe spaces inside them

So, it seems that the double brackets gives us a bit of flexibility more than the old command, but before using it widely think about the audience of your scripts. If you want them available across different shells and, inside the same Bash, across different versions try to avoid using commands or built-ins that are only available in some of them. Sticking with the POSIX standard will make your scripts widely shareable, but as a drawback, they will lack the advanced features that some keywords such as double brackets have to offer. So, wisely balance your writing style and adopt the strategy that best matches your goals. We, when possible, will use the single bracket notation just to be as compatible as we can.

Testing files

There is quite a lot to say about testing and one of the most common tasks is checking files on the filesystem or if a directory is available or has some rights. So, imagine a script that has to write some data in a file inside a directory: first, we should check whether the directory exists, then if we can write into it, and finally if there is no name collision between the file we are going to open for writing and an already existing file. So let's have a look at which operators we use to execute some tests on files and devices and remember that they return true if the condition is met:

- -e: Returns true if a file exists:

    ```
    zarrelli:~$ ls test-files.sh
    test-files.sh
    ```

We just verified that the file `test-files.sh` exists since `ls` shows it:

```
zarrelli:~$ if [ -e test-files.sh ] ; then
echo "Yes, this is a file!" ; fi
Yes, this is a file device!
```

Our test confirms it with a nice message.

Let's verify now that a file named `aaaaa` is not present in our current directory:

```
zarrelli:~$ lsaaaaa
ls: cannot access 'aaaaa': No such file or directory
```

OK, there is no file with such a name; let us do a test:

```
zarrelli:~$ if [ -e aaaaa ] ; then echo "Yes, this is a file!";
else
echo "There is not such a file!" ; fi
There is not such a file!
```

Well, as you can see, we used a semicolon to divide the different parts of the statement. In a script, we would have seen the following:

```
#!/bin/bash
if [ -e aaaaa ]
then
echo "Yes, this is a file!"
else
echo "There is not such a file!"
fi
```

Each single command must be properly terminated either by a new line or a `;`. Each chunk of code delimited by a `;` will be executed before the following without the need for a new line.

- `-a`: This has the same purpose of `-e`, but it is deprecated.
- `-b`: This checks whether the file is actually a block device, like a disk, a CD-ROM, or a tape device:

```
zarrelli:~$ if [ -b /dev/nvme0n1p1 ] ;
then
echo "Yes, this is a block device!" ; fi
Yes, this is a block device!
```

- `-d`: This checks whether a file is actually a directory or not:

  ```
  zarrelli:~$ if [ -d test ] ;
  then echo "Yes, this is a directory!" ;
  else echo "There is not such a directory!" ; fi
  Yes, this is a directory!
  ```

- `-f`: This checks whether a file is a regular file and does not represent something like a character device or a directory or a block device:

  ```
  zarrelli:~$ if [ -f /dev/tty7 ] ;
  then echo "Yes, this is a regular file!" ;
  else echo "There is not a regular file!" ; fi
  There is not a regular file!
  ```

  Well, this is a file that represents a terminal, so it is clearly not a regular file as `test.file` could be:

  ```
  zarrelli:~$ touch test.file
  zarrelli:~$ if [ -f test.file ] ;
  then echo "Yes, this is a regular file!" ;
  else echo "There is not a regular file!" ; fi
  Yes, this is a regular file!
  ```

- `-c`: This tests if the argument is a character file:

  ```
  zarrelli:~$ if [ -c /dev/tty7 ] ;
  then echo "Yes, this is a character file!" ;
  else echo "There is not a character file!" ; fi
  Yes, this is a character file!
  ```

- `-s`: This is true if the file is not of 0 size:

  ```
  zarrelli:~$ if [ -s test.file ] ;
  then echo "Yes, the size of this file is not 0!" ;
  else echo "The size of this file is 0!" ; fi
  The size of this file is 0!
  ```

  Well, we just *touched* the file, so we created it with 0 byte size. Let's fill it with a character:

  ```
  zarrelli:~$ echo 1 >>test.file
  ```

And now, let's repeat the test:

```
zarrelli:~$ if [ -s test.file ] ;
then echo "Yes, the size of this file is not 0!" ;
else echo "The size of this file is 0!" ; fi
Yes, the size of this file is not 0!
```

- `-g`: This is true if the directory has a `sgid` flag set. As we saw, the set group ID imposed on a directory forces the files newly created into it to be owned by the group who owns the directory itself:

```
zarrelli:~$ if [ -g test ] ;
then echo "Yes, this dir has a sgid bit" ;
else echo "No sgid bit on this dir" ; fi
No sgid bit on this dir
```

And now:

```
zarrelli:~$ chmodg+s test
zarrelli:~$ if [ -g test ] ;
then echo "Yes, this dir has a sgid bit" ;
else echo "No sgid bit on this dir" ; fi
Yes, this dir has a sgid bit
```

- `-G`: This is true if the group ID is the same as that of yours. Let's test on a file first:

```
zarrelli:~$ if [ -G test.file ] ;
then echo "Yes, this file has your same group owner" ;
else echo "No the group owner is not the same of yours" ; fi
Yes, this file has your same group owner
```

And now on a directory:

```
zarrelli:~$ if [ -G test ] ;
then echo "Yes, this file has your same group owner" ;
else echo "No the group owner is not the same of yours" ; fi
Yes, this file has your same group owner
```

Let's double-check changing the group owner of `test.file`:

```
zarrelli:~$ su
Password:
root:# chgrp root test.file
root:# ls -lahtest.file
-rw-r--r-- 1 zarrelli root 2 Feb  6 18:23 test.file
root:# exit
exit
zarrelli:~$ if [ -G test.file ] ;
then echo "Yes, this file has your same group owner" ;
else echo "No the group owner is not the same of yours" ; fi
No the group owner is not the same of yours
```

- `-O`: This is true if you are the owner:

```
zarrelli$ if [ -O test.file ] ;
then echo "Yes, you are the owner" ;
else echo "No you are not the owner" ; fi
Yes, you are the owner
zarrelli:~$ ls -lahtest.file
-rw-r--r-- 1 zarrellizarrelli 2 Feb  6 18:23 test.file
```

- `-N`: This is true if the file was modified since the last read. This can become handy when you want to backup a file or just see if new information has been added. A typical scenario would be a log file or a data file being fed by a process, a service: if in a certain amount of time, the file has not been modified it probably means that the process is not running or not working properly so we can probably do something like restart it. So, let's have a look at one of our previous scripts:

```
zarrelli:~$ if [ -N userinput-or.sh ] ;
then echo "Yes, it has been modified since last read" ;
else echo "No modifications since last read " ; fi
No modifications since last read
```

OK, the files seems to have not been modified lately, so it is time to modify it:

```
zarrelli:~$ echo 1 >> userinput-or.sh
zarrelli:~$ if [ -N userinput-or.sh ] ;
then echo "Yes, it has been modified since last read" ;
else echo "No modifications since last read " ; fi
Yes, it has been modified since last read
```

That's it. Remember that in all the tests when we say that the test is true when the condition is verified, we imply a second condition that is the file must exist. So in this case, we would say, it is verified if the file exists and has not been modified from last read. Also remember that in Unix everything is a file, so a directory.

- `-u`: This is true if the `suid` bit is flagged. This kind of test can become quite useful for different reasons related to the fact that when you run an executable it usually runs with the privileges of the user who invoked it. With the `suid` bit flagged the executable is run with the privileges of the owner of that executable file not with the ones of the invoker also not with those of the one who invoked it. So, a program owned by root with the `suid` bit flagged can be a real harm to the security of a system since whoever invokes it has the root rights over the system itself. On the other side of the medal some programs, especially those that must have root rights to access a device, need to have the `suid` bit flagged because this allows a normal user to access the devices as root without having to access the full root environment:

    ```
    zarrelli:$ su
    Password:
    root:# chown root test.file
    root:# ls -lahtest.file
    -rw-r--r-- 1 root zarrelli 2 Feb  6 18:23 test.file
    root:# chmod +s test.file
    root:# ls -lahtest.file
    -rwSr-Sr-- 1 root zarrelli 2 Feb  6 18:23 test.file
    root:# exit
    exit
    zarrelli:~$ if [ -u test.file ] ;
    then echo "Yes, it has the suid bit flagged" ;
    else echo "No suid bit found" ; fi
    ```

- `-k`: This is true if the `sticky` bit is flagged. This kind of privilege is really interesting because if imposed on a file, it will have the file held in memory resulting in faster access, but applied to a directory it restricts the user rights: only the directory owner of the owner of the file inside a directory with a sticky bit set will be able to delete the file itself. This comes really handy in a collaborative environment where several users have their working file in the same directory, and applying the sticky bit on it will give the file owners the right to delete their files only:

    ```
    zarrelli:~$ chmod +t test
    zarrelli:~$ if [ -k test ] ;
    then echo "Yes, it has the sticky bit set" ;
    ```

```
else echo "No sticky bit set" ; fi
Yes, it has the sticky bit set
```

- `-r`: This is true if the read permission is set for the user executing the test:

  ```
  zarrelli:~$ if [ -r test.file ] ;
  then echo "Yes, this user can read the file" ;
  else echo "No this user cannot read the file" ; fi
  Yes, this user can read the file
  ```

So, the user can read the file, let's check the following:

```
zarrelli$ ls -lahtest.file
-rwSr-Sr-- 1 root zarrelli 2 Feb  6 18:23 test.file
```

Oh, well, the file is owned by root and root has read access, so why was the test successful if the read is granted to root? Simple:

```
zarrelli:~$ su
Password:
root:# chmodog-r test.file
root:# exit
exit
zarrelli:~$ if [ -r test.file ] ;
then echo "Yes, this user can read the file" ;
else echo "No this user cannot read the file" ; fi
No this user cannot read the file
```

What happened? The first time we tried the test the owner was root, but the user `zarrelli` was still able to read the file through group permission and other permission. So, clearing those bits made the file readable only by the root user, no one else.

- `-w`: This is true if the write bit is set:

  ```
  zarrelli:~$ if [ -w test.file ] ;
  then echo "Yes, this user can write to the file" ;
  else echo "No this user cannot write to the file" ; fi
  No this user cannot write to the file
  ```

Interesting, let's have a look at the file:

```
zarrelli:~$ ls -lahtest.file
-rw---S--- 1 root zarrelli 2 Feb  6 18:23 test.file
```

Indeed, only the root user can write to it. Would you like to try and fix the issue then run the test again?

- `-x`: This is true if the execution bit is set:

    ```
    zarrelli:~$ if [ -x test.file ] ;
    then echo "Yes, this user can execute it" ;
    else echo "No this user cannot execute it" ; fi
    No this user cannot execute it
    ```

    Let's see what the access permissions on the file are:

    ```
    zarrelli$ ls -lah test.file
    -rw---S--- 1 root zarrelli 2 Feb  6 18:23 test.file
    ```

    So no execute bit for the user. Now, let's test a directory:

    ```
    zarrelli:~$ if [ -x test ] ;
    then echo "Yes, this user can execute it" ;
    else echo "No this user cannot execute it" ; fi
    Yes, this user can execute it
    ```

    Interesting, time to see the permissions on the directory:

    ```
    zarrelli:~$ ls -lah test
    total 8.0K
    drwxr-sr-t 2 zarrellizarrelli 4.0K Feb  6 18:12 .
    drwxr-xr-x 3 zarrellizarrelli 4.0K Feb  7 08:12 ..
    ```

    What are those dots and double dots? Let's have a closer look:

    ```
    zarrelli$ ls -lai
    total 8
    5900830 drwxr-sr-t 2 zarrellizarrelli 4096 Feb  6 18:12 .
    5899440 drwxr-xr-x 3 zarrellizarrelli 4096 Feb  7 08:12 ..
    ```

Keep in mind the first column. These are the **inode** numbers related to .. and ..:

```
zarrelli@:~$ cd ..
zarrelli@:~$ ls -lai
total 36
5899440 drwxr-xr-x 3 zarrelli zarrelli 4096 Feb  7 08:12 .
5899435 drwxr-xr-x 3 zarrelli zarrelli 4096 Feb  7 20:47 ..
5900830 drwxr-sr-t 2 zarrelli zarrelli 4096 Feb  6 18:12 test
5899311 -rw---S--- 1 root     zarrelli    2 Feb  6 18:23 test.file
5899447 -rwxr--r-- 1 zarrelli zarrelli  319 Feb  5 11:42 test-files-not.sh
5899450 -rwxr--r-- 1 zarrelli zarrelli  317 Feb  5 11:21 test-files.sh
5898796 -rw-r--r-- 1 zarrelli zarrelli    0 Feb  7 08:00 test.modified
5899448 -rwxrwxr-x 1 zarrelli zarrelli  352 Feb  5 12:31 userinput-and.sh
5899449 -rwxr-xr-x 1 zarrelli zarrelli  190 Feb  5 12:41 userinput-and-simple.sh
5899444 -rwxrwxr-x 1 zarrelli zarrelli  305 Feb  7 08:07 userinput-or.sh
```

The inode of . inside the `test` directory has the value of 5900830, so now we go up one directory, and we can see that the test directory has an inode value of 5900830. So, we can safely say that . points to the directory we are in. And what about ..? Look at the value of . in the parent directory, it is 5899440. Now look inside the `test` directory to the value of .., it is 5899440, and so we can safely say that .. points to the parent directory since both point to the same inode.

Briefly, to understand what relates an inode to a file, we can say that in a Unix style file system, an inode is a metadata structure describing file and directories attributes, such as type timestamp, size, access rights, links count, and pointers to the disk block holding the data that make up a file or directory content. Each inode number is practically an index that allows the kernel to access a file or directory, its content and attributes, such as an index in an array. And actually, you can know quite a bit of a file if you know how to look at it:

```
zarrelli:~$ stat test
  File: test
  Size: 4096       Blocks: 8          IO Block: 4096   directory
Device: fd01h/25025a Inode: 5900830     Links: 2
Access: (3755/drwxr-sr-t)  Uid: ( 1200/zarrelli)   Gid: ( 1200/zarrelli)
```

```
Access: 2017-02-06 18:12:53.376827639 +0000
Modify: 2017-02-06 18:12:53.376827639 +0000
Change: 2017-02-07 19:26:15.936253432 +0000
 Birth: -
```

So, what we can say is that something pointing to the same inode number is pointing to the same data structure, the same file or directory, and that is what links the .. and . to the representation of the parent and local directory as we proved by following the inode numbers.

- `-h -L`: This is true if a file is a link. A link is a pointer to another file and you can have either a soft or hard link:
    - A soft link is a reference to a file that can span across different filesystems. It is a special kind of file holding a reference to another file, so when the operating system tries to access the link, it recognizes it as a link and redirects all the operations to the actual file pointed by it. If the target is removed the link remains, but points to nothing. The main limits of a soft link is that it creates an overhead in the operations; the OS must redirect all the operations from it to the target.
    - A hard link is another file pointing to the same inode and because inodes are a metastructure of a file system, a hard link cannot span across filesystems. Once the original file is deleted, the hard link is not affected since it points to a valid inode, which actually remains on the file system even if the file is deleted. A limit is that it cannot point to a directory.

So, to make it easy, we can say that the soft link is a pointer by name to a file, whereas a hard link is a pointer by inode. Let's see some differences in play starting with a soft link:

```
zarrelli:~$ ln -s test.filenew.test.file
zarrelli@:~$ ls -lah | grep new
lrwxrwxrwx 1 zarrellizarrelli    9 Feb  7 21:48 new.test.file
->test.file
```

Let's `cat` the link:

```
zarrelli:~$ su
Password:
root:# chmoda+rtest.file
root:# exit
exit
zarrelli:~$ cat new.test.file
1
```

Now, let's remove the original file:

```
zarrelli:~$ rmtest.file
```

And verify if we can access the content through the link:

```
zarrelli:~$ cat new.test.file
cat: new.test.file: No such file or directory
```

The problem is clear with `ls`:

```
zarrelli:~$ ls -lah
total 32K
drwxr-xr-x 3 zarrellizarrelli 4.0K Feb  7 22:06 .
drwxr-xr-x 3 zarrellizarrelli 4.0K Feb  7 22:02 ..
lrwxrwxrwx 1 zarrellizarrelli    9 Feb  7 21:48 new.test.file ->test.file
drwxr-sr-t 2 zarrellizarrelli 4.0K Feb  6 18:12 test
-rwxr--r-- 1 zarrellizarrelli  319 Feb  5 11:42 test-files-not.sh
-rwxr--r-- 1 zarrellizarrelli  317 Feb  5 11:21 test-files.sh
-rw-r--r-- 1 zarrellizarrelli    0 Feb  7 08:00 test.modified
-rwxrwxr-x 1 zarrellizarrelli  352 Feb  5 12:31 userinput-and.sh
-rwxr-xr-x 1 zarrellizarrelli  190 Feb  5 12:41 userinput-and-simple.sh
-rwxrwxr-x 1 zarrellizarrelli  305 Feb  7 08:07 userinput-or.sh
```

The link is still there, but the original file is gone, so when the OS tries to reach it, it fails. Let us recreate the original file and the link:

```
zarrelli:~$ rmnew.test.file
zarrelli:~$ rmnew.test.file
zarrelli:~$ echo 1 >test.file
zarrelli:~$ ln -s test.filenew.test.file
```

Now, let's link across the /boot filesystem. First, let's check that /boot is mounted on its own partition and filesystem:

```
zarrelli:~$ mount | grep boot
/dev/nvme0n1p1 on /boot type ext2
(rw,relatime,block_validity,barrier,user_xattr,acl)
```

OK, it is really another filesystem, so let's soft link:

```
zarrelli:~$ su
Password:
root:# ln -s test.file /boot/boot.test.file
```

And access the link:

```
root:# cat /boot/boot.test.file
cat: /boot/boot.test.file: No such file or directory
```

Well, something has gone wild. What is happening? Have a look with `ls -lah`:

```
root:# ls -lah /boot/boot.test.file
lrwxrwxrwx 1 root root 9 Feb  7 22:19 /boot/boot.test.file
->test.file
```

Well, the link points to `test.file` in `/boot` even though we linked from another directory. We need an absolute reference:

```
root:# ln -s /home/zarrelli/test.file /boot/new.test.file
root:# cat /boot/new.test.file
1
```

And now it works. Finally, let's see what happens if we try to link a directory:

```
zarrelli:~$ ln -s test new.test
```

We linked `new.test` to the `test` directory and now just check that the `test` directory is empty:

```
zarrelli:~$ ls -lah test
total 8.0K
drwxr-sr-t 2 zarrellizarrelli 4.0K Feb  7 22:29 .
drwxr-xr-x 3 zarrellizarrelli 4.0K Feb  7 22:26 ..
```

Now, let's create a file using the link:

```
zarrelli:~$ echo 2 >new.test/testing
zarrelli:~$ cat test/testing
2
```

And let's see what is in test:

```
zarrelli:~$ cat test/testing
2
```

Here we are; we can reach the data inside test using the `new.test` soft link.

Now it is time to hard link across filesystems:

```
zarrelli:~$ su
Password:
root:# ln  /home/zarrelli/test.file /boot/hard.test.file
ln: failed to create hard link '/boot/hard.test.file'
=>'/home/zarrelli/test.file': Invalid cross-device link
```

No way! We cannot reference with a hard link across filesystems; the inode restriction is preventing us from doing it.

Now, let's try to link a directory:

```
zarrelli:~$ ln test hard.test
ln: test: hard link not allowed for directory
```

Again, no good to go. Now, let us try to hard link in the same filesystem:

```
zarrelli:~$ lntest.filehard.test.file
```

No problem, but let's have a look at the inodes:

```
zarrelli:~$ ls -lai
total 40
5899440 drwxr-xr-x 3 zarrellizarrelli 4096 Feb  7 22:35 .
5899435 drwxr-xr-x 3 zarrellizarrelli 4096 Feb  7 22:33 ..
5899465 -rw-r--r-- 2 zarrellizarrelli    2 Feb  7 22:11
hard.test.file
5899355 lrwxrwxrwx 1 zarrellizarrelli    4 Feb  7 22:26
new.test -> test
5900839 lrwxrwxrwx 1 zarrellizarrelli    9 Feb  7 22:12
new.test.file ->test.file
5900830 drwxr-sr-t 2 zarrellizarrelli 4096 Feb  7 22:31
test
5899465 -rw-r--r-- 2 zarrellizarrelli    2 Feb  7 22:11
test.file
5899447 -rwxr--r-- 1 zarrellizarrelli  319 Feb  5 11:42
test-files-not.sh
5899450 -rwxr--r-- 1 zarrellizarrelli  317 Feb  5 11:21
test-files.sh
5898796 -rw-r--r-- 1 zarrellizarrelli    0 Feb  7 08:00
test.modified
5899448 -rwxrwxr-x 1 zarrellizarrelli  352 Feb  5 12:31
userinput-and.sh
5899449 -rwxr-xr-x 1 zarrellizarrelli  190 Feb  5 12:41
userinput-and-simple.sh
5899444 -rwxrwxr-x 1 zarrellizarrelli  305 Feb  7 08:07
userinput-or.sh
```

The hard link points to the same inode of the original file, the soft link does not. Now remove the original file again and try to `cat` the hard and soft link:

```
zarrelli:~$ rmtest.file
zarrelli:~$ cat new.test.file
cat: new.test.file: No such file or directory
zarrelli:~$ cat hard.test.file
1
```

As we expected, the soft link failed because there is no filename to point to, the hard link succeeded because the inode is still there:

```
zarrelli$ ls -lahi
total 36K
5899440 drwxr-xr-x 3 zarrellizarrelli 4.0K Feb  7 22:40 .
5899435 drwxr-xr-x 3 zarrellizarrelli 4.0K Feb  7 22:33 ..
5899465 -rw-r--r-- 1 zarrellizarrelli    2 Feb  7 22:11 hard.test.file
5899355 lrwxrwxrwx 1 zarrellizarrelli    4 Feb  7 22:26 new.test -> test
5900839 lrwxrwxrwx 1 zarrellizarrelli    9 Feb  7 22:12 new.test.file ->test.file
5900830 drwxr-sr-t 2 zarrellizarrelli 4.0K Feb  7 22:31 test
5899447 -rwxr--r-- 1 zarrellizarrelli  319 Feb  5 11:42 test-files-not.sh
5899450 -rwxr--r-- 1 zarrellizarrelli  317 Feb  5 11:21 test-files.sh
5898796 -rw-r--r-- 1 zarrellizarrelli    0 Feb  7 08:00 test.modified
5899448 -rwxrwxr-x 1 zarrellizarrelli  352 Feb  5 12:31 userinput-and.sh
5899449 -rwxr-xr-x 1 zarrellizarrelli  190 Feb  5 12:41 userinput-and-simple.sh
5899444 -rwxrwxr-x 1 zarrellizarrelli  305 Feb  7 08:07 userinput-or.sh
```

Testing

A quick rule of thumb is do not use soft link to reference frequently accessed files, such as web pages, use them for `config` files for instance, as they are just read at the startup. Soft links are slow. Hard links are good for referencing files and preserve their content despite what happens to the origin:

- `-p`: This is true if the file is a pipe. Recall for a while what we said in the first chapter about pipes and named pipes; they are a way to get different processes to communicate between each other. If a process is spawned by a parent is not a big deal, they share the same environment and the same file descriptors, on the open descriptor of the parent process, the child will be able to read data in the same order it was written with a buffer kernel to host the bits waiting to be read. For processes that do not share a common environment we can use a pipe that leverages a file that the processes can cling to: this file can last longer than the processes that make use of it, usually until a reboot and can be deleted or redirected. These kinds of interprocess communication structures are called **named pipes** or **First In First Out** (**FIFO**) pipes, based on the order of the data processed. Let us make an example and create a pipe, either with `mkfifo` or `mknode`:

    ```
    zarrelli:~$ mkfifomyfifo
    ```

    Now, let's open a second terminal and issue, in the same directory, the command:

    ```
    zarrelli:~$ cat myfifo
    ```

    The process will hang waiting for something to read. Now, let's go back to the first terminal and write something to the named pipe:

    ```
    zarrelli:~$ echo hello >myfifo
    ```

    Now back to the second terminal to check what happened:

    ```
    zarrelli:~$ cat myfifo
    hello
    ```

    We will see more on named pipes in one of the next chapters, now we will just check if `myfifo` is really a named pipe:

    ```
    zarrelli:~$ if [ -p myfifo ] ;
    then echo "Yes, it is a named pipe" ;
    else echo "No it is not a pipe" ; fi
    Yes, it is a named pipe
    ```

- `-S`: This is true if it is a socket. As we already saw, a socket is an endpoint between two devices on the same system or across the network and it allows the devices to exchange data, quite as we saw for pipes and named pipes. As you can easily guess, a Linux system has quite a bunch of sockets:

```
zarrelli:~$ if [ -S /tmp/OSL_PIPE_1000_SingleOfficeIPC_39e ] ; then echo "Yes, it is a named pipe" ; else echo "No it is not a pipe" ; fi
Yes, it is a named pipe
```

And we can double-check looking for and in the property of the file as listed by `ls`:

```
zarrelli:~$ ls -lah /tmp/OSL_PIPE_1000_SingleOfficeIPC_39e
srwxr-xr-x 1 zarrellizarrelli 0 Feb 12 09:02
/tmp/OSL_PIPE_1000_SingleOfficeIPC_39e
```

We can see an *s* character at the beginning of the permissions list, and this is what tells has that this file is exactly a socket, as we expected.

- `-t`: This is true if a file is linked to a terminal. A classic use for this test, as you will find almost in all guides, is to check if a `stdin` or a `stderr` in a script is linked to a terminal. Let's check what the `stdout` of our shell:

```
zarrelli:~$ if [ -t 1 ] ;
then echo "Yes, it is associated to a terminal" ;
else echo "No it is not associated to a terminal" ; fi
Yes, it is associated to a terminal
```

Need to double-check it? Simple, since the output of our command issued in the current shell has been printed to our monitor, which is connected to the terminal.

- `file -ntother_file`: This is true if the file is newer than other files, comparison made on their modification dates. Let's have a look:

```
zarrelli:~$ touch other_file ;
for i in {1..10}; do : ; done ; touch file;
if [ file -ntother_file ] ;
then echo "Yes, file is newer then other_file" ;
else echo "No file is not newer than other_file" ; fi
Yes, file is newer then other_file
```

So, what did we do? We simply chained some commands, and since `other_file` must be the older piece, we started off creating it. Then, we setup a simple "for" loop iterating between 1 and 10 doing nothing, as implied by the double colon, since we had to let some time pass before creating the newer file. Passed 10 iterations we created a new file and compared the two. One thing that appears interesting in this example is the use of:

```
{1..10}
```

This is a construct available since Bash newer than 3.0. Let us quickly set up a range writing the starting number and the ending one. From Bash newer than 4.0, we can also define a range with increments, in the form of:

```
{start..end..step}
```

Like in the following example:

```
zarrelli:~$ touch other_file ;
for i in {1..120..2}; do if [ $(($i%5)) -eq 0 ] ;
then echo "Waiting...cycle $i" ; fi ; sleep 1 ; done ;
touch file; if [ file -ntother_file ] ;
then echo "Yes, file is newer then other_file" ;
else echo "No file is not newer than other_file" ; fi
Waiting...cycle 5
Waiting...cycle 15
Waiting...cycle 25
Waiting...cycle 35
Waiting...cycle 45
Waiting...cycle 55
Waiting...cycle 65
Waiting...cycle 75
Waiting...cycle 85
Waiting...cycle 95
Waiting...cycle 105
Waiting...cycle 115
Yes, file is newer then other_file
```

Well, added few things here: the cycle now goes from 1 to 120 in steps of 2 and prints out a message only if the cycle number can be divided by 5, so we will not clutter the screen. Finally, we wait for one sec at each cycle using the sleep command to ensure that at the end of the cycle we spent 60 seconds before creating the last file and making the comparison.

We can also modify the date of a file using a specific date, even back in the past, using touch with the format -t YYMMDDHHmm:

```
zarrelli:~$ ls -lahtest.file
-rw-r--r-- 3 zarrellizarrelli 0 Feb 12 14:56 test.file
touch -t 8504251328 test.file
zarrelli:~$ ls -lahtest.file
-rw-r--r-- 3 zarrellizarrelli 0 Apr 25 1985 test.file
```

- `file -otother_file`: This is true if the file is older than `other_file`:

    ```
    zarrelli:~/$ if [ userinput-or.sh -otother_file ] ;
    then echo "Yes, the first file is older than the second" ;
    else echo "No the first file is not older than the second" ; fi
    ```

    And indeed:

    ```
    zarrelli:~/$ ls -laht userinput-or.sh other_file
    -rw-r--r-- 1 zarrellizarrelli   0 Feb 12 14:16 other_file
    -rwxrwxr-x 1 zarrellizarrelli 305 Feb  7 08:07 userinput-or.sh
    ```

    Now just touch the `userinput-or.sh`:

    ```
    zarrelli:~$ if [ userinput-or.sh -otother_file ] ;
    then echo "Yes, the first file is older than the second" ;
    else echo "No the first file is not older than the second" ; fi
    No the first file is not older than the second
    ```

- `file -efother_file`: This is true if the file and other files share the same inode number and device. Have you already heard about files with the same inode number and that they cannot be on different devices? Yes, we call them hard links:

    ```
    zarrelli$ rmtest.file
    zarrelli:~$ rmnew.test.file
    zarrelli:~$ touch test.file
    zarrelli$ lntest.filenew.test.file
    zarrelli$ lntest.fileother.new.test.file
    zarrelli:~$ if [ new.test.file -efother.new.test.file ] ;
    then echo "Yes, the files share the same inode number and device" ;
    else echo "No the files do not share the same inode number and device" ; fi
    Yes, the files share the same inode number and device
    ```

Now let's double-check:

```
zarrelli:~$ lls -laihtest.fileother.new.test.fileother
.new.test.file
5900839 -rw-r--r-- 3 zarrellizarrelli 0 Feb 12 14:56
other.new.test.file
5900839 -rw-r--r-- 3 zarrellizarrelli 0 Feb 12 14:56
other.new.test.file
5900839 -rw-r--r-- 3 zarrellizarrelli 0 Feb 12 14:56
test.file
```

All three files share the same inode and, since the inode is a metastructure of a file system, a single file system.

We are done with the file comparison, but there is some more that we have to see, for instance how we can test integers since they are quite a common presence in all the script we see around the Internet.

Testing integers

As we saw with comparisons between files, we can do much the same thing with integers using some binary operators. This comes handy in case we want to take a decision based on the value a variable has taken, as we saw in earlier examples, and it is a type of action widely performed when dealing with scripts:

- `-eq`: This is true if the first integer is equal to the second:

```
#!/bin/bash
echo "Hello user, please type in one integer and press enter:"
read user_input1
echo "Now type in the number again and press enter:"
read user_input2
if [ ${user_input1} -eq ${user_input2} ]
then
echo "Great! The integer ${user_input1} is equal to ${user_input2}"
else
echo "The integer ${user_input1} is not equal to ${user_input2}..."
fi
```

The code is quite simple, it does not sports any checks on the input but even though it is so bare bones it fits our purposes:

```
zarrelli:~$ ./eq.sh
Hello user, please type in one integer and press enter:
10
```

```
Now type in the number again and press enter:
10
Great! The integer 10 is equal to 10
zarrelli:~$ ./eq.sh
Hello user, please type in one integer and press enter:
10
Now type in the number again and press enter:
20
The integer 10 is not equal to 20...
```

- `-ne`: This is true if the first integer is not equal to the second integer. Let's just modify the previous script a bit:

```
if [ ${user_input1} -ne ${user_input2} ]
then
echo "Great! The integer ${user_input1} is not equal to ${user_input2}"
else
echo "The integer ${user_input1} is equal to ${user_input2}..."
fi
```

And now, let's execute the new bunch of code:

```
zarrelli:~$ ./ne.sh
Hello user, please type in one integer and press enter:
100
Now type in the number again and press enter:
50
Great! The integers 100 is not equal to 50
```

- `-gt`: This is true if the fist integer is greater than the second integer. Again, let's modify a bunch of lines:

```
if [ ${user_input1} -gt ${user_input2} ]
then
echo "Great! The integer ${user_input1} is greater than ${user_input2}"
else
echo "The integer ${user_input1} is not greater than ${user_input2}..."
fi
```

Now, let's try it out:

```
zarrelli:~$ ./gt.sh
Hello user, please type in one integer and press enter:
999
Now type in the number again and press enter:
```

Testing

```
333
Great! The integer 999 is greater than 333
zarrelli:~$ ./gt.sh
Hello user, please type in one integer and press enter:
222
Now type in the number again and press enter:
888
The integer 222 is not greater than 888...
```

- `-ge`: This is true if the first integer is greater than or equal to the second integer. Here are a few amendments:

```
if [ ${user_input1} -ge ${user_input2} ]
then
echo "Great! The integer ${user_input1} is greater than or
equal to ${user_input2}"
else
echo "The integer ${user_input1} is not greater than or
equal to ${user_input2}..."
fi
```

And now here are some tests:

```
zarrelli:~$ ./ge.sh
Hello user, please type in one integer and press enter:
10
Now type in the number again and press enter:
5
Great! The integer 10 is greater than or equal to 5
zarrelli@moveaway:~/Documents/My books/Mastering bash/Chapter
3/Scripts$ ./ge.sh
Hello user, please type in one integer and press enter:
10
Now type in the number again and press enter:
10
Great! The integer 10 is greater than or equal to 10
zarrelli@moveaway:~/Documents/My books/Mastering bash/Chapter
3/Scripts$ ./ge.sh
Hello user, please type in one integer and press enter:
10
Now type in the number again and press enter:
11
The integer 10 is not greater than or equal to 11...
```

- `-lt`: This is true if the first integer is less than the second integer. So, another small amendments are as follows:

  ```
  if [ ${user_input1} -lt ${user_input2} ]
  then
  echo "Great! The integer ${user_input1} is less than ${user_input2}"
  else
  echo "The integer ${user_input1} is not less than ${user_input2}..."
  fi
  ```

  And now a couple of tests:

  ```
  zarrelli:~$ ./lt.sh
  Hello user, please type in one integer and press enter:
  10
  Now type in the number again and press enter:
  5
  The integer 10 is not less than 5...
  zarrelli:~$ ./lt.sh
  Hello user, please type in one integer and press enter:
  10
  Now type in the number again and press enter:
  20
  Great! The integer 10 is less than 20
  ```

- `-le`: This is true if the first integer is less than or equal to the second:

  ```
  if [ ${user_input1} -le ${user_input2} ]
  then
  echo "Great! The integer ${user_input1} is less than or equal to ${user_input2}"
  else
  echo "The integer ${user_input1} is not less than or equal to ${user_input2}..."
  fi
  ```

  And now the usual tests are:

  ```
  zarrelli:~$ ./le.sh
  Hello user, please type in one integer and press enter:
  30
  Now type in the number again and press enter:
  20
  The integer 30 is not less than or equal to 20...
  zarrelli:~$ ./le.sh
  Hello user, please type in one integer and press enter:
  ```

```
60
Now type in the number again and press enter:
70
Great! The integer 60 is less than or equal to 70
zarrelli:~$ ./le.sh
Hello user, please type in one integer and press enter:
70
Now type in the number again and press enter:
70
Great! The integer 70 is less than or equal to 70
```

We also have a bunch of operators that can be used with the double parenthesis notation, which performs an arithmetic expansion and evaluation:

- <: This is true if the first integer is less than the second. Here is the modified code:

    ```
    #!/bin/bash
    echo "Hello user, please type in one integer and press enter:"
    read user_input1
    echo "Now type in the number again and press enter:"
    read user_input2
    if (($user_input1 < $user_input2))
    then
    echo "Great! The integer $user_input1 is less than $user_input2"
    else
    echo "The integer $user_input1 is not less than $user_input2..."
    fi
    ```

And now, let's test it:

```
zarrelli:~$ ./minor.sh
Hello user, please type in one integer and press enter:
100
Now type in the number again and press enter:
50
The integer 100 is not less than 50...
zarrelli:~$ ./minor.sh
Hello user, please type in one integer and press enter:
10
Now type in the number again and press enter:
100
Great! The integer 10 is less than 100
```

- <=: This is true if the first integer is less than or equal to the second. Just a small change to the previous code:

    ```
    if (($user_input1 <= $user_input2))
    then
    echo "Great! The integer $user_input1 is less than or equal to $user_input2"
    else
    echo "The integer $user_input1 is not less than or equal to $user_input2..."
    fi
    ```

  And the usual tests:

    ```
    zarrelli:~$ ./minequal.sh
    Hello user, please type in one integer and press enter:
    10
    Now type in the number again and press enter:
    20
    Great! The integer 10 is less than or equal to 20
    zarrelli:~$ ./minequal.sh
    Hello user, please type in one integer and press enter:
    20
    Now type in the number again and press enter:
    10
    The integer 20 is not less than or equal to 10...
    zarrelli:~$ ./minequal.sh
    Hello user, please type in one integer and press enter:
    20
    Now type in the number again and press enter:
    20
    Great! The integer 20 is less than or equal to 20
    ```

- >: This is true if the first integer is greater than the second. Just a small change:

    ```
    if (($user_input1 > $user_input2))
    then
    echo "Great! The integer $user_input1 is greater than $user_input2"
    else
    echo "The integer $user_input1 is not greater than $user_input2..."
    fi
    ```

And the usual tests because we are testing all we are writing:

```
zarrelli:~$ ./greater.sh
Hello user, please type in one integer and press enter:
10
Now type in the number again and press enter:
20
The integer 10 is not greater than 20...
zarrelli:~$ ./greater.sh
Hello user, please type in one integer and press enter:
10
Now type in the number again and press enter:
5
Great! The integer 10 is greater than 5
```

- >=: This is true if the first integer is greater than or equal to the second:

```
if (($user_input1 >= $user_input2))
then
echo "Great! The integer ${user_input1} is greater than or equal to ${user_input2}"
else
echo "The integer ${user_input1} is not greater than or equal to ${user_input2}..."
fi
```

And now, let's run some checks:

```
zarrelli:~$ ./greaqual.sh
Hello user, please type in one integer and press enter:
10
Now type in the number again and press enter:
10
Great! The integer 10 is greater than or equal to 10
zarrelli:~$ ./greaqual.sh
Hello user, please type in one integer and press enter:
10
Now type in the number again and press enter:
5
Great! The integer 10 is greater than or equal to 5
zarrelli:~$ ./greaqual.sh
Hello user, please type in one integer and press enter:
10
Now type in the number again and press enter:
20
The integer 10 is not greater than or equal to 20...
```

Testing strings

We just saw some interesting comparisons, but now things start to become more interesting because we are going to introduce some tests on strings, and this brings us a step forward in what we can do to make our scripts more reactive:

- =: This is true if the first string is equal to the second string:

```
#!/bin/bash
echo "Hello user, please type a string and press enter:"
read user_input1
echo "Now type another string and press enter:"
read user_input2
if [ ${user_input1} = ${user_input2} ]
then
echo "Great! The string ${user_input1} is equal to ${user_input2}"
else
echo "The string ${user_input1} is not equal to ${user_input2}..."
fi
```

And now some tests:

```
zarrelli:~$ ./equal.sh
Hello user, please type a string and press enter:
hello
Now type another string and press enter:
hello
Great! The string hello is equal to hello
zarrelli:~$ ./equal.sh
Hello user, please type a string and press enter:
hello
Now type another string and press enter:
Hello
The string hello is not equal to Hello...
```

Now, look at this:

```
if [ ${user_input1}=${user_input2} ]
then
echo "Great! The string ${user_input1} is equal to ${user_input2}"
else
echo "The string ${user_input1} is not equal to ${user_input2}..."
fi
```

Testing

And now some checks:

```
zarrelli:~$ ./equal-wrong.sh
Hello user, please type a string and press enter:
hello
Now type another string and press enter:
hello
Great! The string hello is equal to hello
zarrelli:~$ ./equal-wrong.sh
Hello user, please type a string and press enter:
hello
Now type another string and press enter:
Hello
Great! The string hello is equal to Hello
```

Something weird, isn't there? We just got rid of spaces around the equal sign and now it does not work anymore:

```
zarrelli:~$ ./equal-wrong.sh
Hello user, please type a string and press enter:
hello
Now type another string and press enter:
cat
Great! The string hello is equal to cat
```

Those spaces are actually more important than you could think. Our comparison became an assignment! So, be careful!

- ==: This is true if the first string is equal to the second string, but it has a different behavior than = when it comes to double brackets:

```
#!/bin/bash
echo "Hello user, please type a string and press enter:"
read user_input1
echo "Now type another string and press enter:"
read user_input2
if [[ ${user_input1} == ${user_input2}* ]]
then
echo "Great! The string ${user_input1} is equal to ${user_input2}"
else
echo "The string ${user_input1} is not equal to ${user_input2}..."
fi
```

Matches as long as the first string starts with the character entered for the second string, the * will match whatever characters in the second string after what you entered:

```
zarrelli:~$ ./equalequal.sh
Hello user, please type a string and press enter:
match
Now type another string and press enter:
mi
The string match is not equal to mi...
```

And now we match with spaces:

```
zarrelli:~$ ./equalequal.sh
Hello user, please type a string and press enter:
this should match
Now type another string and press enter:
this
Great! The string this should match is equal to this
```

Be careful, with single brackets, the behavior of this operator changes due to file globbing and word split being in action.

- !=: This is true if the first string is not equal to the second, but keep in mind that there is a pattern matching in place; so we are going to change the previous script a bit:

```
if [[ ${user_input1} != ${user_input2}* ]]
then
echo "Great! The string ${user_input1} is not equal
to ${user_input2}"
else
echo "The string ${user_input1} is equal
to ${user_input2}..."
fi
```

And now the tests are:

```
zarrelli:~/Documents/My books/Mastering bash/Chapter 3/Scripts$
./equalnot.sh
Hello user, please type a string and press enter:
this should match
Now type another string and press enter:
this
The string this should match is equal to this...
zarrelli:~$ ./equalnot.sh
Hello user, please type a string and press enter:
```

Testing

```
this should match
Now type another string and press enter:
not this
Great! The string this should match is not equal to not this
```

- `<`: This is true if the first string is less than the second in ASCII alphabetical order. So, let's modify the script:

```
if [[ ${user_input1} < ${user_input2} ]]
then
echo "Great! The string ${user_input1} is less than ${user_input2}"
else
echo "The string ${user_input1} is not less than ${user_input2}..."
fi
```

Now, here are some tests:

```
zarrelli:~$ ./less.sh
Hello user, please type a string and press enter:
abcd
Now type another string and press enter:
bcde
Great! The string abcd is less than bcde
zarrelli:~$ ./less.sh
Hello user, please type a string and press enter:
zcf
Now type another string and press enter:
rst
The string zcf is not less than rst...
```

> Be careful, with single brackets, the < sign must be escaped, so the condition becomes:
> `if [ ${user_input1} \< ${user_input2} ]`

- `>`: This is true if the first string is greater than the second in ASCII alphabetical order. So, let's modify the script:

```
if [[ ${user_input1} > ${user_input2} ]]
then
echo "Great! The string ${user_input1} is greater than ${user_input2}"
else
echo "The string ${user_input1} is not greater than ${user_input2}..."
fi
```

And now some tests:

```
zarrelli:~$ ./greater.sh
Hello user, please type a string and press enter:
@
Now type another string and press enter:
A
The string @ is not greater than A...
```

Well, actually the @ sign has a value of 40 in the ASCII table and A has a value of 41, so A is greater than @.

Be careful, with single brackets, the > sign must be escaped so the condition becomes:
`if [ ${user_input1} \> ${user_input2} ]`

- -z: This is true if the string is null. Here are a bunch of lines to verify this condition:

```
#!/bin/bash
echo "Hello user, please type a string and press enter:"
read user_input1
if [[ -z ${user_input1} ]]
then
echo "Great! The string ${user_input1} is null"
else
echo "The string ${user_input1} is not null..."
fi
```

And now a couple of checks:

```
zarrelli:~$ ./null.sh
Hello user, please type a string and press enter:
Great! The string  is null
zarrelli:~$ ./null.sh
Hello user, please type a string and press enter:
Hello
The string Hello is not null...
```

As you can see, in case of a null value, nothing is printed on the screen when we echo the variable value.

- `-n`: This is true if the string is not null. Just a minor change to the previous code:

```
if [[ -n ${user_input1} ]]
then
echo "Great! The string ${user_input1} is not null"
else
echo "The string ${user_input1} is null..."
fi
```

And now some tests

```
zarrelli:~$ ./notnull.sh
Hello user, please type a string and press enter:
The string  is null...
zarrelli:~$ ./notnull.sh
Hello user, please type a string and press enter:
Hello
Great! The string Hello is not null
```

 Whenever you test a variable, quote it! Unquoted variables can lead to weird results, especially when dealing with null values.

Have a look at how the results change with a test with single brackets and unquoted variables. Keep in mind that `user_input2` is not instanced, so its value is `null`:

```
#!/bin/bash
echo "Hello user, please type a string and press enter:"
read user_input1
if [ -n ${user_input1} ]
then
echo "Great! The string ${user_input1} is not null"
else
echo "The string ${user_input1} is null..."
fi
echo "But look at this..."
if [ -n ${user_input2} ]
then
echo "Great! The string ${user_input2} is not null"
else
echo "The string ${user_input2} is null..."
fi
echo "And now at this..."
if [ -n "${user_input2}" ]
then
```

```
echo "Great! The string ${user_input2} is not null"
else
echo "The string ${user_input2} is null..."
fi
```

And now, let's run it:

```
zarrelli:~$ ./nullornot.sh
Hello user, please type a string and press enter:
Great! The string  is not null
But look at this...
Great! The string  is not null
And now at this...
The string  is null...
```

Well, as you can see, quoting matters!

More on tests

We just saw some tests with one condition checked at a time, but we also have the equivalent of `&&` and `||`, so we can have compound checks and test more conditions at once, as follows:

- `-a`: It is a logical AND, so it is true when both conditions checked are true. We use this operator with the test command or in single brackets. Let's rewrite one of the previous scripts:

```
#!/bin/bash
echo "Hello user, please give me a number between 10 and 20,
it must be even: "
read user_input
if [ ${user_input} -ge 10 -a ${user_input} -le 20 -a
$(( $user_input % 2 )) -eq 0 ]
then
echo "Great! The number ${user_input} is what we were looking for!"
else
echo "The number ${user_input} is not what we are looking for..."
fi
```

And now some tests are:

```
zarrelli@moveaway:~/Documents/My books/Mastering bash
/Chapter 3/Scripts$ ./userinput-a.sh
Hello user, please give me a number between 10 and 20,
it must be even:
10
Great! The number 10 is what we were looking for!
zarrelli@moveaway:~/Documents/My books/Mastering bash
/Chapter 3/Scripts$ ./userinput-a.sh
Hello user, please give me a number between 10 and 20,
it must be even:
13
The number 13 is not what we are looking for...
```

- `-o`: It is a logical OR and true if either conditions are true. We use this operator with the test command or in single brackets. Let's rewrite some lines from the previous example:

```
if [ ${user_input} -ge 10 -a ${user_input} -le 20 -o
$(( $user_input % 2 )) -eq 0 ]
```

And now some checks:

```
zarrelli:~$ ./userinput-o.sh
Hello user, please give me a number between 10 and 20 OR even:
15
Great! The number 15 is what we were looking for!
zarrelli:~$ ./userinput-o.sh
Hello user, please give me a number between 10 and 20 OR even:
70
Great! The number 70 is what we were looking for!
```

So, now a number is acceptable if it is between 10 and 20 or it is even:

```
zarrelli:~$ ./userinput-o.sh
Hello user, please give me a number between 10 and 20 OR even:
23
The number 23 is not what we are looking for...
zarrelli:~$ ./userinput-o.sh
Hello user, please give me a number between 10 and 20 OR even:
24
Great! The number 24 is what we were looking for!
```

Summary

We finally got into something interesting. Not that the previous chapters were less important, but with the tests, we just saw that we are now able to create some conditional statements and let our script react to different situations. It is not just an echo of a variable, but we get to its value, work on it, decide what to do, and act accordingly. In this chapter, we had a quick bite of what flexibility means in a script: it must be a tool and that makes one of the main goals of writing a script: it must be a tool that makes decisions on our behalf and react as we want it to do based on the conditions that we crafted in advance.

4
Quoting and Escaping

Not everything is what it looks like. We must bear in mind that when dealing with operators and variables, sometimes we get unexpected results based on how we use them. A small example will make this advice more clear:

```
zarrelli:~$ ls
```

The directory has no content, so it is our starting point:

```
zarrelli:~$ touch *
```

We just created a file named star:

```
zarrelli:~$ ls *
*
```

When we do `ls *`, we actually see it:

```
zarrelli:~$ ls
*
```

We see this even if we issue a simple `ls` without any arguments:

```
zarrelli:~$ touch 1 2 3
```

Now, we created three empty files:

```
zarrelli:~$ ls *
* 1 2 3
```

Well, we tried to list only the star file, but we saw all of them. How to show only the star named file? We can do so as follows:

```
zarrelli:~$ ls "*"
*
```

So, now that we have quoted the star symbol, we can see the file named after it. Why is this? Well, as I said, there are some characters that have a special meaning for the shell, such as the star, which is expanded by the shell into *ALL* characters. This is why if we issue `ls *`, we will see all the files held into the directory, because we are asking to show any file whose name is made up of any characters or numbers (except for filenames starting with a dot). Quoting the star symbol prevents the shell from actually interpreting the special character ,and so take it literally, we want to see the file whose name is simply *.

Special characters

We have already used some of these special characters in the previous chapters by giving a hint of what was their meaning. Now, we will be closely looking at each of them and examining their special value for the shell and how they can be used in our scripts.

The hash character (#)

This represents a comment. Each line beginning with # is taken as a comment and not interpreted by the shell. Let's have a look at the following script:

```
#!/bin/bash
# I am a comment at the beginning of a line'
ls # I am a comment after a command
#I am a comment preceeding a command and so it is not interpreted ps
```

The first pound sign is not really a comment, but it is associated to the following exclamation mark and is interpreted as a *sha-bang*. The second line shows a typical comment line, the third a comment after a command, the fourth line is still a comment, and the `ps` command is not interpreted and executed. Let's run it:

```
zarrelli:~$ ./comment.sh
* 1 2 3 comment.sh
```

We see the output of the `ls` command, but not of `ps` as expected. Also notice that the comments are not printed to `stdout`. Since we use it inside the code to comment, it is not something to be shown at runtime. Let's add a couple of lines:

```
echo # I am a comment but you cannot see me
echo \# I am a comment but you can see me
```

Run the script again:

```
zarrelli:~$ ./comment.sh
* 1 2 3 comment.sh
# I am a comment but you can see me
zarrelli:~$
```

As you can see, the first `echo` command creates a blank line and the comment is not taken in account; so, it is as if we had no argument to the `echo` command. The second comment is even more interesting. We escaped the pound sign placing a back slash in front of it. So, being escaped the pound sign is just a pound sign followed by a bunch of characters, and all together, they get printed to `stdout` as the `echo` command arguments. So, be careful since you will find the pound sign used with different meaning, as we already saw in the paragraphs dealing with a parameter substitution and a pattern matching on variables.

The semicolon character (;)

The semicolon is a command separator, and it allows us to chain one command after the other, just as we did for the if construct. For instance, look at this:

```
zarrelli:~$ echo TEST > test.txt ; cat test.txt
TEST
```

We created a `test.txt` file, and we cat its content right after it. Be careful with the find -exec command, as the semicolon must be escaped. The `-exec` option allows us to perform a command on the files provided by find:

```
zarrelli:~$ echo TEST > test_1.txt ; ls test_1.txt ; find -name test_1.txt -exec rm {} 
\; ; ls
test_1.txt
* 1 2 3 comment.sh test.txt
```

With the find `-exec` object, the semicolon is the command sequence terminator and not a command separator, so it must be escaped in order to avoid the shell to interpret it as a special character. After the first escaped semicolon, we then added a second semicolon to separate the `find` command from the subsequent `ls`. Notice that `{}` in the command is substituted by `find` with the full path to the file found.

Quoting and Escaping

The double semicolon character (;;)

The double semicolon is a case construct option terminator. We will see the case constructor later in this book, but as of now, just think of it as a sequence of if/then/else, which is widely adopted to create a user menu:

```
#!/bin/sh
clear
echo "Please choose between these options:"
echo "ls for listing files"
echo "procs for listing processes"
echo "x for exit"
read input
case "$input" in
  "ls" | "LS" )
    echo "Listing files:"
    ls
    exit 0
    ;;
"procs" | "PROCS")
    echo "Listing processes:"
    ps
    exit 0
    ;;
  "x" | "X" )
    echo "exiting"
    exit 0
    ;;
  * )
    # Default catchall option
    echo "exiting"
    exit 0
    ;;
  esac
```

As you can see, the case construct starts with the case keyword and is closed by the reverse of it: esac. What it does is try to verify each condition into the different options that we defined. Each option is separated from the other by the double colon. The last option is usually a star, which means *whatever you type,* and it is a catchall option just in case any other option did not trap what the user typed in. Let's have a look:

```
Please choose between these options:
ls for listing files
procs for listing processes
x for exit
ls
Listing files:
```

```
* 1 2 3 comment.sh menu.sh test.txt
```

Use this for the default option:

```
Please choose between these options:
ls for listing files
procs for listing processes
x for exit
aahadie
exiting
```

Have you noticed that the screen has been cleared out of any content? This is thanks to the `clear` command that we wrote at the beginning of the file, as it clears out the screen so that whatever you write to the customer, it will appear at the top of the screen without any other content distracting the user.

The case terminator (;;&) and (;&))

These are enhanced case terminators too, but they are only available in Bash from a version higher than 4.0. Here are the differences between the three operators:

- `;;`: If the condition is matched, the other options will not be tested
- `;&`: This makes the execution continue with the commands associated to the next condition
- `;;&`: This makes the shell check the option and execute the associated commands if the condition is matched

If no matches are found, the exit status is 0; otherwise, the exit status is the one from the last command executed. We will see more about these terminators and the case constructor in the next chapter.

The dot character (.)

The dot command is a shell builtin, and it has the same function of the source; when executed into the shell, it executes a file. And if it is used inside a script, it loads the referenced file content:

```
zarrelli:~$ comment.sh
bash: comment.sh: command not found
zarrelli:~$ . comment.sh
* 1 2 3 comment.sh menu.sh test.txt
# I am a comment but you can see me
```

As we can see from this example, the first try was not successful because `comment.sh` is not in the search path; but the second time, we were successful since the dot command executed the script. Now, let's see how to include some code from an external file into a script. Let's start writing the external file that we will source from the following code:

```
zarrelli:~$ cat external-data
var1="Hello"
var2="Nice to see you"
```

Now, we have to write the script that will source from this file:

```
#!/bin/bash
echo "We now source external-data file and get the variables content"
echo ". external-data"
 . external-data
echo "Now that we sourced the external file, we have access to variables content"
echo "The content of var1 is: ${var1}"
echo "The content of var2 is: ${var2}"
```

Now, it is just a matter of having a look at what happens:

```
zarrelli:~$ ./sourcing.sh
We now source external-data file and get the variables content
. external-data
Now that we sourced the external file, we have access to variables content
The content of var1 is: Hello
The content of var2 is: Nice to see you
```

So, as we can see, we actually sourced the variables content from the external-data file. But there is more since if we source an external script, its code gets executed and can also return values to the main script:

```
#!/bin/bash
echo "Hello from the inner script, can you give me a number?"
read number
case "$number" in
        [[:digit:]] )
            echo "$number is a digit!"
            exit 0
            ;;
        * )
            # Default catchall option
            echo "Sorry, $number is not a digit"
            exit 1
            ;;
esac
```

This is a simple menu that asks the user for a digit and then checks it; do not worry, as we will see how to match digits and characters later on:

```
zarrelli:~$ ./external-script.sh
Hello from the inner script, can you give me a number?
1
1 is a digit!
zarrelli:~$ ./external-script.sh
Hello from the inner script, can you give me a number?
d
Sorry, d is not a digit
```

There is a quick way to match characters by using a POSIX character class:

- `[:alnum:]` matches both alphabetic and numeric characters
- `[:alpha:]` matches only alphabetic characters
- `[:blank:]` matches only a tab or a space
- `[:cntrl:]` matches any control characters
- `[:digit:]` matches only digits between 0 to 9
- `[:graph:]` matches any the character that has a value between 33 and 126 in the ASCII table
- `[:lower:]` matches alphabetic characters in lower case
- `[:print:]` matches the graph, but also matches the range is from 32 to 126, including the space characters too
- `[:space:]` matches the space and horizontal tabs
- `[:upper:]` matches alphabetic characters in upper case
- `[:xdigit:]` matches digits, but in a hexadecimal notation

Now, let's do something nicer and modify the previous external script in the following way:

```
#!/bin/bash
echo "Hello from the inner script, can you give me an integer between 0 and 9?"
read number
case "$number" in
        [[:digit:]] )
           return 0
           ;;
        * )
           # Default catchall option
           return 1
           ;;
esac
```

Quoting and Escaping

Instead of exiting, we are returning a value to the caller script so that the execution once ended on the child script will continue on the main one. Now a new main script is here:

```
#!/bin/bash
echo "We now source external-script-return.sh file and ask the customer for a digit between 0 and 9"
echo ". external-script-return.sh"
. external-script-return.sh
return=$?
if [ "$return" -eq 0 ]
        then
                echo "The value returned is a digit between 0 and 9, the exit code was $return"
        else
                echo "The value returned is not a digit between 0 and 9, the exit code was $return"
fi
```

Now let's see a couple of tests:

```
zarrelli:~$ ./sourcing-return.sh
```

We will now source the `external-script-return.sh` file and ask the customer for a digit between 0 to 9:

```
. external-script-return.sh
Hello from the inner script, can you give me an integer between 0 and 9?
6
The value returned is a digit between 0 and 9, the exit code was 0
zarrelli:~$ ./sourcing-return.sh
```

We will now source the `external-script-return.sh` file and ask the customer for a digit between 0 to 9:

```
. external-script-return.sh
Hello from the inner script, can you give me an integer between 0 and 9?
25
The value returned is not a digit between 0 and 9, the exit code was 1
zarrelli:~$ ./sourcing-return.sh
```

We will now source the `external-script-return.sh` file and ask the customer for a digit between 0 to 9:

```
. external-script-return.sh
Hello from the inner script, can you give me an integer between 0 and 9?
asry
The value returned is not a digit between 0 and 9, the exit code was 1
```

We used the builtin command return to stop the execution of the inner script once a condition is met and returned an exit status to the parent script. Usually, we can use return without any exit code, and it will serve back the exit status of the last command executed, or we can use an integer between 0 to 255. Would it not be nice to have in return something different from a simple number? Well, you can't. Actually you can with a little trick. Let's modify the previous child script:

```
#!/bin/bash
echo "Hello from the inner script, can you give me an integer between 0 and 9?"
read number
case "$number" in
        [[:digit:]] )
           echo "This is the integer the user gave us: $number"
           exit
           ;;
        * )
           # Default catchall option
           echo "The user did not give us an integer between 0 and 9 but this: $number"
           exit
           ;;
esac
```

Now let's call the script:

```
#!/bin/bash
echo "We now source external-script-return-whatever.sh file and ask the customer for a digit between 0 and 9"
echo ". external-script-return-whatever.sh"
returning=$(. external-script-return-whatever.sh)
echo "The value of returning is: $returning"
```

What did we do? We got rid of return and echoed on the standard output of our message. Then, from the calling script, we used a command substitution. What does this do? It simply reassigns the output of a command; in our case, we reassigned the output of the sourced script to the variable returning. You can do a command substitution using ...: the classic backtics, which has been superseded by $(...). So, use the latter form, since it is the most actual and also allows you to nest multiple command substitutions. Let's give it a try:

```
zarrelli:~$ ./sourcing-return-whatever.sh
We now source external-script-return-whatever.sh file and ask the customer
for a digit between 0 and 9
. external-script-return-whatever.sh
3
The value of returning is: Hello from the inner script, can you give me an
```

```
integer between 0 and 9?
This is the integer the user gave us: 3
```

Oh well, nice! It gave us the echoed string from the first case option, but unfortunately, we also trapped the message printed to the user asking to input a integer. Well, how do you get rid of it? You should already know this; just keep in mind that we are getting everything printed to `stdout`, and so we will need a tiny alteration to the inner script:

```
>&2 echo "Hello from the inner script, can you give me an integer between 0 and 9?"
read -s number
```

We need one modification to the calling script so that the last line will be this:

```
echo "$returning"
```

It is time to test our modifications:

```
zarrelli:~$ ./sourcing-return-whatever.sh
We now source external-script-return-whatever.sh file and ask the customer for a digit between 0 and 9
. external-script-return-whatever.sh
Hello from the inner script, can you give me an integer between 0 and 9?
This is the integer the user gave us: 4
zarrelli:~$ ./sourcing-return-whatever.sh
We now source external-script-return-whatever.sh file and ask the customer for a digit between 0 and 9
. external-script-return-whatever.sh
Hello from the inner script, can you give me an integer between 0 and 9?
The user did not give us an integer between 0 and 9 but this: dirthe
```

What did we do? First, we redirected `stdout` to `stderr`; and both are attached to the terminal, so the user will still see the question asked by the script, but the sentence will not be caught by the command substitution since this latter works only with `stdout`. Then, we silenced the read builtin so that it will not `echo` to the `stdout` and the value typed by the customer; and at the end, we just printed the returned value without any comments. This gave us a neat output. This trick can be used when you have to return a value from a function to the main script body, and you do not want to be limited by the 0-255 value restriction of the returned builtin. A file can be sourced passing by it positional parameters with the following syntax:

```
. file arg1 arg2 argn
```

The sourced script will access the parameters value using $1, $2, and $n. From the 10th parameter, the value must be accessed bracketing the ${15} variable. Before ending the description of the dot character, we should recall what we said in the previous chapter: a single dot is a link to the current directory. It is also widely used in filenames to specifically define file extensions. Finally, in the regular expressions context, the dot matches any single character except for the new line.

The double quotes ("...")

Double quotes are also known as partial or weak quoting, which avoid the interpretation of most of the special characters by the shell. We will see more about them in the next section.

The single quotes ('...')

The single quote, also known as a full or strong quote, avoids the interpretation of all special characters by the shell. More information on it is mentioned in the next section.

The comma character (,)

The comma operator chains together arithmetic operations or strings:

```
zarrelli:~$ x=$((5 + 10)) ; echo $x
15
zarrelli:~$ x=$((5 + 10, 6-1)) ; echo $x
5
zarrelli@moveaway:~$ x=$((y=25, 6-1)) ; echo "The value of x is $x and the value of y is $y"
The value of x is 5 and the value of y is 25
```

What we can see here is that even though the operations are concatenated, only the value of the last one is returned. So, x is instanced with the value of just 6-1. But, as I mentioned before, we can use the comma character to concatenate strings:

```
zarrelli@moveaway:~$ for i in {,1}1 ; do echo $i ; done
1
11
zarrelli@moveaway:~$ for i in {,1}2 ; do echo $i ; done
2
12
zarrelli@moveaway:~$ for i in {,1,}2 ; do echo $i ; done
2
```

```
12
2
zarrelli@moveaway:~$ for i in {,1,,}2 ; do echo $i ; done
2
12
2
2
zarrelli@moveaway:~$ for i in {,1,3,}2 ; do echo $i ; done
2
12
32
2
```

As you can see, you can concatenate a list of values to create new strings and do some funny stuff in the process:

```
zarrelli:~$ for i in {"Hello ","Maybe hello ","Ok, I decided, hello "}world
 ; do echo $i ; done
Hello world
Maybe hello world
Ok, I decided, hello world
```

This is funny, but it is up to you how to use it. You can cycle in a for statement and construct a list of paths to examine; for instance, the applications of a string concatenation is really up to your creativity.

The ,, and , () case modificators

This is new in Bash 4.0, and it forces a lower case conversion in the parameter substitution.

The ^^ and ^ () case modificators

This is new in bash 4.0, it forces upper case conversion in the parameter substitution:

```
zarrelli:~$ cat parm-sub.sh
 #!/bin/bash
echo "Hello, can you give me a string of characters?"
read my_string
if [[ "$my_string" =~ ^[[:alpha:]]*$ ]]
    then
        echo "Printing the variable \$my_string as \${my_string}:
${my_string}" "| No modifications"
        echo "Printing the variable \$my_string as \${my_string^}:
${my_string^}" "| The first char is uppercase"
```

```
            echo "Printing the variable \$my_string as \${my_string^^}:
${my_string^^}" "| All chars are uppercase"
            echo "Printing the variable \$my_string as \${my_string,}:
${my_string,}" "| The first char is lowercase"
            echo "Printing the variable \$my_string as \${my_string,,}:
${my_string,,}" "| All chars are lowercase"
        else
            echo "Please, input characters only"
fi
```

Now, we will do a couple of tests, starting with a lowercase string:

```
zarrelli:~$ ./parm-sub.sh
Hello, can you give me a string of characters?
sdoijweoi
Printing the variable $my_string as ${my_string}: sdoijweoi | No
modifications
Printing the variable $my_string as ${my_string^}: Sdoijweoi | The first
char is uppercase
Printing the variable $my_string as ${my_string^^}: SDOIJWEOI | All chars
are uppercase
Printing the variable $my_string as ${my_string,}: sdoijweoi | The first
char is lowercase
Printing the variable $my_string as ${my_string,,}: sdoijweoi | All chars
are lowercase
```

Now, we will test an upper case string:

```
zarrelli:~$ ./parm-sub.sh
Hello, can you give me a string of characters?
CSEPTKAS
Printing the variable $my_string as ${my_string}: CSEPTKAS | No
modifications
Printing the variable $my_string as ${my_string^}: CSEPTKAS | The first
char is uppercase
Printing the variable $my_string as ${my_string^^}: CSEPTKAS | All chars
are uppercase
Printing the variable $my_string as ${my_string,}: cSEPTKAS | The first
char is lowercase
Printing the variable $my_string as ${my_string,,}: cseptkas | All chars
are lowercase
```

This comes in handy when you want to *normalize* a string that you retrieved for a previous operation or from a user input.

The backslash (\)

This escape character is used to prevent the special characters interpretation by the shell. We saw an example of its usage in the previous bunch of code where we escaped `\${my_input}` so that the echo was able to print it literally as a string and not trying to output its value. Using \ has the same effect as surrounding a variable with single quotes, so this is a strong quotation useful to literally print the " and ' characters, which are usually interpreted as quotation characters.

The forward slash (/)

The forward slash has two different uses:

- It is a file name separator in paths, as we can see in the `/usr/lib/dbus-1.0/dbus-daemon-launch-helper` example. Every bit between a forward slash is a directory until the last leaf, which is a file.
- It is the arithmetic operator for the division.

'...'

This is the command substitution, and we just used it a few pages ago; it assigns the `stdout` command to a variable.

The colon character (:)

The colon does actually nothing except expanding arguments and performing redirection. It can be handy in cycles and tests to actually do nothing if a condition is met. It is also interesting to see how it can be used to evaluate a series of variables using the parameter substitution:

```
#!/bin/bash
x=32
y=5
: ${x?} ${y?} ${z?}
And now let's execute it:
zarrelli:~$ ./test-variable.sh
./test-variable.sh: line 5: z: parameter null or not set
```

Here is a bite on redirection:

```
zarrelli:~$ echo "012345679" > test.colon.2
zarrelli:~$ ls -lah test.colon.2
-rw-r--r-- 1 zarrelli zarrelli 10 Feb 19 14:18 test.colon.2
zarrelli:~$ : > test.colon.2
zarrelli:~$ ls -lah test.colon.2
-rw-r--r-- 1 zarrelli zarrelli 0 Feb 19 14:18 test.colon.2
```

So, what we see here is that the combining of the colon with > gives us a quick method for truncating a regular file without changing the permission. If the file does not exist, it gets created; but if we use >>, it only creates a file and does not truncate a preexisting file. You will find more *strange* uses for a colon, such as a field separator in the /etc/passwd file or as a legit function name.

The exclamation (!)

The exclamation mark is a keyword that negates or reverses a test or an exit status. For instance, take a look at this:

```
zarrelli:~$ ls -lah test.colon.2 ; echo $?
-rw-r--r-- 1 zarrelli zarrelli 10 Feb 19 14:22 test.colon.2
0
```

The exit code of ls is 0, true, since it was successful. But let's reverse it:

```
zarrelli:~$ ! ls -lah test.colon.2 ; echo $?
-rw-r--r-- 1 zarrelli zarrelli 10 Feb 19 14:22 test.colon.2
1
```

Keywords

A *keyword* is a reserved word that has a special meaning to the shell and is hardwired in it such as the builtins; but differing from the latter, the keywords are not full-blown commands, but parts of a command construct, and you can have a list of these by just typing this:

- compgen -k
- if
- then
- else
- elif

Quoting and Escaping

- fi
- case
- esac
- for
- select
- while
- until
- do
- done
- in
- function
- time
- {
- }
- !
- [[
-]]

From the command line, but not from a script, the exclamation mark triggers the bash history.

The asterisk (*)

The asterisk, also known as a wildcard, when used in a file name expansion, matches all the file names in a directory. The file name expansion is also known as **Globbing**. It takes into account some special characters as *, which is expanded to all, and ?, which expands to any single character along with some character lists in brackets:

```
zarrelli:~$ ls -lah [es]*
-rw-r--r-- 1 zarrelli zarrelli  36 Feb 17 07:50 external-data
-rwxr--r-- 1 zarrelli zarrelli 211 Feb 17 17:40 external-script-return.sh
-rwxr--r-- 1 zarrelli zarrelli 373 Feb 18 11:58 external-script-return-whatever.sh
-rwxr--r-- 1 zarrelli zarrelli 257 Feb 17 08:22 external-script.sh
-rwxr--r-- 1 zarrelli zarrelli 391 Feb 17 17:37 sourcing-return.sh
-rwxr--r-- 1 zarrelli zarrelli 235 Feb 19 10:40 sourcing-return-whatever.sh
-rwxr--r-- 1 zarrelli zarrelli 284 Feb 17 07:53 sourcing.sh
```

As we can see in the example, we listed all the * files whose names started either with e or s. But it also interprets the ^ character as negation:

```
zarrelli@moveaway:~/Documents/My books/Mastering bash/Chapter 4/Scripts$ ls -lah [^es]*
-rw-r--r-- 1 zarrelli zarrelli   0 Feb 16 08:35 *
-rw-r--r-- 1 zarrelli zarrelli   0 Feb 16 08:35 1
-rw-r--r-- 1 zarrelli zarrelli   0 Feb 16 08:35 2
-rw-r--r-- 1 zarrelli zarrelli   0 Feb 16 08:35 3
-rwxr--r-- 1 zarrelli zarrelli 249 Feb 16 13:24 comment.sh
-rwxr-xr-x 1 zarrelli zarrelli 409 Feb 16 14:59 menu.sh
-rwxr--r-- 1 zarrelli zarrelli 700 Feb 19 11:22 parm-sub.sh
-rw-r--r-- 1 zarrelli zarrelli   0 Feb 19 14:16 test.colon
-rw-r--r-- 1 zarrelli zarrelli  10 Feb 19 14:22 test.colon.2
-rw-r--r-- 1 zarrelli zarrelli   5 Feb 16 14:07 test.txt
-rwxr-xr-x 1 zarrelli zarrelli  42 Feb 19 14:14 test-variable.sh
```

In this case, we listed all the files in the current directory whose names did not start with either e or s. Be careful as the * in file globbing does not trap file names starting with a dot:

```
zarrelli:~$ mkdir test
zarrelli:~$ cd test/
zarrelli:~$ touch file
zarrelli:~$ touch .another_file
zarrelli:~$ ls -l *
-rw-r--r-- 1 zarrelli zarrelli 0 Feb 19 15:08 file
```

Something is clearly missing, so let's try this:

```
zarrelli:~$ ls -lah
total 8.0K
drwxr-xr-x 2 zarrelli zarrelli 4.0K Feb 19 15:08 .
drwxr-xr-x 3 zarrelli zarrelli 4.0K Feb 19 15:08 ..
-rw-r--r-- 1 zarrelli zarrelli    0 Feb 19 15:08 .another_file
-rw-r--r-- 1 zarrelli zarrelli    0 Feb 19 15:08 file
```

You could also try this for some nice effects:

```
ls -l .*
```

Final remarks, you will find the asterisk used as a wild card in regular expressions as well with the same meaning and also as a multiplication operator in arithmetic operations.

The double asterisk (**)

The double asterisk is being used in two different contexts:

- It is used as a exponentiation operator in an arithmetic context
- It is used as an extended file match globbing operator from Bash 4, meaning it matches filenames and directories recursively

So, we have this:

```
zarrelli:~$ for i in * ; do echo "$i" ; done
file
test2
```

This is different from the following:

```
zarrelli:~$ for i in ** ; do echo "$i" ; done
file
test2
test2/file2
```

The double star matched all files and directories globally. If the double star does not work for you, enable the globstar shell options with `zarrelli:~$ shopt -s globstar ; for i in ** ; do echo "$i" ; done`. The `globstar` value changes the way the shell interprets the double star, which, in a file name expansion, matches all files and any subdirectories. If the pattern is followed by a /, only the directories and subdirectories will be matched:

```
zarrelli:~$ for i in **/ ; do echo "$i" ; done
test2/
```

Test operators (?)

The test operator can be used in a few different scenarios. We already saw in the parameter substitution that it is used to check whether a variable has a value or not. In arithmetic operations, it can be used to implement the trinary or ternary operator in a C-style notation:

```
#!/bin/bash
x=20
y=30
w=40
z=50
k=100
echo 'Usually you would write a control loop in the following way:'
```

```
echo 'if [[ $x -gt $y ]]'
echo '    then'
echo '        z="$w"'
echo '        echo "The value for z is: $z"'
echo '    else'
echo '        z="$k"'
echo ' echo "The value for z is: $z"'
echo 'fi'
if [[ $x -gt $y ]]
    then
        z="$w"
        echo "The value for z is: $z"
    else
        z="$k"
        echo "The value for z is: $z"
fi
echo 'But you can also use the C-style trinary operator to achieve the same result:'
echo '(( z = x>y?w:k ))'
echo 'echo "The value for z is: $z"'
(( z = x>y?w:k ))
echo "The value for z is: $z"
```

As you can see, the C-style notation is more compact even though it is not as readable as a standard loop notation. Let's try it here:

zarrelli:~$ ./c-style.sh

Usually, you would write a control loop in the following way:

```
if [[ $x -gt $y ]]
    then
        z="$w"
        echo "The value for z is: "$z""
    else
        z="$k"
        echo "The value for z is: "$z""
fi
The value for z is: 100
```

But you can also use the C-style trinary operator to achieve the same result:

((z = x>y?w:k))
echo "The value for z is: $z"
The value for z is: 100

Quoting and Escaping

As you can see, we reached the same result but with a more compact code. Essentially, we give a condition that ends with the ? character and then, alternative results follow, which are separated by a : character.

We see that the C-style is widely used in loops and can be defined as a compound command used to evaluate mathematical expressions in a loop, and as seen in the previous example, assign a variable. It is made of three blocks: the first initializes a variable before the first iteration, the second checks for a condition that exits the look, and the third modifies the initial condition. Sounds strange? Look at this, it will look really familiar:

```
#!/bin/bash
for ((i = 0 ; i < 3 ; i++)); do
   echo "Counting loop number $i"
done
```

Now, let's execute it:

```
zarrelli:~$ ./c-style-counter.sh
Counting loop number 0
Counting loop number 1
Counting loop number 2
```

Finally, you can find the quotation mark used for file name expansion in globbing as a wild card matching any one characters; in regular expressions, use it as a single character match.

The substitution ($)

We already know this and have used it for the variable substitution that allows us to access the content of a variable:

```
zarrelli:~$ x=10 ; echo $x
10
```

But it is also used in a regular expression to match at the end of a line:

```
ls | grep [[:digit:]]$
1
2
3
test.colon.2
```

In this example, the output of `ls` is filtered on that file whose name ends with a single integer.

The parameter substitution (${})

This gives us a parameter substitution, which we have already seen earlier in this book.

The quoted string expansion ($'...')

This is a quoted string expansion, and it is used to expand escaped octal or hex values in Unicode or ASCII:

```
zarrelli:~$ x=$'\110\145\154\154\157' ; echo "$x"
Hello
```

We just concatenated some escaped octal values to get a nice and welcoming ASCII string assigned to the variable x.

The positional parameters ($* and $")

The first ($*) represents all the positional parameters as a single string and the second ($") represents all the positional parameters as follows:

```
#!/bin/bash
counter=0
echo "First trying the \$*"
for i in "$*"
do
(( counter+=1 ))
echo $counter
done
counter=0
echo "And now \$@"
for i in "$@"
do
(( counter+=1 ))
echo $counter
done
```

Now, let's test it:

```
zarrelli$ ./positional-single.sh 1 2 3 4 5
First trying the $*
1
And now $@
1
2
```

```
3
4
5
```

As we can see in the first case, the parameters are passed as single words, but beware, `$*` must be quoted to avoid weird side effects of the expansion. `$@` passes each parameter as a quoted string without any interpretation.

The exit status ($?)

We already saw this representing the exit status of a command, function, and script:

```
zarrelli:~$ ls 2&>1 ; echo $?
0
```

The process ID ($$)

This holds the **Process ID (PID)** of the script that appears in the following:

```
#!/bin/bash
echo $$
```

Let's execute it:

```
zarrelli:~$ ./pid.sh
4772
```

Grouping the command (command1 ; command2 ; commandn)

Grouping the commands into parenthesis have them executed in a subshell, and this has a subtle but outstanding implication: whatever you do in the subshell will not be reachable from the calling shell, so if you execute a subshell from a script with commands inside, what you will do in the subshell will not be available to the calling script:

```
#!/bin/bash
x=10
echo "The initial value of x is: $x"
(x=$(( x*x )) ; echo "The value of x is: $x")
echo "But outside the subshell the value of x is untouched: $x"
```

Now, let's execute the code:

```
zarrelli:~$ ./subshell.sh
The initial value of x is: 10
The value of x is: 100
But outside the subshell the value of x is untouched: 10
```

It comes quite straightforward if we recall what we read in the first chapters: the subshell inherits the environment of the calling shell from the script, and so, it can access the value of the x variable, but it cannot inject back anything. So, after having multiplied the value of x for itself and reassigning it to the variable, we could print the result, 100, in the subshell. But once we exited it, we were left with the original value of x and 10. The value of x never changed in the main script; it changed only into the subshell. As we will see later in this book, () is also used to initialize an array:

```
array= (element1 element2 elementn)
{a,b,c}
```

The brace expansion can come handy to address multiple items at once:

```
zarrelli:~$ ls *.{[[:digit:]],txt}
test.colon.2 test.txt
```

In this case, we expanded * in files starting with whatever characters, and then ending with a dot, followed either by a single integer or a txt postfix. But we can actually apply a command to a list of files having the globbing taking effect:

```
zarrelli:~$ wc -l {test.txt,test.colon.2,*-data}
1 test.txt
1 test.colon.2
2 external-data
4 total
```

Or simply, we can do as follows:

```
zarrelli:~$ echo {1,2,3}
1 2 3
```

But be careful; use no spaces inside the braces unless you escape or quote them; otherwise you could face weird issues:

```
{element1..elementn}
```

Quoting and Escaping

The extended brace expansion, available from Bash 3, is an easy way to create iterators:

```
zarrelli:~$ for i in {0..5} ; do echo $i ; done
0
1
2
3
4
5
```

Or create something fancier, as follows:

```
zarrelli:~$ for i in {1..3} ; do for k in {a..c} ; do echo $i,$k ; done ; done
1,a
1,b
1,c
2,a
2,b
2,c
3,a
3,b
3,c
{ command1 ; command2 ; commandn ;}
```

The curly brackets are widely used to create the so-called anonymous functions, which have an interesting property: the code inside these kinds of functions are visible to the rest of the script. There is another way of grouping commands, but with some interesting differences:

- The commands are executed in the same shell, no subshell spawned
- Because of this, all the variables instanced inside the brackets are available from the calling shell, that is, from the calling script
- Braces are reserved words and must be separated from the elements enclosed using spaces or a metacharacter
- A newline or ; is required at the end of the commands list

Here is an example of how to use the curly brackets:

```
#!/bin/bash
x=10
echo "The initial value of x is: $x"
multiplier () {
local y=$(( x*x ))
echo "The value of y in the function is: $y"
}
echo "We now trigger the function..."
```

```
multiplier
echo "The value of y right after the function execution is: $y"
{ z=$(( x*x )) ;
echo "The value of z in the function is: $z" ; }
echo "The value of z right after the function execution is: $z"
```

Now, let's run it:

```
zarrelli:~$ ./curly.sh
The initial value of x is: 10
We now trigger the function...
The value of y in the function is: 100
The value of y right after the function execution is:
The value of z in the function is: 100
The value of z right after the function execution is: 100
```

As you can see, we did not have to call the anonymous function to execute it differently from a normal function. We did not use the local scope for the variable since it is not allowed, and it will throw an error. We will see more about functions and scopes in a while.

Braces support I/O redirection for the code enclosed into it.

Braces ({})

Again, braces have another meaning: using braces with xargs -i (replace string) can be a placeholder for names:

```
zarrelli:~$ ls *.{[[:digit:]],txt} | xargs -i echo "Found file: {}"
Found file: test.colon.2
Found file: test.txt
```

The full path ({} \;)

Used with find -exec, this holds the full path to the file located by find. It is not a shell builtin, and the semicolon at the end of the command sequence must be escaped to avoid shell interpretation:

```
find . -name *.txt -exec cp {} copy.txt \;
zarrelli:~$ ls -lah test.txt copy.txt
-rw-r--r-- 1 zarrelli zarrelli 5 Feb 21 16:12 copy.txt
-rw-r--r-- 1 zarrelli zarrelli 5 Feb 16 14:07 test.txt
```

Expression ([])

This tests the expression between brackets. It is the shell builtin test and not the command called /usr/bin/[.

[[-f copy.txt]] && echo "file found

Expression ([[]])

Again, this tests expressions between brackets, but in a more flexible way. We have already seen this in the previous chapters.

The array index ([])

This points us to the object located into the array at the index specified between the brackets:

```
fruit=(apple banana lemon) ; echo ${fruit[1]}
banana
```

We will see what an array is later on, as of now, just bear in mind that an array index starts from 0, so 1 is the second element into it.

Characters range ([])

This defines a range of characters matched in regular expressions:

```
zarrelli:~$ ls | grep ^[c-m]
comment.sh
copy.txt
c-style-counter.sh
c-style.sh
curly.sh
external-data
external-script-return.sh
external-script-return-whatever.sh
external-script.sh
menu.sh
```

In this case, we matched all the filenames starting with a character in the range between c and m.

Integer expansion ($[...])

This is an integer expansion, deprecated and substituted by ((...)).

Integer expansion (((..)))

This is an integer expansion. We have already seen in the previous chapters how to use it.

>, &>, >&, >>, < and <>

We saw this at the beginning of this book, and we know they are used for redirections. You will find more details on how to use it in the examples provided.

The here document (<<)

A here document is a form of redirection that forces the shell to read the input from the subsequent block of characters up to a user-defined delimiter, and then it uses this bunch of characters as a standard input for a command or a file descriptor. As we can see in the next example, the argument for the `cat` command is not provided on the command line or asked to the user, but it is written into the script between the two DELIMITER words:

```
#!/bin/bash
cat << DELIMITER
This is a string
followed by another
date $(date +%Y.%m.%d)
until the
DELIMITER
```

Now, let's run it:

```
zarrelli:~$ ./here-date.sh
This is a string
followed by another
date 2017.02.21
until the
```

Quoting and Escaping

The delimiter at the right of << can be whatever string you want as long as it matches with the last line: everything between the two delimiters will be used as standard input for, in our example, `cat`. Be aware that the delimiter is not subject to any command substitution, arithmetical, or pathname expansion. But if the delimiter is not quoted, then the lines between the delimiters are subject to the arithmetic and file expansions and the command substitution.

A nice touch is to add – at the right side of <<so that the trailing tab characters get stripped from the input, and this makes it possible to create indented here documents:

```
#!/bin/bash
cat << DELIMITER
This is a string
        followed by an indented one
            with an indented date: $(date +%Y.%m.%d)
until the
DELIMITER
```

You will now get this:

```
zarrelli:~$ ./here-date-indented.sh
This is a string
        followed by an indented one
            with an indented date: 2017.02.21
until the
```

If you swap << with <, you will get an unindented input:

```
zarrelli:~$ ./here-date-indented.sh
This is a string
followed by an indented one
with an indented date: 2017.02.21
until the
```

The here string (<<<)

The *here* string is a simple version of the *here* document, and it consists of a single line where the delimiter is expanded to feed the command:

```
#!/bin/bash
today=$(date +%Y.%m.%d)
cat <<< $today
```

The output is here:

```
zarrelli:~$ ./here-date-string.sh
2017.02.21
```

The ASCII comparison operators (<) and (>)

This is an ASCII comparison between strings. We already saw how to use these in the previous chapter.

Delimiters (\< and \>)

Are delimiters are used to identify a word in a regular expression. Let's create a file:

```
zarrelli:~$ echo "barnaby went to the bar to see the barnum musical" > text.file
```

Now, we will `grep` with the word delimiter set to `bar` with the -o option, which will output only the fragment that matched and not all the lines containing it:

```
grep -o '\<bar\>' text.file
bar
```

This is correct. There is only one single word called `bar`; the others are composite words, and we can double check this:

```
zarrelli:~$ grep -o bar text.file
bar
bar
bar
```

If we do not look for the word named `bar`, but only for the matches of a three character string bar, we see that we can match it three times in the file.

The pipe character (|)

The pipe is a classic example of inter process communication: it passes the `stdout` of a process to the `stdin` of another process:

```
zarrelli:~$ ls -lah | wc -l
35
```

Quoting and Escaping

In this example, we just listed the content of the current directory and fed the output as the `stdin` of the `wc` utility, which counted how many lines there were in data just fed in. The command after the pipe runs in a subshell, so it will not be able to return any modified value to the parent process; and if one of the commands in the pipe aborts somehow, this leads to the so-called broken pipe and the execution of the pipe stops.

The force redirection (>|)

This forces redirection even if a `noclobber` option is set for the shell. Clobbering means the act of overwriting the content of a file, and this is something we have already seen with the redirection, but let's have a look at this example:

```
zarrelli:~$ echo "123" > override.txt
zarrelli:~$ cat override.txt
123
zarrelli:~$ echo "456" > override.txt
zarrelli:~$ cat override.txt
456
```

Everything goes as expected. We redirected the output of the echo, and on the second run, we overwrote the content of the file. But let's now set the `noclobber` option for the shell:

```
zarrelli:~$ set -o noclobber
```

We will try to overwrite the content of the file:

```
zarrelli:~$ echo "789" > override.txt
bash: override.txt: cannot overwrite existing file
```

No way, we are prevented from the accidental overwriting by the `noclobber` option set for the shell:

```
zarrelli:~$ cat override.txt
456
```

In fact, the content of the file is still the same, but now, it is this:

```
zarrelli:~$ echo "789" >| override.txt
zarrelli:~/$ cat override.txt
789
```

We forced the redirection and now the content of the file has changed:

```
zarrelli:~$ set +o noclobber
```

Let's revert the `noclobber` option.

Have a look at `man bash` for some interesting options that you can set with the `set -o` option to alter the Bash behavior. For instance, take a look at this:

- `+B` disables the brace expansion
- `-f` disables the file name expansion, also known as globbing.
- `-i` runs a script in the interactive mode
- `-n` reads the commands in a script but does not execute them; it is a classical dry run mode for syntax check
- The `-o posix` makes everything a POSIX compliant
- The `-p` script runs as SUID
- The `-r` script runs with a restricted shell
- `-s` the commands are read from the `stdin`
- The `-v` commands are printed to `stdout` before their execution
- `-x` is similar to `-v`, but the commands get expanded

The logical OR (||)

We have already understood them, so have a look at the previous pages.

&

This sends a process into the background. Look at this:

```
zarrelli:~$ echo "Hello, see you in 5 seconds" ; sleep 5
Hello, see you in 5 seconds
```

It will hold the prompt for 5 seconds only if you put sleep in the background:

```
zarrelli:~$ echo "Hello, see you in 5 seconds" ; sleep 5 &
Hello, see you in 5 seconds
[1] 8163
```

The shell will give you back control immediately, since the sleep process will not get any more input from the terminal, leaving the command line available to the user. One of the benefits of this is that while you are limited to a single foreground process at time. Since during its execution, you will not be able to enter any other commands with background processes, you can spawn as many as you wish, given the system resources.

Quoting and Escaping

You can manually force a foreground process to go to the background by pressing *Ctrl + Z* and then `fg`:

```
zarrelli:~$ echo "Hello, see you in 50 seconds" ; sleep 50
Hello, see you in 50 seconds
^Z
[6]+ Stopped    sleep 50
zarrelli:~$ fg
sleep 50
```

Logical AND (&&)

This is the logical AND, and it returns `true` in a test if both the conditions are true.

The dash character (-)

The dash is the option character, and usually, it denotes an optional parameter on a command line:

```
ps -ax
```

It is also used in parameter substitution as the prefix for the default parameter, and it is also used to redirect from/to stdin/stdout:

```
zarrelli:~$ cat -
1
1
2
2
3
3
^C
```

Or, it can do this:

```
zarrelli:~$ tar cvzf - $(ls text.file) > zipped.tgz
zarrelli:~$ tar -tf zipped.tgz
text.file
```

What we did is get the file name on the `stdout` using the command substitution, have it read from the `stdin` with the -, then the result of the `tar` operation redirected to the `stdout` to create the zipped file.

We can also use the dash to go back to our previous directory as held in the environmental $OLDPWD variable:

```
zarrelli:~$ mkdir -p dir1/dir2
zarrelli:~$ cd dir1/
zarrelli:~$ cd dir2/
zarrelli:~$ cd -
zarrelli:~$ pwd
dir1
```

Finally, in an arithmetic operations context, the dash means minus, so we can subtract a number from another.

The double dash (--)

The double dash usually stands for long options for a command. For instance, in the next example, we use the short option called -a and the long option called --all to enable the same behavior for ls; the long option being usually a more human readable form of the shorter one. While the short option starts with a single dash, the long option starts with a double dash:

```
zarrelli:~$ ls -a
. .. dir2
zarrelli:~$ ls --all
. .. dir2
```

It is also used, as we saw a few pages ago, with the set command to set Bash options.

Operator =

It can be an assignment operator:

```
zarrelli:~$ x=10 ; echo $x
10
```

It can also be a string comparison operator:

```
zarrelli:~$ x=10 ; y=10 ; if [[ "$x" = "$y" ]] ; then echo "Success" ; fi
Success
```

Operator +

This can be used as an operator in an arithmetic context to add a number to another one. In a regular expression scenario, it matches one or more of the previous regular expressions:

```
zarrelli:~$ echo "Hello" | grep 'Hel\+o'
Hello
```

The plus character is also used by some built-ins to enable some options in the parameter substitution context to mark the alternate value that a variable expands to:

```
zarrelli:~$ x=10 ; y=${x+20} ; echo $y
20
```

If x is set, it will be use the value of 20 otherwise a null string.

The modulo operator (%)

It is the arithmetic operator for modulo, the remainder of a division. The modulo operator is also used as the operator for pattern matching in a parameter substitution context:

```
zarrelli:~$ x="highland" ; y=${x%land} ; echo $y
high
```

Operator ~

This holds the same value of the environment variable called $HOME:

```
zarrelli:~$ echo ~
/home/zarrelli
zarrelli:~$ ls /home/zarrelli/
Desktop Documents Downloads Music Pictures Public Templates test.file test.sh tmp Videos
zarrelli:~$ ls ~/tmp/
setting.sh
zarrelli:~$ cd ~
zarrelli:~$ pwd
/home/zarrelli
```

Operator ~+

This is the current working directory whose value is held by the env variable named $PWD.

Operator ~-

This is the previous working directory whose value is held by the env variable named `$OLDPWD`.

Operator ~=

This is the matching operator for regular expressions inside double brackets. It has been introduced in Bash 3.

Operator ^

In regular expressions it matches the given pattern starting from the beginning of the line. We saw some examples in the previous pages.

The control characters (^ and ^^)

Introduced in Bash 4, they deal with the uppercase conversion in a parameter substitution context.

Apart from the special characters that we saw so far, there is a combination of keys. They are usually called control characters that are not actually used in a script, but ease your interaction with the terminal. They are a combination of two characters, *Ctrl* and another one, pressed together; but they can also be written in escaped hexadecimal or octal notation:

- *Ctrl*+*A*: This moves the cursor at the beginning of a string of characters on the command line.
- *Ctrl*+*B*: This is a backspace, but it does not erase anything.
- *Ctrl*+*C*: This breaks out of a foreground job, terminating it.

Quoting and Escaping

- *Ctrl+D*: This exits on a shell. If the user is in a terminal window and typing, it erases the character the cursor is on. If there is nothing in the window, it gets closed.
- *Ctrl+E*: This moves the cursor at the end of a string of characters on the command line.
- *Ctrl+F*: This moves the cursor forward of one position on the command line.
- *Ctrl+G*: In a terminal window, this could raise a beep.
- *Ctrl+H*: This backspaces and deletes the character under the cursor while backspacing, also known as **rubout**.
- *Ctrl+I*: This is a horizontal tab.
- *Ctrl+J*: This is the newline and it can also be expressed as the `\012` octal and the `\x0a` hexadecimal.
- *Ctrl+K*: This is a vertical tab. In a terminal window, it deletes all the characters from under the cursor to the end of the line.
- *Ctrl+L*: This is the formfeed, and it clears the screen from all the content.
- *Ctrl+M*: This is the carriage return.
- *Ctrl+N*: This deletes a line called back from the history on the command line.
- *Ctrl+O*: Given on the command line, it brings you to a new line executing the current command on CLI .
- *Ctrl+P*: This restores the last command from the history on the command line.
- *Ctrl+Q*: This resumes `stdin` in a terminal window.
- *Ctrl+R*: This searches for text in the history, backwards.
- *Ctrl+S*: This suspends `stdin` in a terminal window, resumed by *Ctrl+Q*.
- *Ctrl+T*: This swaps the character under the cursor with the preceding one on the command line.
- *Ctrl+U*: This deletes all characters between the cursor position and at the beginning of the command line. In some configurations, it deletes all the characters on the command line.
- *Ctrl+V*: This is used mostly in editors, and it allows to enter control characters while inserting text.
- *Ctrl+W*: In a terminal or X term, it deletes characters backwards from under the cursor to the first whitespace; in some configurations, it deletes until the first non alphanumeric character is reached.
- *Ctrl+X*: You will find it in quite a number of word processors, as a way to cut and paste text from the editor to the clipboard.

- *Ctrl+Y*: This pastes the text erased with *Ctrl+U* or *Ctrl+W* back.
- *Ctrl+Z*: This pauses a job that is in the foreground.
- Whitespace: This is often used as a field separator. It is sometimes required in some context and forbidden in others, as we saw in some of the examples available in the previous chapters.

Quoting and escaping

We've already seen how important quoting and escaping is in Bash, and this is due to the fact that some characters are not just what they look like, but they hold some special meaning for the shell, which interprets them whenever it meets them. But sometimes, we want these characters for just what they are; we want to keep whitespaces in a string and not split it up in words, or we just want to see if there is a * file name. Or we want to `echo` a double quote and not start a quote. So, we quote and escape to preserve what we see from what the shell could think it is.

The backslash (\)

The backslash is the character we use to escape all the others. Great. What does it mean? Simply put, each character preceded by a backslash keeps its literal value or meaning. The backslash does not apply to an entire string, but just to its following character, and it is widely used to escape spaces in file names:

```
zarrelli:~$ mkdir this is a directory with spaces in the name
total 44K
drwxr-xr-x 11 zarrelli zarrelli 4.0K Feb 23 09:50 .
drwxr-xr-x  3 zarrelli zarrelli 4.0K Feb 23 09:44 ..
drwxr-xr-x  2 zarrelli zarrelli 4.0K Feb 23 09:48 a
drwxr-xr-x  2 zarrelli zarrelli 4.0K Feb 23 09:48 directory
drwxr-xr-x  2 zarrelli zarrelli 4.0K Feb 23 09:48 in
drwxr-xr-x  2 zarrelli zarrelli 4.0K Feb 23 09:48 is
drwxr-xr-x  2 zarrelli zarrelli 4.0K Feb 23 09:48 name
drwxr-xr-x  2 zarrelli zarrelli 4.0K Feb 23 09:48 spaces
drwxr-xr-x  2 zarrelli zarrelli 4.0K Feb 23 09:48 the
drwxr-xr-x  2 zarrelli zarrelli 4.0K Feb 23 09:48 this
drwxr-xr-x  2 zarrelli zarrelli 4.0K Feb 23 09:48 with
```

Quoting and Escaping

Well, not exactly the result we wanted, but it is what we should have expected: the whitespace has been interpreted by the shell as a separator, so `mkdir` created as many directories as the words given as arguments. We need to have `mkdir` to parse a string complete with whitespaces and not a series of words split by spaces:

```
zarrelli:~$ mkdir this\ is\ a\ directory\ with\ spaces\ in\ the\ name
zarrelli:~$ ls -lah
total 48K
drwxr-xr-x 12 zarrelli zarrelli 4.0K Feb 23 09:52 .
drwxr-xr-x  3 zarrelli zarrelli 4.0K Feb 23 09:44 ..
drwxr-xr-x  2 zarrelli zarrelli 4.0K Feb 23 09:48 a
drwxr-xr-x  2 zarrelli zarrelli 4.0K Feb 23 09:48 directory
drwxr-xr-x  2 zarrelli zarrelli 4.0K Feb 23 09:48 in
drwxr-xr-x  2 zarrelli zarrelli 4.0K Feb 23 09:48 is
drwxr-xr-x  2 zarrelli zarrelli 4.0K Feb 23 09:48 name
drwxr-xr-x  2 zarrelli zarrelli 4.0K Feb 23 09:48 spaces
drwxr-xr-x  2 zarrelli zarrelli 4.0K Feb 23 09:48 the
drwxr-xr-x  2 zarrelli zarrelli 4.0K Feb 23 09:48 this
drwxr-xr-x  2 zarrelli zarrelli 4.0K Feb 23 09:52 this is a directory with spaces in the name
drwxr-xr-x  2 zarrelli zarrelli 4.0K Feb 23 09:48 with
```

Here we go, we finally have a directory whose name is filled with spaces.

You can also see the backslash used in scripts or on the command line when your instructions are becoming a bit too long. You can see them when you want to go on a new line without triggering a carriage return, which would execute your incomplete command line:

```
zarrelli@moveaway:~$ var="This can become a bit too long \
> so better to go on a new line and print on the next" ; \
> echo \
> $var
This can become a bit too long so better to go on a new line and print on the next
```

Double quotes ("")

Double quotes are the so-called weak quoting, since they prevent the interpretation by the shell of all metacharacters except for $, ", ', and \. This means a few things; the most important is that you can reference a variable value even if it is quoted:

```
zarrelli:~$ x=10 ; echo "$x"
10
```

This also means that you can use backslash to escape $ to print the literal $a string:

```
zarrelli:~$ x=10 ; echo "\$x"
$x
```

So, to use one of the preceding interpreted characters, you have to escape it with a backslash.

Also, double quotes preserve whitespaces, so we can rewrite the command we saw earlier:

`mkdir this\ is\ a\ directory\ with\ spaces\ in\ the\ name` as `mkdir "this is a directory with spaces in the name"`.

So, what if you want to prevent any interpretations at all? You have to rely on a strong quoting.

Single quotes (')

Single quotes enable a strong quoting so that none of the metacharacters we saw before, such as $, ", ', and \ , are interpreted; and everything quoted this way is taken literally except for the single quote itself, which keeps its function of the metacharacter. This means that you cannot use it at all since the usual way of taking the literal value of a character. Using a backslash does not work since inside the single quote, as the backslash itself loses its meta effect. One notable effect of strong quoting is that you cannot reference the value of a variable any longer:

```
zarrelli:~$ x=10 ; echo '$x'
$x
```

That being said, we still have some characters with special meanings even after being escaped; here are some of them:

- \a is the alert
- \b is the backspace
- \n is the newline
- \r is the return
- \t is the tab
- \v is the vertical tab

Summary

Now that we understand how to deal safely with variables and special characters, it is time to move toward something more useful in our everyday programming. In the next chapter, we will have a close look at the case construct, arrays, and functions; and this will allow us to create our first fully-fledged command-line parser.

Menus, Arrays, and Functions

Writing a script often means having to deal with user interaction. You want to know what the user expects from your script, and you want to let the user know what options they have to decide from. So, we give the user some choices, they give us their answers, we evaluate them against some preset values, and decide what to do next. This implies a method to expose some data to the user, gather their answer, cycle between options, and react accordingly. There are different ways to do this, and we will see how to accomplish the task using some standard constructs. At the end of this chapter, we will be able to offer, gather, store, and process data efficiently.

The case statement

When you are given more alternatives, you can process them with a sequence of if else statements:

```
if [condition];
then
command
else
command
fi
```

The `if` clauses can be nested if needed, but in the long run, having more than a few choices messes up the code, making it less readable. One of the basic mantras of coding is exactly keeping the code readable, making it *elegant* since elegance here does not simply mean beautiful, but also consistent over time. Always keep a meaningful indentation so that the clauses will outstand. Try to use as little code as you can, adopt the same notation all through your script, and make it all compact and lean. So, having a cascade of *if/then/else/fi* with a lot of indentation cannot show up as the optimal decision for your script, but there is an alternative available and it is widely adopted to create user menus and process the data provided and it is the `case` statement in the following form:

```
case expression in
condition_1)
command_1
command_n
;;
condition_2)
command_1
command_n
;;
condition_n | z)
command_1
command_n
;;
esac
```

The expression is actually a condition that must match the pattern given in `condition x)`. Once the match is true, the corresponding block of commands are executed:

```
condition_x)
command_1
command_n
;;
```

Each of these block of commands is called a **clause** and is terminated by the `;;` double semicolon. All the case statements are enclosed in `case` and `esac` and each condition can be expressed either as `condition_1)` or `condition_1 | condition_2 | condition_n)`.

Each condition can be an alternative match for triggering the execution of the commands inside the clause.

Let's see two examples of how to deal with the same options using the *if/then/else/fi* and *case/esac* constructs:

```
#!/bin/bash
echo "Please, give me some input"
read input
if [[ $input =~ ^[[:digit:]]+$ ]];
then
echo "These are digits"
exit 0
elif [[ $input =~ ^[[:alpha:]]+$ ]];
then
echo "These are chars"
exit 0
else
echo "Dunno..."
exit 1
fi
```

Now, let's look at some tests:

```
zarrelli:~$ ./if-statement.sh
Please, give me some input
123
These are digits
zarrelli:~$ ./if-statement.sh
Please, give me some input
abc
These are chars
zarrelli:~$ ./if-statement.sh
Please, give me some input
12a
Dunno...
zarrelli:~$ ./if-statement.sh
Please, give me some input
!der
Dunno...
```

Menus, Arrays, and Functions

This is not complex code. We are asking for some input, and then we will check for a couple of conditions whether the text entered is all made of digits or characters; otherwise we have `dunno` as the default answer. We used a slightly more complicated version of *if/then/else/fi*. We adopted `elif` to check an alternative option to match for our condition. We could have gone further with a series of `elif` to check if the user input some alphanumerics or other kinds of characters, but as you can see from this tiny example, the code is still becoming a bit difficult to read; it is not so clear. Now, let's try something slightly different using the case statement:

```
#!/bin/bash
echo "Please, give me some input"
read input
case ${input//[[:alpha:]]} in
"")
echo "There were alphabetic chars only"
exit 0
;;
*[[:alnum:]]*)
echo "There were digits in the string"
exit 0
;;
*)
echo "There were non alphanumeric chars"
exit 1
;;
esac
```

What we do here is create a condition, so that we can strip all the alphabetic characters from the input variable value . What's left is checked against `""`. What does it mean? It simply means that if after stripping the string of all alpha characters what's left is an empty string. If the condition is not met we check against a second condition: if in what is left of the original strings there are some alphanumeric characters, it means that in the original string there were numeric characters. If even this second condition is met it means that in the stripped string there are chars other than numbers or alphabetic characters.

Did you ever see or use a `case` statement before ? Yes, probably more often than you think. Let's do something interesting now; we will see later why it is so interesting. Go to the /et/init.d/ directory for Linux distribution, still **SystemV** compatible, and take a look at any of the scripts you find there. These are the scripts that deal with the startup/shutdown of system services such as cron or dbus along with all the additional services that can be offered such as ssh, Apache, and so forth. Looking at these scripts something pops out immediately, they have the following structure:

```
#!/bin/bash
case "$1" in
start)
:
exit 0
;;
stop)
:
exit 0
;;
status)
:
exit 0
;;
restart)
:
exit 0
;;
condrestart)
if $condition
then
exit 0
fi
exit 1
;;
*)
echo $"Usage: $0 {start|stop|restart|condrestart|status}"
exit 1
;;
esac
exit 0
```

Menus, Arrays, and Functions

This can be used as a base for our interactive scripts, since it provides a bare bones structure to deal with user interaction. As you can see, each clause has `:`, as being a base script, nothing gets executed; and for each clause, we graciously exit with a success code except for the conditional restart and the default options. The conditional restart is really optional, but it lets you restart your service based on a condition you will impose, so it is up to you to leave or delete this section. As we saw earlier in this book, the `case` construct is somewhat similar to the *if/then/else/fi* construct with a condition to match against different strings given as options. The construct is enclosed between the `case` and `esac` markers; notice that `esac` is `case` read backwards. Consider the following clause:

```
string1 | string2 | stringn)
do_something
do_somethingn
;;
```

It starts with one or more strings to be matched; each possible match is separated by a `|` and ends with `;;`. If more than one match is true, only the first is taken into account. The last option is usually an asterisk, and this can be considered as a catchall default since `*` matches whatever strings the user inputs. So, if no previous matches trigger a clause, this last one will be matched anyway and is a good place to write help or some command-line utilization messages, since it will always be displayed if the user did not enter the right options.

The string of patterns to match can be optionally preceded by `(`, for example, `(string1 | string2 | stringn)`. Remember that the last `;;` before `esac` can be omitted without causing any issues.

Each string starting the clause is an optional match for case condition in. This is usually a string of text that must be checked for a match against each option string starting a clause. If the condition is a variable, it is expanded using the parameter expansion, variable expansion (tilde), command substitution, process substitution, and quote removal, but no pathname expansion, brace expansion, or word splitting is performed. Given that, you do not need to quote the variable for safe processing.

From Bash 4 a couple of clause terminators were introduced, and we already saw them in the previous chapter:

- `;&` makes the execution continue with the commands associated with the next condition
- `;;&` makes the shell check the option and execute the associated commands if the condition is matched

If no matches are found, the exit status is 0, otherwise the exit status is the one from the last command executed.

Let's see how they word and proceed to modify the base script:

```
#!/bin/bash
case "$1" in
start)
echo "We are starting..."
exit 0
;;
stop)
echo "We are stopping..."
exit 0
;;
status)
echo "We are checking the status..."
exit 0
;;
restart)
echo "We are restarting..."
exit 0
;;
*)
echo $"Usage: $0 {start|stop|restart|status}"
exit 1
;;
esac
exit 0
```

Now, let's try it out:

```
zarrelli:~$ ./terminators.sh
Usage: ./terminators.sh {start|stop|restart|status}
```

Without any arguments, there cannot be any matches on a given option, so the catchall asterisk comes into play and executes the echo printing the usage message on stdout:

```
zarrelli:~$ ./terminators.sh start
We are starting...
zarrelli:~$ ./terminators.sh stop
We are stopping...
zarrelli:~$ ./terminators.sh restart
We are restarting...
zarrelli:~$ ./terminators.sh status
We are checking the status...
```

Menus, Arrays, and Functions

All the other options are straightforward; we deleted the `condrestart` option just to make the script more compact and easy to read.

Now, let's use the ;& terminator on the last clause:

```
restart)
echo "We are checking the status..."
exit 0
;&
```

Now, execute the script with status as the argument:

```
zarrelli:$ ./terminators.sh status
We are checking the status...
```

Ahem, embarrassing, nothing changed. Why? Have a closer look at the clause: the ;& terminator is preceded by `exit 0`, so the execution of the script stops before hitting the terminator. Well, let's delete `exit 0` and invoke the script again with the status argument:

```
zarrelli:~$ ./terminators-last.sh status
We are checking the status...
We are restarting...
```

Interesting, isn't it? We cascaded from one block to the other, so we had the status block commands executed right after the restart block commands got executed. And this is exactly what we expected from the ;& operator, since the execution had to proceed to the next block where once the first condition was met. But now, let's do something else and modify the restart clause as well:

```
restart)
echo "We are restarting..."
;;&
```

Let's execute the script:

```
zarrelli:~$ ./terminators-last.sh status
We are checking the status...
We are restarting...
Usage: ./terminators-last.sh {start|stop|restart|status}
```

What happened? Simply put, once the `status` string was matched, the first `echo` command got executed and the `;&` operator caused the command associated to the restart clause to be invoked without any other string check. In the restart clause, the `;;&` operator caused a string check on the following clause, but this being a string match against a wildcard, it matched anyway so the `echo` command of the `usage` string was executed. But what happens if we invert the operators between the status and restart clauses:

```
zarrelli:~$ ./terminators-last.sh status
We are checking the status...
Usage: ./terminators-last.sh {start|stop|restart|status}
```

We entered the `status` clause, executed the code, and then proceeded to the `restart` code. Here, the command was not executed since `;;&` triggers the command execution only if the string matches, but our `status` argument does not match the `restart` option. In the next line, we have `;&`, which cascades us to the next clause, whose code is executed regardless of any matches. If you want to cause the commands in the `restart` clause to be executed anyway, just modify the matching options:

```
restart | status)
echo "We are restarting..."
;&
```

And now, let's try this:

```
zarrelli:~$ ./terminators-last.sh status
We are checking the status...
We are restarting...
Usage: ./terminators-last.sh {start|stop|restart|status}
```

In this case, we gave two possible matches for the restart clause, `restart` or `status`. The first failed, but the second matched, and the command got executed, and then the next clause command got executed as well.

We saw the `case` construct used in a startup script with minimal interaction with the user, but now, let's start working on this construct to make something more interesting out of it:

```
#!/bin/bash
clear
echo -n "May I create an archive out of the current directory files? [yes or no]: "
read input
case $input in
[yY] | [yY][eE][sS] )
echo -e
echo "Yes, of course...I am proceeding"
echo -e "Archiving the following files\n"
```

```
            now=$(date +%Y.%m.%d.%H.%M.%S)
            filename=${PWD##*/}
            tar cvzf ${now}.${filename}.tgz *
            echo -e
            echo "Archive $now.${filename}.tgz created!"
            ;;
        [nN] | [nN][oO] )
            echo -e
            echo "No, so have a lovely day".;
            echo -e
            exit 1
            ;;
        *)
            echo -e
            echo "Please just answer yes or no, y, n, in lower or capital."
            echo -e
            ;;
    esac
```

This simple script can be used to archive the content of a directory. It asks the user for the content and checks the answer against the lower and upper case y , yes, n , and no. Nothing too difficult here; we are just putting together things we already saw in the previous chapters. We start off with a clear instruction to clean the screen from any previous content, and then we ask the user for yes or no using an echo -n. So, we do not output any new lines, and the user answer will be on the same line after the double colon. The next step is to check against a list of characters.

[yY] | [yY][Ee][Ss]) will match both the lower and capital y but also against yes and YES and all the mix between lower and capital characters in this string. If this matches, we inform the user that we are proceeding to archive the file. Notice echo -e that we used; this enables the interpretation of backslash escapes, so we can use \n to enter a new line and go to the next line on the terminal. The next instruction is a command substitution, so we get the output of the date command assigned to the now variable. What we are doing is creating the bits that will later concatenate to obtain a unique filename for our archive. In this case, we get a date composed by year.month.day.hour.minute.second. We will use this string to prefix our archive, so we will be able to obtain a unique filename every second. But this is also a limit, because if we create two archives at the same moment, the latter will overwrite the former, having both the names the same.

Keep in mind your goals and limits and stick to them. When creating some variables or conditions, you have to think at the scope of your effort and not overthink about what you are doing. An example here is the prefix for the archive name. Giving us a name that is unique in the time range of a second allows us to have a new filename every single second, but it exposes us to the risk of having the archive overwritten if the same script is invoked twice at the same time, for instance, from two different terminals. To avoid this, we could create a function to forge random strings as prefix and avoid this issue or, at least, highly reduce the probability of a name collision. We will see later in this book how to create a random string, but is it worthy now? We are creating an example to show the use of case to process the user input and create an archive, so it is not likely that this script will be run twice at the same time. It could be great to catch this condition, but since it is not in the scope of this project, we will not do so, since the time spent will not be justified by the result and the likeliness of the event that it would prevent. On the opposite side, when writing a script, take your time to clarify to yourself what this script should do, what could be the pitfalls, which errors could occur, and the possible remedies you could code into the script itself.

Professional programming is not just coding, it is planning, trying to understand what could happen, what you want, and how to reach the goal. First, ask yourself what goal you want to accomplish, how to reach it, if you can realistically get to it with your knowledge, means, time, resources, and so on. Then, plan and develop accordingly. This applies to you as well as your clients since most of the time the hardest part is to understand what your customer really wants, being aware or not of it, how much time and resources it takes to code, and if the customer is willing to give you the time required and the resources needed. Finally, ask yourself if you can work on it given all these requisites. Let's say that if you were asked to code a simple calculator in assembly, you probably could do so after learning it, practicing a bit, and then trying a few times. But could you do it if you were given three days, starting from scratch? So, define the goal, its limits and resources, plan the execution, think of the pitfalls your code could face and then, well, take into account a fair contingency: your computer could stop working, you can get a cold, anything can happen so keep a fair amount of time as a contingency because your client has a delivery date in mind, and you have to deliver your code on time, cold, flu, computer gone crazy given. Finally, stick to a routine. Let's say you have four hours a day for coding and you know that in this amount of time, you can code 50 lines; but with exceptional effort, you could code 65 file lines. Do not take 65 lines into account and stick to an average amount. You are confident with this since you are going to code on a daily basis for quite a few days, and you cannot allow yourself to sprint every single day. Create your routine on an effort you know you can carry for a large amount of time so that you and your client do not incur an unpleasant situation.

Menus, Arrays, and Functions

So, after this digression, let's go on and check the last couple of interesting commands in the `yes` clause:

```
filename=${PWD##*/}
tar cvzf ${now}.${filename}.tgz *
```

The first line helps us to find the name of the current directory using parameter expansions: we get the content of the `$PWD` environment variable and delete the longest matching for the pattern, in our case all the path up until the last forward slash, and assign the result to the variable called filename. The second instruction creates an archive from all the files contained in the local directory called * and create the archive name out of the different bits that we prepared beforehand. Note`${}`, which allows us to preserve the variable during the concatenation. So, now is the time to execute the script:

```
May I create an archive out of the current directory files? [yes or no]:
yEs
Yes, of course...I am proceeding
Archiving the following files...
base.sh
case-statement.sh
if-statement.sh
terminators-last.sh
terminators.sh
user-case.sh
Archive 2017.02.26.12.24.55.Scripts.tgz created!
And check if the archive has been really created:
zarrelli:~$ tar -tf 2017.02.26.12.24.55.Scripts.tgz
base.sh
case-statement.sh
if-statement.sh
terminators-last.sh
terminators.sh
user-case.sh
```

We were able to list the files held into the archive and a simple `ls` will double-check the outcome:

```
zarrelli:~$ ls -Al
2017.02.26.12.24.55.Scripts.tgz
base.sh
case-statement.sh
if-statement.sh
terminators-last.sh
terminators.sh
user-case.sh
```

All the files are in place and we can also see the newly created archive. But are we sure that everything is fine? Let's create a `test` directory and copy all our files in it:

```
zarrelli:~$ mkdir test
zarrelli:~$ cp * test
cp: -r not specified; omitting directory 'test'
zarrelli:~$ chmod -R 0550 test
```

We copied the files in the `test` directory and set the directory permissions so that no one will be able to write into it. Now, let's enter the directory and run our script:

```
May I create an archive out of the current directory files? [yes or no]:
yes
Yes, of course...I am proceeding
Archiving the following files...
base.sh
case-statement.sh
if-statement.sh
terminators-last.sh
terminators.sh
user-case.sh
tar (child): 2017.02.27.08.40.03.test.tgz: Cannot open: Permission denied
tar (child): Error is not recoverable: exiting now
tar: Child returned status 2
tar: Error is not recoverable: exiting now
Archive 2017.02.27.08.40.03.test.tgz created!
```

Interesting, we see some error messages, but the script still says we have an archive file, let's check it:

```
zarrelli:~$ ls -A1
base.sh
case-statement.sh
if-statement.sh
terminators-last.sh
terminators.sh
user-case.sh
```

Menus, Arrays, and Functions

No, we do not have any new archive, and this is exactly what we'd expect since our user cannot write anything in the test directory. So, it can happen; sometimes, our script faces an issue, such as it cannot write or read from a directory or some files, and this is what we have to plan now: a contingency method to deal with this possible issue. What we can do is test to check the exit code of the `tar` command: if it is different from 0, it means that the archive creation failed somehow, otherwise everything went fine. So, let's rewrite the `yes` clause adding a test after the `tar` command:

```
tar cvzf $now.${filename}.tgz *
if [ $? -ne 0 ]
then
echo "Sorry there was an issue creating the archive..."
exit 1
else
echo -e
echo "Archive ${now}.${filename}.tgz created!"
exit 0
fi
;;
```

Be careful not to write any command between `tar` and the `test`, since the `$?` traps the exit code of the last command executed. Now, let's check the outcome:

```
May I create an archive out of the current directory files? [yes or no]:
yes
Yes, of course...I am proceeding
Archiving the following files...
tar (child): 2017.02.27.09.20.17.test.tgz: Cannot open: Permission denied
tar (child): Error is not recoverable: exiting now
base.sh
case-statement.sh
if-statement.sh
terminators-last.sh
terminators.sh
user-case.sh
tar: 2017.02.27.09.20.17.test.tgz: Cannot write: Broken pipe
tar: Child returned status 2
tar: Error is not recoverable: exiting now
Sorry there was an issue creating the archive…
```

Not bad! Now, our script is telling us that something has gone wild, and it stopped telling us that the archive was successfully created even though the `tar` command was failing. Anyway, the output is a bit messy. We already know from our error message that there was an error, so let's clean the output by modifying `tar cvzf $now.${filename}.tgz * 2>/dev/null`.

We just redirected the standard error to `/dev/null`, so no errors will be displayed to `stdout`.

Most of the time, it is preferable to mask the system or application errors and provide the customer with a more meaningful error message crafted by you. Bear in mind that not all users are system administrators or programmers and familiar with the operating system, application error messages, or codes.

Let's have a look at the output:

```
May I create an archive out of the current directory files? [yes or no]:
yes
Yes, of course...I am proceeding
Archiving the following files...
base.sh
case-statement.sh
if-statement.sh
terminators-last.sh
terminators.sh
user-case.sh
Sorry there was an issue creating the archive.
```

It is actually cleaner, and we could even go further and rip out the list of files. Do you know how to do it? A tip, the `stdout`...

But then, look at the following clause:

```
[yY] | [yY][eE][sS] )
echo -e
echo "Yes, of course...I am proceeding"
echo -e "Archiving the following files...\n"
now=$(date +%Y.%m.%d.%H.%M.%S)
filename=${PWD##*/}
if tar cvzf $now.${filename}.tgz * 2>/dev/null
then
echo -e
echo "Archive ${now}.${filename}.tgz created!"
exit 0
else
echo "Sorry there was an issue creating the archive..."
exit 1
fi
;;
```

The results are the same, but we used `if` in a more idiomatic way, since its purpose is to test if a condition is true or not, so in this case if the command succeeded or failed. But then, you have many ways to accomplish the same result; take a look here:

```
zarrelli:~$ rm base.sh && echo "File deleted" || echo "File not deleted"
rm: cannot remove 'base.sh': Permission denied
File not deleted
```

The `remove` command, given inside the test directory, fails due to the lack of permissions, but let's go up one directory and create a test file:

```
zarrelli:~$ touch test1
zarrelli:~$ rm test1 && echo "File deleted" || echo "File not deleted"
File deleted
```

I used the logical AND/OR operators to take advantage of what I usually called short circuit. Read the previous examples with the following grammar:

If [command1] is true than we evaluate also command2 [but if the first clause is not true execute command3]

Using the logical AND, both the commands called `rm test1` and `echo "file deleted"` must be true for the overall expression on the left of the OR (||). If the first command does not evaluate to true, the second is not even taken into account (short circuiting).

If the first part called `left_command && right_command` evaluates to be false, the OR comes into play and triggers the execution of the last command. But just in case that the first part, before || is true, then the second part will not be triggered. This is because, for the overall expression `left_command || right_command` to be true, it is enough for one of the two to be true and the first being true, the second command is not even evaluated (short circuiting).

This kind of error handling does not cause a script to exit in case of issues, and this can be desirable behavior most of the time, but sometimes, we could resort to a trick that would throw us out in case of errors:

```
#!/bin/bash -e
```

This will cause the exit from the script if any command, in subshell or braces, exits with a non-zero code. This does not apply if the failing command is part of a command list right after a while or until command, a part of the *fi/elif* test in a *if/then/else/fi* statement, or is part of a set of commands executed following && or ||.

We will see more examples on how to use the case construct later on, as of now we are going to see something interesting that will affect the way you will collect, store, and process data. So, get ready for the arrays.

Arrays

Think of an array as a structure that can hold more than a single object, something like a variable with one or many values. Imagine you have a few friends and you want to write down their names:

```
friend_1=Anthony
friend_2=Mike
friend_3=Noel
friend_4=Tarek
friend_5=Dionysios
```

Once you have the variables instanced, you can then deference them, deferencing being the act of retrieving a value. This is OK, but it somehow cages you into some limitations, such as you must call the exact variable name to access its value, you cannot easily cycle between them, you cannot tell the number of values so quickly, and more. For such operations, there is an appropriate structure, which comes at hand and allows us to work on the values as a single entity--this is the array:

```
friends=(Anthony Mike Noel Tarek Dionysios)
```

The elements inside an array are indexed, and its position is assigned during the assignment, so Anthony will be at the first position and Dionysios at the fifth. But once declared and instanced, we can add elements to the array in a specific position:

```
friends[6]=Claudia
```

How do you check if what is said so far is correct? A good way to do this would be accessing the different elements printing the values at the different positions:

```
zarrelli:~$ friends=(Anthony Mike Noel Tarek Dionysios) ; echo
${friends[0]} ; echo ${friends[4]} ; echo ${friends[5]} ;
friends[5]=Claudia ; echo ${friends[5]}
Anthony
Dionysios
Claudia
```

Menus, Arrays, and Functions

From the previous example, we can see a couple of interesting things:

- The first position of an array has an index of 0
- A value is accessed in the form of `${array_name[index]}`
- If not assigned, a position does not hold any value
- We can assign a value to any position using an index

Let's add another person to the list now:

friends[-2]=Ilaria

Now, it would be fine to have a way to print the whole content of the array at once, since the number of elements is growing, and it is taking a bit of time to echo all the indexed values. So, we can either use `array_name[@]` or `array_name[*]` to access the whole content of the array:

zarrelli:~$ echo ${friends[@]}

Anthony Mike Noel Tarek Ilaria Claudia

What is interesting here is the position of `Ilaria` into the array. We inserted this name at position -2, so using a negative index provides a new feature introduced in Bash 4.2 that allows us to locate a position in the array starting from the end of it. So, -2 means two slots starting from the end of the array. But now, let's go back to the array declaration. We just saw one way to create an array:

array_name=(element_1 element_2 element_n)

There are other ways to create an array:

array_name[index]

In this case, the index must be a positive integer, since we do not have any slots to count backward:

```
zarrelli:~$ test[2]="Here I am!" ; for i in {0..5} ; do echo $i ${test[$i]} ; done
0
1
2 Here I am!
3
4
5
declare -a array_name
```

No index needed here, even if given, it will be ignored. This way of declaring an array can be useful in cases when you do not yet know which values will be stored into it:

```
#!/bin/bash
declare -a friends
clear
echo -n "Can you please tell me the name of some of your friends: "
read -a friends
echo "So, your friends are: ${friends[@]}"
```

Even if you instance an array using another form, placing `declare -a array_name` before the instantiation can speed up subsequent operations on the array itself.

We just declared an array named `friends` and used the read built-in, but this time, we gave the -a option ,which force read to get any words from the user and assigned to the named array indexes in a sequential order. Bear in mind that-a forces the unsetting of the array before the first assignment. Now, let's try this wee script:

```
Can you please tell me the name of some of your friends: Ilaria Max Ron
So, your friends are: Ilaria Max Ron
```

From Bash 4 on, there is a new type of array called an **associative array**. These are a bit different from the indexed arrays that we have seen so far: think of it as a set of two linked arrays:

```
#!/bin/bash
declare -A friends
clear
echo -n "Can you please tell me the name of one of your friends: "
read name
echo -n "And now his email address: "
read address
friends[$name]=${address}
echo -e "So, your friend name is: ${!friends[@]}\nHis email address is: ${friends[@]}"
```

We just declared an associative array called `friends` and asked the user for two values, one a name and the other an email, but we stored them in two different variables instead of inserting them directly in an array. Inserting in the array was the next action. Use the name value as index and the address value as the linked content:

```
Can you please tell me the name of one of your friends: Giorgio Zarrelli
And now his email address: giorgio@whatever.net
So, your friend name is: Giorgio Zarrelli
His email address is: giorgio@whatever.net
```

For our demonstration purposes, we did not check the input, but have a look at this:

```
Can you please tell me the name of one of your friends:
And now his email address:
./declare-array-associative.sh: line 9: friends[$name]: bad array subscript
So, your friend name is:
His email address is:
```

An associative array index cannot be made entirely blank, so we can modify the previous script to add a check on the name value:

```
read name
if [[ -z "$name" ]]
then
echo "The name value cannot be blank"
exit 1
fi
```

We just checked for the name variable not to be unset or empty, and this saved us a lot of trouble.

The standard argument separator on the command line is the space, but you can alter the way your script will read the single word that you give as an argument using the IFS environment variable:

```
#!/bin/bash
IFS=","
declare friends
clear
echo -n "Can you please tell me the name of some of your friends: "
read -a friends
echo "So, your friends are: "
for i in ${!friends[*]}
do
echo "$i - ${friends[$i]}"
done
```

Now, let's execute it and give arguments as Anthony Mike:

```
Can you please tell me the name of some of your friends: Anthony Mike
So, your friends are:
0 - Anthony Mike
```

Both the names are at the same index, so they are not treated as two different friends. So, let's now use a comma to separate the names:

```
Can you please tell me the name of some of your friends: Noel,Tarek
So, your friends are:
0 - Noel
1 - Tarek
```

Here, `Noel` is at index 0 and `Tarek` is at index 1, so they are actually distinct names stored in different positions of the array. But what if the user does not answer to it in a timely manner? Well, another environment variable can help us with this:

```
#!/bin/bash
IFS=","
TMOUT=3
declare friends
clear
echo -n "Can you please tell me the name of some of your friends: "
read -a friends
if [ ${#friends[@]} -eq 0 ]
then
echo "You did not provide me with any names"
exit 1
else
echo "So, your friends are: "
for i in ${!friends[*]}
do
echo "$i - ${friends[$i]}"
done
fi
exit 0
```

We just assigned a value of three seconds to the TMOUT environment variable, which defines the standard timeout period for both the shell and the read built-in. Used in the interactive shell, it causes the shell itself to exit if no input comes to the terminal before the timeout expires. Used with the read built-in, it defines the timeout period after which the commands terminates if no input is given. In our case, when the timeout is hit, we check the number of elements stored into the array: if it is equal to 0, we print a warning message and exit with 1:

```
Can you please tell me the name of some of your friends: You did not
provide me with any names
```

In case we find something in the array, we cycle it and print all the values and associated indexes.

```
Can you please tell me the name of some of your friends: Anthony,Mike,Tarek
So, your friends are:
0 - Anthony
1 - Mike
2 - Tarek
```

Bash 4 introduced a new built-in mapfile, which is used to read lines from the standard input (the file descriptor if a -u option is provided) and load them into an indexed array. What can this be used for? Well, have a look at this--we start off creating a `file.txt` file with a list of our friends:

```
zarrelli:~$ cat friends.txt
Anthony
Dionysios
Ilaria
Mike
Noel
Tarek
```

Now, let's create a script that takes advantage of the mapfile built-in:

```
#!/bin/bash
declare -a friends
echo -e
echo -e "Reading friends list from friends.txt file..."
mapfile friends < friends.txt
echo -e "File content loaded!"
echo -e "So, your friends are: \n${friends[@]}"
```

Finally, let's run the script:

```
zarrelli:~$ ./mapfile-array.sh
Reading friends list from friends.txt file...
File content loaded!
So, your friends are:
Anthony
Dionysios
Ilaria
Mike
Noel
Tarek
```

It's easy to see why `mapfile` is handy: we loaded all the lines from the file without using any loop or having to deal with each single line. In fact, using the built-in `read -a` would have loaded only the first line into the array, and we had to deal with the rest of the text file using some sort of loop. With `mapfile`, you just load everything and that is all.

So, let's recap the different ways we have to store values in an array:

```
array_name[i]=value
```

It is quite straightforward. Select the position in the array using an index and assign the value. I can be any integer out of an arithmetic expression. If it is negative then the `i` positions from the last value are available in the array:

```
zarrelli:~$ my_array[$((3*2))]=my_value ; echo ${my_array[6]}
my_value
```

We can also omit the index, in this case, the value will be assigned to the index 0 slot:

```
my_array=my_other_value ; for i in {0..6} ; do echo $i ${my_array[$i]} ;
done
0 my_other_value
1
2
3
4
5
6 my_value
```

This is true for the associative array as well:

```
zarrelli:~$ my_associative=my_value ; for i in {0..5} ; do echo $i
${my_associative[$i]} ; done
0 my_value
1
2
3
4
5
```

In this case, 0 is actually a string used as a string, as it should be for an associative array.

Menus, Arrays, and Functions

Another method to store data in an array is the compound assignment of values, as we saw before, but it works for indexed arrays only:

```
zarrelli:~$ friends=(Anthony Mike Noel Tarek Dionysios) ; echo
${friends[0]} ; echo ${friends[4]} ; echo ${friends[5]} ;
friends[5]=Claudia ; echo ${friends[5]}
Anthony
Dionysios
```

With this method, we have to be careful since the array is unset before the assignment, so all the previous values get lost:

```
zarrelli:~/$ friends=(Anthony Mike Noel Tarek Dionysios) ; echo -n "Old
array values: ${friends[@]}" ; friends=(Ilaria) ; echo -e ; echo -n "New
array values: ${friends[@]}" ; echo -e
Old array values: Anthony Mike Noel Tarek Dionysios
New array values: Ilaria
```

We can preserve the old content of the array using the += operator:

```
zarrelli:~$ friends=(Anthony Mike Noel Tarek Dionysios) ; echo -n "Old
array values:${friends[@]}" ; friends+=(Ilaria) ; echo -e ; echo -n "New
array values: ${friends[@]}" ; echo -e
Old array values:Anthony Mike Noel Tarek Dionysios
New array values: echo Anthony Mike Noel Tarek Dionysios Ilaria
```

Then, we have a compound assignment using keys:

```
zarrelli:~$ my_array=([2]=first_value [4]=second_value) ; for i in {0..5} ;
do echo $i ${my_array[$i]} ; done
0
1
2 first_value
3
4 second_value
5
```

This holds true for associative arrays as well:

```
#!/bin/bash
declare -A friends
friends=([Mike]="is a friend" [Anthony]="is another friend")
for i in Mike Anthony
do
echo "$i - ${friends[$i]}"
done
And now let's try it:
zarrelli:~$ ./associative.sh
```

```
Mike - is a friend
Anthony - is another friend
```

Notice that an associative array does not imply a specific order in keys; as you can see from the previous example, they are unsorted.

Finally, we see the mapfile method:

```
zarrelli:~$ mapfile < friends.txt ; echo ${MAPFILE[@]}
Anthony Dionisios Ilaria Mike Noel Tarek
```

We used a slightly more compact form of the `mapfile` command, since we did not specify the name of the array to read the file content into. In this case, when no array is provided, `mapfile` stores the data into the default `MAPFILE` array.

Now that we have seen the different methods for storing values, it's time to retrieve them in various ways:

```
${my_array[i]}
```

I can be any integer out of an arithmetic expression. If it is negative, then the i positions from the last value are available in the array:

```
zarrelli:~$ my_array=("first value" "second value" "third value" "fourth value" "fifth value") ; echo "${my_array[-3]}"
third value
```

We can notice a couple of interesting things here.

The -2 index points to the last position in the array, which is filled in by `"fifth value"` minus the two slots, so we count backwards until we reach the 5-2 slot. The third position in the array index 2 (the index count starts from 0) and holds the string `"third value"`.

Second, we used strings with spaces, thanks to the double quotes that preserved them. As a precaution while echoing, we quoted the retrieved value as well.

In a similar way, we can retrieve the value of an element into an associative array using the form called `$my_associative[string]`.

Where the string is one of the keys stored into the array related to the values, we want to retrieve this:

```
my_associative=([George]=first_value [Anthony]=second_value) ; echo ${my_associative[Anthony]}
second_value
```

We can also retrieve all the stored values at once using this:

```
${my_array[@]}
${my_array[*]}
${my_associative[@]}
${my_associative[*]}
```

As we can see from the following examples:

```
zarrelli:~$ echo ${my_array[@]}
first value second value third value fourth value fifth value
zarrelli:~$ echo ${my_array[*]}
first value second value third value fourth value fifth value
zarrelli:~$ echo ${my_associative[@]}
my_value second_value first_value
zarrelli:~$ echo ${my_associative[*]}
my_value second_value first_value
```

But if you do not want all the values, we can get them in *slices* using the following syntax:

```
${my_array[@]:S:O}
${my_array[*]:S:O}
```

With S being the index value we are starting from and O the offset for reading the values:

```
zarrelli:~$ my_array=("first value" "second value" "third value" "fourth value" "fifth value") ; echo "${my_array[@]:3:2}"
fourth value fifth value
zarrelli:~$ my_array=("first value" "second value" "third value" "fourth value" "fifth value") ; echo "${my_array[*]:3:2}"
fourth value fifth value
```

In both the examples, we started reading from the index position 3 and actually read the two following values. If we omit one of the values, the remaining will be taken in account as an offset from position 0:

```
zarrelli:~$ my_array=("first value" "second value" "third value" "fourth value" "fifth value") ; echo "${my_array[*]:2}"
third value fourth value fifth value
```

We can also play with the substring removal operators that we saw earlier in this book:

```
zarrelli:~$ my_array=("first value" "second value" "third value" "fourth value" "fifth value") ; echo "${my_array[@]%%fou*}"
first value second value third value fifth value
```

Or:

```
zarrelli:~$ my_array=("first value" "second value" "third value" "fourth
value" "fifth value") ; echo "${my_array[@]#s?cond}"

first value value third value fourth value fifth value
```

Or:

```
zarrelli:~$ my_array=("first value" "second value" "third value" "fourth
value" "fifth value") ; echo "${my_array[@]/third/forth-1}"

first value second value forth-1 value fourth value fifth value
```

And so forth.

Notice that ${array_name[@]} and ${array_name[*]} follow the same rules as $@ and $* when it comes to the parameters expansion with the first notation seeing the parameters all as a single string and the latter as single words quoted.

Now that we know how to store and retrieve data from an array, we have to see how to delete them. We can use the following commands:

- unset array_name
- unset array_name[@]
- unset array_name[*]

Have a look at the following examples:

```
zarrelli:~$ my_array=(one two three four five) ; echo "The content of the
array is: ${my_array[@]}" ; unset my_array ; echo "Now the content of the
array is: ${my_array[@]}"
The content of the array is: one two three four five
Now the content of the array is:
zarrelli:~$ my_array=(one two three four five) ; echo "The content of the
array is: ${my_array[@]}" ; unset my_array[@] ; echo "Now the content of
the array is: ${my_array[@]}"
The content of the array is: one two three four five
Now the content of the array is:
zarrelli:~$ my_array=(one two three four five) ; echo "The content of the
array is: ${my_array[@]}" ; unset my_array[*] ; echo "Now the content of
the array is: ${my_array[@]}"
The content of the array is: one two three four five
Now the content of the array is:
```

We can unset a single value at a defined index position:

```
zarrelli:~$ my_array=(one two three four five) ; echo "The content of the
array is: ${my_array[@]}" ; unset my_array[2] ; echo "Now the content of
the array is: ${my_array[@]}"
The content of the array is: one two three four five
Now the content of the array is: one two four five
```

This holds true for the associative arrays as well:

```
#!/bin/bash
declare -A friends
friends=([Mike]="is a friend" [Anthony]="is another friend")
unset friends[Mike]
for i in Mike Anthony
do
echo "$i - ${friends[$i]}"
done
```

As you can see from the following output:

```
zarrelli:~$ ./associative-remove.sh
Mike -
Anthony - is another friend
```

You can also assign nothing both to the array and the single values, either for the indexed or associative arrays:

```
zarrelli:~$ my_array=(one two three four five) ; echo "The content of the
array is: ${my_array[@]}" ; my_array[2]="" ; echo "Now the content of the
array is: ${my_array[@]}"
The content of the array is: one two three four five
Now the content of the array is: one two four five
```

Or:

```
zarrelli:~$ my_array=(one two three four five) ; echo "The content of the
array is: ${my_array[@]}" ; my_array=() ; echo "Now the content of the
array is: ${my_array[@]}"
The content of the array is: one two three four five
Now the content of the array is:
```

For the associative array, just change this line in the previous script:

```
friends=([Mike]="is a friend" [Anthony]="is another friend")
friends[Mike]=""
for i in Mike Anthony
```

Now, run it:

```
zarrelli:~$ ./associative-remove.sh
Mike -
Anthony - is another friend
```

Otherwise again, change these lines:

```
friends=([Mike]="is a friend" [Anthony]="is another friend")
friends=()
for i in Mike Anthony
```

Now, run the script:

```
zarrelli:~$ ./associative-remove.sh
Mike -
Anthony -
```

Some final notes are due for some interesting notations that we can use to deal with arrays:

```
${#array_name[index]}
```

The following code explains the length of the array value pointed out at the index:

```
my_array=(one two three four five) ; echo "The length of ${my_array[4]} is
of ${#my_array[4]} characters"
The length of five is of 4 characters
```

Or:

```
#!/bin/bash
declare -A friends
friends=([Mike]="is a friend" [Anthony]="is another friend")
echo "The lenght of \"${friends[Anthony]}"\ is ${#friends[Anthony]}"
And executing it gives us:
zarrelli:~$ ./associative-count.sh
The lenght of "is another friend" is 17
```

Another interesting expansion that we can have on arrays is represented by:

#{#array_name[*]} or #{#array_name[@]}

This can expand to the number of elements in the array:

```
zarrelli:~$ my_array=(one two three four five) ; echo "We have
${#my_array[*]} elements in the array"

We have 5 elements in the array
```

Or:

```
#!/bin/bash
declare -A friends
friends=([Mike]="is a friend" [Anthony]="is another friend")
echo "We have ${#friends[@]} elements in the array"
```

This gives us the following:

```
zarrelli:~$ ./associative-elements.sh
We have 2 elements in the array
```

We have all the elements now to see how we can loop through the content of an array. We can start with something easy that we have already seen:

```
#!/bin/bash
declare -a my_array
my_array=("one" "two" "three" "four" "five")
for (( i=0 ; i<${#my_array[*]} ; i++ ));
do
echo "${my_array[i]}"
done
```

Now, let's execute it:

```
zarrelli:~$ ./loop1.sh
one
two
three
four
five
```

This is a simple method with some restrictions: the index starts from 0 and the progression is expected to be sequential. But we can do something to overcome these limitations:

```
#!/bin/bash
declare -a my_array
my_array=("one" "two" "three" "four" "five")
for i in ${my_array[*]} ;
do
echo "$i"
done
```

We modified the `for` statement and now `i` will be instanced with each of the elements that we got from the `$(my_array[*]}` expansion:

```
zarrelli:~$ ./loop2.sh
one
two
three
four
five
```

So far, so good. We have access to the values, but what about the indexes? Just bear in mind that `${!array_name[@]}` and `${!array_name[*]}` expand to the list of indexes of the array. Just notice that using @ in quotes expands each key into a single word. So, knowing this, we can retrieve both the values and the indexes:

```
#!/bin/bash
declare -A friends
friends=([Mike]="is a friend" [Anthony]="is another friend")
for i in ${!friends[*]}
do
echo "$i - ${friends[$i]}"
done
```

This will give us the following:

```
zarrelli:~$ ./loop3.sh
Mike - is a friend
Anthony - is another friend
```

Finally, something a bit more complex:

```
#!/bin/bash
declare -A friends
friends=([Mike]="is a friend" [Anthony]="is another friend")
indexes=(${!friends[*]})
for ((i=0 ; i<${#friends[*]} ; i++));
do
echo "${indexes[i]} - ${friends[${indexes[i]}]}"
done
```

We stored all the indexes of the friends array in another array called `indexes`, and then we used this latter to retrieve the content from the former one:

```
zarrelli:~$ ./loop4.sh
Mike - is a friend
Anthony - is another friend
```

We will see more on iterations shortly, but what we will focus on next is how to make our code clean, tidy, and reusable by taking advantage of another construct that Bash provides us with: the functions.

Functions

At this point of the book, we know enough to write our own code, process variables, interact with the user, and the environment, many things altogether, and so we are ready to make a mess. We know how to write a bunch of lines, but we still do not know how to keep things clean and tidy and, moreover, how to make our code reusable. As we can easily guess from the examples seen so far, a script or a command line is a one way processed flow of code; the characters making up our commands are read from left to right, from top to bottom. So, when you pass a construct or an assignment, it is done and if you want to process something the same way you did before; you have to rewrite the code that carried on the procedure again. So, if you are coding more than a small script you risk to end up with a huge amount of repetitive code, sloppy layout; and inefficiency; but Bash, like any other programming language, provides us with a method to overcome these issues. We are talking of functions. What are functions? An example will clarify what a function is better than many words. Let's create a small fragment of code:

```
#!/bin/bash
if (("$1" < "$2"))
then
echo "Great! The integer $1 is less than $2"
else
echo "The integer $1 is not less than $2..."
fi
```

It takes two positional arguments as input to check if the first argument is less than the second assuming that the input is an integer:

```
zarrelli:~$ ./minor-no-function.sh 1 2
Great! The integer 1 is less than 2
Now, let's move part of the code into a function:
#!/bin/bash
minor()
{
```

```
if (("$1" < "$2"))
then
echo "Great! The integer $1 is less than $2"
else
echo "The integer $1 is not less than $2..."
fi
}
minor "$1" "$2"
```

Time to try our brand new function:

```
zarrelli:~$ ./test.sh 1 2
Great! The integer 1 is less than 2
```

What did we do? First, we see that a function declaration has the following structure:

```
function_name()
{
instruction_1
...
instruction_n
}
```

But it can also have the following structure:

```
function _name() {
instruction_1
...
instruction_n
}
```

It can even have a declared notation using the `function` keyword as follows:

```
function function_name {
instruction_1
...
instruction_n
}
```

We can also have a one-line definition:

```
zarrelli:~$ print_me() { echo "This is your input:"; echo "$1"; } ;
print_me 1
This is your input:
1
```

Notice the ; after the last command. We also saw in Chapter 4, *Quoting and Escaping*, the use of anonymous functions.

Whatever kind of declaration you want to use, a function is triggered simply by calling its name and accepting positional parameters such as follows:

```
function_name arg1 argn
```

As we saw in the previous chapter, a function can return a value, because bear in mind that the values processed inside a function are available only after the function itself has been triggered:

```
#!/bin/bash
minor()
{
if (("$1" < "$2"))
then
echo "Great! The integer $1 is less than $2"
echo "Assigning \$1 to the variable \"var\""
var="$1"
echo "The value of var inside the function is: $var"
else
echo "The integer $1 is not less than $2..."
fi
}
echo "The value of var outside the function before it is triggered is: $var"
minor "$1" "$2"
echo "The value of var outside the function after it is triggered is: $var"
```

In this example, we assigned the value of the first positional variable to the variable named `var`, and then printed this value from inside and outside the function, before it gets triggered and finally after it is triggered:

```
zarrelli:~$ ./minor-function.sh 1 2
The value of var outside the function before it is triggered is:
Great! The integer 1 is less than 2
Assigning S1 to the variable "var"
The value of var inside the function is: 1
The value of var outside the function after it is triggered is: 1
```

We notice a couple of interesting things.

If we try to print the value of `var` before the function is triggered, we do not get anything. This is because even though the code for the function is read before the command, the echo itself `echo "The value of var outside the function before it is triggered is: $var"` is executed before the function is triggered and has the chance to work on variables and assign a value to `var`.

Second, just because `echo "The value of var outside the function before it is triggered is: $var"` is executed before the function itself, it actually is the first message printed on the terminal.

The content assigned or created inside a function is available outside of it, because the function runs in the same shell context of the script, so they share the same environment and variables. But what if I wish to create variables that are available only inside the function itself? Let's alter the assignment instruction by adding the local built-in before the variable:

```
local var= "$1"
```

We run the script once again:

```
zarrelli:~$ ./minor-function.sh 1 2
The value of var outside the function before it is triggered is:
Great! The integer 1 is less than 2
Assigning S1 to the variable "var"
The value of var inside the function is: 1
The value of var outside the function after it is triggered is:
```

We can hide variables from the main body of the script, but we can also get the function to return us something:

```
#!/bin/bash
OK=10
NOT_OK=50
minor()
{
if (("$1" < "$2"))
then
echo "Returning the value of OK"
return "$OK"
else
echo "Returning the value of NOT_OK"
return "$NOT_OK"
fi
}
print_return()
{
if (("$3" == "$OK")) ; then
echo "Great! The integer $1 is less than $2"
exit 0
elif (("$3" == "$NOT_OK")) ; then
echo "The integer $1 is not less than $2..."
exit 1
else
```

```
echo "Something gone wild..."
echo "The first integer has the value of $1 and the second of $2..."
exit 1
fi
}
minor "$1" "$2"
print_return "$1" "$2" "$?"
```

In this example, we had a bit of fun creating a new function to print the actual messages shown to the user, and we can see on initial benefit of using functions: the code evaluating, if an integer is minor then another is now clean, holds less rows, and it is more readable. On the other hand, the print return takes as input the first two positional variables and takes the third as the return code ($?) of the minor function. Another benefit of introducing a function focused on printing messages to the user is that we introduced something else with it, a separation between the presentation layer, the `print_return` function, the elaboration layer, and the `minor` function. So, each time we want to modify how the information is shown to the user, we do not have to tinker with the core function, so we do not risk introducing any error in its code. On the other hand, if we want to work on the core function, we can make any modifications, and we do not have to modify the presentation layer as long as the output from the core remains the same.

If you have some functions that you think you can use in many of your scripts, it would be a good idea to write all of them in file, and then source the file from within your script and use them from there. This way you will have your own library of functions that you will reuse over time when needed without the burden of having to write them every single time.

But can we pass to a function variable that references other variables? Let's try this:

```
zarrelli:$ cat inference.sh
#!/bin/bash
FIRST_VALUE=SECOND_VALUE
SECOND_VALUE=20
print_value()
{
echo "The value of \$1 is: $1"
}
print_value "${FIRST_VALUE}"
exit 0
```

So, FIRST_VALUE references SECOND_VALUE, which has a value of 20, so we would expect to see 20 when we try to print $FIRST_VALUE:

```
zarrelli:~$ ./inference.sh
The value of $1 is: SECOND_VALUE
```

It is not what we were expecting, was it? This happens because Bash treats the variable name SECOND_VALUE as a bunch of characters. A mere is a string taken in its literal value and not as a pointer to a value called (20). We can overcome this issue anyway; let's just add print_value "${!FIRST_VALUE}" to the previous script before exit 0, and now we run it again:

```
zarrelli:~$ ./inference.sh
The value of $1 is: SECOND_VALUE
The value of $1 is: 20
```

We used what is called indirect referencing to actually reference the value of a value. This kind of notation called ${!variable_name} introduced in Bash 2 makes indirect referencing not so difficult to write down, but sometimes, you will find the old version:

```
zarrelli:~$ a=b ; b=c ; echo $a ; eval a=\$$a ; echo $a
b
c
```

What we see as $$a is actually the value of the value, and then we escape it and with eval, we force its evaluation and assignment it to a.

How about dereferencing a variable after it has been passed to a function? Here are some lines of code to play with:

```
#!/bin/bash
a10=20
print_value()
{
echo -e
echo -e "The name of the variable passed as \$1 to the function is: $1\n"
b20=\$"$1"
echo -e "b20 holds the reference to the content of the variable passed on the command line: $b20\n"
c30=${b20//[[:punct:]][[:alpha:]]}
echo -e "But playing with parameter substitution we got an untyped value out of it: $c30\n"
eval d40=\$$1
e50=$(($d40+$c30))
echo "And we used it as in integer to add to the original value we received"
echo -e "as input so the integer extracted from the name of the variable added to the variable value is: $e50\n"
eval $1=$e50
echo -e "Thanks to eval we assign the new value to the original input\n"
echo -e "The value of \$1 now is: $e50\n"
}
echo -e
```

```
echo "The value of a10 before triggering the function is: $a10"
print_value a10
echo -e "The value of a10 after triggering the function is: $a10\n"
exit 0
```

So we started with a variable called a10 holding the value of 10. Then, we printed its value before triggering the function, and right afterwards, we called the function passing the name of the variable. The first step in the print_value function prints the value of the first positional argument passed to the function itself. Now, you have all the knowledge to read the code and get what has been done. We played a bit with indirect reference, deference, and a parameter substitution, so the simple output of the script should make it all clear:

```
zarrelli:~$ ./dereference.sh
The value of a10 before triggering the function is: 20
The name of the variable passed as $1 to the function is: a10
b20 holds the reference to the content of the variable passed on the
command line: $a10
But playing with parameter substitution we got an untyped value out of it:
10
And we used it as in integer to add to the original value we received as
input so the integer extracted from the name of the variable added to the
variable value is: 30
Thanks to eval we assign the new value to the original input
The value of $1 now is: 30
The value of a10 after triggering the function is: 30
```

And here we are: the value of a10 changed from the original 20 to the new 30, and now we know why and how. Before leaving the functions chapter, just a couple of notes: we already talked about anonymous functions:

```
zarrelli:~$ x=10 ; y=5 ; { z=$(($x*$y)) ; echo "Value of z inside the
function: $z" ; } ; echo "Value of z outside the function: $z"
Value of z inside the function: 50
Value of z outside the function: 50
```

Just remember the last semicolon before the ending brace and also see the returned values:

```
zarrelli:~$ cat minor-function-return-message.sh
#!/bin/bash
OK=10
NOT_OK=50
minor()
{
if (("$1" < "$2"))
then
echo "Returning the value of OK"
return "$OK"
```

```
else
echo "Returning the value of NOT_OK"
return "$NOT_OK"
fi
}
message=$(minor "$1" "$2")
echo "$message"
```

Once invoked, the script outputs a meaningful error message overcoming the limitations of the return built-in, which can only return integers:

```
zarrelli@moveaway:~/Documents/My books/Mastering bash/Chapter 5/Scripts$
./minor-function-return-message.sh 1 2
```

The previous code returns the value of OK, and being a block of code, a function stdin and stdout can be redirected easily:

```
zarrelli:~$ cat redirect.sh
#!/bin/bash
file=friends.txt
parse()
{
while read lineofile
do
echo $lineofile
done
}<$file
parse
```

This gives us the following:

```
zarrelli:~$ ./redirect.sh
Anthony
Dionisios
Ilaria
Mike
Noel
Tarek
```

And that's all for now, it's time to move on and add some spice to our scripts.

Summary

You learned how to interact with users, read their input, and store it in appropriate structures, cycle though values, and take advantage of the functions to make our code tidy and reusable. So now it is time to explore some structures that we have already used a bit: we are talking about iterations.

6
Iterations

What we have seen so far enables us to interact with the user, process the input, and provide some output based on conditions we imposed. All of this is fine; and if the user calls our scripts with some arguments, we can store them in an array and process given that we know how many options they are passing to the command line. We must know in advance how many items the user will provide us with, otherwise we will lose those in excess. This is where an iterative construct comes in play. Since we already saw some examples, it can enumerate the content of an array and let us process its content without knowing in advance the number of items stored. In this chapter, we will have a look at how to use the `for` loop and *while/until* loop to get a strong grip on the data the user provides us with.

The for loop

The `for` loop is one of the most used structures when it comes to a Bash script and enables us to repeat one of more actions on each single item in a list. Its basic structure can be outlined as follows:

```
for placeholder in list_of_items
do
  action_1 $placeholder
  action_2 $placeholder
  action_n $placeholderdone
```

So, we use a placeholder, which will take at each round of the loop one of the values in the list of items, which will then be processed in the do section. Once all the list is scanned through, the loop is done, and we exit it. Let's start with a simple and nice example:

```
#!/bin/bash
for i in 1 2 3 4 5
do
   echo "$i"done
```

And now let's execute it:

```
zarrelli:~$ ./counter-simple.sh
1
2
3
4
5
```

Actually, quite straightforward, but notice that the list can be the result of any kind of operations:

```
#!/bin/bash
for i in {10..1..2}
do
   echo "$i"done
```

In this case, we used a brace expansion to get a countdown with a step of 2:

```
zarrelli:~$ ./counter-brace.sh
10
8
6
4
2
```

We can have a for loop on one line as well:

```
zarrelli:~$ for i in *; do echo "Found the following file: $i"; done
Found the following file: counter-brace.sh
Found the following file: counter-simple.sh
```

Nice, isn't it? Now let's do something a bit more complex. Let's say we want to write the following list:

```
Belfast is in UK
Redwood is in USA
Milan is in ITALY
Paris is in FRANCE
```

How can we do this? Let's try with a simple loop and see what happens:

```
#!/bin/bash
for cities in Belfast UK Redwood USA Milan ITALY Paris FRANCE
do
   echo "$cities is in $cities"
done
exit 0
```

Now let's run it:

```
zarrelli:$ ./for-pair.sh
Belfast is in Belfast
UK is in UK
Redwood is in Redwood
USA is in USA
Milan is in Milan
ITALY is in ITALY
Paris is in Paris
FRANCE is in FRANCE
```

Not exactly what we wanted. Well, not at all because the script does not know how to tell what is a city, what is a nation, and what goes with what. We have to find a way to qualify our items; and we can do it using their position. Here we have the set built-in, which enables us to assign the content of a variable to a positional parameter. We will just use it in a fancy way:

```
#!/bin/bash
for cities in "Belfast UK" "Redwood USA" "Milan ITALY" "Paris FRANCE"
do
   set -- $cities
   echo "$1 is in $2"
done
exit 0
```

And now let's run the script:

```
zarrelli:~$ ./for-pair-set.sh
   Belfast is in UK
   Redwood is in USA
   Milan is in ITALY
   Paris is in FRANCE
```

Iterations

This is much better, and it is exactly what we were looking for; but how did we reach our goal? The first step was grouping the related items into double quotes, so for instance, `Belfast` goes with `UK`. The tricky part was using the set built-in with `--`, which forces the values following it to be assigned to positional parameters even though they start with a dash and if no arguments are given the positional parameters get unset. So, since we have groups of two: city and nation, we have `$1` and `$2`; one holding the city and the other having the nation. From there on, it was just a matter of printing the positional parameters. We can go even further without specifying a list:

```
zarrelli:~$ cat for-pair-input.sh
#!/bin/bash
i=0
for cities
do
   echo "City $((i++)) is: $cities"
done
exit 0
```

Then, we can provide the arguments on the command line; the script will take its input from `$@`):

```
zarrelli:~$ ./for-pair-input.sh Belfast Redwood Milan Paris
City 0 is: Belfast
City 1 is: Redwood
City 2 is: Milan
City 3 is: Paris
```

As we discussed before, the list can be anything: a variable, a brace expression, fixed values, the result of a command substitution, anything that creates a list of value through which we iterate:

```
zarrelli:~/$ cat counter-function.sh
#!/bin/bash
counter()
{
   echo {10..0..2}
}
for i in $(counter)
do
   echo "$i"
done
```

In this example, the list is provided by the counter function, which prints out the result of a brace expansion. We then take the value returned by the function through the `echo` command and use it as a list to iterate on:

```
zarrelli:~$ ./counter-function.sh
10
8
6
4
2
0
```

Do not forget the C-style:

```
zarrelli:~$ cat c-for.sh
#!/bin/bash
for ((i=20;i > 0;i--))
{
if (( i % 2 == 0 ))
then
    echo "$i is divisible by 2"fi
}
exit 0
```

So, we have a decreasing counter:

```
zarrelli:~$ ./c-for.sh
20 is divisible by 2
18 is divisible by 2
16 is divisible by 2
14 is divisible by 2
12 is divisible by 2
10 is divisible by 2
8 is divisible by 2
6 is divisible by 2
4 is divisible by 2
2 is divisible by 2
```

What we saw so far allows us to cycle through structures of data and work on them as long as we have some items to process, but we do not know yet how to work on something until a condition is met or not, so this is the topic for the next paragraph where we will see how to keep our script alive until something happens.

Let's do something while, until...

The `for` loop is a great option to enumerate the contents provided by the user, but it is not so handy when it comes to handling a number of options whose number is not known beforehand. In this case, we would find more interesting kinds of loops, which would allow us to cycle until a certain condition is met or while a certain situation persists, for instance, while the user inputs something or until a threshold is met. So, let's see which constructs can help us:

```
while condition
do
   command_1
   command_2
   command_n
done
```

At a first glance, the difference between the `while` and `for` loops is evident: the latter is based on a placeholder that each time takes a value from a list and we work on that value, the former is triggered while conditions last. Let's make an example starting with a `for` loop:

```
#!/bin/bash
for i in 1 2 3 4 5
do
   echo "$i"
done
```

It is a simple counter, from 1 to 5, and we already saw it:

```
zarrelli:~$ ./counter-simple.sh
1
2
3
4
5
```

Now, let's rewrite it using a `while` loop:

```
#!/bin/bash
i=1
while (( i <= 5))
do
   echo "$i"((i++))
done
```

Let's see if the output is the same:

```
zarrelli:~$ ./while-simple.sh
1
2
3
4
5
```

Well, the output is exactly the same. Now, we will speak about another loop constructor, the until loop, which cycles on a list until a condition is met. Its structure is as follows:

```
until condition
do
   command_1
   command_2
   command_n
done
```

The structure is similar to the while loop, just the conditions change: while lasts as long as a condition is met, until lasts until a condition is met. To better understand the difference, let's rewrite the example in the until form:

```
#!/bin/bash
i=1
until (( i > 5))
do
echo "$i"((i++))done
```

As we can see from the code, until we do not reach a value of i higher than 5, we print its value and increase it:

```
zarrelli:~$ ./until-simple.sh 12345
```

Looks familiar, doesn't it? So we can recap the three kinds of loop under the following conditions:

- for iterates on the values taken from a list
- while executes the loop until the condition is false
- until executes the loop while the condition is false

Exiting the loop with break and continue

This gives us some nice opportunities, such as infinite loops:

```
while true ; do echo "Hello" ; done
```

Since `true` always evaluates as true, the condition is always verified so we have an infinite execution of the do/done clause; press *Ctrl+ C* to exit from the loop. An infinite loop looks like something nasty, but it opens a new scenario for our scripts, since we can make them run or wait for something for as long as we want. Actually, if we do not use a couple of loop control commands: `break` will exit the loop and `continue` will restart it, jumping over the remaining commands. Let's see an example of creating a hypothetical backup program menu:

```
#!/bin/bash
while true
do
  clear
  cat <<MENU
BACKUP UTIL v 1.0
-----------------
1. Backup a file/directory
2. Restore a file/directory
0. Quit
-----------------
MENU
  read -p "Please select an option, 0 or Q to exit: " option
  case $option in
  1 | [Bb])
  echo "You chose the first option, Backup"
  sleep 3
  ;;
  2 | [Rr])
  echo "You chose the second option, Restore"
  sleep 3
  ;;
  0 | [Qq])
  echo "You chose the third options, Quit, so we quit!"
  break
  ;;
  *)
  echo "Not a valid choice, please select an option..."
  sleep 3
  ;;
  esac
done
```

Let's see what we did. We opened a `while true` loop, so whatever is inside it will be executed over and over. We then used a *here* document to have a nice menu to display to the user and a `read` option to ask the user for a choice to evaluate the input. Any choice except for `quit` will do nothing but display a message and wait for 3 seconds, after which the cycle restarts, clearing the screen and showing the menu once again (this is the reason for the `sleep` command). The only exception is if the customer hits 0,Q, or q: in this case a message is displayed and the loop is exited:

```
zarrelli:~$ ./menu.sh
  BACKUP UTIL v 1.0
  ------------------
  1. Backup a file/directory
  2. Restore a file/directory
  0. Quit
  ------------------
  Please select an option, 0 or Q to exit: 0
  You chose the third options, Quit, so we quit!
```

Notice that we exit a loop, not necessarily the entire script. This is a nice old style menu, which has its advantages over graphical ones: easier to code, easier to maintain, and less resources consumed, but most of all, it does not require a graphical monitor to be displayed: it works well on character monitors and over serial connections. For the `continue` instruction, the action flow is quite different, since it resumes iteration for the main `for`, `while`, `until`, or `select` loop. When used in a `for` loop the variable takes the value of the next element in the list of conditions:

```
zarrelli:~$ cat for-continue.sh
#!/bin/bash
for i in {0..10}
do
   if (( i == 4 ))
   then
   continue
   else
   echo $i
   fi
done
exit 0
```

Our code will enumerate from 0 to 10 and print the values met, except when it hits the number 4: in this case, the `continue` will force the `for` loop to skip the value and proceed from 5:

```
zarrelli:~$ ./for-continue.sh
0
1
```

```
2
3
5
6
7
8
9
10
```

Time to give our client a menu

In this chapter, we are looking at different ways to play with loops in order to work on the pieces of information the user provides us with. From a simple menu, we moved onto something fancier and better looking; and now, it is time to take a step further and have a look at the `select` construct whose task is to let us create menu in an effortless way. Its syntax is similar to the for construct:

```
select placeholder [in list]
do
command_1
command_2
command_n
done
```

So, as we can see, this construct is very similar to `for` and sports a list, which gets expanded on the standard error in a series of elements preceded by a number. If we omit the `in list` part, the list gets constructed from the positional parameters given on the command line, such as if we used `[in $@]`. Once the elements in the list are printed, a `PS3` prompt is shown and a line from the `stdin` is read and stored into the REPLY variable. If something is read on the line, each word is displayed along with a number; if the line is empty the prompt is displayed again, but `if` and `EOF` characters are given as an input (*Ctrl+D*) the loop is exited. As a shortcut, you can use `break` to exit. Let's see an example:

```
#!/bin/bash
echo "Just select the fruit you like:"
select fruit in apple banana orange mango
do
    echo "You picked $fruit (Option $REPLY)"
done
```

This easy script will show you a menu of choices taken from the `in list` and wait for a selection. Once the user inputs a selection, it is echoed and the loop starts again showing the available options:

```
zarrelli:~$ ./simple-select.sh
Just select the fruit you like:
1) apple
2) banana
3) orange
4) mango
#? 3
You picked orange (Option 3)
#? o
You picked  (Option o)
#? pear
You picked  (Option pear)
#?
```

As we can see, there is no control on what the user provided us with, so this is something we have to implement by ourselves. Also, the prompt is the least sexy thing we have ever seen, but we can alter it giving a value to the PS3 variable, so just add PS3="Your choice is: " right below the sha-bang. Save and rerun the script:

```
Just select the fruit you like:
Enter the number of the file you want to protect:
1) apple
2) banana
3) orange
4) mango
Your choice is:
```

Way better now. Great, now another small issue: the script never exits, so how can we force it to exit? Let's see some interesting modifications:

```
zarrelli:~$ cat case-select.sh
#!/bin/bash
PS3="Your choice is: "
echo "Just select the fruit you like:"
select fruit in apple banana orange mango
do
   case "$fruit" in
           mango)
                echo "You chose $fruit, so we wanna break free!"
                break
                ;;
           *)
                echo "You chose $fruit"
                ;;
   esac
done
```

We nested a case construct inside the `select` so that we can evaluate the choice given by the user and react accordingly. In any case, we just print out the choice made by the user, but if he selects 4, we print the choice and exit with `break`:

```
zarrelli:~$ ./case-select.sh
Just select the fruit you like:
1) apple
2) banana
3) orange
4) mango
Your choice is: 2
You chose banana
Your choice is: 4
You chose mango, so we wanna break free!
```

But we can do something more interesting than this, especially if we want to interact with the system. Let's again aim to make a backup script and take advantage of what we just did:

```
#!/bin/bash
while true
do
   clear
   cat <<MENU
BACKUP UTIL v 1.0
------------------
   1. Backup a file/directory
   2. Restore a file/directory
   0. Quit
------------------
MENU
PS3="Which file do you want to backup? "
touch EXIT
   read -p "Please select an option, 0 or Q to exit: " option
   case $option in
      1 | [Bb])
      echo "You chose the first option, Backup"
      clear
      select file in *
      do
         case "$file" in
               EXIT)
               echo "Ok, we exit!"
               rm EXIT
               break
               ;;
      *)
            echo "Compressing file $file"
            tar cvzf "${file}".tgz "$file" || exit 1
```

```
                        echo "File $file compressed."
                        ls "${file}".tgz
                        echo "Press a key to return to main menu..."
                        read
                        break
                        ;;
                esac
            done
            ;;
        2 | [Rr])
            echo "You chose the second option, Restore"
            sleep 3
            ;;
        0 | [Qq])
            echo "You chose the third options, Quit, so we quit!"
            break
            ;;
        *)
            echo "Not a valid choice, please select an option..."
            sleep 3
            ;;
    esac
done
rm EXIT
```

We used `while true` to make the main loop so that the script will be always running unless we explicitly exit from it, then with a *here* document, we show a neat menu to the user and then a case construct to provide a way to evaluate the answers given by the user in the next step. The first option in the `case` statement clears the screen and embeds a select structure, also it provides a list of files to work on using a filename expansion. Since we do not know in advance how many files we will have in the current directory, and we cannot modify the list, we can rely on a trick, creating a file called `EXIT` at the beginning of the script and deleting at the end of it. The output will be something like this:

```
BACKUP UTIL v 1.0
------------------
1. Backup a file/directory
2. Restore a file/directory
0. Quit
------------------
Please select an option, 0 or Q to exit:
```

Iterations

And select option 1:

```
1) backup-menu.sh      6) counter-simple.sh   11) for-pair.sh
2) case-select.sh      7) EXIT                12) simple-select.sh
3) c-for.sh            8) for-continue.sh     13) until-simple.sh
4) counter-brace.sh    9) for-pair-input.sh   14) while-simple.sh
5) counter-function.sh 10) for-pair-set.sh
Which file do you want to backup?
```

The files are automatically numbered along without the EXIT placeholder. The files in the directory are all numbered, and our EXIT strategy shows up even though it is not the last option; but renaming it would allow us to place it wherever we want. Inside `select`, we find another case, since we want to evaluate the answer given by the user and work on the right file. So, if the user does not select the option corresponding to EXIT, we do not break out from the loop clearing out the file, but proceed by compressing it and exiting to the main loop, which will show up the main menu. All of this is nice, but did you realize that there is a big issue at play here? What happens if you select one option that is not really available in the select menu?

```
1) backup-menu.sh
2) case-select.sh
3) c-for.sh
4) counter-brace.sh
5) counter-function.sh
6) counter-simple.sh
7) EXIT
8) for-continue.sh
9) for-pair-input.sh
10) for-pair-set.sh
11) for-pair.sh
12) simple-select.sh
13) until-simple.sh
14) while-simple.sh
Which file do you want to backup? 15
Compressing file
tar: Substituting `.' for empty member name
tar: : Cannot stat: No such file or directory
tar: Exiting with failure status due to previous errors
```

Well, it is to be expected since we did not provide a real check on the input, or better, we are checking only what we expected to receive, not the unexpected. So let's modify the default option for the inner case statement:

```
*)
    if [ -z "$file" ]
    then
```

```
        echo "Please, select one of the number displayed"
        sleep 3
        continue
        fi
    echo "Compressing file $file"
        tar cvzf "${file}".tgz "$file" || exit 1
        echo "File $file compressed."
        ls "${file}".tgz
        echo "Press a key to return to main menu..."
        read
        break
        ;;
```

We simply added a check to the content passed through $file variable: if the variable does not hold anything and does not point to any filename, we display a message, wait for three seconds, and then restart the loop. We could also use read instead of just waiting to force the user to press a key to continue; and this would leave the warning message displayed until the user reacts.

As we can see from the various examples, there is more than one way to create a user menu in Bash; and in the coming chapters, we will use them and make them even more fancier. But talking about user interaction, we have one topic left to face and it is quite interesting: dealing with how to manage the command line argument passed to our scripts. So, if we do not want to show a menu, but want to receive arguments on the command line, how do we do it? We already saw something, but there is a nice built-in that can ease our job, so it is time to have a look at getops.

CLI, passing the arguments to the command line

Geopts is a Bash built-in widely used to efficiently parse switches and arguments passed on the command line of a script. We already saw other ways to accomplish this task, but getops makes it quite easy to handle it, since it can automatically recognize the switches and argument passed to the script. Its syntax is as follows:

```
getops options variable
```

Iterations

The first thing we pass to `getops` is a string of options, the classical -a -x -f of whatever you want, without any leading dash, such as `getops axf` or also `getops ax:f`. If you see an option followed by a colon, this means that the option is meant to have an argument such as follows:

./our_script.sh -x our_argument -a

In our example, -x has an argument while -a is a simple switch, or we can also call it **flag** that can just be there or not, but it does not require any arguments. The options can be specified as lower or upper characters or digits. The `getops` built-in has some predefined variables for its internal use:

- `OPTARG` holds the argument for an option or the flag for an unknown option.
- `OPTBIND` holds the index for the next option to parse.
- `OPTERR` holds 0 or 1 and sets the display of error messages from `getops`. The default value is 1, so messages are displayed here.

As it is quite clear, `getops` is useful for parsing short options, but it cannot process the long style options, so -a is okay, but --all will not be parsed. It's a limit, but it is just a matter of style. Let's see a simple example and by commenting on it, we will have a look at how `getops` works on the field:

```
#!/bin/bash
while getopts ":ax:f" option
do
  case $option in
  a | f)
echo "You selected $option!"
;;
  x)
echo "You selected $option with argument $OPTARG"
;;
  ?)
echo "Invalid switch: -$OPTARG"
  ;;
  :)
echo "No arguments provided: -$OPTARG"
  ;;
  esac
done
```

So, our script starts with a while loop, and this is due to the fact that `getops` exits with a status called `fail` when there is nothing to parse, and this condition is met when it reaches the first non option argument or when it hits a `--`. Next, we see the `getops` built-in followed by `ax:f`, which means it expects this:

```
-a
-x argument
-f
```

`getops` will read all the options up to the first non-option argument and store them in a variable that in our case is named option. Now, the last part is a bit tricky. Have a look at `getopts ":ax:f"`.

Did you notice : before the first option? It disables the standard error messages for getops and alters the way the standard variables are used.

In case of an invalid option, the variable (`option` in our example) is used to store the ? character, which highlights the error; and `OPTARG` is instanced with the invalid character provided by the user.

In case of an argument, the variable is instanced with a colon : and `OPTARG` holds the option character. Let's run this script with the different options to see how it works:

```
zarrelli:~/$ ./getops-simple.sh -a
You selected a!
zarrelli:~/$ ./getops-simple.sh -f
You selected f!
zarrelli:~/$ ./getops-simple.sh -f -a
You selected f!
You selected a!
zarrelli:~/$ ./getops-simple.sh -x
No arguments provided: -x
zarrelli:~/$ ./getops-simple.sh -x hello
You selected x with argument hello
zarrelli:~/$ ./getops-simple.sh -x hello -a -f
You selected x with argument hello
You selected a!
You selected f!
zarrelli:~/$ ./getops-simple.sh -z
Invalid switch: -z
```

Nice, but do not get fooled, we have two main issues here, do you see them? Let's have a look at the first one:

```
zarrelli:~/$ ./getops-simple.sh
zarrelli:~/$
```

Iterations

Well, no switches were given, no output at all, and this is not good at all: remember not to leave your user without a feedback, never. Always have your script to show something to the user, so he knows he did something and will not try to invoke it repeatedly. We can manage this situation adding just before the while loop a small fragment of code, which counts the arguments on the command line:

```
if (( $# == 0 ))
then
    echo "Please, give at least one option on the command line"
exit 1
fi
```

Nothing special, we just checked if the number of arguments passed to the command line is equal to 0 and whether this is the case we echo a message and exit with an error:

```
zarrelli:~$ ./getops-arguments.sh
Please, give at least one option on the command line
Is it this all about our errors? Not precisely:
zarrelli:~$ ./getops-arguments.sh -a Hello
You selected a!
```

Hello is an argument passed to the command line, but -a does not accept the options argument, so how do we retrieve Hello? Notice that there is a difference between these two invocations:

```
zarrelli:~$ ./getops-arguments.sh -x Hello
You selected x with argument Hello
zarrelli:~$ ./getops-arguments.sh -a Hello
You selected a!
```

The first Hello is the argument of an option and the second is a simple argument on the command line, which is not related to an option, since -a does not accept any arguments. And so, we were able to reach Hello the first time, but not on the second scenario. How can we overcome this limitation? Let's rewrite the previous example adding the following lines at the end of the script:

```
echo "And the argument was $*"
shift "$((OPTIND-1))"
echo "And the argument was $*"
```

Now let's run the script again:

```
zarrelli:~$ ./getops-arguments.sh -x whatever -a Hello
You selected x with argument whatever
You selected a!
And the argument was -x whatever -a Hello
And the argument was Hello
```

And here we are. Notice the use of shift that helped us in retrieving the argument; this trick is based upon the value hold by OPTIND, which corresponds to the number of options parsed by the last call of getops. If we recall how getops works: each time it is invoked, it puts the next option in the variable used to hold them, initializing it if does not exist and the index of the next argument to parse into the OPTIND variable. So, OPTIND at the first run has 1 as its argument. Bear in mind that OPTIND is never reset by the shell, so if you have to make multiple calls to getops, it is up to you to reinitialize the variable to 1. Then, we use shift to deal with the positional parameter, since this built-in is able to shift the positional parameters on the left by the number specified as its argument. So shift "$((OPTIND-1))" shifts the positional parameter of the next argument of getops back to one position. Let's rewrite a part of the previous script:

```
case $option in
    a | f)
echo "You selected $option with $OPTIND=$OPTIND and the command line argument $*!"
;;
x)
echo "You selected $option with argument $OPTARG with $OPTIND=$OPTIND and the command line $*!"
    ;;
    ?)
    echo "Invalid switch: -$OPTARG with $OPTIND=$OPTIND"
    ;;
    :)
    echo "No arguments provided: -$OPTARG with $OPTIND=$OPTIND"
    ;;
    esac
done
echo "$OPTIND at the end of the loop is $OPTIND"
shift "$((OPTIND-1))"
echo "But at the end of the script we have this left on the command line: $*"
```

Now, run it again:

```
zarrelli:~$ ./getops-arguments.sh -f -a Hello
You selected f with $OPTIND=2 and the command line argument -f -a Hello!
You selected a with $OPTIND=3 and the command line argument -f -a Hello!
$OPTIND at the end of the loop is 3
```

But at the end of the script, we have this left on the command line: Hello.

Iterations

So, what happens? When you run the script, `OPTIND` starts with a value of `1` and gets incremented by `1` each time `getops` gets called. So, since we have two options to process on the command line, at the end of the `getops` loop, the value of `OPTIND` will be 2+1, so we have 3. Now, if we shift the command line of "`$((OPTIND-1))`", it means that we move the command-line arguments of 2 slots (3-1) to the left. Bear in mind that when you shift the positional arguments to the left, they get essentially lost and so what you are left with is the rest of the arguments. In our case, if we move the positional arguments of 2 on the left, we get rid of `-f` and `-a`; and we are left with the first non-option argument, "`Hello`". Here we are! If we now print the content of the command line `$@` after the loop, we are left exactly with `Hello`. Now, it's time to build up the tools we will use in the next chapters and pull together all the bits and parts you learned so far. First things first: the script will become more complex, and it will tend to clutter a bit, so if we recall what we saw in the first chapters about sourcing a file, what we will do now is create a library to hold all the common functions and settings that we are going to use frequently. Adopting this style will help to keep our scripts neat and simple and to master their content with less effort. So, first things first, let's create a library file that we will call `library.lib` and start writing some functions in it:

```
# Library file holding common functions and setting
# Functions
non_zero_input()
{
  if (( $1 == 0 ))
    then
    echo "Please, give at least one option on the command line"
    exit 1
  fi
}
```

Now, let's rewrite the first part of the previous script in the following way:

```
#!/bin/bash
source library.lib
non_zero_input "$#"
```

And time to run the script without any options:

```
zarrelli:~$ ./getops-library.sh
Please, give at least one option on the command line.
```

As we can see, the check on the zero length input has been moved to the library, then sourced back to the main script. So, now, we have two advantages:

- Less rows in our primary script
- The `non_zero_function` is now available to all the scripts that will source the library we just created

But now, it is time for something fancy. Ever wanted to give some spice to your output? Just modify this library in the following way:

```
# Library file holding common functions and setting
# Functions
#----------
non_zero_input()
{
  if (( $1 == 0 ))
    then
    echo "Please, give at least one option on the command line"
    exit 1
    fi
}
color_print()
{
  printf "$1$2${CReset}n"
}
# Colors - foreground
#--------------------
Black='33[0;30m'
Red='33[0;31m'
Green='33[0;32m'
Yellow='33[0;33m'
Blue='33[0;34m'
Purple='33[0;35m'
Cyan='33[0;36m'
White='33[0;37m'
# Colors - Reset
#---------------
CReset='33[0m'
```

Iterations

We added some ANSI color code to our library assigning them to a meaningful variable name and also created a small `color_print` function. ANSI escape code or sequences are methods to manage colors and attributes on text terminals and are represented by a string starting with the ESC character (033 in octal), followed by a character between 64 to 95 in the ASCII range. W just added a few foreground colors, but by googling, you will find a lengthy list of escaped characters that you can assign to background colors, bold characters, reverse, and so forth. The `color_print` function is just a tiny example of what can be done with these control codes and it makes use of `printf`, which is a bit more flexible than `echo` even though `echo -e` will deal with escaped characters and will be good enough to print colors and attributes. Notice that the `color_print` functions ends `printf` with `'33[0m'`, which is a reset control character that will revert to default all the changes you made to the output: once you modify a color or an attribute, everything will be printed with that alteration until you explicitly reset to default using the reset escape sequence. Now, it is time to take advantage of what we just saw and modify the script we just created so that it ends this way:

```
done
echo "$OPTIND at the end of the loop is $OPTIND"
shift "$((OPTIND-1))"
echo $@
echo -e "${Green}But${CReset} at the end of the script we have this left on
the command line: ${Red}$@${CReset}"
color_print ${Yellow} "But we can use our color_print function to have a
fancy output: $@"
```

There are two different examples on how to use the escape codes to manage the output:

```
echo -e "${Green}But${CReset} at the end of the script we have this left on
the command line: ${Red}$@${CReset}"
```

The word But is preceded by the value of the variable Green that we sourced from the library and it is closed by the CReset variable value, so echo will turn the output to green foreground right before writing But and revert to the standard color, usually white, right after thanks to the reset escape sequence. Then, right before printing the command-line arguments, it switches to Red to revert back once finished. The last line is printed using the color_print function sourced from the library file:

```
color_print ${Yellow} "But we can use our color_print function to have a
fancy output: $@"
```

As we can see from the function definition, it accepts two arguments, the escape code and the string to print trailing them with a reset code; in our case we selected Yellow, so let's see what is the outcome in the following screenshot:

```
zarrelli@moveaway:~$ ./getops-library.sh -x bench -a Hello
You selected x with argument bench with $OPTIND=3 and the command line -x bench -a Hello!
You selected a with $OPTIND=4 and the command line argument -x bench -a Hello!
$OPTIND at the end of the loop is 4
Hello
But at the end of the script we have this left on the command line: Hello
But we can use our color_print function to have a fancy output: Hello
zarrelli@moveaway:~$
```

Inline escape codes or ad hoc functions kicks up our output

Nice, isn't it? There are actually many ways to color your output using Bash, from interacting with the dialog program, which will give you curses such as interface:

```
zarrelli:~$ dialog --begin 10 30 --backtitle "Example menu" --title "This
is a Message Box" --msgbox 'Your message goes here!' 10 30
```

This is a simple message box, which reminds me of the old Linux installers to zenity that will give you a GTK+ interface:

```
zarrelli:~$ ls -l | zenity --text-info --height=600 --width 800
```

```
total 68
-rwxr-xr-x 1 zarrelli zarrelli 1158 Mar  9 09:20 backup-menu.sh
-rwxr-xr-x 1 zarrelli zarrelli  277 Mar  8 11:09 case-select.sh
-rwxr--r-- 1 zarrelli zarrelli  138 Mar  7 08:07 c-for.sh
-rwxr-xr-x 1 zarrelli zarrelli   52 Mar  6 09:18 counter-brace.sh
-rwxr-xr-x 1 zarrelli zarrelli   83 Mar  6 10:42 counter-function.sh
-rwxr-xr-x 1 zarrelli zarrelli   51 Mar  6 09:15 counter-simple.sh
-rwxr-xr-x 1 zarrelli zarrelli   99 Mar  7 12:01 for-continue.sh
-rwxr-xr-x 1 zarrelli zarrelli   78 Mar  6 10:20 for-pair-input.sh
-rwxr-xr-x 1 zarrelli zarrelli  134 Mar  6 09:57 for-pair-set.sh
-rwxr-xr-x 1 zarrelli zarrelli  120 Mar  6 09:47 for-pair.sh
-rwxr--r-- 1 zarrelli zarrelli  772 Mar 10 11:09 getops-arguments.sh
-rwxr--r-- 1 zarrelli zarrelli  845 Mar 11 11:34 getops-library.sh
-rwxr--r-- 1 zarrelli zarrelli  374 Mar  9 11:35 getops-simple.sh
-rw-r--r-- 1 zarrelli zarrelli  518 Mar 10 12:23 library.lib
-rwxr-xr-x 1 zarrelli zarrelli  174 Mar  8 11:03 simple-select.sh
-rwxr-xr-x 1 zarrelli zarrelli   63 Mar  7 09:26 until-simple.sh
-rwxr-xr-x 1 zarrelli zarrelli   64 Mar  7 08:54 while-simple.sh
```

Zenity allows you to create beautiful interfaces using GTK+ decorations

What we can use depends on the level of interaction we want to have with the customer; for instance, scripts dealing with services probably will not need any fancy stuff. And on our concerns about portability: to use dialog and zenity you have to install them; they are not shipped by default with a Linux system. For zenity, keep in mind that it only show its goodness on a graphical interface; if you go over serial or text-based terminals, it will show you curses such as interface at best. If you want to use something more advanced than ANSII escape code, you can resort to the `tput` command, which is shipped with Linux; and by using the `terminfo` or `termcap` databases, it enables you to interact with the terminal in a more interesting way:

```
#!/bin/bash
fred=$(tput setaf 1)
fgreen=$(tput setaf 2)
fwhite=$(tput setaf 7)
bblue=$(tput setab 4)
esmso=$(tput smso)
xsmso=$(tput rmso)
dim=$(tput dim)
reset=$(tput sgr0)
hide=$(tput civis)
box() {
printf ${hide}
printf ${bblue}
width=$(tput cols)
height=$(tput lines)
```

Iterations

```
message="Width is: ${esmso}${fgreen}$width${fwhite} Height is:
${dim}${fred}$height${reset}"
length=${#message}
clear
tput cup $((height / 2)) $(((width / 2) - ((length - 29) / 2)))
printf "$message"
}
trap box WINCH
box
while true
do
    :
done
```

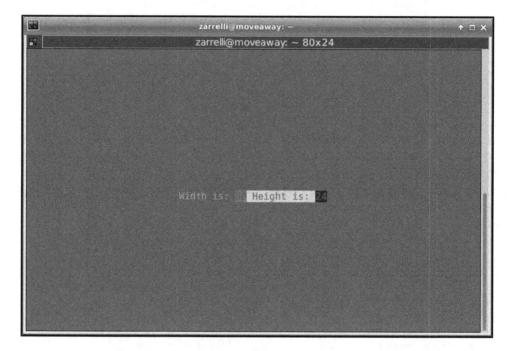

An auto updating message displayed using tput

This simple script uses `tput` with a series of numbers to change the color of the output. `tput setaf x` sets the foreground color to the value corresponding to the x integer:

```
0 black
1 red
2 green
3 yellow
4 blue
```

[234]

```
5 magenta
6 cyan
7 white
```

For the background, we use `tput setbg x` with the same list of codes. We used the command substitution to get the output of the command and use it with `printf` to modify the output accordingly. The values for the rest of the `tput` commands are quite obvious:

- `tput smso` enters the standout mode
- `tput rmso` exits the standout mode
- `tput dim` makes the output less bright
- `tput sgro` reverts back to the standard terminal output
- `tput cvis` hides the cursor

Then, we created a function named `box`, which hides the cursor, and then sets the background to blue. The interesting parts are here:

- `tput cols` gets the number of columns of the terminal
- `tput lines` gets the number of lines of the terminal

We stored the output of the two commands in the width and height variables and used the message variable to compose a string, which outputs the dimensions of our terminal, using the `tput` colors to format the output, which has a nice flag as a background. We used the various attributes in an unconventional way, but you can play with them and see what kind of output you can get.

Look into `man terminfo`, `man termcap`, and `man tput` to have an idea of all that you can do with `tput`. Continuing with the script, we get the length of the message and clear the script, clear the screen, and finally with `tput cup x y`.

We move the cursor to the right position to center the message on the terminal. We had to compensate the characters used for the `tput` attributes. Outside the function, we then use a trap that intercepts the window change signal sent to the process when the terminal, which controls it, changes its size. This way the trap will invoke the function box each time the user changes the size of the window, so the new height and width will be calculated and printed to the terminal. We left an infinite loop at the end, which kicks in play once the first box iteration has been completed: the infinite loop keeps the script running idle waiting for the winch signal to be trap. And as soon as it is trapped, the box function is called, a new height and width values calculated, and an up-to-date message is displayed.

Summary

Our scripts are starting to get more complex and ever interesting; we are moving from dealing with the shell to programming, to making something handy out of it. The next part of the book will dive into a bit of real-world programming, creating some applications that will show us how to create some sound and reliable tools for our everyday life as sysadmins or curious users.

7
Plug into the Real World

We are moving into the real world now, creating something that can turn out handy for your daily routine; during this process, we will have a look at the common pitfalls in coding and how to make our script reliable. Be it a short or long script, we must always ask ourselves the same questions:

- What do we really want to accomplish?
- How much time do we have?
- Do we have all the resources needed?
- Do we have the knowledge required for the task?

We will start coding with a Nagios plugin, which will give us a broad understanding of how this monitoring system is and how to make a script dynamically interact with other programs.

What is Nagios?

Nagios is one of the most widely adopted open source IT infrastructure monitoring tools, whose main interesting feature is the fact that it does not know how to monitor anything. Well, it sounds like a joke, but actually Nagios can be defined as an evaluating core, which takes some information as input and reacts accordingly. How is this information gathered? It is not the main concern of this tool and this leads us to an interesting point: Nagios leaves the task of getting the monitored data to an external plugin, which knows the following details:

- How to connect to the monitored services
- How to collect the data from the monitored services
- How to evaluate the data

Inform Nagios if the values gathered are beyond or in the boundaries to raise an alarm.

So, a plugin does a lot of things and one would ask oneself what does Nagios do then? Imagine it as an exchange pod where information is flowing in and out and decisions are taken based on the configurations set; the core triggers the plugin to monitor a service; the plugin itself returns some information and Nagios takes a decision about:

- Whether to raise an alarm
- Send a notification
- Whom to notify
- For how long
- What, if any action is taken in order to get back to normality

The core Nagios program does everything except actually knock at the door of a service, ask for information, and decide whether this information shows some issues or not.

Active and passive checks

To understand how to code a plugin, we have first to grasp how, on a broad scale, a Nagios check works. There are two different kinds of checks.

Active checks

Based on a time range, or manually triggered, an active check sees a plugin actively connecting to a service and collecting information. A typical example could be for a plugin to check the disk space: once invoked, it interfaces with (usually) the operating system, executes a `df` command, works on the output, extracts the value related to the disk space, evaluates it against some thresholds, and reports back a status, such as **OK**, **WARNING**, **CRITICAL**, or **UNKNOWN**.

Passive checks

In this case, Nagios does not trigger anything but waits to be contacted by some means by the service, which must be monitored. It seems quite confusing, but let's make a real-life example. How would you monitor if a disk backup has been completed successfully? One quick answer would be: knowing when the backup task starts and how long it lasts, we can define a time and invoke a script to check the task at that given hour.

Nice, but when we plan something, we must have a full understanding of how real life goes, and a backup is not our little pet in the living room, it's rather a beast, which does what it wants. A backup can last a variable amount of time depending on an unpredictable factor.

For instance, your typical backup task would copy 1 TB of data in 2 hours, starting at 03:00, out of a 6 TB disk. So, the next backup task would start at 03:00+02:00=05:00 AM, give or take some minutes. And you set up an active check for it at 05:30, and it works well for a couple of months. Then, one early morning, you receive a notification on your smartphone that the backup is in **CRITICAL**. You wake up, connect to the backup console and see that at 06:00 in the morning, you are asleep and the backup task has not even been started by the console. Then, you have to wait until 08:00 AM until some of your colleagues show up at the office to find out that the day before the disk, your backup has been filled with 2 extra TB of data due to an unscheduled data transfer. So, the backup task preceding the one you are monitoring lasted not for a couple of hours but 6 hours, and the task you are monitoring then started at 09:30 AM.

Long story short, your active check has been fired up too early; that is why it failed. Maybe your are tempted to move your schedule some hours ahead, but simply do not do it, as these time slots are not sliding frames. If you move your check ahead, you should then move all the checks for the subsequent tasks ahead. You do it in one week, the project manager will ask someone to delete the 2 TB excess (useless for the project now), and your schedules will be 2 hours ahead, making your monitoring useless. So, as we insisted before, planning and analyzing the context is the key factor in making a good script and, in this case, a good plugin. We have a service that does not run 24/7 like a web service or a mail service; what is specific to the backup is that it is run periodically, but we do not know exactly when.

The best approach to this kind of monitoring is letting the service itself notify us when it finished its task and what was its outcome. This is usually accomplished using the ability of most backup programs to send a **Simple Network Monitoring Protocol** (**SNMP**) trap to a destination to inform it of the outcome; and in our case it would be the Nagios server, which would have been configured to receive the trap and analyze. Add to this an event horizon so that if you do not receive the specific trap in, let's say, 24 hours, we raise an alarm anyway and you are covered: whenever the backup task gets completed or when it times out, we receive a notification.

Plug into the Real World

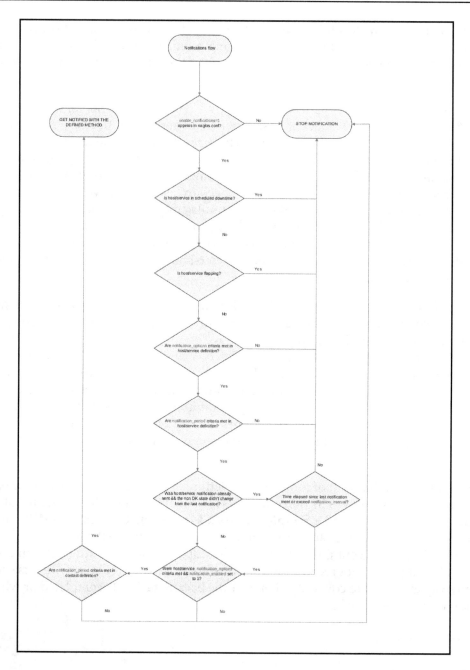

Nagios notifications flowchart

Returning code and thresholds

Before coding a plugin, we must face some concepts that will be the stepping stone of our Nagios code base, one of these being the return codes of the plugin itself. As we already discussed, once the plugin collects the data about how the service is going, it evaluates these data and determines if the situation falls under one of the following status:

Return code	Status	Description
0	OK	The plugin checked the service and the results that are inside the acceptable range.
1	WARNING	The plugin checked the service and the results that are above a **WARNING** threshold. We must keep an eye on the service.
2	CRITICAL	The plugin checked the service and the results that are above a **CRITICAL** threshold or the service not responding. We must react now.
3	UNKNOWN	Either we passed the wrong arguments to the plugin or there is some internal error in it.

So, our plugin will check a service, evaluate the results, and based on a threshold, will return to Nagios one of the values listed in the tables and a meaningful message, like we can see in the description column in the following screenshot:

Notice the service check in red and the message in the preceding screenshot.

In the screenshot, we can see that some checks are green, meaning okay, and they have an explicative message in the description section. What we see in this section is the output of the plugin written in the `stdout`; and it is what we will craft as a response to Nagios.

Pay attention to the **SSH** check: it is red and is failing because it is checking the service at the default port, which is 22, but on this server the `ssh` daemon is listening on a different port. This leads us to a consideration: our plugin will need a command line parser able to receive some configuration options and some threshold limits as well, because we need to know what to check, where to check, and what are the acceptable working limits for a service:

- **Where**: In Nagios, there can be a host without service checks (except for the implicit host alive carried on by a ping), but no services without a host to be performed onto. So, any plugin must receive on the command line the indication of the host to be run against, be it a dummy host but there must be one.
- **How**: This is where our coding comes in; we will have to write the lines of code that instruct the plugin how to connect to the server, query, collect, and parse the answer.
- **What**: We must instruct the plugin, usually with some meaningful options on the command line, on what are the acceptable working limits so that it can evaluate them and decide to notify us with an **OK**, **WARNING**, or **CRITICAL** message.

That is all for our script: who to notify, when, how, how many times, and so forth. These are tasks carried on by the core; a Nagios plugin is unaware of all of this. What it really must know for effective monitoring is what are the correct values that identify a working service. We can pass to our script two different kinds of value:

- **Range**: This is a series of numeric values with a starting and ending point, like from 3 to 7 or from one number to infinite
- **Threshold**: It is a range with an associated alert level

So, when our plugins perform checks, they collect a numeric value that is within or outside a range, based on the threshold we impose; then, based on the evaluation, it replies to Nagios with a return code and a message. How do we specify some ranges on the command line? Essentially in the following way:

```
[@] start_value:end_value
```

If the range starts from 0, the part from : to the left can be omitted. The `start_value` must always be a lower number than `end_value`.

If the range starts with `start_value`, it means from that number to infinity. Negative infinity can be specified using ~.

An alert is generated when the collected value resides outside the range specified, comprised of the endpoints.

If @ is specified, the alert is generated if the value resides inside the range.

Let's see some practical examples of how we would call our script, imposing some thresholds:

Plugin call	Meaning
./my_plugin -c 10	**CRITICAL** if less than 0 or higher than 10
./my_plugin -w 10:20	**WARNING** if less than 10 or higher than 20
/my_plugin -w ~:15 -c 16	**WARNING** if between -infinite and 15, critical from 16 and higher
./my_plugin -c 35:	**CRITICAL** if the value collected is below 35
./my_plugin -w @100:200	**CRITICAL** if the value is from 100 to 200, **OK** otherwise

We covered the basic requirements for our plugin that in its simplest form should be called with the following syntax:

```
./my_plugin -h hostaddress|hostname -w value -c value
```

We already talked about the need to relate a check to a host; we can do this either by using a hostname or hostaddress. It is up to us what to use, but we will not fill in this piece of information, because it will be drawn by the service configuration as a standard macro. We just introduced a new concept, service configuration, which is essential in making our script work in Nagios, so let's briefly see what we are talking about. A caveat before starting our journey on Nagios configurations: this is not a book on Nagios, so we will not cover all the complex bits and parts. We will touch all the topics needed to make our script do its job and with a working Nagios installation; we will be able to activate our new plugin quickly. Let's see now how to configure a plugin to make it work under Nagios, so then we will be able to focus on our script without any distractions.

Command and service definitions

At the base of everything in Nagios is a plugin, the minion who carries out the job of retrieving the information, evaluating it, raising the alarm, and providing a meaningful message. Left alone, Nagios does not know how to call a plugin, what options to pass to it or how to handle it, so we need a command definition, which defines how the script will be called.

Let's take as an example the command definition for the `ssh` service check, which is failing because the port used for the check is not the one the daemon is listening on:

```
# 'check_ssh' command definition
define command{
command_name check_ssh
command_line /usr/lib/nagios/plugins/check_ssh '$HOSTADDRESS$'
}
```

We can see here a command definition named `command_name check_ssh`.

Let's keep `check_ssh` in mind, because it will be the handle we will use to refer to this command definition later on. As we can see, this definition is really short; it defines a handle, and, most importantly, the command line to call the plugin. In this case, it is really easy: the plugin accepts the host address and that is enough for a basic check. Look at `$HOSTADDRESS$`. This is one of the so-called **Nagios standard macros:** essentially a place holder, which will be instantiated by Nagios with the host address of the host you will associate the service making use of this command. Nothing complicated so far, let's move onto the service definition, making use of this command definition:

```
# check that ssh services are running
define service {
use generic-service
host_name localhost
service_description SSH
check_command check_ssh
}
```

The `ssh` service definition introduces something new, and this is the inheritance of properties by the Nagios objects. As we discussed previously, the script carries out the checking, evaluation, and alarm raising; the core does all the rest, and lots of stuff. Looking at this service definition, it does not seem a lot, but focus on the first line named `use generic-service`. This rings a bell. Looking at the definition, it seems that `generic-service` is actually a template, doesn't it?

```
# generic service template definition
define service{
name generic-service ; The 'name' of this service template
active_checks_enabled 1 ; Active service checks are enabled
passive_checks_enabled 1 ; Passive service checks are enabled/accepted
parallelize_check 1 ; Active service checks should be parallelized
(disabling this can lead to major performance problems)
obsess_over_service 1 ; We should obsess over this service (if necessary)
check_freshness 0 ; Default is to NOT check service 'freshness'
notifications_enabled 1 ; Service notifications are enabled
event_handler_enabled 1 ; Service event handler is enabled
```

```
flap_detection_enabled 1 ; Flap detection is enabled
failure_prediction_enabled 1 ; Failure prediction is enabled
process_perf_data 1 ; Process performance data
retain_status_information 1 ; Retain status information across program
restarts
retain_nonstatus_information 1 ; Retain non-status information across
program restarts
 notification_interval 0 ; Only send notifications on status change by
default.
is_volatile 0
check_period 24x7
normal_check_interval 5
retry_check_interval 1
max_check_attempts 4
notification_period 24x7
notification_options w,u,c,r
contact_groups admins
register 0 ;
DONT REGISTER THIS DEFINITION - ITS NOT A REAL SERVICE, JUST A TEMPLATE!
}
```

Well, as we can see, there is a lot we can define service-wise, just so much to clutter a service definition so we hide the complexity in a template and recall it, like sourcing a library. Once the template is imported, all its definition will apply to the service that called it and if we want to modify some values from the template, we just write them in the service definition with the new values, because if we have multiple definitions with the same name and different values, the closest to the final object wins. So, a definition at the service level wins over a definition in the template. We will not explain all the definitions in the template, as they are not useful for our goal, since our script will rely on the generic service definition without any alterations.

Let's go back to the service definition and have a look at the second line `host_name` localhost. We already mentioned the fact that each service check must refer to one (or more) host, so here is where we see what host this service applies to. We could also have used `hostgroup_name name_of_the_hostgroup`.

To apply a single check to multiple hosts enclosed in a host group definition. Let's move onto the `service_description` ssh. As for the command definition, this is the handle used to refer to this service definition throughout Nagios:

check_command check_ssh

Plug into the Real World

This is where we call the command definition passing optional arguments. In our predefined configuration, there are no parameters to give to the command, so nothing special. With this line, the service definition recalls the syntax defined in the command definition called by the handled, and optionally passes some arguments to it. All the configurations for services, commands, hosts, and templates follow the same structure:

```
define object {
definitions_1
definitions_2
definitions_n
}
```

You can then have the different definitions on one files closed in their snippets.

We just saw how the ssh check works in Nagios, but it actually does not work, since it throws us an error. What we would need is a way to change the port that the service is being checked on. How do we accomplish this task? By simply bearing in mind that the actual plugin is the star here, it will drive all our efforts, so let's invoke it and see what it has to say. Let's have a look at the command line definition:

```
command_line /usr/lib/nagios/plugins/check_ssh '$HOSTADDRESS$'
```

From here, we know where the script is, so let's call it:

```
root:~$ /usr/lib/nagios/plugins/check_ssh
check_ssh: Could not parse arguments
Usage:
check_ssh [-4|-6] [-t <timeout>] [-r <remote version>] [-p <port>] <host>
```

What we see here is that the script accepts some arguments and options on the command line, but each script is usually coded with a full help message invoked by a -h option:

```
root:~$ /usr/lib/nagios/plugins/check_ssh -h
check_ssh v2.1.1 (monitoring-plugins 2.1.1)
Copyright (c) 1999 Remi Paulmier <remi@sinfomic.fr>
Copyright (c) 2000-2007 Monitoring Plugins Development Team
<devel@monitoring-plugins.org>

Try to connect to an SSH server at specified server and port

Usage:
check_ssh [-4|-6] [-t <timeout>] [-r <remote version>] [-p <port>] <host>

Options:
-h, --help
Print detailed help screen
-V, --version
```

```
Print version information
--extra-opts=[section][@file]
Read options from an ini file. See
https://www.monitoring-plugins.org/doc/extra-opts.html
for usage and examples.
-H, --hostname=ADDRESS
Host name, IP Address, or unix socket (must be an absolute path)
-p, --port=INTEGER
Port number (default: 22)
-4, --use-ipv4
Use IPv4 connection
-6, --use-ipv6
Use IPv6 connection
-t, --timeout=INTEGER
Seconds before connection times out (default: 10)
-r, --remote-version=STRING
Warn if string doesn't match expected server version (ex: OpenSSH_3.9p1)
-P, --remote-protocol=STRING
Warn if protocol doesn't match expected protocol version (ex: 2.0)
-v, --verbose
Show details for command-line debugging (output may be truncated by
the monitoring system)

Send email to help@monitoring-plugins.org if you have questions regarding
use of this software. To submit patches or suggest improvements, send email
to devel@monitoring-plugins.org
```

Let's keep in mind this help, because it is something we will have to implement in our plugin. Anyway, what we see, among other options is that we can actually change the port the service is being checked on using the option: -p.

Let's check where our `ssh` server is listening for connections:

```
root:~$ netstat -tapn | grep ssh
tcp 0 0 0.0.0.0:1472 0.0.0.0:* LISTEN 685/sshd
tcp6 0 0 :::1472
```

Now we know that our `ssh` daemon is listening on port `1472`. So we have to make a manual check to be sure on how to invoke the plugin with the new parameters and values:

```
root:~$ /usr/lib/nagios/plugins/check_ssh -H localhost -p 1472
SSH OK - OpenSSH_6.7p1 Debian-5+deb8u3 (protocol 2.0) |
time=0.011048s;;;0.000000;10.000000
```

Plug into the Real World

It worked we processed `-H localhost` to identify which host we are executing our check against and `-p 1472` to query the correct port for this `ssh` daemon configuration. Now, let's pay attention to the reply from the plugin:

```
SSH OK - OpenSSH_6.7p1 Debian-5+deb8u3 (protocol 2.0) |
time=0.011048s;;;0.000000;10.000000
```

This is the standard structure of the message provided by a Nagios plugin:

1. The name of the service (SSH).
2. Service status (OK).
3. Message given by the service being checked (or a message we crafted ourselves).

Then there is something we never saw before:

```
| time=0.011048s;;;0.000000;10.000000
```

This is a pipe, followed by one or more labels, time in our example, and some values usually related to how the service is working. Whatever is written, it is not a Nagios concern, since it will not process this part of the output line. These values are there for third-party applications such as `pnp4nagios` or Nagios graph to process them and eventually draw out some performance graphics.

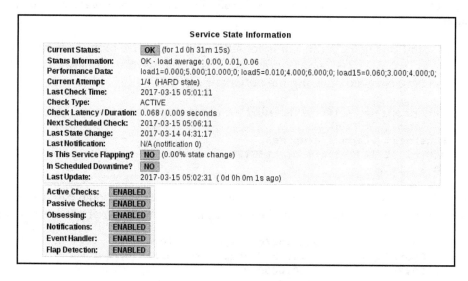

Nagios shows the performance data but does not really make use of it

[248]

We will see later how a graph for a service looks like, now let's remember one thing: the output of a plugin is usually one line long and even though you have a multiline output, it is always better to stick to a simple message.

Now, let's go back to the definition of the SSH service check, and let's see how to modify it to enable a different port check. This is the `check_ssh` command that we have already seen:

```
# 'check_ssh' command definition
define command{
command_name check_ssh
command_line /usr/lib/nagios/plugins/check_ssh '$HOSTADDRESS$'
}
```

To enable the definition of an arbitrary port check, we have to modify the `command_line` row so that it will accept the new -p parameter with an argument:

```
# 'check_ssh' command definition
define command{
command_name check_ssh
command_line /usr/lib/nagios/plugins/check_ssh '$HOSTADDRESS$' -p $ARG1$
}
```

What we did is simple: we just added a -p followed by $ARG1$. What is this new bit? In Nagios, you can pass whatever arguments you want to a script, and you refer to them using a positional variable. Think of $ARG1$ as $1 for a standard bash script; it identifies the first argument passed to the command line. Bear in mind that options like -p are not counted as arguments. So $ARG2$ will be the second positional argument, $ARG3$ the third, and so on. Do not forget the leading and trailing dollar signs. So, we modified the way Nagios can call the plugin, and now we can pass it an extra argument. What is left is to actually provide the extra argument to the script; this is done by modifying the service definition for ssh. We previously had this:

```
# check that ssh services are running
define service {
use generic-service
host_name localhost
service_description SSH
check_command check_ssh
}
```

This definition must be modified so that we can store and pass the port number to the command, so this is how we do it:

```
# check that ssh services are running
define service {
use generic-service
host_name localhost
service_description SSH
check_command check_ssh!1472
}
```

The exclamation mark (!) after the command name is a standard field separator and identifies the different positional arguments passed to the plugin. Let's make an example modifying the command_line of ssh to accept it:

```
-p 1472
-4
-P 2.0
-t 30
```

We must modify the command line to accept five parameters instead of one:

```
# 'check_ssh' command definition
define command{
command_name check_ssh
command_line /usr/lib/nagios/plugins/check_ssh '$HOSTADDRESS$' -p $ARG1$ -$ARG2$ -r $ARG3$ -P $ARG4$ -t $ARG5$
}
```

The modification is quite straightforward, we just wrote down all the switches and their arguments using the positional $ARGn$ variables. Now that the command line is ready to accept the new values, we must fill in the placeholders:

```
# check that ssh services are running
define service {
use generic-service
host_name localhost
service_description SSH
check_command check_ssh!1472!4!2.0!30
}
```

Not so complicated; each argument must be written in the order expected by the command line:

-p	-	-P	-t
1472	4	2.0	30

One thing to bear in mind is that the standard macros do not play a positional parameters so they do not have to be taken in to account when counting the slot indexes.

Now that we have all the bits in order, with the right switches and values, we have to write our new configuration down. Okay, but where? The location of the configuration files differs from distribution to distribution and the way the files are fragmented too: some distributions have commands and service definitions inside a host file along with the host definition, some others have fragmented in single files. How do we deal with it? Let the Nagios process tell you how it reads the information:

```
root:~$ ps ax | grep nagios
803 ? SNs 0:02 /usr/sbin/nagios3 -d /etc/nagios3/nagios.cfg
2502 pts/1 S+ 0:00 grep nagios
```

A `ps` command shows us that Nagios is reading its main configuration directives from /etc/nagios3/nagios.cfg. So, it is worth having a look at it:

```
# Commands definitions
cfg_file=/etc/nagios3/commands.cfg


# Debian also defaults to using the check commands defined by the debian
# nagios-plugins package
cfg_dir=/etc/nagios-plugins/config

# Debian uses by default a configuration directory where nagios3-common,
# other packages and the local admin can dump or link configuration
# files into.
cfg_dir=/etc/nagios3/conf.d

# OBJECT CONFIGURATION FILE(S)
# These are the object configuration files in which you define hosts,
# host groups, contacts, contact groups, services, etc.
# You can split your object definitions across several config files
# if you wish (as shown below), or keep them all in a single config file.

# You can specify individual object config files as shown below:
#cfg_file=/etc/nagios3/objects/commands.cfg
#cfg_file=/etc/nagios3/objects/contacts.cfg
#cfg_file=/etc/nagios3/objects/timeperiods.cfg
#cfg_file=/etc/nagios3/objects/templates.cfg

# Definitions for monitoring a Windows machine
#cfg_file=/etc/nagios3/objects/windows.cfg

# Definitions for monitoring a router/switch
#cfg_file=/etc/nagios3/objects/switch.cfg
```

```
# Definitions for monitoring a network printer
#cfg_file=/etc/nagios3/objects/printer.cfg

# You can also tell Nagios to process all config files (with a .cfg
# extension) in a particular directory by using the cfg_dir
# directive as shown below:

#cfg_dir=/etc/nagios3/servers
#cfg_dir=/etc/nagios3/printers
#cfg_dir=/etc/nagios3/switches
#cfg_dir=/etc/nagios3/routers
```

This is a standard section in the Nagios main configuration file, and you will find it in each and every installation, so pay attention to the lines that are not commented out by a # character:

```
# Commands definitions
cfg_file=/etc/nagios3/commands.cfg

# Debian also defaults to using the check commands defined by the debian
# nagios-plugins package
cfg_dir=/etc/nagios-plugins/config

# Debian uses by default a configuration directory where nagios3-common,
# other packages and the local admin can dump or link configuration
# files into.
cfg_dir=/etc/nagios3/conf.d
```

So, from the main configuration file, we can see that the configurations are stored in one file and two directories. Since we are dealing with a command plugin modification, we start from `cfg_dir=/etc/nagios-plugins/config`.

Looking for a file that cold bear an `ssh` configuration, let's move to `root:~$ cd /etc/nagios-plugins/config` and `grep` for `ssh` in each file:

```
root:~$ egrep -lr ssh *
disk.cfg
ssh.cfg
```

Just `egrep -l` will print only the names of the files where a match has been found; if you are not sure and want to see the actual matched line, use `-ir` instead of `-lr`, and you will see a lot more information. Anyway, between the two files, it seems pretty clear that the one we will have to modify is `ssh.cfg`.

Let's open it and go to the end of the file, adding our new command definition:

```
define command{
command_name check_ssh_arguments
command_line /usr/lib/nagios/plugins/check_ssh '$HOSTADDRESS$' -p $ARG1$ -
$ARG2$ -P $ARG3$ -t $ARG4$
}
```

As appears evident, we changed `command_name`; since there cannot be two command definitions with the same handle, we just chose something unique for our purposes. It will not be displayed to users, so it does not need to be fancy, just useful and meaningful. Let's save the file and proceed to define a new service configuration; from the main configuration file, it seems quite clear we have to look into `cfg_dir=/etc/nagios3/conf.d`.

So, let's move to this directory: `root:~$ cd /etc/nagios3/conf.d`, and `grep` for `ssh` again:

```
root:~$ egrep -lr ssh *
hostgroups_nagios2.cfg
services_nagios2.cfg
```

In this case, it is not clear what is bearing what, so an extended `grep` will be handy:

```
root:~$ egrep -ir ssh *
hostgroups_nagios2.cfg:# A list of your ssh-accessible servers
hostgroups_nagios2.cfg:  hostgroup_name ssh-servers
hostgroups_nagios2.cfg:  alias SSH servers
services_nagios2.cfg:# check that ssh services are running
services_nagios2.cfg:  hostgroup_name ssh-servers
services_nagios2.cfg:  service_description SSH
services_nagios2.cfg:  check_command check_ssh
```

Now, it is clear that `hostgroups_nagios.cfg` bears the configurations related to the host groups, and among those, the configuration of the group of hosts that are being checked for the `ssh` service. The second file, `services_nagios2.cfg`, holds the configuration for the ssh service check, so let's open it:

```
# check that ssh services are running
define service {
hostgroup_name ssh-servers
service_description SSH
check_command check_ssh
use generic-service
notification_interval 0 ; set > 0 if you want to be re-notified
}
```

Here is the `ssh` service check configuration we were looking for. In a production environment, we would have to estimate the impact of our configuration, since if we now modify this definition, it will apply to all the servers we are checking against.
Notice `hostgroup_name ssh-servers`, we are checking a group of servers being this group populated by one or one thousand servers is not important.

In a production or a staging scenario, we would have to see which servers we are checking for the ssh service, understand if our modifications will have some odd effects on some of them, and if so, tear these servers out of the new check and create a special group for them using the old definition for them. In our case, since this is a demo installation and has `localhost` as the only group member, we can just modify the existing configuration and go with it:

```
# check that ssh services are running
define service {
hostgroup_name ssh-servers
service_description SSH
check_command check_ssh_arguments!1472!4!2.0!30
use generic-service
notification_interval 0 ; set > 0 if you want to be renotified
}
```

This definition is quite similar to the one we crafted before; just here we are in a real scenario. Nagios is configured to apply this check on a hostgroup instead of a single server, but since the hostgroup is made by one server only, the localhost, the two definitions have the same scope. What we are left with is to force Nagios to reload the definitions so that our new configurations will be read by the core. A reload or restart will suffice:

```
service nagios3 reload
```

Now edit the `/etc/nagios3/nagios.cfg` file and enable the following configuration bit:

```
check_external_commands=1
```

With 0 meaning disabled and 1 enabled, we just told Nagios to accept external command, so we can reload the configuration `service nagios3 reload`, go to the service name, and enter the server details page. Here we just have to click on **Re-schedule the next check of this service.**

Let's select **Force check and commit**; a new check will be forced whatever schedule is at play.

In the Debian and Ubuntu standard Nagios installation, you could face `Error: Could not stat() command file '/var/lib/nagios3/rw/nagios.cmd'!`

When you try to force a check. You can solve it with the following procedure:

```
service nagios3 stop
dpkg-statoverride --update --add nagios www-data 2710 /var/lib/nagios3/rw
dpkg-statoverride --update --add nagios nagios 751 /var/lib/nagios3
service nagios3 start
```

If you face any issues with your plugin, enable `debug` mode in `/etc/nagios3/nagios.cfg` by setting the following configuration bit:

```
debug_level=-1
debug_verbosity=2
```

This will generate a lot of information written in the `debug` file, which in our installation is in `/var/log/nagios3/nagios.debug` file, which is important to understand what is going on, but they will slow down the system a bit, so we must keep the debug on only for the time it is needed, then we must revert to the normal logging.

A Nagios reload will enforce the activation of the new configuration. But let's have a look at what the debug log has to say about our new modified command:

```
[1489655900.213562] [016.0] [pid=13954] Checking service 'SSH' on host 'localhost'...
[1489655900.213602] [2320.2] [pid=13954] Raw Command Input: /usr/lib/nagios/plugins/check_ssh -p $ARG1$ -$ARG2$ -P $ARG3$ -t $ARG4$ '$HOSTADDRESS$'
[1489655900.213787] [2320.2] [pid=13954] Expanded Command Output: /usr/lib/nagios/plugins/check_ssh -p $ARG1$ -$ARG2$ -P $ARG3$ -t $ARG4$ '$HOSTADDRESS$'
[1489655900.213825] [2048.1] [pid=13954] Processing: '/usr/lib/nagios/plugins/check_ssh -p $ARG1$ -$ARG2$ -P $ARG3$ -t $ARG4$ '$HOSTADDRESS$''
[1489655900.213839] [2048.2] [pid=13954] Processing part: '/usr/lib/nagios/plugins/check_ssh -p '
[1489655900.213846] [2048.2] [pid=13954] Not currently in macro. Running output (37): '/usr/lib/nagios/plugins/check_ssh -p '
[1489655900.213906] [2048.2] [pid=13954] Uncleaned macro. Running output (41): '/usr/lib/nagios/plugins/check_ssh -p 1472'
[1489655900.213911] [2048.2] [pid=13954] Just finished macro. Running output (41): '/usr/lib/nagios/plugins/check_ssh -p 1472'
[1489655900.213921] [2048.2] [pid=13954] Not currently in macro. Running output (43): '/usr/lib/nagios/plugins/check_ssh -p 1472 -'
[1489655900.214051] [2048.2] [pid=13954] Uncleaned macro. Running output (44): '/usr/lib/nagios/plugins/check_ssh -p 1472 -4'
[1489655900.214064] [2048.2] [pid=13954] Just finished macro. Running output (44): '/usr/lib/nagios/plugins/check_ssh -p 1472 -4'
[1489655900.214074] [2048.2] [pid=13954] Not currently in macro. Running
```

```
output (48): '/usr/lib/nagios/plugins/check_ssh -p 1472 -4 -P '
[1489655900.214109] [2048.2] [pid=13954] Uncleaned macro. Running output
(51): '/usr/lib/nagios/plugins/check_ssh -p 1472 -4 -P 2.0'
[1489655900.214114] [2048.2] [pid=13954] Just finished macro. Running
output (51): '/usr/lib/nagios/plugins/check_ssh -p 1472 -4 -P 2.0'
[1489655900.214123] [2048.2] [pid=13954] Not currently in macro. Running
output (55): '/usr/lib/nagios/plugins/check_ssh -p 1472 -4 -P 2.0 -t '
[1489655900.214161] [2048.2] [pid=13954] Uncleaned macro. Running output
(57): '/usr/lib/nagios/plugins/check_ssh -p 1472 -4 -P 2.0 -t 30'
[1489655900.214175] [2048.2] [pid=13954] Just finished macro. Running
output (57): '/usr/lib/nagios/plugins/check_ssh -p 1472 -4 -P 2.0 -t 30'
[1489655900.214200] [2048.2] [pid=13954] Not currently in macro. Running
output (59): '/usr/lib/nagios/plugins/check_ssh -p 1472 -4 -P 2.0 -t 30 ''
[1489655900.214263] [2048.2] [pid=13954] Uncleaned macro. Running output
(68): '/usr/lib/nagios/plugins/check_ssh -p 1472 -4 -P 2.0 -t 30
'127.0.0.1'
[1489655900.214276] [2048.2] [pid=13954] Just finished macro. Running
output (68): '/usr/lib/nagios/plugins/check_ssh -p 1472 -4 -P 2.0 -t 30
'127.0.0.1'
[1489655900.214299] [2048.2] [pid=13954] Not currently in macro. Running
output (69): '/usr/lib/nagios/plugins/check_ssh -p 1472 -4 -P 2.0 -t 30
'127.0.0.1''
[1489655900.214310] [2048.1] [pid=13954] Done. Final output:
'/usr/lib/nagios/plugins/check_ssh -p 1472 -4 -P 2.0 -t 30 '127.0.0.1''
```

It is clear how Nagios builds up the command line piece by piece, so we can understand how it parses all our definitions and how it allocates the value we passed through the service definition itself. If we take the last row, copy and paste the command line of the final output, and execute it on the server, we are monitoring the service onto this:

```
/usr/lib/nagios/plugins/check_ssh -p 1472 -4 -P 2.0 -t 30 '127.0.0.1'
SSH OK - OpenSSH_6.7p1 Debian-5+deb8u3 (protocol 2.0) |
time=0.015731s;;;0.000000;30.000000
```

We get the service checked, a status (**OK**), and performance data as well:

	Service State Information	
Current Status:	OK (for 0d 0h 7m 51s)	
Status Information:	SSH OK - OpenSSH_6.7p1 Debian-5+deb8u3 (protocol 2.0)	
Performance Data:	time=0.011270s;;;0.000000;30.000000	
Current Attempt:	1/4 (HARD state)	
Last Check Time:	2017-03-16 05:23:20	
Check Type:	ACTIVE	
Check Latency / Duration:	0.174 / 0.017 seconds	
Next Scheduled Check:	2017-03-16 05:28:20	
Last State Change:	2017-03-16 05:18:20	
Last Notification:	N/A (notification 0)	
Is This Service Flapping?	NO (11.71% state change)	
In Scheduled Downtime?	NO	
Last Update:	2017-03-16 05:26:10 (0d 0h 0m 1s ago)	
Active Checks:	ENABLED	
Passive Checks:	ENABLED	
Obsessing:	ENABLED	
Notifications:	ENABLED	
Event Handler:	ENABLED	
Flap Detection:	ENABLED	

Our SSH service check now works and we have performance data too.

Performance data is a useful bit of information that can give you some ready-made projections on service running pattern, once you plot it on a chart. With such data and charts we can do this:

- **Adopt a service capacity management strategy**: Since we can easily forecast the consumption curve for a service, we can predict when it will be time to upgrade the hardware needed to provision it.
- **Find out usage patterns**: A service can be used in a uneven pattern. For example, a company mail server is most used during office hours and less during the night or weekends; disk space for a data warehouse server is used more during the data consolidation batches than during other moments. So, a service that appears adequate while you are checking it can be under-equipped in other moments: a graph will show you how the usage curve moves over time.
- **Find failures at a glance**: Watching at the gaps into the graph, you can easily spot service interruptions, and selecting the piece of graph you want to inspect can be exploded in detail.
- **Create fancy reports for management**: Seems a joke but busy management prefers to have a comprehensive glance at services than pages and pages of numeric data.

So, let's quickly see how to install one of this graphing tools. Since this is not a book on Nagios, we will not go into much detail, but we are going to see only what is needed to enable this third-party service and have our plugin performance data graphed.

Let's start editing the /etc/nagios3/nagios.cfg file.

Look for the following snippets of configuration and modify them so the final result will be this:

```
process_performance_data=1
host_perfdata_command=process-host-perfdata
service_perfdata_command=process-service-perfdata
```

We enabled the performance processing data and defined the name of the commands, which will deal with them; the next logical step is to define the commands we just pointed out. Edit the /etc/nagios3/commands.cfg file and add the following snippet:

```
# 'process-host-perfdata' command definition
define command{
command_name process-host-perfdata
command_line /usr/bin/perl /usr/lib/pnp4nagios/libexec/process_perfdata.pl -d HOSTPERFDATA
}
# 'process-service-perfdata' command definition
define command{
command_name process-service-perfdata
command_line /usr/bin/perl /usr/lib/pnp4nagios/libexec/process_perfdata.pl
}
```

We are working on a Debian installation, so the paths and file names may differ when using some other distribution or installing from sources.

Comment out any pre-existing snippets sporting `command_name process-host-perfdata` and `command_name process-service-perfdata`.

We will use the new ones, as the old ones are useless for our purposes, so again comment them out. Now that we have the command in place and the data will be processed as intended, we have to tell Nagios how to trigger the chart visualization. So, time to edit `/etc/nagios3/conf.d/services_nagios2.cfg` and modify the previously edited ssh service check configuration so that now it appears as this:

```
# check that ssh services are running
define service {
hostgroup_name ssh-servers
service_description SSH
check_command check_ssh_arguments!1967!4!2.0!30
action_url /pnp4nagios/index.php/graph?host=$HOSTNAME$&srv=$SERVICEDESC$
use generic-service
notification_interval 0 ; set > 0 if you want to be renotified
}
```

We added an action URL configuration line so that Nagios will draw a small clickable icon close to the service name. So, let's restart Nagios and go to the service page just to find out something new:

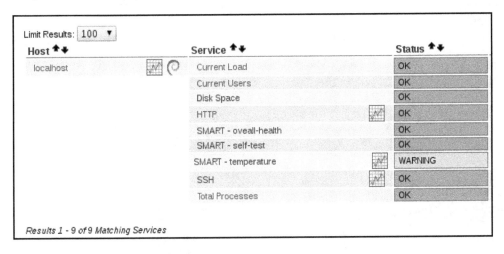

Adding the action_url string to any service configurations will make this new icon appear

[259]

Plug into the Real World

The icon is clickable, so we just click it and the result is similar to the one in the next screenshot:

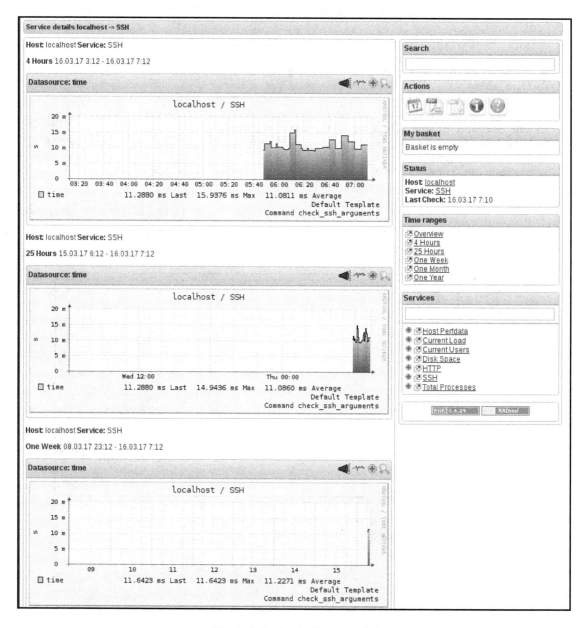

SSH service check performance data are now graphed

From now on, our performance data will be graphed, so our Nagios environment is ready to host our first Nagios plugin.

Our first Nagios plugin

It's time now to start working to our first Nagios plugin, and it does not really matter what we are going check here, since what we are interested in is how to deal with the exchange between Nagios and the plugin, more than how and what we are going to monitor. Once we are done with the script, we will be able to reuse its framework to create whatever script we want, so let's start.

Our project involves checking the status of the local disk using the **Self-Monitoring, Analysis, and Reporting Technology (S.M.A.R.T.)**, which we can think of as a system embedded in most hard disks and solid state disks, whose task is to anticipate and prevent issues and failures. So, a plugin able to query the S.M.A.R.T. system can be used to trap some forthcoming failures, notify the user, and even take advantage of the response mechanism in Nagios to trigger some scripts or programs, for example copying all the data from the soon to fail disk to somewhere else before it get lost.

Our first step in this project will be installing the smartmontools package in our distribution. In Debian and Ubuntu, the package is called smartmontools; it can be different in other distribution. What we are looking for is a package holding the smartctl utility.

This is the program our plugin will rely on, and it is the actual utility querying the for the disk information, so our first step will be to find which disks are attached to our system:

```
zarrelli:~$ lsblk -d
sda  8:0  0  119.2G  0 disk
sr0  11:0  1  1024M  0 rom
```

Here we are; our system has one disk and its name is sda. If we want to find out something more about our disk, we can install hwinfo and run it as root:

```
root:~$ hwinfo --disk
27: IDE 00.0: 10600 Disk
  [Created at block.245]
  Unique ID: 3OOL.eNwxL8uda61
  Parent ID: w7Y8.FuT6qrC8mT0
  SysFS ID: /class/block/sda
  SysFS BusID: 0:0:0:0
  SysFS Device Link:
  /devices/pci0000:00/0000:00:1f.2/ata1/host0/target0:0:0/0:0:0:0
```

```
Hardware Class: disk
Model: "TS128GSSD720"
Device: "TS128GSSD720"
Revision: "2"
Serial ID: "REDACTED"
Driver: "ahci", "sd"
Driver Modules: "ahci"
Device File: /dev/sda
Device Files: /dev/sda, /dev/disk/by-id/ata-TS128GSSD720_REDACTED
Device Number: block 8:0-8:15
BIOS id: 0x80
Geometry (Logical): CHS 15566/255/63
Size: 250069680 sectors a 512 bytes
Capacity: 119 GB (128035676160 bytes)
Config Status: cfg=new, avail=yes, need=no, active=unknown
Attached to: #20 (SATA controller)
```

Now that we have been introduced to our disk, we have to see if it is polite enough to answer our S.M.A.R.T requests:

```
root:~$ smartctl --all /dev/sda
smartctl 6.4 2014-10-07 r4002 [x86_64-linux-3.16.0-4-amd64] (local build)
Copyright (C) 2002-14, Bruce Allen, Christian Franke, www.smartmontools.org

=== START OF INFORMATION SECTION ===
Model Family:     SandForce Driven SSDs
Device Model:     TS128GSSD720
Serial Number:    REDACTED
LU WWN Device Id: 0 023280 000000000
Firmware Version: 5.0.2
User Capacity:    128,035,676,160 bytes [128 GB]
Sector Size:      512 bytes logical/physical
Rotation Rate:    Solid State Device
Device is:        In smartctl database [for details use: -P show]
ATA Version is:   ATA8-ACS, ACS-2 T13/2015-D revision 3
SATA Version is:  SATA 3.0, 6.0 Gb/s (current: 3.0 Gb/s)
Local Time is:    Fri Mar 17 16:34:30 2017 GMT
SMART support is: Available - device has SMART capability.
SMART support is: Enabled

=== START OF READ SMART DATA SECTION ===
SMART overall-health self-assessment test result: PASSED

General SMART Values:
...
Self-test execution status: (0) The previous self-test routine completed
                                without error or no self-test has ever been run.
...
```

```
SMART Attributes Data Structure revision number: 10
Vendor Specific SMART Attributes with Thresholds:
ID# ATTRIBUTE_NAME FLAG VALUE WORST THRESH TYPE UPDATED WHEN_FAILED
RAW_VALUE
...
SMART Error Log not supported

SMART Self-test Log not supported

SMART Selective self-test log data structure revision number 1
SPAN MIN_LBA MAX_LBA CURRENT_TEST_STATUS
...
Selective self-test flags (0x0):
After scanning selected spans, do NOT read-scan remainder of disk.
If Selective self-test is pending on power-up, resume after 0 minute delay.
```

That is a lot of information taken from you hard disk and, bottom line, most of it is useless to you. For the sake of our little project, we will take just a little information into account and this is here:

```
SMART overall-health self-assessment test result: PASSED
194 Temperature_Celsius 0x0022 036 060 000 Old_age Always - 36 (Min/Max
12/60)
Self-test execution status: ( 0) The previous self-test routine completed
```

So, our plugin will take just these three pieces of information into account with three different thresholds:

Control	OK	WARNING	CRITICAL
SMART overall-health self-assessment test result	PASSED		!CRITICAL
Temperature	40:	@41:49	:50
Self-test execution status	0		!0

We start planning our script. For the `overall-health`, we have an OK value, but no **WARNING** since whatever value we have different from `PASSED` means to us a critical situation. For the temperature, we can adjust the threshold to our working environment. Usually a value up to 40 degrees Celsius is considered optimal. From 41 to 50 is deemed acceptable, meaning it can cause some damage to the disk in the long run, so we are in a **WARNING** condition--not yet lethal, but we must keep an eye on it.

Everything from 50 Celsius and above is considered extremely dangerous to the health of your disk, so we shall trigger a CRITICAL condition and have someone to react as soon as possible. `Self-test execution status` tells us if the last self test on the drive was successful or completed with errors, and so anything other than 0 (successful) will trigger a critical condition.

We identified the information that will trigger the status in Nagios; we planned our threshold, now before actually writing the plugin we need to find a way to reliably collect the data that will be evaluated against the threshold. Here some regular expressions will come in handy, so let's start with the overall health, calling the `smartctl` utility with a filter:

```
root:~$ smartctl --all /dev/sda | grep -i overall-health | awk '{print $6}'
PASSED
```

This simple one liner gets the full output from `smartctl`, then pipes it to the input of `grep`, which selects and outputs only the line containing the words `overall-health`. The output is finally passed to `awk`, which takes the input and divides it into columns, each field separated by blanks, and then prints out the sixth field, which shows `PASSED`. Then something like this would trap the result of the overall check:

```
root:~$ H_CHECK=$(smartctl --all /dev/sda | grep -i overall-health | awk '{print $6}')
```

In fact, we can double-check this with the following line:

```
root:~$ H_CHECK=$(smartctl --all /dev/sda | grep overall-health | awk '{print $6}') ; echo $H_CHECK
PASSED
```

That is, the command substitution got the output of the whole command line into the `H_CHECK` variable, and we could print it too.

One recommendation here. When it comes to variables, you can use whatever notation you want, it is up to you, but bear in mind some rules of thumb:

- **Keep the variable name short and meaningful**: A variable name like `THIS_IS_THE.OVER-ALL.RESULT` will clutter your code, so `H_HEALTH` is compact and meaningful
- **Use lower, capital, or camelcase like** `OverAllHealth`**, but be consistent with your choice**: Stick to whatever you chose throughout your script, so it will be easier to identify variables in your code
- **Do not use keywords, utility of built-in names, or anything reserved for your variable names**: It will make your script unreliable

Now it is time to get the value of the temperature in our disk:

```
root:~$ smartctl --all /dev/sda | grep -i Temperature | awk '{print $10}'
35
```

So, let's get this into a variable:

```
root:~$ T_CHECK=$(smartctl --all /dev/sda | grep -i Temperature | awk '{print $10}') ; echo $T_CHECK
35
```

Finally, we have to check for `Self-test execution status`:

```
root:~$ smartctl --all /dev/sda | grep -i "Self-test execution status" | awk '{print $5}' | tr -d ")"
```

And trap the resulting value in a variable:

```
S_CHECK=$(smartctl --all /dev/sda | grep -i "Self-test execution status" | awk '{print $5}' | tr -d ")") ; echo $S_CHECK
0
```

Now that we have a way to gather the information we want, it is time to put some boundaries on our investigations. What if the disk does not exist? What if it does not support S.M.A.R.T.? And our script will need to call `smartctl` as root, so we will get advantage of `sudo` to ease the process. So, let's start with the first lines of the script, which holds the sha-bang, license, author, and first variables. Remember to change the code to whatever suits you:

```
#!/bin/bash
# License: GPL
#
# Author: Giorgio Zarrelli <zarrelli@linux.it>
#
# This program is free software; you can redistribute it and/or modify
# it under the terms of the GNU General Public License version 2 as
# published by the Free Software Foundation.
#
# This program is distributed in the hope that it will be useful,
# but WITHOUT ANY WARRANTY; without even the implied warranty of
# MERCHANTABILITY or FITNESS FOR A PARTICULAR PURPOSE.  See the
# GNU General Public License for more details.
#
# You should have received a copy of the GNU General Public License
# along with this program. If not, see <http://www.gnu.org/licenses/>.
#
```

This is the sha-bang and a licence with author, nothing special, so let's move on:

```
SMARTCTL="/usr/sbin/smartctl"
```

Since the path for each utility we use the command substitution with which: this latter will give us back the path to the utility. The only drawback is that it will give no path if the utility is not in the $PATH environment of the user, but this is not a big deal except for smartctl, which is not in $PATH ; we just give the full path manually. We do not check echo command, since it is a built-in:

```
# Nagios return codes
STATE_OK=0
STATE_WARNING=1
STATE_CRITICAL=2
STATE_UNKNOWN=3
```

Who remembers the correct status codes returned by a Nagios plugin? Better have them stored in some handy variables:

```
# Default WARNING and CRITICAL values
WARNING_THRESHOLD=${WARNING_THRESHOLD:=41}
CRITICAL_THRESHOLD=${CRITICAL_THRESHOLD:=50}
```

Now, a bit of a caution. If the script does not receive a value for the **WARNING** and **CRITICAL** thresholds, it will be assigned automatically from a predefined value.

Now that we have some headings in place, let's check if our utilities are correctly pointed to by the variables:

```
# Check if we have all the system tools we need
path_exists()
{
for i in "$@"
do
if [ -e "$i" ];
then
echo "$i is a valid path"
else
echo "$i is not reachable, is this the correct path?"
exit 1
fi
done
}
path_exists "$SMARTCTL"
```

This is the first function of our script, and its job is quite straightforward: it checks if the path pointed by #SMARTCTL leads to a file; if not, it prints a **WARNING** message and exits with an error. In our prototype, we print a message even if the path is valid, but in the final stage, we will put a debug condition to activate or deactivate this kind of extra message, since Nagios does not accept such a message. We will also have a debug option that will make visible the inner computation of our script, if needed. Let's test what's done so far, making the script executable and running:

```
zarrelli:~$ ./check_my_smart.sh
/bin/echo is a valid path
/usr/sbin/smartctl is a valid path
```

Now let's check adding two fake variables to the script:

```
TEST1=""
TEST2="/blah/blah"
```

Now let's check again:

```
path_exists "$SMARTCTL" "TEST1" "TEST2"
```

And then run the script again:

```
zarrelli:~$ ./check_my_smart.sh
/bin/echo is a valid path
/usr/sbin/smartctl is a valid path
TEST1 is not reachable, is this the correct path?
```

The script exits at the first variable that does not hold a correct path to a file, so let's delete it, remove it from the function, and run the script again:

```
zarrelli:~$ ./check_my_smart.sh ; echo $?
/bin/echo is a valid path
/usr/sbin/smartctl is a valid path
TEST2 is not reachable, is this the correct path?
1
```

Again, the script exits at the first variable met that does not hold a path to a file with an error code; and we printed it on the standard out. This behavior suits us since we want the script to stop its execution if something prevents it from running correctly, and we want meaningful advice, so we can amend it using the hints it provides. We do not need fake variables anymore, so let's clear them out.

Next, check whether the disk we are inspecting really exists, so let's add some more stuff to our script. First, a variable to hold the path to the disk we want to monitor:

```
# Disk to check
DISK=${DISK:="/dev/sda"}
```

Then, let's check if the path we just specified leads to a real block device:

```
# Check for the path to bring us to a block device with SMART capability
disk_exists()
{
if [ -b "$DISK" ]
then
echo "$DISK is a block device"
else
echo "$DISK does not point a block device"
fi
}
```

A simple file test on the path tells us whether this is a block device or not. Is it enough just to know if a path leads to a block device? No, because a disk is a block device, but a block device is not necessarily a disk, it can be a tape drive for instance. Anyway, we do not need a specific test looking for a disk, since the next function will check S.M.A.R.T. capabilities for the device. Only a S.M.A.R.T.-enabled hard disk will pass this test, and no other kinds of block device have this capability, so here we will sort out which is which. Before proceeding, let's write a verbosity switch for our functions so that we will be able to print informative messages on `stdout`. Let's start creating a variable, which will hold the status value for the verbosity switch:

```
# Enable verbose; 0 for disabled, 1 for enabled
VERB=${VERB:=1}
```

And now, let's rewrite the `path_exists` function:

```
path_exists()
{
for i in "$@"
do
if [ -e "$i" ];
then
(( VERB )) && echo "$i is a valid path"
:
else
if (( VERB ));
then
echo "$i is not reachable, is this the correct path?"
exit 1
```

```
    fi
  fi
done
}
```

Well, time to test the script:

```
zarrelli:~$ ./check_my_smart.sh
/bin/echo is a valid path
/usr/sbin/smartctl is a valid path
/dev/sda is a block device
```

All the messages are printed out, but what happens if we change the value of verbosity to 0 like VERB=${VERB:=0}?

Let's call the script again:

```
zarrelli:~$ ./check_my_smart.sh
/dev/sda is a block device
```

All the messages from the path_exists function are now silenced. How did we do it? Simply using the the arithmetic (( )) operator, which returns true as exit status if it evaluates to a non-zero value. We used two different ways to manage the verbosity:

```
(( VERB )) && echo "$i is a valid path"
```

This compact notation has a smaller impact on the flow of our script and is prefered when we have to execute a short list of commands. In this case, if $VERB evaluates to not zero, a simple echo is executed, so this notation fits the case. When we have to execute a longer list of commands, we can choose a more readable notation:

```
if (( VERB ));
then
echo "$i is not reachable, is this the correct path?"
command_2
command_n
fi
```

In this case, we can append more commands under the echo, and they all will be executed if $VERB evaluates to a non-zero value: cascading more commands on a list will make the code more readable and easy to maintain. But, well, the second verbose switch is not really useful because that part of the code traps an issue and comes into play when the path does not point to a file, and we always want to see an error message when we have an issue, regardless of the verbosity.

Plug into the Real World

So, clear it out, as it was just an example:

```
if (( VERB ));
then
echo "$i is not reachable, is this the correct path?"
fi
```

Now, let's add the verbosity switch to the `disk_exists` function:

```
disk_exists()
{
if [ -b "$DISK" ]
then
(( VERB )) && echo "$DISK is a block device"
:

else
echo "$DISK does not point a block device"
exit 1
fi
}
```

Notice (:) in the code. It is a placeholder for us to fill in with a S.M.A.R.T. capability checking code. As of now, if the path leads to a block device, the script does nothing (:). How do we check if a device is S.M.A.R.T. enabled? We can rely on the `smartctl` output:

```
root:~$ smartctl -a /dev/sda | grep "^SMART support is:"
SMART support is: Available - device has SMART capability.
SMART support is: Enabled
```

Great, the output of `smartctl` sports two lines, on one we have the info about whether the device has S.M.A.R.T. capability or not and the second informs us whether it is enabled or not.

Be wary while working with the output of a command: it can change upon different versions, so always check first the full output of the command itself before trying to trap some information.

Once we know where to look, it is just a simple matter to trap the bits of information we want:

```
root:~$ SMART=$(smartctl -a /dev/sda | grep "^SMART support is:" | awk '{print $4}') ; echo $SMART
Available Enabled
```

Cutting the output of smartctl and grabbing the content of the fourth field only gave us the two keywords we were looking for:

```
Available
Enabled
```

Both of them must be in the output for our check to pass, so let's rewrite the first part of our script:

```
# Retrieve the full path to the system utilities
AWK=$(which awk)
ECHO=$(which echo)
GREP=$(which grep)
SMARTCTL="/usr/sbin/smartctl"

# AWK field to print
A_FIELD='{print $4}'
```

We will make use of awk and grep, so we added them to a couple of handy variables. Notice that we are parsing the output of the utility (smartctl) and this can change in the future releases of the program, so we store in variables the fields we are working on. This way, if the output-related keywords change, we will modify them just once in our script. Now, just before the disk_exists function, we create a new code snippet:

```
smart_enabled()
{
  SMART=($($SMARTCTL -a "$1" | "$GREP" "$IS_SMART" | "$AWK" "$A_FIELD"))
}
```

We are just putting in a function that we did on the command line, but now, we store the output into an array. We start with simple constructs and check whether they work correctly. Once we are confident, we move to more complex solutions. Now, we must call the function with an argument; let's do it at the end of the script:

```
path_exists "$SMARTCTL"
disk_exists "$DISK"
smart_enabled "$DISK"
```

So far, so good. Our script is grabbing the two keywords we were looking for. Now, we can go further and work on the keyword so that if they are not in the output of smartctl, our script will exit with an error; and we start adding something at the beginning of our script:

```
# SMART CAPABILITY INDICATOR
IS_SMART="^SMART support is:"
SMART_IND=(Available Enabled)
```

The SMART_IND array contains the keyword we need to trap to be sure we have a drive with S.M.A.R.T. capabilities, so now we have to craft our function to take an advantage of this new array:

```
smart_enabled()
{
SMART=($($SMARTCTL -a "$1" | "$GREP" "$IS_SMART" | "$AWK" "$A_FIELD"))
for i in "${SMART[@]}"
do
for j in "${SMART_IND[@]}"
do
if [[ "$i" == "$j" ]];
then
(( COUNTER++ ))
fi
done
done
if (( COUNTER != ${#SMART_IND[@]} ))
then
ALT_SMART="$($SMARTCTL -a "$1" | "$GREP" "$ALT_IS_SMART")"           if !
[[ -z $ALT_SMART ]]
then
(( VERB )) && echo "$DISK has SMART capability"
smart_check "$B_SEL" "$DISK"
else
(( VERB )) && echo "Check the device, it seems it does not support SMART"
(( VERB )) && echo "The counter matched: $COUNTER times"           echo
exit "$STATE_UNKNOWN"
fi
else
(( VERB )) && echo "$DISK has SMART capability"
smart_check "$B_SEL" "$DISK"
fi
}
```

So, basically we grep the output of smartctl on the IS_SMART value, then hold the results in the IS_SMART array. We have two nested loops: the outer cycles through the values of IS_SMART and the inner through the values of SMART_IND. Every time two indicators match, a counter is incremented. At the end of the loop, if the counter is not equal to the length of SMART_IND, we know that we could not match the exact number of indicators. In some cases, you will not have that nice smart support string, so we can use an alternative indicator to match, in case the first string is not shown:

```
ALT_IS_SMART="=== START OF SMART DATA SECTION ==="
```

Maybe less, maybe more, better to exit with an error and check.

Now, let's see what happens if we run this script on a system with a disk, which does not support SMART:

```
root:~$ ./check_my_smart.sh
/bin/echo is a valid path
/usr/sbin/smartctl is a valid path
/dev/sda is a block device
Check the device, it seems it does not support SMART
The counter matched: 0 times
```

Fair enough, when the script detects no SMART capabilities, it exits cleanly giving us a meaningful message. Now, since the smart check can be carried on only if there is a valid disk, we will call the `smart_enabled` function from inside the `disk_exists` function. So, let's move the `smart_enabled` function call from the bottom of our script to the `disk_exists` function:

```
disk_exists()
{
if [ -b "$DISK" ]
then
(( VERB )) && echo "$DISK is a block device"
smart_enabled "$DISK"

else
echo "$DISK does not point a block device"
exit 1
fi
}
```

To be available inside the `disk_exists` function, the `smart_enable` function must be defined beforehand.

We made a good amount of checks, now it is time to create our check function, which will deal with three different times of measurements:

- Overall health
- Temperature
- Self-test

Plug into the Real World

So, our function must accept at least three parameters:

- The type of check
- Warning threshold
- Critical threshold

Let's start with something easy, implementing just the overall-check monitoring, starting with some new variables:

```
# AWK field to print
A_FIELD='{print $4}'
H_FIELD='{print $6}'
# SMART check keywords
H_KEY="overall-health"
# SMART matches
H_MATCH="PASSED"
```

Now, just before the smart_enabled function, let's create a new function:

```
smart_check()
{
H_CHECK=$($SMARTCTL -a "$1" | "$GREP" "$H_KEY" | "$AWK" "$H_FIELD")
if [[ "$H_CHECK" == "$H_MATCH" ]];
then
echo "SMART OK: Overall-health check $H_MATCH"
exit "$STATE_OK"
else
echo "SMART CRITICAL: Overall-health check NOT $H_MATCH"
exit "$STATE_CRITICAL"
fi

}
```

Nothing really difficult, we just grep the output, put it into a variable, and see whether it matches our anchor (`PASSED`). If it does, the script exits with a `STATE_OK` value, and if not, it throws `STATE_CRITICAL`. Let's have a look, but change the verbosity to 0 beforehand:

```
root:~$ ./check_my_smart.sh
SMART OK: Overall-health check PASSED
```

This is an acceptable plugin response, and if we passed this to Nagios, it would show a green OK field on the web UI, so we reached a milestone: we have our first good plugin reply. Now, since all the errors must be trapped by Nagios, let's allocats `exit 1` with this:

```
echo "SMART UNKNOWN: Please check the plugin"
exit "$STATE_UNKNOWN"
```

So, all the previous error message must now become optional like in the `path_exists()` function:

```
path_exists()
{
for i in "$@"
do
if [ -e "$i" ];
then
(( VERB )) && echo "$i is a valid path"
disk_exists "$DISK"
else
(( VERB )) && echo "$i is not reachable, is this the correct path?"
echo "SMART UNKNOWN: Please check the plugin"
echo "SMART UNKNOWN: Please check the plugin"
exit "$STATE_UNKNOWN"
fi
done
}
```

We can see a slight change in the function; since we called `disk_exists` from inside `path_exists()`, we chained the functions so that when we have a successful outcome, we call the next function in a row.

Great, we have a function to check the `overall-health` parameter, and it also gives us a correct Nagios message and exit code; but this is one out of three possible checks, so we have to make this one element in our series. So, what should we do if we want to make this a part of a wider range of tests? Since these are three checks only, we can easily group them in a `if/then/elif/fi` construct, but let's start with a new variable:

```
# BRANCH selector
B_SEL=${B_SEL:="HEALTH"}
```

This is a branch selector; if we do not specify anything, it will take the value of `HEALTH` and trigger one of the three checks; now let's see the new code:

```
smart_check()
{
if (("$#" != 2));
then
echo
exit "$STATE_UNKNOWN"
else
if [[ "$1" == "HEALTH" ]];
then
H_CHECK=$($SMARTCTL -a "$2" | "$GREP" "$H_KEY" | "$AWK" "$H_FIELD")      if
[[ "$H_CHECK" == "$H_MATCH" ]];
```

```
then
    echo "SMART OK: Overall-health check $H_MATCH"
    exit "$STATE_OK"
else
    echo "SMART CRITICAL: Overall-health check NOT $H_MATCH"
    exit "$STATE_CRITICAL"
fi
elif [[ "$1" == "TEMPERATURE" ]];
then
    if (( $(echo "scale=2; "$WARNING_THRESHOLD" >= "$CRITICAL_THRESHOLD"" | $BC ) ));
    then
        echo "SMART UNKNOWN: The value of WARNING ($WARNING_THRESHOLD) must be lower than CRITICAL ($CRITICAL_THRESHOLD)"      exit "$STATE_UNKNOWN"
    else
        T_CHECK=$($SMARTCTL -a "$2" | "$GREP" "$T_KEY" | "$AWK" "$T_FIELD")    if ! [[ "$T_CHECK" = *[[:digit:]]* ]];
        then
            echo "SMART UNKNOWN: The $T_KEY check is not available on $DISK"
            exit "$STATE_UNKNOWN"
        fi
        if (( T_CHECK < WARNING_THRESHOLD ));
        then
            echo "SMART OK: Temperature is $T_CHECK | TEMP=$T_CHECK"
            exit "$STATE_OK"
        elif (( T_CHECK < CRITICAL_THRESHOLD ));
        then
            echo "SMART WARNING: Temperature is $T_CHECK | TEMP=$T_CHECK"
            exit "$STATE_WARNING"
        else
            echo "SMART CRITICAL: Temperature is $T_CHECK | TEMP=$T_CHECK"
            exit "$STATE_CRITICAL"
        fi
    fi
elif [[ "$1" == "SELFCHECK" ]];
then
    S_CHECK=$($SMARTCTL -a "$2" | "$GREP" "$S_KEY" | "$AWK" "$S_FIELD" | "$TR" -d "$S_DEL")
    if ! [[ "$S_CHECK" = *[[:digit:]]* ]];                          then
        echo "SMART UNKNOWN: The $S_KEY check is not available on $DISK"
        exit "$STATE_UNKNOWN"
    fi
    if (( S_CHECK == S_MATCH ));
    then
        echo "SMART OK: Overall-health check $S_MATCH"
        exit "$STATE_OK"
    else
```

```
        echo "SMART CRITICAL: Overall-health check NOT $S_MATCH"
        exit "$STATE_CRITICAL"
    fi
    else
    echo
    exit "$STATE_UNKNOWN"
    fi
fi
}
```

The new code checks for how many arguments have been passed as input, if they are not exactly two, it throws an error and exit with STATE_UNKNOWN. If we have two arguments, then it goes on checking if the first argument is a function selector and what its value. We filled in just the first function, created some placeholders for the other two, and got a catchall in case none of the acceptable values for a function selector have been entered.

We can now proceed with the self-check function, which is quite similar to the overall-health, but first some variables:

```
TR=$(which tr)
S_FIELD='{print $5}'
S_KEY="Self-test execution status"
S_MATCH=0
```

You can already figure out what these are used for; we just to have to keep in mind we are using a lot of variable to customize the commands as much as we can, since we are working with a utility output, and this output can change from version to version. It usually stays quite the same over minor releases, but by using plenty of variable, we will be able to modify our script quickly if needed:

```
    eelif [[ "$1" == "SELFCHECK" ]];
    then
    S_CHECK=$($SMARTCTL -a "$2" | "$GREP" "$S_KEY" | "$AWK" "$S_FIELD" | "$TR"
    -d "$S_DEL")
    if ! [[ "$S_CHECK" = *[[:digit:]]* ]];
    then
    echo "SMART UNKNOWN: The $S_KEY check is not available on $DISK"
    exit "$STATE_UNKNOWN"
    fi
    if (( S_CHECK == S_MATCH ));
    then
    echo "SMART OK: Overall-health check $S_MATCH"
    exit "$STATE_OK"
    else
    echo "SMART CRITICAL: Overall-health check NOT $S_MATCH"
    exit "$STATE_CRITICAL"
    fi
```

Plug into the Real World

We filled in our placeholder. This function is similar to the first one, the only real difference is the arithmetic evaluation performed and a check on the value to match and that must be a number. Calling the function with the SELFCHECK keyword will show us this:

```
root:~$ ./check_my_smart.sh
SMART OK: Overall-health check 0
```

Great, now it is time for the last check, which is quite different from the other two, since it requires a check against some thresholds. We start with some variables as usual:

```
BC=$(which bc)
T_FIELD='{print $10}'
T_KEY="Temperature"
```

And now we use the code itself:

```
    elif [[ "$1" == "TEMPERATURE" ]];
    then
    if (( $(echo "scale=2; "$WARNING_THRESHOLD" >= "$CRITICAL_THRESHOLD"" | $BC
) ));
    then
    echo "SMART UNKNOWN: The value of WARNING ($WARNING_THRESHOLD) must be
lower than CRITICAL ($CRITICAL_THRESHOLD)"
    exit "$STATE_UNKNOWN"
    else
    T_CHECK=$($SMARTCTL -a "$2" | "$GREP" "$T_KEY" | "$AWK" "$T_FIELD")
    if ! [[ "$T_CHECK" = *[[:digit:]]* ]];
    then
    echo "SMART UNKNOWN: The $T_KEY check is not available on $DISK"
    exit "$STATE_UNKNOWN"
    fi
    if (( T_CHECK < WARNING_THRESHOLD ));
    then
    echo "SMART OK: Temperature is $T_CHECK | TEMP=$T_CHECK"
    exit "$STATE_OK"
    elif (( T_CHECK < CRITICAL_THRESHOLD ));
    then
    echo "SMART WARNING: Temperature is $T_CHECK | TEMP=$T_CHECK"
    exit "$STATE_WARNING"
    else
    echo "SMART CRITICAL: Temperature is $T_CHECK | TEMP=$T_CHECK"
    exit "$STATE_CRITICAL"
    fi
    fi
    fi                                                                      fi
```

This is a bit more complex than the other two checks. First, we check that the value of WARNING_THRESHOLD is lower than CRITICAL_THRESHOLD; and we do it using a small command line calculator and an arithmetic evaluation. Then, we check that T_CHECK holds a numeric value since we are talking about degrees Celsius (the hard disk temperature is commonly reported in Celsius). Once we are free from such hindrances, we can proceed to check the value of T_CHECK against the threshold in the following way:

```
$T_CHECK < $WARNING_THRESHOLD IS OK
$T_CHECK < $CRITICAL_THRESHOLD IS WARNING
EVERYTHING ELSE IS CRITICAL
```

Let's test the script with different values for the **WARNING** and **CRITICAL** thresholds:

```
WARNING_THRESHOLD=${WARNING_THRESHOLD:=41}
CRITICAL_THRESHOLD=${CRITICAL_THRESHOLD:=50}ro
ot:~$ ./check_my_smart.sh
SMART WARNING: Temperature is 41 | TEMP=41

WARNING_THRESHOLD=${WARNING_THRESHOLD:=45}
CRITICAL_THRESHOLD=${CRITICAL_THRESHOLD:=50}
root:~$ ./check_my_smart.sh
SMART OK: Temperature is 41 | TEMP=41

WARNING_THRESHOLD=${WARNING_THRESHOLD:=35}
CRITICAL_THRESHOLD=${CRITICAL_THRESHOLD:=40}
root:~$ ./check_my_smart.sh
SMART CRITICAL: Temperature is 41 | TEMP=41

WARNING_THRESHOLD=${WARNING_THRESHOLD:=50}
CRITICAL_THRESHOLD=${CRITICAL_THRESHOLD:=40}
root:~$ ./check_my_smart.sh
SMART UNKNOWN: The value of WARNING (50) must be lower than CRITICAL (40)
```

As we can see, our thresholds are set pretty well and the same is for the precedence of values, so we are quite fine. Notice the performance data; since this is a temperature indicator, we can later have it plotted on Nagios if we wish. The last step here is to create a command line parser to get all the required values:

```
# Print help and usage
print_help()
{
cat << HERE

MY SMART CHECK v1.0
---------------------

Please enter one or more of the following options:
```

```
-d | --disk
eg. /dev/sda
-t | --test
HEALTH
TEMPERATURE
SELFCHECK
-w | --warning
eg. -w 41
-c | --critical
eg. -c 50
HERE
}
```

We started with the print usage. In case the user does input some wrong options, we give them a hint of what to do:

```
root:~$ ./check_my_smart.sh -T ITISWRONG
Unknown argument: -T

 MY SMART CHECK v1.0
 -------------------

Please enter one or more of the following options:
-d | --disk
eg. /dev/sda
-m | --module
HEALTH
TEMPERATURE
SELFCHECK
-w | --warning
eg. -w 41
-c | --critical
eg. -c 50
```

Nice, isn't it? But how do we call that function and manage the input? Let's see:

```
# Parse parameters on the command line
while (( $# > 0 ))
do
case "$1" in
-h | --help)
print_help
exit "${STATE_OK}"
;;
-d | --disk)
shift
DISK="$1"
;;
```

```
-m | --module)
shift
B_SEL="$1"
;;
-w | --warning)
shift
WARNING_THRESHOLD="$1"
;;
-c | --critical)
shift
CRITICAL_THRESHOLD="$1"
;;
*) echo "Unknown argument: $1"
print_help
exit "$STATE_UNKNOWN"
;;
esac
shift
done
```

What do we do in this block? While the number of arguments on the command line is higher than zero, we parse the command line itself, and check the options using the case construct. Every time we match a value, we instantiate a variable and shift the command line, so we are ready to process the next option; this is our command line parser.

Now that our plugin is ready to serve our purposes, we have to copy it to the plugins directory `root:~$ cp check_my_smart.sh /usr/lib/nagios/plugins/`; now let's check the ownership and access right to it. The one shown here should suffice:

```
root:~$ cd /usr/lib/nagios/plugins/
root:~$ ls -lah check_my_smart.sh
-rwxr-xr-x 1 root root 6.2K Mar 22 09:32 check_my_smart.sh
```

Once the script is in place, we have to tell Nagios how to call it, so a command definition is needed. Let's move to the command configurations directory `cd /etc/nagios-plugins/config/` and create the `check_my_smart.cfg` file with the following content:

```
# 'check_my_smart' command definition
define command{
command_name check_my_smart
command_line /usr/lib/nagios/plugins/check_my_smart.sh -d $ARG1$ -m $ARG2$ $ARG3$ $ARG4$
}
```

We won't repeat it, but always check for the user access rights on files. If you are not confident about which rights to use, look at the similar files in the directory you are working on. But be aware of what you concede.

We are going to use `sudo` since the `smartctl` utility needs the root privileges to access disk information. The disk and module options must be given on the service configuration, but the **WARNING** and **CRITICAL** values are optional. Time to modify `/etc/sudoers` and add the following line:

```
# SMART Nagios plugin sudo
nagios ALL=(root) NOPASSWD: /usr/sbin/smartctl
```

So, the Nagios user now is able to call the `smartctl` utility as root without being asked for any passwords. This, though, requires a little change in our script:

```
SUDO=$(which sudo)
SMARTCTL="$SUDO /usr/sbin/smartctl"
```

This will enable our script to call `smartctl` as the root user. A little homework: try to trap and deal with the chance we did not enable `sudo` for the Nagios user. How would your manage this problem? Let's move on and write our services definitions in `/etc/nagios3/conf.d/localhost_nagios2.cfg`, and add the following lines:

```
# SMART - Check overall-health
define service{
use generic-service
host_name localhost
service_description SMART - oveall-health
check_command check_my_smart!/dev/sda!HEALTH
}

# SMART - Check self-test
define service{
use generic-service
host_name localhost
service_description SMART - self-test
check_command check_my_smart!/dev/sda!SELFCHECK
}

# SMART - Check temperature
define service{
use generic-service
host_name localhost
service_description SMART - temperature
action_url /pnp4nagios/index.php/graph?host=$HOSTNAME$&srv=$SERVICEDESC$
```

```
check_command check_my_smart!/dev/sda!TEMPERATURE!-w 41!-c 50
}
```

We configured three new service checks, but only one needs an `action_url`, as only the temperature check gives us some values that change over time and can be usefully graphed. Now, all that is left is to restart Nagios using `service nagios3 restart` and check whether everything is fine, as we can see in the following screenshot:

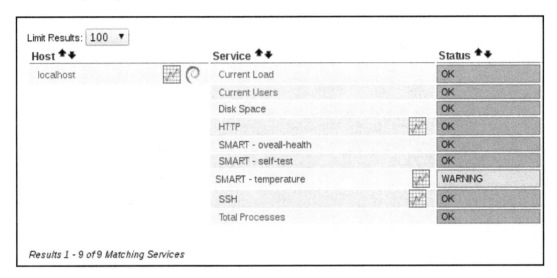

Our new three checks are online and the disk seems a bit overheated.

Plug into the Real World

Let's just check whether our temperature check is producing some performance data and it is being graphed:

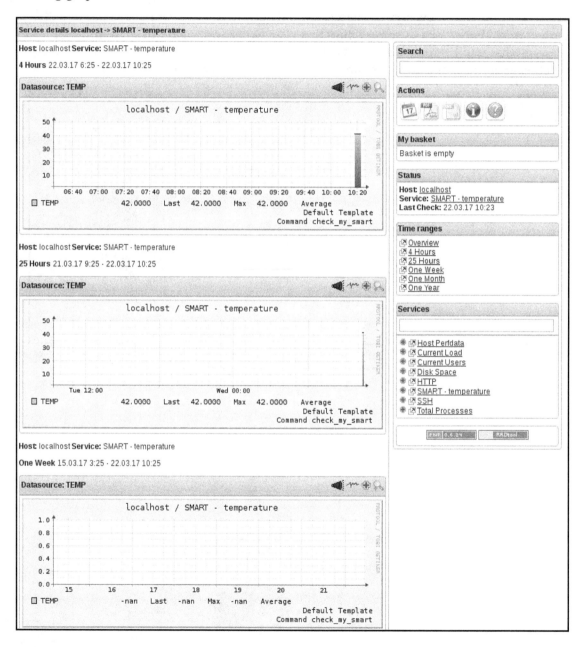

We are keeping an eye on the temperature, thanks to our new graph.

Summary

We just saw how to handle a problem in a real scenario by analyzing our goal, planning the methods and tools we needed to accomplish it, and taking care of the issues on the path to our solution. We worked on our outcome in small steps, consecutive and joined all the bits once ready, so we did not face a cumbersome whole big problem, but solved what we encountered at each step by learning how to proceed and avoid overthinking. Now, we are ready to proceed and work on something quite useful nowadays: our personal Slack poster utility.

8
We Want to Chat

In the previous chapter, we just had a dive through the planning and coding of a Nagios plugin. We studied the bits needed to understand what is a plugin, what is expected from it, and how to integrate it with the monitoring system; and this is because creating a script or program is not just the coding itself: this is the last step of a long and complex workflow.

Now, we will venture into something a bit different, creating a small client to send information to a Slack channel. This will allow us to touch on some new topics, such as JSON, and have a look at how to interact with a cloud-based service. We will not write a fully-fledged client with the capability to read and write, but just the sending bit, since Bash is not the optimal tool to build a whole interactive client. The goal here is to write a tool that we could use to send notifications to a channel so that we can, for instance, notify the members of the channel of the outcome of a task, a cronjob, and so on.

The Slack messaging service

Slack is the acronym of **Searchable Log of All Conversation and Knowledge** and it is a collaboration tool widely used by small and large teams to share information, documentation, and ideas. Slack, at a glance, offers the following:

- **Chat rooms:** Public or private, the chat rooms allow team mates to discuss any topic without interfering with other people. A channel is persistent, can have a topic, and anyone invited can take part in it.
- **Direct messages:** People can send direct messages to other people or groups so that they can have private direct conversations.
- **Integrated searches:** Everything in Slack is searchable, from the messages shared in a chat, to the files uploaded to it, and to the people we dealt with; and this is probably one of the most interesting features of this platform.

- **Calls:** Direct or group calls can be made from inside a channel or on a direct message; and this is without the need of an external application, so there is no need to leave the platform.
- **Teams:** Anyone can join a team using a URL or invitation provided by a team owner; and this is probably the most community-like feature of this tool.
- **Integration with external services:** Slack can connect to a variety of external services so to enhance its offering, from Google Drive to Dropbox, from GitHub to Zendesk, just to name a few.
- **Clients:** The platform has plenty of clients, native or via web, for many platforms such as Windows, macOS, Linux, Android, just to name some, so we do not need another client.

So we want to interact with Slack by sending messages to one channel and having them displayed nicely. The first step will be to create a new team at the URL:

https://slack.com/

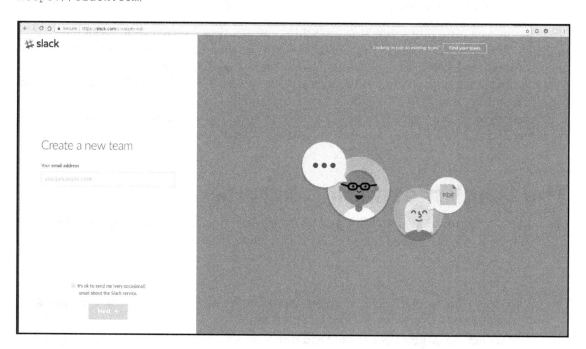

Creating a new team

In our first step, we are going to create a new team. We have to do all the usual stuff, insert an email, the confirmation code, and choose a team URL:

A team URL will gather people with shared interests, invite some friend if you are done; your team is ready to fill the ranks!

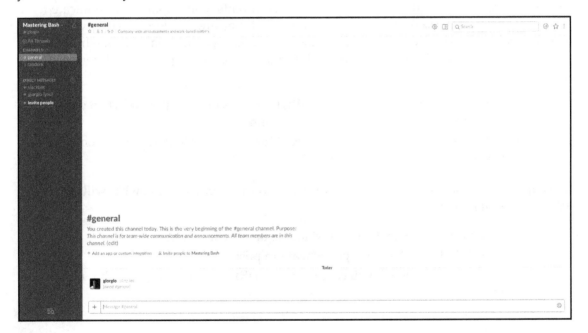

We are ready to share our messages. Once you are done creating the team space, we will have two default channels available:

```
#general
#random
```

We can use the default channel or create a new one; in our case, we will create a brand new public channel called `#test`.

There we will send there all the messages created by our script and conveyed by a WebHook. Now, we have introduced a new term, WebHook, and this is crucial to our script, since it is a method we use to interact with Slack. So, it is better for us to stop a moment and deepen the concept of WebHook for Slack

Slack WebHooks

What is a WebHook? We could define it as a method to make some web pages reactive to user input based on a simple HTTP POST method to support a user-defined HTTP callback. Still a bit obscure, isn't it? Let's put it this way: Slack has some endpoints, sensitive URLs; and when you post something through HTTP to endpoints, you actually communicate with Slack. What makes these WebHook interesting is that they are stateless, since they do not rely on a continuously open connection to the service; and you just ping Slack whenever you need to post or retrieve some pieces of information. Slack supports two different kinds of WebHooks:

- **Incoming WebHook:** This is the URL that we will be posting to when we want some messages to appear on our test channel
- **Outgoing WebHook:** This is the URL that Slack uses to notify us of some events in a channel

We will be using the Incoming WebHook for our notification script. So, what will we need? We will need the following things:

- Slack incoming WebHook linked to one of our channels.
- A JSON holding the message we want to post.
- An application, which will connect to the URL and post the JSON. It will be our script.

Chapter 8

1. Our first task will be to create a new incoming WebHook and link it to our test channel. As the administrator of the team login, we have to log in at `https://my.slack.com/services/new/incoming-webhook/`. And from the dropdown menu, we must select our test channel as shown here:

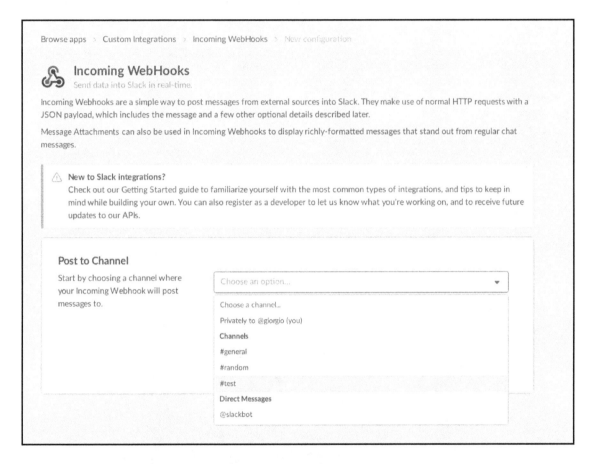

2. Select the **#test** channel from the drop-down menu.

We Want to Chat

3. Now, let's click on the **Add Incoming WebHooks Integration** button; and we are led to the Incoming WebHooks page, where we will find the URL that we have to call to send a message to our test channel.

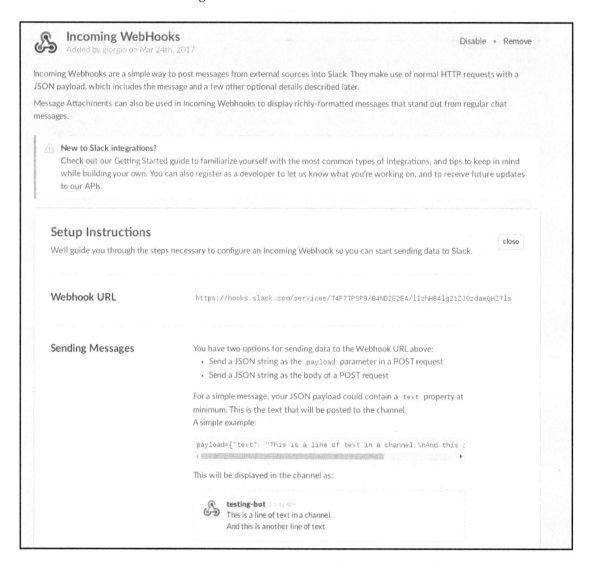

4. In the Incoming WebHooks page, you can find your newly created WebHook.

In our case, the WebHook has the following URL: `https://hooks.slack.com/services/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`.

As explained earlier, we have two options to send a message through this WebHook:

- As a JSON string in the payload parameter of a POST request
- As a JSON string in the body of a POST request

So, JSON is something crucial for our messaging system, but what exactly is a JSON?

What is a JSON?

JSON, or **JavaScript Object Notation**, is an open, standard format (ECMA-404) widely used to exchange data between applications. Created in 2007 as a subset of the JavaScript programing language, it quickly became adopted by many languages as a means to deliver data regardless of the language of the sending and receiving applications to be a neutral conveyor. We can find a JSON file modeled on two different structures.

An object composed by name: value pairs, opened and closed by a bracket with each name separated from the corresponding value by a colon and each pair separated by a comma, such as the following example:

```
{
"name" : "Janet",
"state" : "California",
"cake" : "Toffee sticky pudding"
}
```

An ordered list of values inside an array opened and closed by a square bracket and the values separated by a comma: `[ "1", "2", "3"]`.

A value in JSON can be a number, object, array, string, true, false, or null.

We Want to Chat

So, JSON will be the format that we will use to transmit our messages to the channel using the WebHook, and it will be structured in an object made of name:value pairs. The simplest message in Slack would bear a simple `"text"` keyword as the name part of the JSON and the message to deliver as its value:

```
{
    "text": "This is the first line of a message This is
             the second line."
}
```

Now that we have our first message formatted into a neat JSON, we must proceed to deliver this content to our `#test` channel.

Do you like cURLing?

One of the easiest ways to post JSON content is to use an external utility, such as a cURL, whose task is to transfer data over URLs. We have two ways to transfer data:

- Directly as a JSON in the body of an HTTP POST request, with a specific content-type header, and this is the preferred method
- As a URL-escaped JSON inside the payload parameter as part of the POST body

In the first case, we are going to use cURL with the following bits:

`-X POST`

It specifies the method to use to communicate with an HTTP server. The default method is `GET`, but here, we have to `POST` some information:

`-H 'Content-type: application/json'`

This option allows us to send extra headers to the HTTP server. In our case, we are sending a **Multipurpose Internet Mail Extensions** (**MIME**) type, informing the Slack server that it has to expect a JSON (rfc4627) application type object in the body:

`--data '{"text":"This is our first message,.n which continues on another line."}'`

The `--data` option allows us to send the JSON object in the body of the `POST` request so that it can be passed to the HTTP server to be processed:

https://hooks.slack.com/services/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

This is the final bit: the address of the WebHook that cURL will call to make its POST request. Now, we have all we need, so it's just a matter of creating our command line. Install it if you do not have it already; the cURL utility and issue the following command on a single line:

```
cURL -X POST -H 'Content-type: application/json' --data
'{
"text":"This is a line of text.nAnd this is another one.
"}'
https://hooks.slack.com/services/T4P7TPSP9/B4ND2E2E4/
lIzhH84lg21ZJ0zdaeQHZ7ls
```

And here is our first message to the channel:

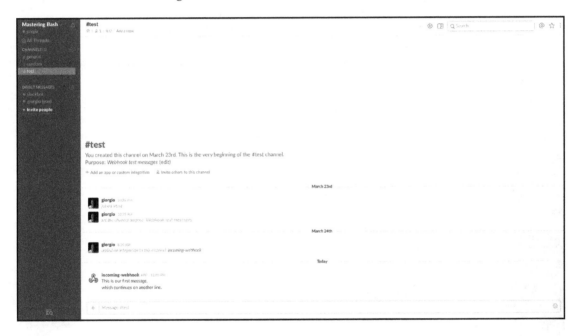

A simple cURL gave us the first message to the channel.

The second way to send a message with cURL is to have its URL encoded inside the payload parameter of the POST body. Your URL will become a messy string filled by a bunch of percentage characters, but it is more of a traditional way, so you could feel more confident using it.
To send a JSON file inside the payload parameter, we need the following bits:

```
-X POST
```

We Want to Chat

This specifies the method to use to communicate with an HTTP server. The default method is `GET`, but here, we have to `POST` some information:

```
--data-URLencode 'payload={"text":"This is our second message."}'
```

This URL encodes our JSON, so it can be posted. The structure of the data part is a bit different because to be CGI compliant; it must begin with a keyword:

```
https://hooks.slack.com/services/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
```

Finally, we have the URL, which is the same as for the first method. Let's assemble our command line and try it out:

```
cURL -X POST --data-URL
encode 'payload={"text":"This is our second message."}'
https://hooks.slack.com/services/T4P7TPSP9/B4ND2E2E4/lI
zhH84lg21ZJ0zdaeQHZ7ls
```

Creating a new team.

That's it, our second message is being displayed on the channel. It is still in a basic form without any whistles and bells, but it does its job and helps us in understanding how to interact with the Slack server. Anyway, basic is fine, but why not try to embellish our conversations with some special effects?

Formatting our messages

We can add some style to our messages, from text properties to links and buttons, so that they can become something more than a simple bunch of text. Actually, modifying by hand all the payloads to check what combinations of attributes best suits your messages can be too much hassle, but Slack helps us with an online *Message Builder* that lets you customize and preview your messages without the need to post it anywhere. Just head to your browser at `https://api.slack.com/docs/messages/builder`, and let's start having fun:

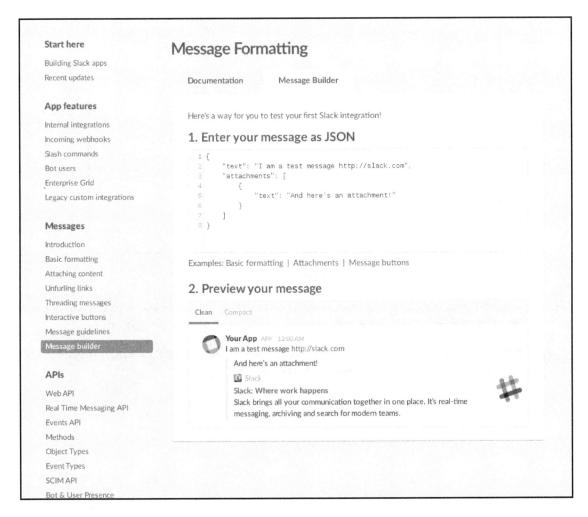

We Want to Chat

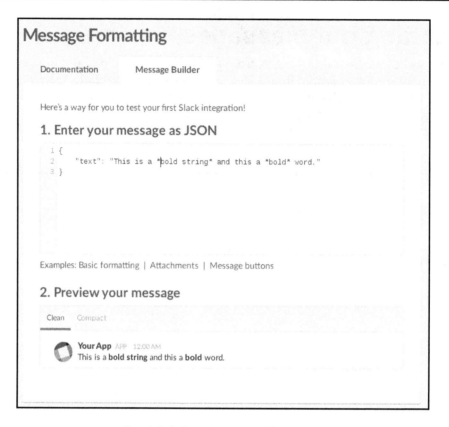

The payload editor lets you try your message before sending it.

Inside the upper box, we can forge our payload as we wish and preview it in the lower box, so let's see some of the more interesting bits that we can add to our messages:

- **Bold:** Well, this is a classic. You can turn any strings of text in bold simply by wrapping it between two asterisks, try out this payload:

```
{
    "text": "This is a *bold string* and this a *bold* word"
}
```

[298]

Here is how our bold lines appear in the **Message Builder**.

- **Italics:** This stresses the importance of a word or a sentence, and you can get this effect simply by wrapping a string between the two underlines:

    ```
    {
        "text": "This is a _string in italics_."
    }
    ```

- **Code:** If you are writing some text that belongs to a command line or a some kind of code, you can enclose it between to back tickles and have it outstanding:

  ```
  {
      "text": "We can use the code attribute to write some code
               like:n`x=y+1`"
  }
  ```

  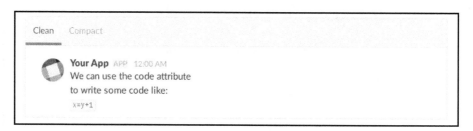

  Here is how your code is shown in the channel.

- **Code block:** But how do you enclose a `multi line` code block? Let's see:

  ```
  {
      "text": "We can use the block code attribute to write some
               multi line code like:n```y=1nx=y+1nx=2```"
  }
  ```

  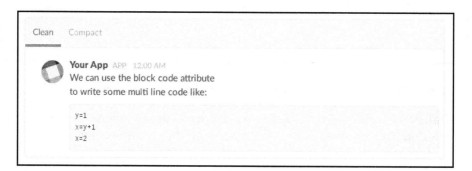

  A `multi line` code block appears a little different compare to a single line code string.

- **URL linking:** You can insert clickable links in a message by enclosing the URL in <>. You can use two different ways to insert a link:
  - Just put the link itself surrounded by <>: `<http://www.packtpub.com>`

- Add to the previous syntax `"|linked"` to make the linked string referring to the URL called `<http://www.zarrelli.org|this>"`

So, our payload with both syntaxes could well be this:

```
{
    "text": "This is a web link <http://www.packtpub.com> and
        <http://www.zarrelli.org|this too>"
}
```

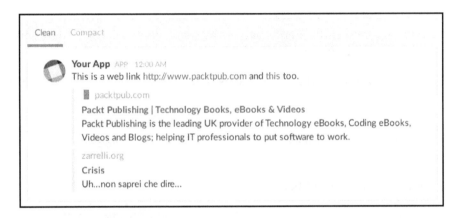

We have two different ways to link a URL:

- **Email address linking:** In a way similar to URL linking, just surround the email link and a `"|linked"` by <>:

```
{
    "text": "Just email the <mail-
to:giorgio.zarrelli@gmail.com|author>."
}
```

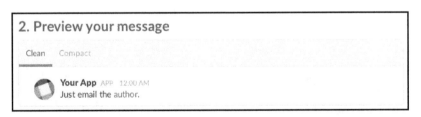

Click on the highlighted word, and your email client will fire up with the email address that is filled in as the recipient.

We Want to Chat

- **Date:** We can format a date in your message using a Unix epoch timestamp and some selector to modify its appearance. We can optionally link a URL, but we always have to provide some fallback text to be displayed to older clients in case the time token conversion fails. The keyword to you in this case is `<!date>`, but with a tad more complex syntax:

    ```
    {
        "text": "<!date^unix_timestamp^ Some optional text
    {date_selector}|Fallback text>"
    }
    ```

    We have a bunch of different selectors available to modify how dates and times will appear in the channel:

- `{date}`: Your date will appear as classic *March 26th*, so try out the following payload:

    ```
    {
        "text": "<!date^1490531695^ {date}|Fallback>"
    }
    ```

    So, our cURL line would be:

    ```
    cURL -X POST -H 'Content-type: application/json' --data
    '{"
    text":
    "<!date^1490531695^ {date}|Fallback>"
    }' https://hooks.slack.com/services/T4P7TPSP9/B4ND2E2E4/
    lIzhH84lg21ZJ
    OzdaeQHZ7ls
    ```

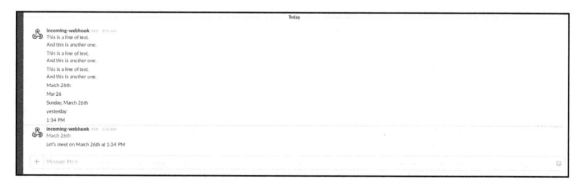

[302]

Here is how our messages will appear in the channel:

- `{date_short}`: As the name states, this is an even more compact `Mar 26`
- `{date_long}`: This gives you an extended date called `Sunday, March 26th`
- `{date_pretty}`: This displays the date as `{date}`, but it uses `"yesterday,` `"today"` or `"tomorrow"` when it fits
- `{date_short_pretty}`: This displays the date as `{date_short}`, but it uses `"yesterday,` `"today"`, or `"tomorrow"` when it fits
- `{date_long_pretty}`: This displays the date as `{date_long}`, but it uses `"yesterday,` `"today"`, or `"tomorrow"` when it fits
- `{time}`: This displays the time in a 12-hour format, and in our example, it is `1:34 PM`; but if the client is set on a 24-hour format, it would be displayed as `13:34`
- `{time_secs}`: This displays the time to the seconds bit in a 12-hour format `1:34:55 PM`; but if the client is set on a 24-hour format, it would be displayed as `13:34:55`

We can also add a URL to the date so that when you click on the date/time, you will be brought the website pointed as follows:

```
{
    "text": "<!date^1490531695^{date}^http://www.packtpub.com|Fallback>"
}
```

Obviously, you can mix the formatter to have a more meaningful message as follows:

```
{
    "text": "<!date^1490531695^Let's meet on {date} at {time}|Meeting info>"
}
```

And the complete cURL line would be as follows:

```
cURL -X POST -H 'Content-type: application/json' --data '{"text":
"<!date^1490531695^Let's meet on {date} at {time}|Meeting info>"}'
https://hooks.slack.com/services/T4P7TPSP9/B4ND2E2E4/lIzhH84lg21ZJ
0zdaeQHZ7ls
```

We Want to Chat

Apart from the dates, we can use some special commands in your messages to get our audience to head up and pay attention to us:

- `<!here>`: This will notify all our team members in the channel who are active:

    ```
    {
      "text":
    "<!here><!date^1490531695^{date}^http://www.packtpub.com|Fallback>"
    }
    ```

- `<!channel>`: This will notify all our team members in the channel regardless of their status. A notify icon will appear close to the channel name.
- `<!group>`: This is a synonym of `<!channel>` and both can be used inside a channel or a group.
- `<!everyone>`: This notifies all of our team members. This can be used in the team wide channel, which is usually called **#general**.

Using one of the notification tags will cause a notification icon to appear closer to the channel name.

If we want to have the attention of our audience, we can make use of the classical tools that are popular in the social networks: the so-called emojis. Slack will let us display any emoji we like, so let's just go to `https://unicodey.com/emoji-data/table.htm`, and choose the little drawings you like the most.

Once we have chosen our emojis, we can then forge a payload like this:

```
{
    "text": "Guys, read carefully the examples:bangbang:, take
your time :hourglass:, be :b:rave and love the :shell:"
}
```

And cURL it:

```
cURL -X POST -H 'Content-type: application/json' --data '{ "text": "Guys,
read carefully the examples:bangbang:, take your :hourglass:, be :b:rave
and love the :shell:"}'
https://hooks.slack.com/services/T4P7TPSP9/B4ND2E2E4/lIzhH84lg21ZJ0zdaeQHZ7
ls
```

The results, in the following screenshot, are really nice: they attract attention in a fancy way, so our team members will not be haunted by our messages!

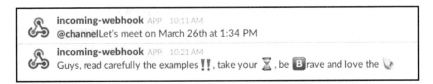

A fancy message can nicely convey the urgency of a statement. Finally, we can address a single user just using `<@user| Optional handle>`, and we can also override the channel we want to send the message to using this:

```
"channel": "#name_of_channel"
```

So, we could address the user called `Giorgio` who is in the channel called `#general`, asking him to join the test channel:

```
{
    "text": "Hey <@giorgio|Giorgio> did you join the
       <#test|Test>  channel?", "channel": "#general"
}'
```

So, the complete cURL line would be as follows:

```
cURL -X POST -H 'Content-type: application/json' --data '{ "text": "Hey
<@giorgio|Giorgio> did you join the <#test|Test> channel?", "channel":
"#general"}'
https://hooks.slack.com/services/T4P7TPSP9/B4ND2E2E4/lIzhH84lg21ZJ0zdaeQHZ7
ls
```

We Want to Chat

With this message, the user Giorgio will receive a notification in the `#general` channel; and the content will be brought to his attention.

> You do not need to convert in HTML the entire text of your message, but there are three characters that must be necessarily turned into HTML entities:
> & must be replaced with &amp
> < must be replaced with &lt
> > must be replaced with &gt

What we did so far was pretty--all you can do with a plain JSON without any hurdles, but if we want to further spice up our messages, we have to reply to message attachments, which will enable us to send images, attach buttons, and much more. So, our next step will be the message attachments to see not only how to embellish our messages, but how to make them more useful and effective.

Message attachments

A message attachment lets us convey more content to the user, and lets it be displayed with more whistles and bells; but we have to keep an eye on a restriction imposed by Slack: no more than 20 attachments per message. It makes sense, otherwise our messages would be so messy that it would distract the average user.

What we have seen so far is a simple JSON: a one-level object, which is more or less like this example:

```
{
    "text": "This is the first line of a messagen
    This is the second line."
}
```

In a message attachment, though we are going to see more details, more content modifier, and a flat structure like the one we just saw that has not enough complexity to convey all the information. We need structured container, still a JSON; but this time, it will be an array holding several properties, which will resemble this snippet:

```
{
    "attachments": [
        {
            "fallback": "Text to be displayed in case of client
                        not supporting formatted text",
            "color": "#ff1493",
            "pretext": "This goes above the attachment",
```

```
            "author_name": "Giorgio Zarrelli",
            "author_link": "http://www.zarrelli.org",
            "author_icon":
"https://www.zarrelli.org/blog/wp-content/uploads/2017/03/IMG_20161113_1500
52.jpg",
            "title": "Title example",
            "title_link": "http://www.zarrelli.org",
            "text": "This text is optional and it is shown in the
                  attachment",
            "fields": [
                {
                    "title": "Priority",
                    "value": "Medium",
                    "short": false
                }
            ],
            "image_URL":
"http://www.zarrelli.org/path/to/image.jpg",
            "thumb_URL":
"https://www.zarrelli.org/blog/wp-content/uploads/2017/03/IMG_20161113_1500
52-1-e1490610507795.jpg",
            "footer": "Slack API",
            "footer_icon":
"https://www.zarrelli.org/blog/wp-content/uploads/2017/03/IMG_20161113_1500
52.jpg",
            "ts": 1490531695
        }
    ]
}
```

What does this snippet look like? We can see in the following screenshot how the attachment gets displayed:

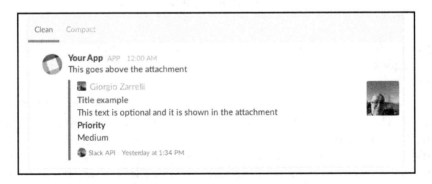

Lots of things in a single message, with a touch of pink!

This is a nice output, much better than the previous basic examples; but things get a bit more complicated, since the structure of the JSON becomes more complex, and we have more fields available. So, let's have a look at the main directives, so we can use their meaning and limitations.

What we are looking at is one out of 20 possible attachments, which start with a fallback. As the name states, it is plain text without any markup, which is to be displayed if a client does not support formatted text:

- `color`: You can color code your message giving a hue to the left-side bar. This can be useful either to make your message stand out in the discussion flow or to have a quick glance at its severity. The color can have three predefined attributes:
    - `good`: This turns the side bar to green
    - `warning`: This turns the side bar to yellow
    - `danger`: This turns the side bar to red

  Apart from these predefined settings, you can use whatever color defined in hex code to turn your left-side bar into an attractive highlighted sign:

- `Pretext`: This is optional text that is shown above the attachment.
- `author_name`: This is the name of the author of the message.
- `author_link`: Any valid URL and it will turn the author's name content into a link. It only works if author_name is available.
- `author_icon`: Any valid URL pointing to a 16x16 pixels image, which will be displayed to the left of `author_name`: This only works if the author's name is available.

  The author's information, if available, will be displayed at the very beginning of each message.

- `title`: As the name states, this is the title of the message and it gets displayed in a bigger size and bold text at the top of the message, but preceding the author's information.
- `title_link`: This is a full blown URL that will turn the tile in a clickable link.
- `Text`: This is the actual body of the message, and the content can be formatted with the basic attributes that we saw in the previous pages. If the content exceeds the 500 characters of 5 line breaks, the content will collapse and a **Show more** link will allow the user to expand the content. Any URLs inside the text field will not unfurl.

- `Fields`: This is an array in the main array, and the bits inside it will be displayed in a table in the attachment. You can have more than one hash inside the array, just separate them with a comma, such as in the following example:

    ```
    "fields": [
            {
                    "title": "Who's in charge",
                    "value": "Giorgio",
                    "short": true
            },
            {
                    "title": "Priority",
                    "value": "Medium",
                    "short": true
            }
    ]
    ```

- `title`: This is plain text shown in bold just above the value. It cannot contain any markup.
- `value`: This can contain multiline text formatted with the markups that we saw in the previous pages.
- `short`: This optional bit will mark the value short enough to be displayed side by side with other values as shown here:

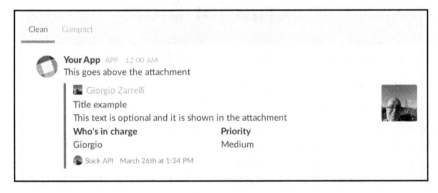

Values can be displayed side by side.

- `image_URL`: This is any valid URL of our choice, which points to a valid image in the PNG, JPEG, GIF, and BMP formats. The displayed size is of 400 x 500 pixels, and any wider or higher images will be automatically resized keeping the original aspect ratio. The image will be displayed inside the message attachment.

- `thumb_URL`: This is any URL pointing to an image file in the PNG, JPEG, GIF, and BMP format. It will be displayed on the right side of the message of the attachment, and it will be rescaled to 75 x 75 pixels keeping the aspect ratio. There is a file size limit to less than 500 KB.
- `footer`: This is the small chunk of text, limited to 300 characters to give some extra information to the readers.
- `footer_icon`: Provide a valid URL to an image, and it will be displayed beside your footer text. The image will be displayed with a fixed size of 16 x 16 pixels and only if you provided a footer.
- `ts`: Each message has its own timestamp when published, but we can attach a specific timestamp to an event or happening mentioned into the message attachment using the ts field and time info expressed in epoch time.

For what we are interested in, it is all about the message formatting. There are some fancy things such as buttons, but that would require a full-blown application able to read from the channel and react to the user actions. As of now, we will stick to a simpler interaction with our script by just sending nicely formatted information to the channel; but no one will prevent you from starting off this example and build up some more complex and suited to your needs.

Our wee chatty script for Slack

Time to start planning our script for Slack, and the first step is to ask ourselves what do we want out of it. Let's recap our requirements, the script has to do as follows:

- Accept the text message to display: required
- Accept a title for the message: required
- Accept a title_link: optional and only if a title is available
- Accept a fallback message: required
- Accept an author_name: optional
- Accept an author_link: optional and only if an author_link available
- Accept an author_icon: optional and only if an author_link available
- Accept a color: required
- Accept a pretext: optional
- Accept fields: required and required title, value and short
- Accept image_URL: optional
- Accept thumb_URL: optional

- Accept footer: optional
- Accept footer_icon: optional and only if the footer is available
- Accept ts: optional

Now, we have a matrix to start building our bits and to parse the command line, and we are ready to start coding. We know what to do, but due to the complexity of the task, we will proceed step by step, adding bits to bits; and since the core of our message is the JSON, we will start coding its structure. But what to do before the first step? We have to think about which utilities we are going to use. As a start, we would say at least cURL, so check if you have it installed on your system; and if you don't, install it. The first lines of our script will have a sha-bang, and try to locate the utility in our PATH:

```
#!/bin/bash
# License: GPL
#
# Author: Giorgio Zarrelli <zarrelli@linux.it>
#
# This program is free software; you can redistribute it and/or modify
# it under the terms of the GNU General Public License version 2 as
# published by the Free Software Foundation.
#
# This program is distributed in the hope that it will be useful,
# but WITHOUT ANY WARRANTY; without even the implied warranty of
# MERCHANTABILITY or FITNESS FOR A PARTICULAR PURPOSE. See the
# GNU General Public License for more details.
#
# You should have received a copy of the GNU General Public License
# along with this program. If not, see <http://www.gnu.org/licenses/>.
#
# Retrieve the full path to the system utilities
cURL=$(which cURL)
```

These first lines resemble the previous Nagios plugin, and this script starts off with a license statement as well. It can be quite useless to state a license, but if we plan to make our scripts available to the public, it is upon us to let the potential user know what they can do with our scripts. The author of this book encourages distributing the software under the GNU GPL license, as it makes it easier to use it to create new programs from it and reutilizing the code. But it is up to the creator of the program what kind of license to use. To have a glance at the various GNU licenses available, we can just go to https://www.gnu.org/licenses/licenses.html and have a look at the numerous licenses on one of them, which will surely fit our purposes. Notice that for this script, we will use lower case variables just to get used to the different kinds of notations adopted by different coders.

We Want to Chat

So, we pointed to the `cURL` utility, but how can we be sure that it is installed and we can reach it? Well, we have to bear in mind that the command substitution given to the variable the output of which and this latter will print out something only if the argument passed to it is reachable in one of the directories pointed out by the user $PATH environment variable. Just for a test, let's call which with cURL as an argument:

```
zarrelli:~$ which cURL
/usr/bin/cURL
```

Now, let's call which with some blurb:

```
zarrelli:~$ which cr234a
zarrelli:~$
```

We get nothing in the output, so our `cURL` variable will bear no value. One more check, let's test ifconfig as the root:

```
root:# which ifconfig
/sbin/ifconfig
```

Then, let's check it again as a non-privileged user:

```
zarrelli:~$ which ifconfig
zarrelli:~$
```

So, since the path to `ifconfig` is in the $PATH variable of the root user only, which, for the non-privileged user, will return nothing. Based on this, we can implement a check with just a few lines:

```
if [ -z "$cURL" ]
    then
        echo "Cannot reach the utility, is it in the $PATH or
even installed?"
        exit 1
    else
        echo "The utility is reachable"
fi
```

So, if the $cURL variable is not empty, the utility is reachable; if not, we receive a warning and exit from the script with an error:

```
zarrelli:~$ ./my_slack.sh
The utility is reachable
```

Great, it seems to work. Now let's change cURL=$(which cURL) into cURL=$(which curl12).

Let's run the script again:

```
zarrelli:~$ /bin/bash -x my_slack.sh
++ which curll2
+ cURL=
+ '[' -z '' ']'
+ echo 'Cannot reach the utility, is it in the $PATH or even in
stalled?'
Cannot reach the utility, is it in the $PATH or even installed?
+ exit 1
```

Correct, the script exits because which cannot find that non sense string in the user $PATH variable. So, this check can come in handy, but as it is written it is not so useful, so let's make a function out of it:

```
# Check if which comes back with a path to a utility
check_which()
{
   for i in "$@"
   do
         if [ -z "$i" ];
             then
                    echo "Cannot reach the utility $i, is it in
the $PATH or even installed?"
                    exit 1
             else
                 :
             fi
   done
}
check_which "$cURL"
```

We simply check if which outputs the path to the utility checked; if it outputs nothing, then the variable is empty and we exit with a message and an exit code. If the variable holds something, then we do nothing since we assume this is the path to the utility. This check resembles the one we used for the Nagios plugin:

```
# Check if we have all the system tools we need
path_exists()
{
for i in "$@"
do
       if [ -e "$i" ];
           then
                   (( VERB )) && echo "$i is a valid path"
                   disk_exists "$DISK"
           else
```

We Want to Chat

```
                        (( VERB )) && echo "$i is not reachable,
is this the correct path?"
                        echo "SMART UNKNOWN: Please check the
plugin"
                        exit "$STATE_UNKNOWN"
        fi
done
}
```

This other one check tests if the content of the variable actually points to a file. Which is better? Depends on what you are checking for. If we need to verify that the variable points to a real file, then `[ -e "$i" ]` is what we are looking for. Otherwise, when we want a more generic check, `[ -z "$i" ]` will do the job for us.

What do we need next in our script? Let's recall a `cURL` that we made a few pages ago:

```
cURL -X POST -H 'Content-type: application/json' --data '{"text":
"<!date^1490531695^ {date}|Fallback>"}'
https://hooks.slack.com/services/T4P7TPSP9/B4ND2E2E4/lIzhH84lg21ZJ0zdaeQHZ7
ls
```

Once we deal with the `cURL` command, we have to manage the headers:

```
-X POST
-H 'Content-type: application/json'
--data
```

These are static and will not change, so we can use them without enclosing in a variable.

We must not forget our WebHook URL:

```
# WebHook
URLwebhook="https://hooks.slack.com/services/T4P7TPSP9/B4ND2E2E4/lIzhH84lg2
1ZJ0zdaeQHZ7ls"
```

Now, it is time to build our first, static payload; and here comes the tricky part. Since the payload is a long multiline JSON, writing it in a single long line would be cumbersome, so we are going to give this burden to a function, which will create this content on our behalf; and it will be nicely formatted too:

```
generate_payload()
{
   cat <<MARKER
{
    "attachments": [
        {
            "fallback": "Text to be displayed in case of client
```

```
                            not supporting formatted text",
            "color": "#ff1493",
            "pretext": "This goes above the attachment",
            "author_name": "Giorgio Zarrelli",
            "author_link": "http://www.zarrelli.org",
            "author_icon":
"https://www.zarrelli.org/blog/wp-content/uploads/2017/03/IMG_20161113_1500
52.jpg",
            "title": "Title example",
            "title_link": "http://www.zarrelli.org",
            "text": "This text is optional and it is shown in the
                    attachment",
            "fields": [
                {
                    "title": "Priority",
                    "value": "Medium",
                    "short": false
                }
            ],
            "image_URL":
"http://www.zarrelli.org/path/to/image.jpg",
            "thumb_URL": "https://www.zarrelli.org/blog/wp-
content/uploads/2017/03/IMG_20161113_150052-1-e1490610507795.jpg",
            "footer": "Slack API",
            "footer_icon":
"https://www.zarrelli.org/blog/wp-content/uploads/2017/03/IMG_20161113_1500
52.jpg",
            "ts": 1490531695
        }
    ]
}
MARKER
}
```

We used a *here* document which, as we saw previously, is one of the best ways to deal with multiline content in Bash scripts. The function will create the content for us, so let's check whether this is true by adding `generate_payload` at the bottom of our script; and let's run it:

```
zarrelli:~$ ./my_slack.sh
{
    "attachments": [
        {
            "fallback": "Text to be displayed in case of client
                        not supporting formatted text",
            "color": "#ff1493",
            "pretext": "This goes above the attachment",
            "author_name": "Giorgio Zarrelli",
```

```
                "author_link": "http://www.zarrelli.org",
                "author_icon": "https://www.zarrelli.org/blog/wp
content/uploads/2017/03/IMG_20161113_150052.jpg",
                "title": "Title example",
                "title_link": "http://www.zarrelli.org",
                "text": "This text is optional and it is shown in the
                        attachment",
                "fields": [
                    {
                        "title": "Priority",
                        "value": "Medium",
                        "short": false
                    }
                ],
                "image_URL":
"http://www.zarrelli.org/path/to/image.jpg",
                "thumb_URL": "https://www.zarrelli.org/blog/wp
content/uploads/2017/03/IMG_20161113_150052-1-e1490610507795.jpg",
                "footer": "Slack API",
                "footer_icon": "https://www.zarrelli.org/blog/wp
content/uploads/2017/03/IMG_20161113_150052.jpg",
                "ts": 1490531695
            }
        ]
    }
```

Great, it works! Our content is here, and so we can proceed in building the command line. Let's delete the call to the function at the bottom of the script and add the following line:

```
"$cURL" -f -X POST -H 'Content-type: application/json' --data
"$(generate_payload)" "$webhook"
```

`$(generate_payload)` is a command substitution that will give `--data` the output generated by the function; but do not forget to enclose it in double quotes, or your output will be taken line by line and not as a single object. Time to save and execute the script and check our `#test` channel:

```
zarrelli:~$ ./my_slack.sh
ok
```

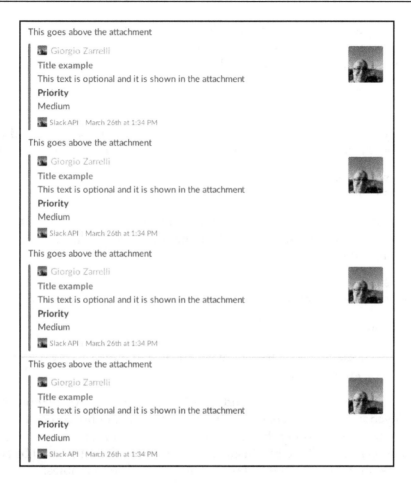

We checked our script just to be sure that it works as intended.

Nice, the script works, we can see the results in the #test channel and a tiny OK in the command line. Well, nice, but we cannot rely on a third-party output to know if anything went wrong, so let's modify our command line to get some useful response:

```
"$cURL" -f -X POST -H 'Content-type: application/json' --data
"$(generate_payload)" "$webhook" && echo " - Success exit code: $?" || echo
"There was an error, exit code: $?"
```

We added a `-f` flag to cURL so that it exits silently in case of error, letting us write something meaningful on the output. It is not 100% failsafe and, as we will see, sometimes an error message slips through, but it is still usable. Then we add this:

```
&& echo " - Success exit code: $?" || echo "There was an error, exit code: $?"
```

We have already seen this kind of test before. We are checking if the command was successful or not and echoing the exit code called "$?" to the stdout. Let's have a look:

```
zarrelli:~$ ./my_slack.sh
ok - Success exit code: 0
```

Great! cURL just printed ok on the command line, and since the execution went fine, we printed a Success message with exit code. Now, let's remove k from $webhook on the last line and execute the script again:

```
zarrelli:~$ ./my_slack.sh
cURL: (3) <URL> malformed
```

There was an error, exit code: 3.

It should have failed silently, but anyway, we were able to write our meaningful error message; and this is all we want.

Our first step is accomplished: we can send a static message to our WebHook and have the message displayed in the #test channel. This is interesting, but not so flexible. What we really want is to be able to modify the message based on our input. To reach this goal, we have to turn into variables all the bits inside our attachment so that we will be able to pass the values on the command line. Let's start creating a couple of variables:

```
# Message attachment variables
fallback=${fallback:="This is a text shown on older clients"}
text=${text:="This line of text is optional"}
```

Now, we just have to modify the payload:

```
{
            "fallback": "$fallback",
            "color": "#ff1493",
            "pretext": "This goes above the attachment",
            "author_name": "Giorgio Zarrelli",
            "author_link": "http://www.zarrelli.org",
            "author_icon": "https://www.zarrelli.org/
            blog/wp-content/uploads/2017/03/IMG_20161113_150052.jpg",
            "title": "Title example",
            "title_link": "http://www.zarrelli.org",
```

```
            "text": "$text",
            "fields": [
                {
                    "title": "Priority",
                    "value": "Medium",
                    "short": false
                }
            ],
                "image_URL":
               "http://www.zarrelli.org/path/to/image.jpg",
                "thumb_URL": "https://www.zarrelli.org/
                  blog/wpcontent/uploads/2017/03/IMG_20
                  161113_150052-1-e1490610507795.jpg",
            "footer": "Slack API",
            "footer_icon": "https://www.zarrelli.org/blog/wpcontent/
              uploads/2017/03/IMG_20161113_150052.jpg",
                "ts": 1490531695
    }
```

Now, let's run the script to see if our modifications are taken into account:

```
zarrelli:~$ ./my_slack.sh
ok - Success exit code: 0
```

It seems it worked; a check to the `#test` channel will confirm the outcome, as we can see in the following screenshot:

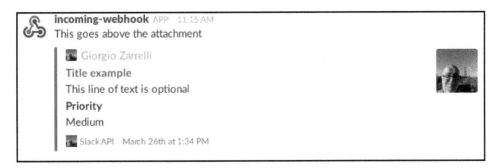

Our variables are being taken into account by the script.

Since our variables seem to be working, let's create a new whole bunch of them:

```
# Message attachment variables
fallback=${fallback:="This is a text shown on older clients"}
color=${color:="good"}
pretext=${pretext:="Announcement:"}
author_name=${author_name:="Giorgio Zarrelli"}
```

```
author_link=${author_link:="http://www.zarrelli.org"}
author_icon=${author_icon:="https://www.zarrelli.org/blog/wp
content/uploads/2017/03/IMG_20161113_150052.jpg"}
title=${title:="New message"}
title_link=${title_link:="Announcement:"}
text=${text:="This line of text is optional"}
fields_title=${fields_title:="Priority"}
fields_value=${fields_value:="Medium"}
fields_short=${fields_short:="true"}
image_URL=${image_URL:="http://www.zarrelli.org/path/to/image.jpg"}
thumb_URL=${thumb_URL:="https://www.zarrelli.org/blog/wp-content/uploads/20
17/03/IMG_20161113_150052-1-e1490610507795.jpg"}
footer=${footer:="Mastering Bash"}
footer_icon=${footer_icon:="https://www.zarrelli.org/blog/wp-content/upload
s/2017/03/IMG_20161113_150052.jpg"}
ts=${ts:="1490531695"}
```

Obviously, the payload must be modified accordingly:

```
{
    "fallback": "$fallback",
    "color": "$color",
    "pretext": "$pretext",
    "author_name": "$author_name",
    "author_link": "$author_link",
    "author_icon": "$author_icon",
    "title": "$title",
    "title_link": "$title_link",
    "text": "$text",
    "fields": [
        {
            "title": "$fields_title",
            "value": "$fields_value",
            "short": "fields_short"
        }
    ],
    "image_URL": "$image_URL",
    "thumb_URL": "$thumb_URL",
    "footer": "$footer",
    "footer_icon": "$footer_icon",
    "ts": "$ts"
}
```

Again, let's test our code:

```
zarrelli:~$ ./my_slack.sh
ok - Success exit code: 0
```

The screenshot here shows our newly formatted message:

It seems that our new payload works well.

Now that we have all the variables in place, it is time to create a menu that will help us manage the user input. Let's start writing a help function; we already saw how to do this in the previous chapter, but this time, we have a lot of options to deal with, so we start associating a switch to each variable:

```
-f --fallback
-c --color
-p --pretext
-an --author_name
-al --author_link
-ai --author_icon
-t --title
-tl --title_link
-tx --text
-ft --fields_title
-fv --fields_value
-fs --fields_short
-iu --image_URL
-tu --thumb_URL
-fr --footer
-fi --footer_icon
-ts --timestamp
```

What we use as short and long options is up to us, but we must keep in mind a golden rule: these must be meaningful not for us, but for the potential users of the script, so we have to take a step aside and try to think as our users. Once we have decided on the best options, we must proceed creating the actual command-line parser:

```
# Parse parameters on the command line
while (( $# > 0 ))
   do
             case "$1" in
```

```
            -h | --help)
                print_help
                    exit 1
                    ;;
            -f | --fallback)
                shift
                fallback="$1"
                ;;
        -c | --color)
                shift
             color="$1"
                ;;
            -p | -pretext)
                shift
                pretext="$1"
                    ;;
            -an | --author_name)
                    shift
                author_name="$1"
                    ;;
        -al | --author_link)
                shift
                author_link="$1"
                    ;;
    -ai | --author_icon)
                shift
                author_icon="$1"
                    ;;
        -t | --title)
                shift


                    ;;
            -tl | --title_link)
                    shift
                    title_link="$1"
                        ;;
            -tx | --text)
                shift
                author_icon="$1"
                    ;;
            -ft | --fields_title)
                shift
                fields_
                    ;;
            -fv | --fields_value)
                shift
                fields_value="$1"
                    ;;
```

```
                -fs | --fields_title)
                        shift
                        fields_short="$1"
                        ;;
                -iu | --image_URL)
                        shift
                        image_URL="$1"
                        ;;
                -tu | --thumb_URL)
                        shift
                        thumb_URL="$1"
                        ;;
                -fr | --footer)
                        shift
                        footer="$1"
                        ;;
                -fi | --footer_icon)
                        shift
                        image_URL="$1"
                        ;;
                -ts | --timestamp)
                        shift
                        ts="$1"
                        ;;
            *) echo "Unknown argument: $1"
                        print_help
                        exit 1
                        ;;
        esac
        shift
    done
```

And now the `print_help` function:

```
# Print help and usage
print_help()
{
    cat << HERE

    Slack sender v1.0
    ---------------
Please enter one or more of the following options:
            -h  | --help
            -f  | --fallback
            -c  | --color
            -p  | -pretext
            -an | --author_name
```

```
            -al |  --author_link
            -ai |  --author_icon
             -t |  --title
            -tl |  --title_link
            -tx |  --text
            -ft |  --fields_title
            -fv |  --fields_value
            -fs |  --fields_title
            -iu |  --image_URL
            -tu |  --thumb_URL
            -fr |  --footer
            -fi |  --footer_icon
            -ts |  --timestamp
HERE
}
```

Now, let's comment the last line of the script: the one calling cURL. Then, let's call the script with the -h switch:

```
zarrelli:~$ ./my_slack.sh -h

Slack sender v1.0
------------------
Please enter one or more of the following options:
             -h |  --help
             -f |  --fallback
             -c |  --color
             -p |  -pretext
            -an |  --author_name
            -al |  --author_link
            -ai |  --author_icon
             -t |  --title
            -tl |  --title_link
            -tx |  --text
            -ft |  --fields_title
            -fv |  --fields_value
            -fs |  --fields_title
            -iu |  --image_URL
            -tu |  --thumb_URL
            -fr |  --footer
            -fi |  --footer_icon
            -ts |  --timestamp
```

There is a small issue: even the Nagios plugin had it, so it is time to solve it. Let's call the script without any parameters:

```
zarrelli:~$ ./my_slack.sh -h
zarrelli:~$
```

Nothing, we do not have anything as feedback, so we do not even know if we can use a -h switch to get more information. How do we solve this hindrance? Well, we have different options available; we could modify the while clause for instance or adopt a different strategy:

```
if (( $# == 0 ))
    then
        echo "No options provided, you can use -h for help but this time I will do it for you..."
        print_help
fi
```

We have to put these lines before the menu creation, and they will check the input: if nothing is given on the command line, it will write an error message and call the `print_help` function. Time to test our script now and see what happens:

```
./my_slack.sh -c warning -an Me -t "My cli test" -tx "This is a cli text"
ok - Success exit code: 0
```

It seems it worked, and the screenshot of the `#test` channel confirms our guess:

Our script now accepts the command-line parameters.

[325]

Summary

We are now able to send formatted messages to the `#test` channel, but is this all we can do with this script? No, as you will learn over time with a bit more experience, programming is also setting a scope to our efforts: we must define our goals, plan accordingly, accomplish them, and assess the results. Overdoing, in a professional environment, breaks one of the fundamental rules of the project management, the so-called *iron triangle* that defines the quality of a project as the intersection between scope, time, and costs that are the top three constrains driving us in creating our programs. Spend too long on a program or exceed the goals, the cost will levitate and the overall quality, not the quality of the code, but of our project, will be impacted.

This script was an example on how to plan and execute, how to check for the information we need to code a working script, and how to write down our steps. There are many ways to improve this framework, for example, by allowing the user to pass a date on the command line, not as epoch time, but in one format allowed by the date command, and then translating it with a tiny function or even inline into the code. We can, for instance, put a check on the option arguments so that the user will be forced to pass an argument if they specify an option on the command line. This is a play field and these can be advises on how to have fun and develop the script further. We are now moving further to deepen what we can do with a subshell, how to execute a bunch of processes in parallel and, as always, how to have fun!

9
Subshells, Signals, and Job Controls

Whatever we have seen so far was pretty straightforward. We launched a script that executed some commands, instances, variables, and made something out of it, that is all-- one command after the other, one instruction piled on the previous one. This is what we would call a serial execution, one command after the other just like domino tiles: the first coming in and the first being processed; and this brings to mind the concept of the FIFO queue, **First In First Out**.

What if we wanted to process more than one instruction at a time? Well, we cannot do this and it would not be incorrect: a CPU is a serial device and it can process only one instruction at a time. What we use to give us the *taste* of multitasking is having the CPU switching between an instruction and the other really fast. So, instead of completely processing an instruction before passing on to the other, the CPU will work a bit on the first one, pass it to work a bit on the second, and then again back to the first for a while. It is this back and forth idea that gives us the illusion that our CPU is working on more than one thing at the same time. And then, we have systems with multiprocessors, and we can take advantage of this kind of architecture so that we can distribute processes on different CPU, so they can really be elaborated in parallel.

Whatever we decide to do, everything starts from an invocation, a leap of faith into a new instance of the main shell so that a new child shell is given birth, and it will be devoted to our tasks. So, first, what is a subshell?

What is a subshell?

Let's start with a more basic question. What is a shell? To make it simple, a shell is an interface between the user and the underlying operating system. It can be a command-line interpreter or a graphic interface, but the purpose of a shell is to be an intermediary between the user and the core of the system, allowing the former to access the services offered by the latter. So, for instance, a bash shell gives us a command-line interface access through a Terminal and a series of commands that allows us to communicate with the operating system and make use of its services to perform tasks.

In a shell, each command is usually executed after the former has concluded its task, but we can change to some extent this behavior leveraging some key concepts: background process, signals, and subshells.

Background processes

Let's start with an intuitive definition of a background process, and define it as a process with no interaction with the terminal it is launched from. This practically means that a background process has no interaction with the user and that's it. Technically, we can say that a background process is the one whose process ID group differs from the one of the terminal it has been launched from. We can define a process group as a bunch of processes sharing the same process group ID, which is an identifier allowing the system to manage all the processes as a whole. A process group ID is determined by the process ID of the first process of the group, also called process group leader; each subsequent process in the group will be the process group ID drawn from the process ID of the leader; and each child process is placed in the process group ID of its parent. Similarly, a session is a collection of process groups; and the first process in the session is also the session leader, which is the only process allowed to control a terminal, if any is available. Thus, the process that prepares the login session for the user is also the session leader for all the processes spawned during the "user session", and all the processes will be in a process group under the session. When a user session is closed, the kernel sends a **Signal Hang Up** (**SIGHUP**) signal to the leader of the session holding the terminal foreground process group. This is because when the user closes its interactive session, the connection to the terminal is closed and the foreground processes have no longer a terminal to access to, so they must be killed. That being said, a background process will be barred from reading or writing from the terminal with a **SIGnal due to TeleType INput** (**SIGTTIN**) in case it attempts to read from it and **SIGnal due to TTY OUtput** (**SIGTTOU**) in case it attempts to write to it.

Signals

In the early days of computing, signals were a means to deal with unusual events, and usually, their job was to reset a condition to a default state. Nowadays, with facilities such as job control, signals are used to actually instruct processes on what to do and are now more an interprocess facilities than a reset mechanism, as they were originally conceived. Each signal is associated to an action that must be performed by the process receiving it, so here is a brief list with some of the more interesting signals that the kernel can send to a process:

- SIGCHLD: This signal is sent to a parent process when a child terminates or stops.
- SIGCONT: This tells the process that has been put on hold by SIGSTOP or SGSTP to resume its execution. These three signals are used in job controlling.
- SIGHUP: This signal is sent to a process when its terminal is closed and kills it. It owes its name to the old good times when connections were held over serial line, which hang up due to a line drop. If sent to a daemon, it usually forces them to reload the configuration file and reopen the log file.
- SIGINT: This is the signal given to the process when a user presses *Ctrl + C*, and it interrupts the process, terminating it. This signal can be ignored by the process.
- SIGKILL: This terminates a process immediately. This cannot be ignored, and the process has to die immediately without closing or saving anything. (kill -9)
- SIGQUIT: When the process receives this signal, it quits performing a core dump. A core dump is a dump, a copy, of the memory used by the process, so we can find in it a lot of useful information such as a processor, registers, flags, data, which are useful to debug the working state of the process itself.
- SIGSTOP: This signal is sent to stop a process. It cannot be ignored.
- SIGTERM: It is a termination request. This is the preferable way to kill a process since it allows the process to shut down nicely, releasing the resources and saving state and also killing all the child processes in an orderly way. It can be ignored by the process (kill -15).
- SIGTRAP: This is a signal sent to a process when an exception or a trap arises. We already had a glimpse of traps, and we will see more about them now.
- SIGTSTP: This is an interactive stop, and it can be sent by the user pressing *Ctrl+Z*. It can be ignored by the process. The process pauses in its current state.
- SIGTTIN: This signal is sent to a background process when it tries to read from the terminal.

Subshells, Signals, and Job Controls

- **SIGTTOU**: This signal is sent to a background process when it tries to write to the terminal.
- **SIGSEV**: This is sent to a process when it goes on segmentation fault, and this happens when a process attempts to access a memory location; it is not allowed to access or in a way it is not permitted.

So, we have signals, and we have process groups and sessions and this leads us to Unix job control. What is it? In Unix, we can control what we call jobs, and we are already familiar with those since this is another term to refer to process groups. A job is not a process, it is a group of processes. But what does control mean? Simply, we can suspend, resume, or terminate a job and send signals to it.

When a shell session is started on a terminal, its process group is granted access to it, and it becomes the foreground process group for that terminal. This means that the processes belonging to the foreground group can read and write from the terminal, while the processes belonging to other process groups are barred from accessing the terminal and stopped if they try to. So, from the shell, you can interact with the terminal and perform different actions, for example, retrieve a list of processes and their job ID:

```
zarrelli:~$ ps -fj | awk '{print $2 " -> " $4 " -> " $10 }'
PID -> PGID -> CMD
1422 -> 1422 -> /bin/bash
7886 -> 7886 -> ps
7887 -> 7886 -> awk
```

As we can see, the `ps` and `awk` processes have the same process group ID, which is the process ID of the first command in the group, `ps`. Now, what about the job control? Let's see how to start a process in the background:

```
zarrelli:~$ sleep 10 &
[1] 8163
```

The sleep command just waits for the amount of seconds we specify as an argument, but the ampersand is the key; it will put the process in the background. What we get in return is a job number `[1]` and a process ID; `ps` will show us more details:

```
zarrelli:~$ ps -jf
UID PID PPID PGID SID C STIME TTY TIME CMD
zarrelli 1422 1281 1422 1422 0 08:46 pts/0 00:00:00 /bin/bash
zarrelli 8163 1422 8163 1422 0 10:25 pts/0 00:00:00 sleep 10
zarrelli 8166 1422 8166 1422 0 10:25 pts/0 00:00:00 ps -jf
```

Now, let's have a look at this:

```
zarrelli:~$ (sleep 100 &) ; sleep 20 &
[1] 8632
zarrelli:~$:~$ ps -jf
UID PID PPID PGID SID C STIME TTY TIME CMD
zarrelli 1422 1281 1422 1422 0 08:46 pts/0 00:00:00
/bin/bash
zarrelli 8631 1 8630 1422 0 10:39 pts/0 00:00:00 sleep
100
zarrelli 8632 1422 8632 1422 0 10:39 pts/0 00:00:00 sleep
20
zarrelli 8637 1422 8637 1422 0 10:40 pts/0 00:00:00 ps -jf
```

Here, we put one sleep process in the background but used the () to execute it in the subshell, and it actually was executed in the foreground; but now, the main shell did not report any job or process ID because the child shell could not report back any information to the parent shell. The only job information we received was for the second sleep instruction performed in the parent shell, and interestingly, both the sleep processes have the same group ID.

Job controls

So, we have the job ID, process ID, foreground, and background processes, but how do we control these jobs? We have a bunch of commands available, let's have a look at how to use them:

- `kill`: We can pass the job ID to this command, which will send the SIGTERM signal to all the processes belonging to the job itself:

    ```
    zarrelli:~$ sleep 100 &
    [1] 9909
    zarrelli:~$ kill %1
    zarrelli:~$
    [1]+ Terminated sleep 100
    ```

    You can also pass to kill a specific signal to send to the process. For instance, `kill -15` will nicely terminate a process with a SIGTERM signal, and if it refuses to die, `kill -9` will send a SIGKILL, which will instantly terminate a process. Which signals can we send to a process? Either `kill -l` or `cat /usr/include/asm-generic/signal.h` will give us a list of all the signals supported.

- `killall`: If we know what is the name of the process, the easiest way to kill it is through the `killall` command followed by the name of the process:

```
zarrelli:~$ sleep 100 &
[1] 10595
zarrelli:~$ killall sleep
[1]+ Terminated sleep 10
```

But `killall` has another interesting to use. Let's run the sleep command for four times, each time with a different argument:

```
zarrelli:~$ sleep 100 &
[1] 10672
zarrelli:~$ sleep 200 &
[2] 10689
zarrelli:~$ sleep 300 &
[3] 10690
zarrelli:~$ sleep 400 &
[4] 10693
```

Now, let's check the list of processes:

```
zarrelli:~$ ps -jf
UID PID PPID PGID SID C STIME TTY TIME CMD
zarrelli 1422 1281 1422 1422 0 08:46 pts/0 00:00:00
/bin/bash
zarrelli 10672 1422 10672 1422 0 11:16 pts/0 00:00:00 sleep
100
zarrelli 10689 1422 10689 1422 0 11:16 pts/0 00:00:00 sleep
200
zarrelli 10690 1422 10690 1422 0 11:16 pts/0 00:00:00 sleep
300
zarrelli 10693 1422 10693 1422 0 11:16 pts/0 00:00:00 sleep
400
zarrelli 10699 1422 10699 1422 0 11:16 pts/0 00:00:00 ps -jf
```

We can see the four processes: same name and different argument. Now, let's use `killall` giving the process name, sleep, as its argument:

```
zarrelli:~$ killall sleep
[1] Terminated sleep 100
[2] Terminated sleep 200
[4]+ Terminated sleep 400
[3]+ Terminated sleep 300
```

All the processes have been killed at once. Quite handy, isn't it? Let's make the last check:

```
zarrelli:~$ ps -jf
UID PID PPID PGID SID C STIME TTY TIME CMD
zarrelli 1422 1281 1422 1422 0 08:46 pts/0 00:00:00
/bin/bash
zarrelli 10709 1422 10709 1422 0 11:16 pts/0 00:00:00 ps -jf
```

No more instances of sleep running now; we killed everything with one single run of `killall`.

- `jobs`: This shows the processes running in the background along with their job ID:

```
zarrelli:~$ sleep 100 &
[1] 8892
zarrelli:~$ sleep 200 &
[2] 8893
zarrelli:~$ jobs
[1]-  Running sleep                   100 &
[2]+  Running sleep                   200 &
```

- `fg`: This sends a background running job to the foreground. It accepts the job ID as an argument. If no job ID is provided, the current job is affected:

```
zarrelli@moveaway:~$ sleep 100 &
[1] 9045
zarrelli@moveaway:~$ fg %1
sleep 100
```

- `bg`: This sends a foreground job to the background. If no job ID is provided, the current job is affected.
- `suspend`: This suspends the shell until a SIGCONT signal is received.
- `logout`: This logs out from the login shell.
- `disown`: This removes a job from the shell table of active jobs.

- `wait`: This interesting command stops the execution of a script until all the background jobs have terminated or, if passed as an argument, until a job ID or a PID terminates, and returns the exit status of the process it was waiting for.

Job ID	Meaning	Example
%n	Job number	Kill %1
%s	String the command executed starts with	sleep 200 & [1] 9486 kill %sl [1]+ Terminated sleep 200
%?s	String the command executed contains	sleep 200 & [1] 9504 kill %?ee [1]+ Terminated sleep 200
%%	Last job that has been either stopped in the foreground or started in the background	sleep 200 & [1] 9536 kill %% [1]+ Terminated sleep 200
%+	Last job that has been either stopped in foreground or started in the background	sleep 200 & [1] 9618 fg %+ sleep 200
%-	Last job	sleep 200 & [1] 9626 kill %- [1]+ Terminated sleep 200
$!	Last process in the background	sleep 200 & [1] 9646 sleep 300 & [2] 9647 sleep 400 & [3] 9648 kill $! [3]+ Terminated sleep 400

- `times`: We saw this command at the opening of this book. It gives us statistics on time elapsed during the execution of a command.
- `builtin`: This execute a builtin command disabling functions and non-builtin commands, which have the same name as the builtin.
- `command`: This disables all the aliases and functions for the specified command:

    ```
    zarrelli@moveaway:~$ ls
    Desktop Documents Downloads First session Music Pictures
    progetti Projects Public Templates tmp Videos
    [1]- Done    sleep 200
    [2]+ Done    sleep 300
    zarrelli:~$ ls
    Desktop Documents Downloads First session Music Pictures
    progetti Projects Public Templates tmp Videos
    zarrelli:~$ alias ls="ps -jf"
    zarrelli:~$ ls
    UID PID PPID PGID SID C STIME TTY TIME CMD
    zarrelli 1373 1267 1373 1373 0 07:36 pts/0 00:00:00
    /bin/bash
    zarrelli 10738 1373 10738 1373 0 10:17 pts/0 00:00:00 ps -jf
    zarrelli:~$ command ls
    Desktop Documents Downloads First session Music Pictures
    progetti Projects Public Templates tmp Videos
    zarrelli@moveaway:~$ ls
    UID PID PPID PGID SID C STIME TTY TIME CMD
    zarrelli 1373 1267 1373 1373 0 07:36 pts/0 00:00:00 /bin/bash
    zarrelli 10742 1373 10742 1373 0 10:17 pts/0 00:00:00 ps -jf
    ```

- `enable`: This enables or disables the -n builtin command, so if we have a builtin and an external command, then when invoked, the builtin will be ignored and the external command will be executed. Specifying the -a option will show a list of all the builtins along with their status, while the -f switch will load a builtin as a shared library module from a compiled object file.
- `Autoload`: This is not enabled by default in Bash and it must be loaded through enabling -f. It marks a name as a function name and not a builtin or an external command reference. The named function must reside in an external file and it will be loaded from there.

So, we had a look at the foreground and background processes and at the job controlling commands; now, we can see how to work with subshells and what benefit they can bestow on our scripts.

Subshells and parallel processing

We already talked a bit about subshells in the opening chapters of this book; they can be defined as child processes of their main shell. So, a subshell is a command interpreter inside a command interpreter. When does this happen? Well, usually when we run a script, this spawns its own shell and from there executes all the commands listed; but notice this nice detail: an external command, unless invoked using `exec`, spawns a subprocess, but a builtin doesn't. And this is the reason why the bultins execution time is faster than the execution time for the corresponding external command, as we saw in the previous pages of this book.

Well, what can be useful for a subshell? Let's see a small example that will make everything easier:

```
#!/bin/bash
echo "This is the main subshell"
(echo "And this is the second" ; for i in {1..10} ; do echo $i ; done)
```

Nothing special. We echo in the first subshell spawned by the script, and then open a subshell from inside the subshell and echo the $i variable using a range between `1` and `10`:

```
zarrelli:~$ ./subshell.sh
This is the main subshell
And this is the second
1
2
3
4
5
6
7
8
9
10
```

As I just said, there is nothing really special in this script other than the way we called a subshell using `(command_1; command_2; command_n)`.

Whatever is inside the parentheses is executed in a new subshell isolated from the parent shell since; whatever happens inside the subshell is local to this environment:

```
#!/bin/bash
a=10
echo "The value of a in the main subshell is $a"
(echo "The value of a in the child subshell is $a"; echo "...but
now it changes"...; a=20; echo "and now a is $a")
echo "But coming back to the main subshell, the value of a has not
been altered here since the subshell variables are local, a: $a"
```

Now, let's run this piece of code:

```
zarrelli:~$ ./local.sh
The value of a in the main subshell is 10
The value of a in the child subshell is 10
...but now it changes...
and now a is 20
But coming back to the main subshell, the value of a has not been altered
here since the subshell variables are local, a: 10
```

As we can see from the example, this is a one-way inheritance from the parent to the child, nothing climbs up the ladder. But it is possible to spawn subshell from inside a subshell, so to have a nesting structure, this is nice; but we could lose track of where we are. It's better to have a handy variable such as $BASH_SUBSHELL available:

```
#!/bin/bash
(
echo "Bash nesting level: $BASH_SUBSHELL. Shell PID: $BASHPID"
(
echo "Bash nesting level: $BASH_SUBSHELL. Shell PID: $BASHPID"
(
echo "Bash nesting level: $BASH_SUBSHELL. Shell PID: $BASHPID"
)
)
)
```

Firstly, we wrote the code in this fancy way just to highlight the nested structure of the shells; we can use a more compact notation on a production script. Notice the two variables:

- $BASH_SUBSHELL: This internal variable is available from Bash version 3 and holds the subshell level
- $BASHPID: This holds the process ID of the shell instance

Let's run the script and have a look at the output:

```
zarrelli:~$ ./nesting.sh
Bash nesting level: 1. Shell PID: 19787
Bash nesting level: 2. Shell PID: 19788
Bash nesting level: 3. Shell PID: 19789
```

Well, we have the subshell levels nicely printed along with the PID of each shell instance, and this shows us that they are actually different processes spawned by each parent shell. We could be tempted to use the internal $SHLVL variable to keep track of the shell level, but unfortunately this is not affected by the nested shells as the following example highlights:

```
echo "Bash level: $BASH_SUBSHELL - $SHLVL" ; (echo "Bash level:
$BASH_SUBSHELL - $SHLVL"; (echo "Bash level: $BASH_SUBSHELL -
$SHLVL"))
Bash level: 0 - 1
Bash level: 1 - 1
Bash level: 2 - 1
```

Nice, but what happens when we exit from a nested shell? Time for another example:

```
#!/bin/bash
echo "This is the main subshell"
(
echo "This is the second level subshell";
for i in {1..10}; do if (( i==5 )); then exit; else echo $i; fi;
done
)
echo "Out of the second level subshell but still kicking inside
the first level!"
for i in {1..3}
do echo $i
done
```

In the lines of code we spawn an inner subshell counting from 1 to 10 and printing to the stdout until we reach 5: in this case we exit the subshell and jump back to the first level. Will the script continue and print the other three numbers? Running it will reveal the answer:

```
zarrelli:~$ ./exit.sh
This is the main subshell
This is the second level subshell
1
2
3
4
Out of the second level subshell but still kicking inside the
```

```
first level!
1
2
3
```

Yes, the exit call affected the inner subshell only and the rest of the script kept running on the upper level.

Well, we saw some fancy stuff about subshells, but we can use them for parallel execution, but how? Just as usual, let's start with a script:

```
#!/bin/bash
(while true
do
    :
done) &
(for i in {1..3}
do
   echo "$i"
done)
```

The first thing to notice is the & character whose job is to put in background the commands or the shells it follows. In this example, the first subshell has an infinite loop, and if we do not send it in the background, it will prevent the second subshell to be spawned and its content executed. But let's see what happens when we send it in the background:

```
./parallel.sh
1
2
3
```

So, the second subshell was correctly spawned and the for loop executed, but what happened to the first infinite while loop?

```
ps -fj
UID PID PPID PGID SID C STIME TTY TIME CMD
zarrelli 17311 1223 17311 17311 0 09:07 pts/0 00:00:01
/bin/bash
zarrelli 21843 1 21842 17311 99 10:46 pts/0 00:00:16
/bin/bash ./parallel.sh
zarrelli 21863 17311 21863 17311 0 10:47 pts/0 00:00:00 ps -fj
```

Well, it is still there running in memory. You can use & not just for subshells but also for any other command:

```
zarrelli:~$ ls &
[1] 22064
zarrelli:~$ exit.sh local.sh nesting.sh parallel.sh sub
shell.sh
[1]+ Done ls --color=auto
```

Do you want the command you issued to run even after you logged off the system? Just run the following command:

```
nohup command &
```

It will run in a subshell in the background, and nohup will catch the SIGHUP signal that is sent to all the subshells and processes when the main shell is terminated. This way, the subshell and the related command will not be affected by the terminate signal and will continue its execution.

Going back to subshells, why would you want to send in the background an entire subshell and not single commands or compounds? Think of subshells as containers: tear down a problem in less complex tasks, enclose the latter in subshells, and have them to execute in the background, and you will save time having them executed in parallel.

We just said parallel, but actually Bash does not optimize the execution of commands and script for a multicore architecture. If we want something more core wise, we can install a nice program called *parallel*. We will not talk much about this program since it is not really Bash related, but it is a nice tool for the reader to explore, a tool core savy:

```
zarrelli:~$ parallel --number-of-cpus
1
zarrelli:~$ parallel --number-of-cores
4
```

The basic syntax of parallel is quite easy:

```
parallel command ::: argument_1 argument_2 argument_n
```

It is similar to the following example:

```
zarrelli:~$ parallel echo ::: 1 2 3
1
2
3
```

Giving more arguments separated by ::: will cause parallel to pass them to the command in all the combinations possible:

```
zarrelli:~$ parallel echo ::: 1 2 3 ::: A B C
1 A
1 B
1 C
2 A
2 B
2 C
3 A
3 B
3 C
```

The number of jobs executed here is equal to the number of cores available, but we can modify this value with -j+n to add the n jobs to the cores. Fire parallel with -j0, and it will try to execute as many jobs as possible:

```
zarrelli:~$ parallel --eta --joblog sleep echo {} ::: 1 2 3 4 5
10
Computers / CPU cores / Max jobs to run
1:local / 4 / 4Computer:jobs running/jobs completed/%of started
jobs/Average seconds to complete
ETA: 0s Left: 6 AVG: 0.00s local:4/0/100%/0.0s 1
ETA: 0s Left: 5 AVG: 0.00s local:4/1/100%/0.0s 2
ETA: 0s Left: 4 AVG: 0.00s local:4/2/100%/0.0s 3
ETA: 0s Left: 3 AVG: 0.00s local:3/3/100%/0.0s 4
ETA: 0s Left: 2 AVG: 0.00s local:2/4/100%/0.0s 5
ETA: 0s Left: 1 AVG: 0.00s local:1/5/100%/0.0s 10
ETA: 0s Left: 0 AVG: 0.00s local:0/6/100%/0.0s
zarrelli:~$ parallel -j0 --eta --joblog sleep echo {} ::: 1 2 3
4 5 10
Computers / CPU cores / Max jobs to run
1:local / 4 / 6
Computer:jobs running/jobs completed/%of started jobs/Average se
conds to complete
ETA: 0s Left: 6 AVG: 0.00s local:6/0/100%/0.0s 1
ETA: 0s Left: 5 AVG: 0.00s local:5/1/100%/0.0s 2
ETA: 0s Left: 4 AVG: 0.00s local:4/2/100%/0.0s 3
ETA: 0s Left: 3 AVG: 0.00s local:3/3/100%/0.0s 4
ETA: 0s Left: 2 AVG: 0.00s local:2/4/100%/0.0s 5
ETA: 0s Left: 1 AVG: 0.00s local:1/5/100%/0.0s 10
ETA: 0s Left: 0 AVG: 0.00s local:0/6/100%/0.0s
```

What can we do with parallel? Well, a lot of tricky stuff, but it is left to the reader to try and experiment with this nice utility; I am confident that a lot of new ideas will arise while tinkering with it.

Summary

We had a peek into some internals of our Bash, pidfiles, sessions, jobs, and had lots of stuff to play with. We also introduced parallel and subshell. This is probably one of those chapters that requires a bit of practice. Take time to experiment and try whatever comes to our mind to get confident with the job controls and background processes. Now that we had a look at the processes and how to manage them, we will proceed to see how to make them talk to each other and exchange information. Time for IPC!

10
Let's Make a Process Chat

Inter-process Communication (**IPC**) is a nice way to describe the fact that processes talk to each other, exchange data, and can then react accordingly. This kind of chatting can be held between a parent and a child process, between processes on the same host, and between programs on different hosts. Processes exchange data in a different ways; for instance, if we think about it, when we SSH to a remote server, our client is communicating with the remote host and actually exchanging data back and forth. The same happens when you pipe the output of a command into the standard input of another one; these are ways, sometimes monodirectional, sometimes bidirectional, to put different processes into communicating and enhancing what we can do with our Bash environment.

There are different ways to accomplish IPC, some more familiar, some less, but all are effective to a certain extent, and we already saw some examples during this book. So, now we will go through few pages which will describe a bit more in depth how processes can interact and how can use the IPC to enhance our scripts, focusing on those methods that we can access using Bash, starting with the so-called **pipes**.

Pipes

We can describe a pipeline as a sequence of processes tied together by `stdout` and `stdin` so that the output of one process becomes the input of the following one. This is a simple form of IPC, commonly known as anonymous pipe, and it is a one-way form of communicating: whatever comes from standard output of the preceding process flows into the standard input of the following one; nothing comes back from the latter to the former.

Let's see an example that will clarify the concept of anonymous pipe, staring with a simple `ps` command:

```
zarrelli:~$ ps
PID TTY          TIME CMD
1427 pts/0    00:00:00 bash
12112 pts/0   00:00:00 ps
```

We have a simple listing with some commands: `PID`, `TTY`, and `CMD`. Let's say we want to trim down the output to just `PID` and `CMD`. We could alter the output using some `ps` switches, but who remembers them? It's easier to use something that is capable of mangling the text and gives us the result we want, so why not use `awk`? The problem here is that `awk` works on the text it receives from the input, reading a file for instance. But we can cut corners, linking its standard input to the `ps` standard output by means of the pipe character `|`:

```
zarrelli:~$ ps | awk '{print $1, $4}'
PID CMD
1427 bash
12113 ps
12114 awk.
```

Here, `awk` accepted the output of `ps` as the input and printed to the `stdout` the first and fourth field only, being the blank character the standard field separator. As mentioned earlier, we can chain more than two processes:

```
zarrelli:~$ ps | awk '{print $1, $4}' | tail -n +2 | wc -l
5
```

In this case, we piped the output of the previous set of commands through `tail`, which actually got the first line (`PID CMD`) removed and printed to `stdout`. Then, we piped this output through the `stdin` of `wc`, which then printed the count of the lines we received in `stdin`. This is possible because all the processes are in the same environment since each command at the right end of a pipe runs in a subshell of the main shell and shares the same file descriptors. Thus, it is just matter of writing the data to the open descriptor of the parent process; and the child will be able to read them in the same order it was written: with a kernel buffer to hold the bits waiting to be read.

Nice and handy, but there are some serious restrictions:

- The processes must reside on the same host
- The processes must be active on an overlapping span of time: the preceding process must be producing output while the following one is reading

- The communication is one way only: the data descends the chain and never climbs back the ladder

We can overcome some of these restrictions using pipes, which are often referred to as FIFO pipes due to the way they work. They rely on the creating a file, which then any number of processes can access, and this introduces a huge difference with respect to the anonymous pipe. It lasts as long as the processes involved last, while a named pipe lasts as long as the file exists; and this can last as long as the system is not rebooted or the file itself. We can create a file using either `mkfifo` or `mknode`, and use the I/O redirection to read or write as shown in the following example:

```
#!/bin/bash
pipefile="mypipefile"
if [[ ! -p $pipefile ]]
then
mknod $pipefile p
fi
while true
do
read row <$pipefile
if [[ "$row" == 'exit' ]]
then
echo "I read $row so exiting"
break
fi
echo $row
done
```

Let's follow the flow of the script. The first thing we want to be sure of is that our named pipe is in place, so we test for a particular kind of file called -p, a pipe. If it does not exist, the script creates it using `mknod $pipefile p`.

The p added at the end of the command line ensures the creation of the file as a pipe and not as a regular one. Then, we want the script to keep reading from the file we open so we use an infinite loop: *true is always true*. Inside the infinite loop, we have the `read row $pipefile` instruction, which reads from the pipe file line by line and stores the content into the `row` variable. So far, so good. If we jump to the end of the script, we can see that it just echoes whatever we input but there is a tiny check in between; if we input `exit`, the program will exit. Let's run in one terminal our new script:

zarrelli:~$ ./pipe.sh

We will see our prompt flashing without giving us the command line back: the script is trapped in an infinite loop reading from the named pipe and will not terminate until we type `exit` into its standard input. Now, using the output redirection, let's send some stuff into the pipe file:

```
zarrelli:~$ echo "Hello" > mypipefile
zarrelli:~$ echo "Another line" > mypipefile
zarrelli:~$ echo "It is time to quit" > mypipefile
zarrelli:~$ echo exit > mypipefile
```

Let's see what is on the terminal running our script:

```
zarrelli:~$ ./pipe.sh
"Hello"
"It is time to quit"
I read exit so exiting
```

That's it. The script echoed all the text we sent to the `pipe` file; and when it encountered the `quit` string, it just exited, giving us a nice message. This example is quite easy and can be replicated using simple files, but switch the context and think about multiple processes coordinating their actions writing and reading from a pipe, sending and reading data, keywords, commands from the pipe, and doing something in a graceful order. All without using an intermediary temporary file but a pipe that will disappear upon the system reboot without the need for all processes to run at the same time. Processes can be triggered by cron jobs manually, by other applications, or by running indefinitely in a loop. It does not matter, as everything is async. We have a means to connect processes in an asynchronous way and both ways, since each process can both send and receive data. This means, we instruct other processes and feed them with data, or are instructed and get fed with data when needed. All this is really useful but there is something more barebone than this when it comes to IPC, not really an inter-process communication since we are going to use redirections to plain files.

Redirection to a file

Well, redirecting the output of a process is not what an IPC means, but it can be used as such in an asynchronous way: have one process redirect its output to a file and have another one read from the same file later on; and this can be a way to exchange information between the two processes:

```
zarrelli:~$ myfile="myfile.txt" ; touch "$myfile" ; echo "$myfile" >
controller ; while read -r line; do tar cvzf $line.tgz $line ; done <
controller
myfile.txt
```

In this example, we just stored a filename into a variable. We created the file with `touch`, and then stored the filename into the `controller` file. Once we had the filename into the `controller` file, we had it read line by line and each line was stored into the `line` variable. Finally, the content of the line variable is used to zip the file pointed by the `myfile` variable:

```
zarrelli:~$ ls -lah
total 20K
drwxr-xr-x 2 zarrelli zarrelli 4.0K Apr 10 09:18 .
drwxr-xr-x 4 zarrelli zarrelli 4.0K Apr 10 09:17 ..
-rw-r--r-- 1 zarrelli zarrelli  11 Apr 10 09:18 controller
-rw-r--r-- 1 zarrelli zarrelli   0 Apr 10 09:18 myfile.txt
-rw-r--r-- 1 zarrelli zarrelli 123 Apr 10 09:18 myfile.txt.tgz
prw-r--r-- 1 zarrelli zarrelli   0 Apr  9 13:05 mypipefile
-rwxr--r-- 1 zarrelli zarrelli 223 Apr  9 12:44 pipe.sh
```

Here, we have all the files in place and `tar` just followed the instructions stored by `echo` in the `controller` file. This is quite a trivial example, and it can be expanded as much as we wish. Notice that in this way, there are no special files needed, and the processes can be unrelated and can be executed any time without any need for concurrency. Probably this kind of IPC is not so surprising, but if we pay enough attention, we can find other interesting ways to make processes talk to each others, for instance, **command substitution**.

The command substitution

We already saw what a command substitution is:

```
zarrelli:~$ time=$(date +%H:%M) ; echo $time
10:06
```

The output of a command gets stored as a string into a variable, and it is then available to be used in any way we need. So, for instance, we could well do this:

```
zarrelli:~$ myfile="myfile.txt.tgz" ; content=$(tar -tzf $myfile) ; echo $content
myfile.txt
```

In this case, we used the command substitution to perform a test on a `tar` file whose name was provided by means of a variable. The output of the command substitution was then fed as an argument to echo, which showed us the outcome of the `tar` command. We could use an even more complex command inside the command substitution bit, but beware of some issues with escaping since what happens inside the parentheses is not always what we would expect.

Is this a valid way to make processes communicate with each other? Yes, it is. Is it handy? Not so much. Command substitution can be tricky in a complex task, and we have the same limitations we saw for other methods since it is a one-way flow. That said, it is widely used in Bash scripts to provide a quick access to command paths or just store some information in variables, such as the actual date on the system or whatever small bit of information we need. We have other options to feed the output of a process to the standard input of another, but sometimes we do not take enough time to think at all the ways we have to accomplish this goal. For example, using the process substitution.

The process substitution

The **process substitution** is a handy way to feed the output of multiple commands/processes to the input of another process. The standard way to manage a process substitution goes along with the following syntax:

```
>(list_of_commands)
<(list_of_commands)
```

Mind the space between <,>, and the parentheses; there is no space at all:

```
zarrelli:~$ wc -l <(ps -fj)
5 /dev/fd/63
```

In this example, the output of `ps -fj` has been given as an input to `wc -l`, which counted 5 lines in the output. Notice /dev/fd/63.

This is the file descriptor used by the process substitution to feed the results of the process inside the parentheses to another process. So, file descriptors in /dev/fd are used to feed data, and this is useful, especially for those commands that cannot take advantage of pipes, because they expect data to be read from a file and not fed from the standard input. A classic example of a multiprocess feed as follows:

```
zarrelli:~$ mkdir "test 1"
zarrelli:~$ mkdir "test 2"
zarrelli:~$ for i in {1..5}; do touch "test 1/$i"; done
zarrelli:~$ for i in {1..3}; do touch "test 2/$i"; done
zarrelli:~$ diff <(ls "test 1") <(ls "test 2")
4,5d3
< 4
< 5
```

We just created a couple of test directory and in the first directory, we made 5 empty files, in the second, 3. Then, we just fed `diff` with the output of the `ls` command issued on both `test 1` and `test 2` directories. The utility then just showed us all the files available in `test 1` but not in `test 2`, as we had issued it on the two real directories. It is handy, but consider its scope carefully since the command substitution remains available in a function until this returns. Talking about scope, process substitution is a good way to avoid a common pitfall when piping command to a loop in a subshell:

```
#!/bin/bash
main_variable=10
echo "We are outside the loop and the global variable called main_variable
has a value of: $main_variable"
for i in {1..5}
do
echo "$i"
done |
while read j
do
main_variable="$j"
echo "We are inside the loop and main_variable has a value of:
$main_variable"
done
echo "We are now past the loop and main_variable has a value of:
$main_variable"
```

Piping is actually executing the loop inside a subshell, and this will have all the variables inside the loop being available in the subshell only. The value of main_variable will be modified in the inner loop but once we exit it, we go back to the main value since each variable value set in the inner loop cannot be sent back to the calling environment:

```
zarrelli:~$ ./looping.sh
We are outside the loop and the global variable called main_variable has a
value of: 10
We are inside the loop and main_variable has a value of: 1
We are inside the loop and main_variable has a value of: 2
We are inside the loop and main_variable has a value of: 3
We are inside the loop and main_variable has a value of: 4
We are inside the loop and main_variable has a value of: 5
We are now past the loop and main_variable has a value of: 10
```

As we can see, main_variable changes inside the subshell, where the loop after the pipe is executed; but it is unaffected on the main shell. Subshells can be really tricky, because you may not realize you are spawning them and so be unaware of what the real outcome will be. Even setting some environment variable will not help us in preventing this issue.

Environment variables

Let's call it a proof of concept more than a real means to have processes communicate with each other. Who would really want to mess with the environment? Anyway, we are exploring some viable means to IPC, so we can take this in account even though we will not use it in the first instance. Let's have a look at `env`:

```
env
LS_COLORS=REDACTED
XDG_MENU_PREFIX=xfce-
LANG=en_GB.utf8
DISPLAY=:0.0
XDG_VTNR=7
SSH_AUTH_SOCK=/tmp/ssh-MgHTC62oCYDp/agent.1121
GLADE_CATALOG_PATH=:
XDG_SESSION_ID=2
XDG_GREETER_DATA_DIR=/var/lib/lightdm/data/zarrelli
USER=zarrelli
GLADE_MODULE_PATH=:
DESKTOP_SESSION=xfce
PWD=/home/zarrelli
HOME=/home/zarrelli
GUAKE_TAB_UUID=b07321dd-a221-41bd-8ecc-0ae94b9082b9
SSH_AGENT_PID=1159
QT_ACCESSIBILITY=1
XDG_SESSION_TYPE=x11
XDG_DATA_DIRS=/usr/share/xfce4:/usr/local/share/:/usr/share/:/usr/share
XDG_SESSION_DESKTOP=xfce
GLADE_PIXMAP_PATH=:
GTK_MODULES=gail:atk-bridge
TERM=xterm
SHELL=/bin/bash
XDG_SEAT_PATH=/org/freedesktop/DisplayManager/Seat0
XDG_CURRENT_DESKTOP=XFCE
QT_LINUX_ACCESSIBILITY_ALWAYS_ON=1
SHLVL=1
XDG_SEAT=seat0
LANGUAGE=en_GB:en
GDMSESSION=xfce
LOGNAME=zarrelli
DBUS_SESSION_BUS_ADDRESS=unix:path=/run/user/1000/bus
XDG_RUNTIME_DIR=/run/user/1000
XAUTHORITY=/home/zarrelli/.Xauthority
XDG_SESSION_PATH=/org/freedesktop/DisplayManager/Session0
XDG_CONFIG_DIRS=/etc/xdg
PATH=/usr/local/bin:/usr/bin:/bin:/usr/local/games:/usr/games
SESSION_MANAGER=local/moveaway:@/tmp/.ICE-
```

```
unix/1169,unix/moveaway:/tmp/.ICE-unix/1169
OLDPWD=/home/zarrelli
_=/usr/bin/env
```

We trimmed out the content of the `LS_COLORS` variable, but even so, one outstanding issue is that the output is a bit crowded and holds a lot of information, most of it vital for our login session. So, first advice, let's be really cautious when tinkering with the `environment` variable.

One thing we must keep in mind is that there is a big difference between a `shell` variable and an `environment` one; let's see an example:

```
#!/bin/bash
a=10
b=20
echo -e "n"
echo "This is the value of a in the main subshell: $a"
(a=$((a+b)) ; echo "Inside the nested subshell a now has the value of: $a")
echo "Back to the main subshell a has a value of: $a"
echo -e "n"
echo "And now we will tinker with the environment..."
echo "This is the value of a in the main subshell: $a"
(
export a=$((a+b))
b=$((a+b))
echo "Inside the nested subshell a now has the value of: $a"
echo "Inside the nested subshell b now has the value of: $b"
echo "The value of the environment variable a is:"
env | grep ^a
echo "Here is the value of a at this level of subshell using process substitution:"
grep ^a <(env)
echo "And they are the same, since the nested shell share the environment variables of the parent shell"
echo "b is inherited as well: $b"
)
echo "Back to the main subshell the environment variable a has a value of: $a"
echo "Back to the main subshell the shell variable b has a value of: $b"
```

Executing it, we will get this:

```
zarrelli:~$ ./environment.sh
This is the value of a in the main subshell: 10
Inside the nested subshell a now has the value of: 30
Back to the main subshell a has a value of: 10
```

And now we will tinker with the environment:

```
This is the value of a in the main subshell: 10
Inside the nested subshell a now has the value of: 30
Inside the nested subshell b now has the value of: 50
The value of the environment variable a is:
a=30
Here is the value of a at this level of subshell using process
substitution:
a=30
```

And they are the same, since the nested shell shared the environment variables of the parent shell:

```
b is inherited as well: 50
Back to the main subshell the environment variable a has a value of: 10
Back to the main subshell the shell variable b has a value of: 20
```

What we get from this example concerns the normal use of variables. There is no real difference between shell and environment variables: both are accessible by sub processes/shells and both are unaffected by subshell manipulations. The real difference stands out when we have a subprocess which is executed by an `execve()` system call: in this case, the shell variable is not be passed through. We will have to export it to make it available to the subshell. If we want to have fun, there is something even trickier than this. A new keyword introduced with Bash 4.0 can reveal itself as a nice playground for our experiments.

Coprocesses

Introduced with Bash 4.0, the coproc keyword allow allows the user to run a process in the background in an asyncronous subshell. During the execution of the process, a pipe is established between the calling shell and the coprocess. The best results are obtained with programs which can be run in a CLI and can read from `stdin` and write to `stdout`, better if with an unbuffered stream. The syntax for coprocess is here:

```
coproc (NAME) command (redirections)
```

The bits within parentheses are optional, but if you specify a name, `coproc` will create a coprocess with the name. If no name is given, it will be defaulted to COPROC; and we must not define any name if the following is a simple command, otherwise it will be treated as the first word of the command. The process ID of the shell executing the coprocess is stored in a variable called NAME_PID:

```
Let's see an example:
zarrelli:~$ coproc { while true ; do ls ; done }
[2] 31067
```

We executed an infinite loop and its PID is shown as 31067; let's check whether we can read it from COPROC_PID, which is the default name for the variable when no name has been provided:

```
zarrelli:~$ echo $COPROC_PID
31067
```

Here, we can easily get the PID value from the COPROC_PID variable. When coprocess is executed the shell instances an array variable named after NAME, which holds two pieces of information:

- **NAME[0]**: This holds the output file descriptor for coprocess
- **NAME[1]**: This holds the input file descriptor for coprocess

So, we can read and write using the file descriptors, which in our example are here:

```
zarrelli:~$ echo ${COPROC[0]}
62
zarrelli:~$ echo ${COPROC[1]}
58
```

Another way to see what files are open for the current process is this:

```
ls -lah /proc/PID/fd
```

In our case, do this:

```
ls -la /proc/31067/fd
total 0
dr-x------ 2 zarrelli zarrelli 0 Apr 11 16:37 .
dr-xr-xr-x 9 zarrelli zarrelli 0 Apr 11 15:13 ..
lr-x------ 1 zarrelli zarrelli 64 Apr 11 16:37 0 -> pipe:[615372]
l-wx------ 1 zarrelli zarrelli 64 Apr 11 16:37 1 -> pipe:[615371]
lrwx------ 1 zarrelli zarrelli 64 Apr 11 16:37 2 -> /dev/pts/0
lrwx------ 1 zarrelli zarrelli 64 Apr 11 16:37 255 -> /dev/pts/0
```

```
l-wx------ 1 zarrelli zarrelli 64 Apr 11 16:37 60 -> pipe:[608200]
lr-x------ 1 zarrelli zarrelli 64 Apr 11 16:37 63 -> pipe:[608199]
```

These pipes are in place before any redirection a user could specify on the command line, so the file descriptors can be used as arguments for the commands issued on the command line, and redirections can be used to feed or retrieve data; but beware that the file descriptors do not get inherited by subshells. That said, we can feed data to coprocess simply using the following syntax:

```
echo data >&"${COPROC[1]}"
```

While we can use `read` to retrieve data from coprocess as follows:

```
read variable <&"${COPROC[0]}"
```

Before having a look a simple example, we have to keep in mind a few points:

- Most of the commands in Linux are buffered when used without a user interaction. And this fools us into reading from the `coproc` file descriptors. To make some simple experiments, the `bc` util works fine; or use `awk` with `fflush()` or the `unbuffer` command from the `expect` package to have unbuffered output.
- There can be only one active coproc at time.
- We can use the `wait` built-in to wait for coprocess to terminate.

That said, let's see how can we can interact with a process in the background:

```
#!/bin/bash
coproc bc_calc { bc; }
in=${bc_calc[1]}
out=${bc_calc[0]}
echo '10*20' >&$in
read -u $out myvar
echo $myvar
```

To trick `coproc` into letting us use a name we created a list with only one command followed by `;` then we made it a bit easier to work with file descriptors, storing them in two meaningful variables. So, we will not fiddle with 0 and 1. In the next step, we echoed a `bc` multiplication to the `stdin` of `bc` using its file descriptor, and read it with the `-u` option, which is exactly the option needed for reading from file descriptors. As the last step, we printed the out variable in which we previously stored the result of the multiplication, printed by `bc` on its standard output.

There is actually one last way to make different processes talk to each other; can we recall it? Yes, we already saw it at the very beginning of this book.

/dev/tcp and /dev/udp

If we look inside the `/dev` directory, we find lots of files that represent physical devices that can be hardware or not. These device files can represent partitions; loopback is used to access plain files as if they were block devices. ISO files, for example, can be mounted as if they were CD-ROMs. Some of this device files are quite unusual, but we have already heard of them, for instance, `/dev/null`, `/dev/zero`, `/dev/urandom`, `/dev/tcp`, and `/dev/tcp`.

These are called pseudo-devices, and they represent and provide access to some *facilities*. For instance, all this is moved or redirected to the `/dev/null` fall in a *black hole* and disappears, whereas `/dev/urandom` is a good way to get a random string when needed:

```
cat /dev/urandom | head -c 25 | base64
HwUmcXt0zr6a7puLtO1xyKMrAdZrRqIrgw==
```

With `/dev/tcp` or `/dev/udp`, we get access to a socket through which we can communicate to network services locally or remotely. For our examples, we will focus on TCP sockets, since they are more interesting to use for our experiments.

Then what is a socket? Imagine a socket as a pipe between two multistorey buildings. To put this pipe in place, you have to know the civic number of each building and which floor of one must be connected to which floor of the other. The same is for a network socket which is identified by two tuples:

```
origin_ip:origin_port
destination_ip:destination_port
```

So, Bash is able to set up a connection to a network service as long as we provide at least the remote end of the communication channel, the IP or hostname, and the port to cling to. Easy, isn't it, but how to do it? The right syntax is the following:

```
exec file_descriptor_number <> /dev/tcp/ip/port
```

< means opening the socket for reading, > for writing, and <> for both. There isn't a big difference between the IP or hostname, but we must pay attention to which file descriptors we are going to use. We have 10 file descriptors available, from 0 to 9, but since, `0 = stdin, 1 = stdout, 2 = stderr` are already bound, we cannot use them. So, we are left with seven file descriptors, from 3 to 9. So, let's try an easy example:

```
cat </dev/tcp/time.ien.it/13
11 APR 2017 22:00:46 CEST
```

We just read the time over the internet, connecting to an Italian time server in an easy way, but we can do something even more complicated; let's recall an example we made in the first chapter.

Let's open a socket in read/write mode to a web server and assign a file descriptor called 9:

```
zarrelli:~$ exec 9<> /dev/tcp/172.16.210.128/80 || exit 1
```

Then, we are going to write a request to it using the HTTP/1.1 syntax as if we were a real web browser:

```
zarrelli:~$ printf 'GET /index2.html HTTP/1.1nHost: 172.16.210.128nConnection: closenn' >&9
```

We just requested a simple HTML file created for this example; so since we requested it, it is time to read this page through the file descriptor called 9:

```
zarrelli:~$ cat <&9
HTTP/1.1 200 OK
Date: Sat, 21 Jan 2017 17:57:33 GMT
Server: Apache/2.4.10 (Debian)
Last-Modified: Sat, 21 Jan 2017 17:57:12 GMT
ETag: "f3-5469e7ef9e35f"
Accept-Ranges: bytes
Content-Length: 243
Vary: Accept-Encoding
Connection: close
Content-Type: text/html
<!DOCTYPE HTML PUBLIC "-//W3C//DTD HTML 4.01//EN"
"http://www.w3.org/TR/html4/strict.dtd">
<HTML>
<HEAD>
<TITLE>This is a test file</TITLE>
</HEAD>
<BODY>
<P>And we grabbed it through our descriptor!
</BODY>
</HTML>
```

Here, we could interact with a remote server as if it was a local file, using `print` and `cat` to push and pull content. All locally, but definitely remotely.

There is indeed one last way to have fun when we want to tinker with IPC; even though this is not a proper IPC means, it is so much fun that we cannot avoid talking about Netcat.

Netcat

We could even never have been using this tool but no one probably can say they never heard about it being called the *TCP/IP Swiss army knife* and that for its versatility. You can literally have hours of fun just exploring all the possibilities it enables. That said, `netcat` is a utility, which reads and writes over the network using either TCP or UDP protocol; and what makes it really handy is its ability to keep up the connection until the remote side of the connection is shut down. This makes it different from most of the applications, which just stop working after the last bit of data has been delivered. `netcat` is different; it keeps both ends of the communication channel in touch even if there is nothing passing through, so you can use it for repeated dispatches.

The Netcat can be used either in a server or client mode and from inside scripts too by adding network facilities to them. So many things, but the best way to understand what we can do with it is to run some examples. So, the first step will be opening a connection to a remote server inside a term, which can be split in two panels such as *terminator*. Last bit, remember that Netcat cannot be installed by default on our system, but distributions have a package for it. So, once the utility is installed, let's open two `xterm`, or split terminators into two panels and connect to a remote server. On the remote server, check for an open port, usually something around `8000` (`8080` being a port widely used for proxies) or `9000` would be nice; a command like this executed as root can tell us whether the port we are looking for is available:

```
root:# netstat -tapnl | grep 9000
```

Netstat simply lists all the tcp ports in listen mode, showing the numeric port numbers; and then we grep over the port we want to check. If it returns nothing, the port is free. Second step, often forgotten, is that we are sure the port is not blocked by our local firewall. This is because we are mastering Bash and *have* a firewall in place even on our local desktop. We will talk more about securing our boxes later on, but, for now, let's assume we have a simple but reliable firewall in place such as `ufw`. To enable port `900` , we can just give the following command:

```
root:# ufw allow 9000/tcp
Rule added
Rule added (v6)
```

Let's Make a Process Chat

Rule added, it is the sixth in our chain, but it can have any other number depending on how many other rules you have. Remember that to delete a rule, you just have to run this:

```
root:# ufw delete 6
Deleting:
allow 9000/tcp
Proceed with operation (y|n)? y
Rule deleted
```

We used the rule number; you can use the rule name `allow 9000/tcp` as you wish. Now that we have a free port unblocked, we can run `netcat` in listening mode on the remote server:

```
root:# netcat -lvvp 9000
listening on [any] 9000 ...
```

This will start `netcat` in listening mode, and `-l` will be ready to accept connections on port `-p 9000` in a verbose detailed mode `-vv`. We will not have our prompt back because `netcat` keeps running in the foreground, monopolizing the terminal. Now, on the local system, let's run `netcat` in client mode:

```
zarrelli:~$ nc -vv 192.168.0.10 9000
spoton [192.168.0.10] 9000 (?) open
```

Great, the connection is opened on both sides. Notice that we invoked Netcat both with the `netcat` command and `nc`; we can choose whatever we prefer. Once the connection is established, we will see a message like this on the listening side:

```
192.168.0.5: inverse host lookup failed: Unknown host
connect to [192.168.0.10] from (UNKNOWN) [192.168.0.5] 60054
```

The message called `Unknown host` must not bother us; Netcat makes a reverse lookup to check the hostname the connection is coming from. Being a test environment we did not set any internal DNS resolution. If you do not want to tinker with DNS, a simple solution is to open the `/etc/hosts` file on the server side operating system and add a line such as `192.168.0.5 spoton`.

Being `192.168.0.t` the IP address of the client the connection is coming from and `spoton` the hostname we want it to be identified and resolved by `netcat` on the server side. If you don't want the DNS resolution, add `-n` on the server and the client side, and you will work with IP. So now, let's retry the connection:

```
root:# netcat -lvvp 9000
listening on [any] 9000 ...
connect to [192.168.0.10] from spoton [192.168.0.5] 60176
```

This looks better, doesn't it? Let's just type something on the client, and whatever we input will be echoed on the server side. We can pause and type at a later time; meanwhile, the channel will be up and running waiting for our input:

The client is on the left panel and gets echoed on the right panel, onto the server side. Now something spooky; on the server side, type this:

```
root:# netcat -lvvp 9000 -c /bin/date
listening on [any] 9000 ...
```

What we just did is use the `-c` switch to tell `netcat` to execute right after the connection the command specified as argument. The command will be passed to `/bin/sh -c` for execution with no further check, and if you do not have the `sh` shell installed, just use `-e` to have the command executed. Now, on the client side, let's execute this:

```
zarrelli:~$ nc -vv 192.168.0.10 9000
spoton [192.168.0.10] 9000 (?) open
Wed 12 Apr 11:14:07 BST 2017
sent 0, rcvd 29
```

The connection has been established right after the `date` command has been issued; so, in our client, we can see the output of the command and the date and time on the server side. It does not seem spooky, does it? It is just `date`, what harm can it do? Okay, let's modify the server argument and be ready to freak out:

```
root:# netcat -lvvp 9000 -c /bin/bash
listening on [any] 9000 ...
```

Interesting, at each connection, we will execute a Bash shell. Let's open it on the client side:

```
zarrelli:~$ nc -vv 192.168.0.10 9000
spoton [192.168.0.10] 9000 (?) open
```

Now, let's give some innocent commands in the client:

```
date
Wed 12 Apr 11:21:02 BST 2017
```

Okay, this is a date, but where are we?

```
pwd
/root
```

Nice, but who are we?

```
whoami
root
```

So, we are `root` but on which side?

```
hostname -I | awk '{print $1}'
192.168.0.10
```

Ouch, we are `root` on the server, and we issued commands as a superuser with no authentication required. Since this is really dangerous, use this option with extreme care. Maybe just for fun and testing and nothing else, we just showed it to highlight the potentials and the risks.

What else can we do? Let's create a file on the client side:

```
zarrelli:~$ echo "Here I am, a test file" > testfile.txt
```

On the server side, let's start `netcat`, this time with no verbose mode since we do not need it if you do not want to debug the connection and redirect the output to `testfile.txt`:

```
zarrelli:~$ netcat -lp 9000 > testfile.txt
```

We used unprivileged users. We do not need to use `root` if we do not want to bind the so-called reserved or system ports; the ports below `1024` are used for providing service, such as `22` for SSH, `80` for HTTP, and so forth.

Now, back on the client side, let's feed the client with the content of `testfile`:

```
zarrelli:~$ cat testfile.txt | nc -w2 192.168.0.10 9000
```

We added a timeout of 2 seconds for the connection so that once the file content is dispatched, it will close the connection after 3 seconds. Once on the server side, we see this:

```
connect to [192.168.0.10] from spoton [192.168.0.5] 32912
sent 0, rcvd 29
```

We are done and we just have to interrupt Netcat with a *Ctrl + C* and check the content of `filetest.txt`:

```
zarrelli:~$ cat testfile.txt
"Here I am, a test file"
```

And that's it, the content of the file has been transferred to the server and saved on `testfile.txt`. But what if we wanted to transfer whole directories or bunches of file? We cannot adopt the same strategy because all the output would be redirected to a single file, and this won't work. So, on the server side, let's first create a test `dir`:

```
zarrelli:~$ mkdir test
zarrelli:~$ cd test
```

Now, let's run Netcat:

```
zarrelli:~$ nc -lvvp 9000 | tar -xpzf -
```

This will run `tar` on the input with the following:

- `x`: It extracts files from the archive received in input
- `p`: It preserves permissions on files
- `z`: It filters the received archive through `gzp`, essentially uncrompressing it
- `f`: File archive to work on. In our case everything goes to the `stdout`
- `-`: The last dash means it will work on the data coming from the `stdin` instead of looking for a file on the filesystem

On the client side, let's enter a directory with some files and subdirectories we want to transfer and have a look at their properties:

```
zarrelli:~$ ls -lah
total 44K
drwxr-xr-x 4 zarrelli zarrelli 4.0K Apr 12 11:54 .
drwxr-xr-x 4 zarrelli zarrelli 4.0K Apr 12 12:56 ..
-rw-r--r-- 1 zarrelli zarrelli   11 Apr 10 09:20 controller
-rwxr--r-- 1 zarrelli zarrelli  121 Apr 11 18:30 coproc.sh
-rwxr--r-- 1 zarrelli zarrelli  961 Apr 11 12:19 environment.sh
-rwxr--r-- 1 zarrelli zarrelli  382 Apr 11 10:08 looping.sh
-rw-r--r-- 1 zarrelli zarrelli    0 Apr 10 09:20 myfile.txt
-rw-r--r-- 1 zarrelli zarrelli  122 Apr 10 09:20 myfile.txt.tgz
prw-r--r-- 1 zarrelli zarrelli    0 Apr  9 13:05 mypipefile
-rwxr--r-- 1 zarrelli zarrelli  223 Apr  9 12:44 pipe.sh
drwxr-xr-x 2 zarrelli zarrelli 4.0K Apr 10 12:20 test 1
drwxr-xr-x 2 zarrelli zarrelli 4.0K Apr 10 12:20 test 2
-rw-r--r-- 1 zarrelli zarrelli   29 Apr 12 12:06 testfile.txt
```

Now, on the client side, let's run Netcat:

```
tar czf - * | nc -vw2 192.168.0.10 9000
```

The `tar` command is executed with the following:

- `c`: Create an archive.
- `z`: Compress it filtering through `gzip`.
- `f`: File archive to work on. In our case, it will get the name from the input.
- `-`: The last dash means it will work on the data coming from the `stdin` instead of looking for a file on the filesystem.

We gave all the visible files and directories as input to `tar`; we could also use single or multiple files and directory names if we just wanted to copy a few of them. Once the command is given, we should see something like this on the server side:

```
connect to [192.168.0.10] from spoton [192.168.0.5] 33022
sent 0, rcvd 1352
```

It seems the files and directories have been transferred. Let's exit Netcat and check this:

```
zarrelli:~$ ls -lah
total 44K
drwxr-xr-x  4 zarrelli zarrelli 4.0K Apr 12 12:35 .
drwxr-xr-x 70 zarrelli zarrelli 4.0K Apr 12 12:33 ..
-rw-r--r--  1 zarrelli zarrelli   11 Apr 10 09:20 controller
-rwxr--r--  1 zarrelli zarrelli  121 Apr 11 18:30 coproc.sh
-rwxr--r--  1 zarrelli zarrelli  961 Apr 11 12:19 environment.sh
-rwxr--r--  1 zarrelli zarrelli  382 Apr 11 10:08 looping.sh
-rw-r--r--  1 zarrelli zarrelli    0 Apr 10 09:20 myfile.txt
-rw-r--r--  1 zarrelli zarrelli  122 Apr 10 09:20 myfile.txt.tgz
prw-r--r--  1 zarrelli zarrelli    0 Apr  9 13:05 mypipefile
-rwxr--r--  1 zarrelli zarrelli  223 Apr  9 12:44 pipe.sh
drwxr-xr-x  2 zarrelli zarrelli 4.0K Apr 10 12:20 test 1
drwxr-xr-x  2 zarrelli zarrelli 4.0K Apr 10 12:20 test 2
-rw-r--r--  1 zarrelli zarrelli   29 Apr 12 12:06 testfile.txt
```

That's it, all the files and directories are copied and permissions preserved. There are so many things we can do with Netcat that probably it would deserve a book on its own; we are just scratching the surface and having fun:

```
zarrelli:~$ netcat -z -w 1 -vv 192.168.0.10 22
spoton [192.168.0.10] 22 (ssh) open
sent 0, rcvd 0
```

We can just use it as a simple port scanner with -z, which will prevent the reception of any data from the remote server and -w 1 to timeout the connection in case the remote port does not provide a reply. You can add -n to prevent the DNS resolution and specify a port not only by its number but also with its name or specify a range of ports to be checked specifying *lower_port_number:higher_port_number*:

```
zarrelli:~$ netcat -z -w 1 -vv 192.168.0.10 https
spoton [192.168.0.10] 443 (https) : Connection timed out
sent 0, rcvd 0
```

If we do not know or remember the ports associated to the main services, we can retrieve a list from the /etc/services file.

Well, do we need a proxy?

```
zarrelli:~$ ncat -l 9999 -c 'nc 192.168.0.10 80'
```

In this case, we used ncat, a sort of Netcat on steroids, which can overcome a limit in Netcat. It has a one direction pipe, so we can send but not read from the server while proxying. Once ncat executes Netcat, managing the flow, we can connect to port 9999 on localhost and ask for a page:

```
telnet localhost 9999
Trying ::1...
Connected to localhost.
Escape character is '^]'.
GET / HTTP/1.1
Host: 192.168.0.10
Connection: close
HTTP/1.1 200 OK
Date: Wed, 12 Apr 2017 12:41:02 GMT
Server: Apache/2.4.10 (Debian)
Last-Modified: Thu, 01 Dec 2016 18:52:27 GMT
ETag: "29cd-5429d52a85057"
Accept-Ranges: bytes
Content-Length: 10701
Vary: Accept-Encoding
Connection: close
Content-Type: text/html
<!DOCTYPE html PUBLIC "-//W3C//DTD XHTML 1.0 Transitional//EN"
"http://www.w3.org/TR/xhtml1/DTD/xhtml1-transitional.dtd">
<html xmlns="http://www.w3.org/1999/xhtml">
```

We just cut a part of the output with the whole page and highlighted the commands we gave to retrieve the page. Anyway, instead of `ncat`, we could use Netcat with a named pipe:

```
zarrelli:~$ mkfifo mypipe
```

Then, simply use the output redirection to have a bidirectional channel:

```
zarrelli:~$ nc -l 9999 0<mypipe | nc 192.168.0.10 80 1>mypipe
```

Now, telnet to localhost on port `9999` and perform the same get as in the other example or, better, fire up your internet browser and point it to `http://localhost:9999`.

One more thing before leaving this chapter, did you ever fancy a quick, easy server at your disposal? Let's start creating a small HTML page:

```
<!doctype html>
<html lang="en">
<head>
<meta charset="utf-8">
<title>My Netcat Test Page</title>
<meta name="description" content="Test page for Netcat HTTP server">
<meta name="author" content="Giorgio Zarrelli">
<link rel="stylesheet" href="css/styles.css?v=1.0">
</head>
<body>
Hello I am a test page for Netcat used as HTTP server
</body>
</html>
```

Now, an infinite loop will help Netcat to serve us the page:

```
while true; do nc -lp 9999 < my_index.html; done
```

Last step, let's open `http://localhost:9999` in our favorite internet browser.

The page will be served because it was pushed by a web server, as we can see from the following screenshot:

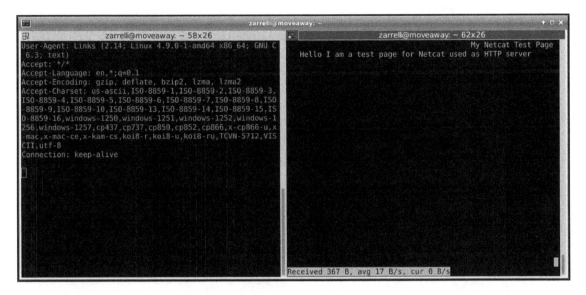

The HTML page we just created is being served as if it was pushed by a real web server.

Summary

Letting services talk to each other is not so difficult and can be real fun, especially if we know how to redirect the flows and spice things up with the right tools. Did we see everything Bash has to offer regarding IPC? No, and this is one of the best things about the shell: we can accomplish the same task in different ways, and there are so many things to do that a chapter would not be enough. Once again, this is the best thing in shell: we start off with some examples, learn how to work with the commands and utilities, and then expand our knowledge trying new experiments, tinkering with options and arguments, and mastering the tools we have been offered.

We pushed IPC so far that Netcat became a simple web server, pushing a page over the network so that we could actually display it in a browser. This is amazing, and it is quite the limit of what Bash can do, but we will try to stretch these boundaries in the next chapter by taking a look at how we can create simple daemons and offer services with Bash.

11
Living as a Daemon

In the journey that we had through the pages of this book, we saw lots of fun stuff, played with processes, sent signals, put things in the background, and wrote complex scripts. Everything done so far has one goal: to make us get the best from our Bash, have it working for us in repetitive tasks, and use built-ins, loops, and external commands to ease our everyday life as a power user. There are some times, though, when we need our scripts getting to work on a long run, maybe staying active indefinitely, so just running it as a normal program would not fit our need. We have to sweep through the obscure path of life as a daemon.

What is a daemon?

Well, what makes a daemon different from a normal program? We usually want to use a daemon to get some of the following features:

- Runs indefinitely
- Offers a service
- Survives even if the calling session ends
- Does not lock a terminal
- Does not lock the any subdirectory

That is, more or less, what a daemon as we know it does. Imagine the SSHD daemon, FTPD, or Apache:

- Runs in the background
- Offers a service you interact with a socket

Living as a Daemon

- Can be started or stopped but no further direct interaction from the command line
- Available when you log in and still there when you log off
- They run in background

You actually have no idea on how they can do all of this.

nohup and &

So, how could we turn one of our scripts into a daemon? One first attempt could be using `&`. The trailing ampersand is a Bash built-in which instructs the shell to run the command in the background inside a subshell. Once the command is executed, the shell does not wait for it to finish but returns a code 0, which means successful, and proceeds further in any other commands that are to be executed:

```
zarrelli:~$ ls -lah & ps -jf
[1] 13704
total 48K
drwxr-xr-x 4 zarrelli zarrelli 4.0K Apr 12 14:12 .
drwxr-xr-x 4 zarrelli zarrelli 4.0K Apr 12 19:37 ..
-rw-r--r-- 1 zarrelli zarrelli  11 Apr 10 09:20 controller
-rwxr--r-- 1 zarrelli zarrelli 121 Apr 11 18:30 coproc.sh
-rwxr--r-- 1 zarrelli zarrelli 961 Apr 11 12:19 environment.sh
-rwxr--r-- 1 zarrelli zarrelli 382 Apr 11 10:08 looping.sh
-rw-r--r-- 1 zarrelli zarrelli   0 Apr 10 09:20 myfile.txt
-rw-r--r-- 1 zarrelli zarrelli 122 Apr 10 09:20 myfile.txt.tgz
-rw-r--r-- 1 zarrelli zarrelli 367 Apr 12 14:12 my_index.html
prw-r--r-- 1 zarrelli zarrelli   0 Apr  9 13:05 mypipefile
-rwxr--r-- 1 zarrelli zarrelli 223 Apr  9 12:44 pipe.sh
drwxr-xr-x 2 zarrelli zarrelli 4.0K Apr 10 12:20 test 1
drwxr-xr-x 2 zarrelli zarrelli 4.0K Apr 10 12:20 test 2
-rw-r--r-- 1 zarrelli zarrelli  29 Apr 12 12:06 testfile.txt
UID        PID  PPID  PGID  SID C STIME TTY      TIME CMD
zarrelli  1385  1272  1385 1385 0 08:14 pts/0 00:00:00 /bin/bash
zarrelli 13705  1385 13705 1385 0 10:55 pts/0 00:00:00 ps -jf
[1]+ Done      ls --color=auto -lah
```

What we saw in the example is that the shell executed the first `ls` command and gave us back this:

```
[1] The job number
13704 The process ID
```

But then, it did not wait for the `ls` process to complete its job; it just forked it in a subshell and proceeded to execute the `ps` command. For our experiments, let's create an empty shell and a script with an infinite loop, which actually does nothing:

```
#!/bin/bash
while true
do
:
done
```

Nothing special, the only thing interesting here is that once launched, the script will execute until we stop it. Now, let's run it:

zarrelli:~$ ./while.sh

Well, we said it does nothing, but it actually does something: it gets hold of your terminal and will not give it back to you until it is terminated or sent into the background. So, here we have two options:

Ctrl + C sends a `SIGKILL` signal to the process and terminates it:

zarrelli:~$ ./while.sh
^C

Ctrl+Z sends `SIGTSTP`, which suspends its execution:

zarrelli:~$ ./while.sh
^Z
[1]+ Stopped   ./while.sh

Once suspended, we can put the job in the background using its job ID, in our case `[1]`:

zarrelli:~$ bg %1
[1]+ ./while.sh &

If now we check the status of the job, it will be this:

zarrelli:~$ jobs
[1]+ Running   ./while.sh &

We can see that the script is no longer stopped, but it is actually running in the background. At this point, you may have forgotten what was the PID of the subshell running the script, or you just do not know that there is a quick way to recall it, since it is stored in the `$!` variable:

```
zarrelli:~$ echo $!
18672
```

Now, let's bring the process into the foreground:

```
zarrelli:~$ fg %1
./while.sh
```

Kill it since it got hold of the terminal once again:

```
zarrelli:~$ ./while.sh
^C
```

Let's see what happens if we run multiple instances of the script directly in the background using the ampersand:

```
zarrelli:~$ ./while.sh & ./while.sh & ./while.sh &
[1] 20167
[2] 20168
[3] 20169
```

So, all of them are in the background with their own job ID:

```
zarrelli:~$ jobs
[1]  Running    ./while.sh &
[2]- Running    ./while.sh &
[3]+ Running    ./while.sh &
```

There is something new in the output of jobs and those are – and + characters, which are close to the job ID:

- +: This identifies the job that `fg` or `bg` will work on by default
- –: This identifies the job that would be the default if the current default job exited.

Let's make a test. First, check the status of the jobs:

```
zarrelli:~$ jobs
[1]  Running    ./while.sh &
[2]- Running    ./while.sh &
[3]+ Running    ./while.sh &
```

All of them are running in the background. Let's recall in the foreground the default one:

```
zarrelli:~$ fg
./while.sh
```

Now, let's suspend it with *Ctrl+Z*:

```
./while.sh
^Z
[3]+ Stopped    ./while.sh
```

So, we just gave the `fg` command without an argument; and as expected, the job with ID 3 and the + trailing character was pulled into the foreground. Now, let's check the status of the jobs:

```
zarrelli:~$ jobs
[1]  Running    ./while.sh &
[2]- Running    ./while.sh &
[3]+ Stopped    ./while.sh
```

The third job is stopped, but we can see the + character. Let's recall the default job to the foreground again, and then stop it:

```
zarrelli:~$ fg
./while.sh
^Z
[3]+ Stopped    ./while.sh
```

Again, the third job is the default one because it never died, it just got suspended. So, time to gracefully kill it:

```
zarrelli:~$ kill -15 %3
[3]+ Terminated    ./while.sh
```

Let's have a look at the status of the job now that we killed the default one:

```
zarrelli:~$ jobs
[1]- Running    ./while.sh &
[2]+ Running    ./while.sh &
```

That's it, the job ID number 2 is now the default one, and the number 1 is the second in the line.

nohup

nohup is a **Portable Operating System Interface** (**POSIX**) command that prevents the process given as an argument from receiving the **Hangup (HUP)** signal. If we run a script preceding it with nohup, it will be shielded by the HUP signal sent to all the processes when the interactive session closes. If the standard output is a terminal, nohup appends it to the `nohup.out` file in the local directory and if it is not possible in the user's home directory while the standard error is redirected to the `stdout`. So something as follows:

```
zarrelli:~$ nohup ./while.sh &
[1] 14247
nohup: ignoring input and appending output to 'nohup.out'
```

The script is running in the background as `jobs` correctly reports:

```
zarrelli:~$ jobs
[1]+ Running   nohup ./while.sh &
```

So, the script is detached and `stdout` is redirected to the `nohup.out` file while `stdin` is ignored:

```
zarrelli:~$ ls -lah
total 12K
drwxr-xr-x 2 zarrelli zarrelli 4.0K Apr 13 14:35 .
drwxr-xr-x 4 zarrelli zarrelli 4.0K Apr 13 14:32 ..
-rw------- 1 zarrelli zarrelli    0 Apr 13 14:35 nohup.out
-rwxr--r-- 1 zarrelli zarrelli   35 Apr 13 11:06 while.sh
```

Now, let's exit our interactive session using `exit` and recreate a new session. We just have to open a new terminal and give the `jobs` command:

```
zarrelli:~$ jobs
```

Nothing, no jobs were listed. Why? Is the process still there? Let's have a look:

```
zarrelli:~$ ps ax | grep while
14247 ?     R  8:49 /bin/bash ./while.sh
14839 pts/0 S+ 0:00 grep while
```

The script is still running and `PID` is the same, so why don't we see it in the job list? Because we closed the old shell and opened a new one; and so the old job list, related to the old shell, got destroyed. This is desirable since without having a job ID, the shell cannot control the process and interfere with it directly. Then, have a look at the second field of the process listing:

```
14247 ?     R  8:49 /bin/bash ./while.sh
14839 pts/0 S+ 0:00 grep while
```

While `grep` has a terminal associated `pts/0`, the `while` script runs without any terminal associated, so we see `?` and that is what we wanted from the beginning. Before proceeding, let's clean up, killing the script:

```
zarrelli:~$ kill 14247
```

Nice, everything is clear, simple, and easy, isn't it? No. Sometimes we just fire an application on a remote server through SSH. We use `nohup` and `&` to detach completely from the terminal, and shield it from the HUP signal on session closure; and then when we try to log off, our connection just hangs indefinitely. What happened? Why does everything seem to hang? This behavior is due to the OpenSSH server that handles the SSH connections: before closing the connection, OpenSSH waits to read the **end-of-file (eof)** on the pipes connected to `stdout` and `stderr` of the process ran by the user. The issue here is related to how a file returns an eof in Unix, and it does so when all the references to it have been closed. But when you run a process in the background of the shell you are working on over an SSH connection, the process gets the standard references to `stdout` and `stderr` of the shell it runs in. When you then close the shell, the OpenSSH server loses these references, because the shell has now died and so it will never see any eof coming from those. So, it will hang the connection indefinitely. So, how to prevent this? Actually either manually closing the process once it has been launched and before logging out or redirecting the references to the standard streams (`stdin`, `stdout`, `stderr`) when launching it:

```
nohup command > foo.out 2> foo.err < /dev/null &
```

Unfortunately, not even redirecting sometimes works since OpenSSH is quite sensitive to a bunch of causes and circumstances and will not send any HUP to the processes.

disown

What if we run a process and then want to keep it alive even after the interactive shell has been closed? Let's recall what happens when a shell exits: before exiting, it sends SIGHUP to all the jobs running. If a job is in stop state, the shell will send it a SIGCONT signal to resume it so that it can receive the SIGHUP signal and gracefully die. To accomplish this task, the shell browses through a table where it keeps all the jobs, and here is the trick. Let's start a script in the background a few times:

```
zarrelli:~$ ./while.sh & ./while.sh & ./while.sh &
[1] 8944
[2] 8945
[3] 8946
```

Now let's have a look at the shell job table:

```
zarrelli:~$ jobs
[1]  Running    ./while.sh &
[2]- Running    ./while.sh &
[3]+ Running    ./while.sh &
```

We can see all three processes running as we expected. Now do the fun stuff:

```
zarrelli:~$ disown %2
```

What just happened to the job with ID 2?

```
zarrelli:~$ jobs
[1]- Running    ./while.sh &
[3]+ Running    ./while.sh &
```

Well, it disappeared from the job table but it's still there:

```
zarrelli:~$ ps -p 8945
PID TTY     TIME CMD
8945 pts/0 00:05:18 while.sh
```

The ps command followed by -p and pid just shows us a process selecting it on PID. It just showed that our disowned job is still up and running. So, with disown, we just removed a job from the shell job list; and thus, when the shell exits, it will not send to this job the SIGHUP signal it would send if no disown was given. We can actually go even further:

```
zarrelli:~$ disown -h %1
zarrelli:~$ jobs
[1]- Running    ./while.sh &
[3]+ Running    ./while.sh &
```

The job is still there but has been marked not to receive a `SIGHUP` signal from the shell when the latter exits. Optionally, you can run `disown` with no `ID` and `-a` so that it removes or marks all the IDs in the job table. No ID and `-r` will restrict the operations to only the running jobs.

Are the background processes not being killed after your interactive shell is closed? Let's check this:

shopt | grep huponexit

`huponexit` is set to off. This can be the reason why the background processes are not being killed on shell exit. We can temporarily set it on with this:

shopt -s huponexit; shopt | grep huponexit

To make it permanent, set it in `~/.bashrc` or `/etc/bashrc` with `shopt -s huponexit`.

Double fork and setsid

There are a couple of methods to daemonize a process, maybe less popular but really interesting ones; and these are the **double fork** and **setsid**.

Double fork is the way a process is usually daemonized and implies a fork, a duplication of the parent process to create a child one. In the case of double forking applied to daemonization, the parent process forks off a child process, then terminates it. Then, the child process forks its own child process and terminates. So, at the end of the chain, the two parent processes die and only the grandchild is alive and running but as a daemon. The reason for this resides in how a controlling terminal for a session is allocated since the child processes that are forked inherit the controlling terminal from their parent process.

In an interactive session, the shell is the first processed to be executed, so it is the controlling process for the terminal and the session leader from which all forked processes in the session inherit their controlling terminal. Forking and killing the parent processes gives us an orphan process, which is automatically reparented to `init`, so it becomes the child of the main process of the system. All of this is to prevent the child process from being a session leader and acquiring a controlling terminal; and this is the reason why we double fork and kill the parent twice: we want to make the child process an orphan so that the system, to prevent it from becoming a zombie process, will reparent it to `init`. Since it is is not the first process in its pipeline, it cannot become a session leader and acquire the controlling terminal. So, the child process is then moved to a different session and has no hold on the controlling terminal, going effectively daemon.

Let's have a look and start our script in the background:

```
zarrelli:~$ ./while.sh &
[1] 17460
```

And have a look at the IDs:

```
zarrelli:~$ ps -Ho pid,ppid,pgid,tpgid,sess,args
PID PPID PGID TPGID SESS COMMAND
10355 1401 10355 17515 10355 /bin/bash
17460 10355 17460 17515 10355 /bin/bash ./while.sh
17515 10355 17515 17515 10355 ps -Ho pid,ppid,pgid,tpgid,sess,args
```

The session ID is the same as the shell from which it forked, but it has its own process group ID and the **Parent Process ID** (**PPID**) equal to its parent process ID. Let's see where the script places itself in the process tree:

```
zarrelli:~$ pstree | grep -B3 while
|   `-{gmain}
|-login---bash-+-grep
|   |-pstree
|   `-while.sh
```

As expected, it is nested inside the login session, so it is part of this session. Now, let's double fork:

```
zarrelli:~$ (./while.sh &) &
[1] 17846
```

Have a look at the process:

```
zarrelli:~$ ps -Ho pid,ppid,pgid,tpgid,sess,args
PID PPID PGID TPGID SESS COMMAND
10355 1401 10355 17970 10355 /bin/bash
17970 10355 17970 17970 10355 ps -Ho pid,ppid,pgid,tpgid,sess,args
17847 1 17846 17970 10355 /bin/bash ./while.sh
```

The PPID of the shell executing `while` is now really interesting; it took the value of `1`. This means that his parent process is no longer the shell spawned at the login session but the `init` process. But notice, it still shares the same session ID and the same terminal. We can double-check with `pstree`:

```
zarrelli:~$ pstree | grep -B3 while
|   `-{probing-thread}
|-upowerd-+-{gdbus}
|   `-{gmain}
|-while.sh
```

We do not have any nesting since we are directly reparented at the first level to init.

With setsid, we get a slightly different outcome. Whenever a process which is not the process group leader calls setsid, this creates a new session and makes the calling process the session leader, the process group leader of a newly created process group, and deprives it of a controlling terminal. So, we essentially come up with a new session that holds a new process group and only one process, the calling process. Both the session and process group ID are set to the calling process ID. We want to daemonize a process but there is a drawback, we do not have any output unless we redirect to a file:

```
setsid command > file.log
```

Let's demonize our script:

```
zarrelli:~$ setsid ./while.sh
zarrelli:~$ ps -e -Ho pid,ppid,pgid,tpgid,sess,args | grep while
22853 10355 22852 22852 10355 grep while
22572 1 22572 -1 22572 /bin/bash ./while.sh
```

This time, we had to use the -e option of ps to show all the processes and the grep to while, because ps, by default, shows only the processes with the same effect user ID as the current user and with the same terminal. In this case, we changed the terminal, so it would not show up. Finally, let's have a look at pstree:

```
zarrelli:~$ pstree | grep -B3 while
 |  `-{probing-thread}
 |-upowerd-+-{gdbus}
 |  `-{gmain}
 |-while.sh
```

As we would expect, since the PPID is 1, we see a nesting on the first level. The process, in our case the shell, executing the script is reparented to init without any controlling terminal.

Now that we have examined a few methods on how to effectively put a process in the background and shield it from a session closure, we can proceed further, having a look at how we can actually write scripts that demonize themselves, going in the background and working without user interaction. Well, there would be some workaround such as using utilities: a screen and a terminal multiplexer, which allow you to detach a session from a terminal so that the process can keep running even if user logs out. Anyway, this is not our goal, we are not reviewing external tools but trying to sort out the best from our Bash, so the next paragraph will dwell a bit on the different methods to have Bash to demonize our scripts.

Becoming a daemon

A life as a daemon is not an easy life and requires a lot of gruesome deaths of parent processes.

The first thing needed for a process to become a daemon is to fork as a new process so the parent can exit, and the the prompt is returned to the invoking shell. This ensures that the new process is not a process group leader, since a process group leader cannot create a new session calling `setsid`. So, the new child process can now be promoted to process group leader and session leader by calling `setsid`. So far, the new session has no controlling terminal, and so does the new child. So, we fork again to be sure that the session and group leader can exit. Now, the grandchild is not a session, so the terminal it is going to open cannot be its controlling terminal. This is how things work in the hard life of a Linux process; if it is not a session leader, the terminal it is going to open is not the controlling terminal for the calling process.

Now, the process is detached from a controlling terminal but we still have an issue: it is locking the directory it has been called from, so if we tried to unmount it, we'd fail. The next step is to have the process change its working directory to `/`, the root directory of the filesystem (`chdir /`), or to any directory holding the files the process requires to be able to run. We are almost there. A good practice is to set `umask 0` for the process, so we reset `umask`. The process could have inherited and will create files with the permissions granted by the `open()` call. We are almost there; the next step for the process is to close the standard file descriptors (`stdin`, `stdout`, `stderr`) inherited from the parent process and open a new set.

Trapping a daemon

Before giving yourselves to the black magic of creating a daemon, you should learn how to shield it from any signals that can doom it to death. As we saw in the previous chapters, if a process dies, it could leave a mess behind since it had no time to clean *the house*. Scary, but we can do something to prevent all this: using traps that will help us deal with the signal and create more robust and well functioning scripts. In our case, the `trap` built-in will be handy to keep an eye on how our script behaves, since it is a signal handler that modifies how a process reacts to a signal. The general syntax of trap is here:

```
trap commands signal_list
```

With commands being a list that can be executed, functions included, upon receiving a signal. We already saw some of the signals and their numeric values, but trap can use some keywords for the most common ones, as listed in the following table:

Signal	Numeric value	
HUP	1	Hang up. Means that the controlling terminal exited.
INT	2	Interrupt, it happens when Ctrl + C is pressed.
QUIT	3	Quit.
KILL	9	This is an untrappable signal. Upon receiving, the process has to exit.
TERM	15	Terminate, is the default kill signal, can be handled, otherwise the process exits gracefully.
EXIT	0	An exit trap is raised on exit.

You can specify one or more signals per single trap, and you can also reset a trap to its default behavior using the trap called - signal.

Signals, how many of them? Who can remember all of them? No one but the kill command:

```
zarrelli:~$ kill -l
 1) SIGHUP	 2) SIGINT	 3) SIGQUIT	 4) SIGILL	 5) SIGTRAP
 6) SIGABRT	 7) SIGBUS	 8) SIGFPE	 9) SIGKILL	10) SIGUSR1
11) SIGSEGV	12) SIGUSR2	13) SIGPIPE	14) SIGALRM	15) SIGTERM
16) SIGSTKFLT	17) SIGCHLD	18) SIGCONT	19) SIGSTOP	20) SIGTSTP
21) SIGTTIN	22) SIGTTOU	23) SIGURG	24) SIGXCPU	25) SIGXFSZ
26) SIGVTALRM	27) SIGPROF	28) SIGWINCH	29) SIGIO	30) SIGPWR
31) SIGSYS	34) SIGRTMIN	35) SIGRTMIN+1	36) SIGRTMIN+2	37) SIGRTMIN+3
38) SIGRTMIN+4	39) SIGRTMIN+5	40) SIGRTMIN+6	41) SIGRTMIN+7
42) SIGRTMIN+8	43) SIGRTMIN+9	44) SIGRTMIN+10	45) SIGRTMIN+11
46) SIGRTMIN+12	47) SIGRTMIN+13	48) SIGRTMIN+14	49) SIGRTMIN+15	50) SIGRTMAX-14	51) SIGRTMAX-13	52) SIGRTMAX-12	53) SIGRTMAX-11	54) SIGRTMAX-10
55) SIGRTMAX-9	56) SIGRTMAX-8	57) SIGRTMAX-7	58) SIGRTMAX-6	59) SIGRTMAX-5
60) SIGRTMAX-4	61) SIGRTMAX-3	62) SIGRTMAX-2
63) SIGRTMAX-1	64) SIGRTMAX
```

Now, let's see how to use a trap for a clean exit with this little example:

```
#!/bin/bash
x=0
while true
```

```
do
    for i in {1..1000}
    do
    x="$i"
    if (( x == 500 ))
    then
        echo "The value of x is: $x" >> write.log
    fi
    done
done
```

This script features an infinite `while` loop, which hosts a nested `for` loop, running through a range between `1` and `1000`. When the value of x reaches `500`, it prints a message on the `write.log` file. Upon exit, the inner loop is relaunched, but the outer structure is an infinite loop and will keep running indefinitely. Let's run it and after a few seconds, let's issue a *Ctrl + C*:

```
zarrelli:~$ ./write.sh
^C
```

So, we had the terminal locked by our script that was running in the foreground, and to regain control, we had to issue a `kill -15`, a *TERM* signal, by pressing *Ctrl+C*. Let's have a look at the directory:

```
zarrelli:~$ ls -lh
total 28K
-rw-r--r-- 1 zarrelli zarrelli   20 Apr 16 07:54 open
-rwxr--r-- 1 zarrelli zarrelli  193 Apr 16 13:27 test.sh
-rwxr--r-- 1 zarrelli zarrelli   35 Apr 16 11:54 while.sh
-rw-r--r-- 1 zarrelli zarrelli 5.2K Apr 16 13:32 write.log
-rwxr-xr-x 1 zarrelli zarrelli  152 Apr 16 13:05 write.sh
-rwxr-xr-x 1 zarrelli zarrelli  293 Apr 16 13:28 write-term.sh
```

It seems that the log was left behind:

```
zarrelli:~$ tail -5 write.log
The value of x is: 500
The value of x is: 500
The value of x is: 500
The value of x is: 500
The value of x is: 500
```

Yes, it is actually our log filled with the message we set up. Being a log, it is not so bad if it is left behind, but what if this were a temporary file? Would we want to litter the filesystem with temp files each time the script exits because of a term or another signal? Let's improve it creating a cleanup function:

```
clean_exit()
{
echo "ouch, we received a iINT signal. Outta here but first a bit of
cleaning"
rm write.log
exit 0
}
```

Once invoked, this function will echo a meaningful message on `stdout`, delete the `write.log` file, and exit with a successful status. The last bit is the actual signal handler:

```
trap 'clean_exit' INT
```

That is all, let's run the script and give a *Ctrl+C* after a while:

```
zarrelli:~$ ./write-term.sh
^Couch, we received a INT signal. Outta here but first a bit of cleaning
```

It seems it worked; let's have a look at the filesystem:

```
zarrelli:~$ ls -lh
ttotal 20K
-rw-r--r-- 1 zarrelli zarrelli  20 Apr 16 07:54 open
-rwxr--r-- 1 zarrelli zarrelli 193 Apr 16 13:27 test.sh
-rwxr--r-- 1 zarrelli zarrelli  35 Apr 16 11:54 while.sh
-rwxr-xr-x 1 zarrelli zarrelli 152 Apr 16 13:05 write.sh
-rwxr-xr-x 1 zarrelli zarrelli 293 Apr 16 13:28 write-term.sh
```

Clean, `write.log` has been cleaned upon exit. This is the expected and desired behavior. We can also go further, shielding the process from a signal so that is essentially ignored. Let's add the following line to our script:

```
trap '' TERM
```

Now, let's execute the script in the background:

```
zarrelli:~$ ./write-term.sh &
[1] 16831
```

Well, since we are going to deal with daemons, we do not have to fear killing innocent processes:

```
zarrelli:~$ kill 16831
```

Haha! We killed you!

```
zarrelli:~$ jobs
[1]+ Running  ./write-term.sh &
```

Ahem, we have to reconsider our statement. It seems that our trap worked very well. In fact, a trap with a signal but with just ' ' as argument simply lets the signal be ignored. Well, we have other means of destruction, as we can invoke INT:

```
zarrelli:~$ kill -INT 16831
zarrelli:~$ ouch, we received a INT signal. Outta here but first a bit of
cleaning

[1]+ Done    ./write-term.sh
```

Finally, we exited the script in an orderly manner, no logs left behind:

```
zarrelli:~$ ls -lh
total 16K
-rw-r--r-- 1 zarrelli zarrelli  20 Apr 16 07:54 open
-rwxr--r-- 1 zarrelli zarrelli  35 Apr 16 11:54 while.sh
-rwxr-xr-x 1 zarrelli zarrelli 152 Apr 16 13:05 write.sh
-rwxr-xr-x 1 zarrelli zarrelli 307 Apr 16 13:39 write-term.sh
```

The filesystem is clean, no `write.log` left on it. Now, let's see a tricky use of a trap adding a few bits to our script. Let's start with y=0 placed at the very opening of the script, followed by a slightly revised loop:

```
for i in {1..3}
do
if (( x == 3 ))
then
y="$x"
echo "The value of x is: $x" >> write.log
fi
trap 'echo "The value of \$y is \"${y}\""' DEBUG
done
```

Now, let's run the script:

```
zarrelli:~$ ./write-debug.sh
The value of $y is "0"
The value of $y is "0"
The value of $y is "0"
The value of $y is "0"
The value of $y is "0"
The value of $y is "0"
The value of $y is "0"
The value of $y is "0"
The value of $y is "3"
The value of $y is "3"
```

 If a signal is received while Bash is waiting for a command to complete, the trap will be executed only after the command is over with its execution. If the built-in `wait` is used, it will return immediately upon receiving a signal for which a `trap` is set and the `trap` itself gets executed. Notice that a `trap` usually exits with a status of 0, but, in this case, the value of the exit status will be higher than 128.

Each time a command is executed, the value of the variable is printed as we can see, debugging the script with the -x option added to the Bash:

```
zarrelli:~$ /bin/bash -x ./write-debug.sh
+ y=0
+ trap clean_exit INT
+ trap '' TERM
+ for i in {1..3}
+ x=1
+ (( x == 3 ))
+ trap 'echo "The value of \$y is \"${y}\""' DEBUG
+ for i in {1..3}
++ echo 'The value of $y is "0"'
The value of $y is "0"
++ echo 'The value of $y is "0"'
The value of $y is "0"
+ x=2
++ echo 'The value of $y is "0"'
The value of $y is "0"
+ (( x == 3 ))
++ echo 'The value of $y is "0"'
The value of $y is "0"
+ trap 'echo "The value of \$y is \"${y}\""' DEBUG
+ for i in {1..3}
++ echo 'The value of $y is "0"'
The value of $y is "0"
```

```
++ echo 'The value of $y is "0"'
The value of $y is "0"
+ x=3
++ echo 'The value of $y is "0"'
The value of $y is "0"
+ (( x == 3 ))
++ echo 'The value of $y is "0"'
The value of $y is "0"
+ y=3
++ echo 'The value of $y is "3"'
The value of $y is "3"
+ echo 'The value of x is: 3'
++ echo 'The value of $y is "3"'
The value of $y is "3"
+ trap 'echo "The value of \$y is \"${y}\""' DEBUG
```

Move around the `trap` line and see how much info you can gather by modifying it to suit your needs. So, play for a while and have fun preparing for the the final touch of magic.

Going dark with the daemon

Do you think doing daemons is a complex task? Yes it is, unless you use a nice utility called *daemon*. The task of this program is to daemonize other commands or script in a simple and neat way. Does this utility take any shortcuts? No, it just goes through all the steps we have already seen to detach a process from the controlling terminal, putting it in background, starting a new session, clearing the umask, and closing the old file descriptors. Well, doing it by ourselves in Bash coding will be quite a difficult task. This program makes everything straightforward, nothing to take care of manually. But there is a drawback: this is not a standard utility and must be installed by the user. Not a big issue indeed since many distributions such as Debian or Red Hat have a package for this utility.

Time to try this utility out, so let's take our `write.sh` script and daemonize it:

```
root:# daemon -r /root/write.sh
```

We just called the daemon program, passing the full path to our script and the `-r` option that will respawn it in case it gets stopped. Let's see what happens on our system:

```
root:# ps -Heo tty,pid,ppid,pgid,tpgid,sess,args | grep write
pts/0 2458 2298 2457 2457 2298 grep write
?     2455    1 2454   -1 2454 daemon -r /root/write.sh
?     2456 2455 2454   -1 2454 /bin/bash /root/write.sh
```

Great, our script has no controlling terminal; it is running in background and writing its log file into the root directory of our filesystem. Now, let's kill it with the -9 option, as no process can ignore it:

```
root:# kill -9 2456
```

So we killed the process; let's verify it:

```
root:# ps -Heo tty,pid,ppid,pgid,tpgid,sess,args | grep write
pts/0 2461 2298 2460 2460 2298 grep write
?     2455    1 2454   -1 2454 daemon -r /root/write.sh
?     2459 2455 2454   -1 2454 /bin/bash /root/write.sh
```

The script is there. We actually killed its process but the -r option for daemon forced it to respawn the script; and here we are, our daemon is up and running even though we killed it. If we really want to read it, we must first kill the daemon program then the script process:

```
root:# kill -9 2455 2459
root:# ps -Heo tty,pid,ppid,pgid,tpgid,sess,args | grep write
pts/0 2481 2298 2480 2480 2298 grep write
```

This is the easiest way to run daemon, which has quite a bunch of options. For instance, let's say we want to run the script as user `zarrelli` and have it change the directory to a subdir:

```
root:# daemon -D /home/zarrelli/tmp/ -u zarrelli /home/zarrelli/write.sh
```

With -D, we gave a new target for `chdir` while -u gives the process a new running user as we can see from `ps`:

```
root:# ps -Heo user,tty,pid,ppid,pgid,args | grep write
zarrelli ? 2607    1 2606 daemon -D /home/zarrelli/tmp/ -u zarrelli
/home/zarrelli/write.sh
zarrelli ? 2608 2607 2606 /bin/bash /home/zarrelli/write.sh
```

As expected, the newly created log files belong to the user called `zarrelli`:

```
root:# ls -lah /home/zarrelli/tmp/
total 780K
drwxr-xr-x 2 zarrelli zarrelli 4.0K Apr 17 04:45 .
drwxr-xr-x 3 zarrelli zarrelli 4.0K Apr 17 04:43 ..
-rw-r--r-- 1 zarrelli zarrelli 769K Apr 17 04:50 write.log
```

Simple, but probably we want a service that runs at the startup of the system and stops when it shuts down. So, why not use `systemd` for our purposes? First step, we create the `/etc/systemd/system/writing.service` file.

We are going to create a basic unit for a `systemd` managed service, so let's write the following unit configuration lines inside the file:

```
[Unit]
Description=Write.sh Daemon
After=syslog.target
[Service]
ExecStart=/root/write.sh
Type=simple
[Install]
WantedBy=default.target
```

Nothing special here; depending on what kind of script we are going to demonize, we can choose our after target. A network script needs to be run after the network is up, so `network.target` is more appropriate here. We could just want to add some logging function, so we gave `syslog.target`. We could also give multiple target, so it really depends on what we are going to demonize. Under `[Service]`, we just point out the script executable and, more importantly, the type of execution: since our script will run indefinitely, it will never exit. So we need to specify the *simple* startup style so that `systemd` will execute the script and move on without waiting for it to exit like in the *fork* style. The rest is quite straightforward, so let's save the file and give the appropriate permission to it:

```
root:# chmod 664 /etc/systemd/system/writing.service
```

Now, time to enable the service:

```
root:# systemctl enable writing.service
```

Create a symlink from `/etc/systemd/system/default.target.wants/writing.service` to `/etc/systemd/system/writing.service`.

Reloading the `systemd` daemon will help to have the new service recognized:

```
root:# systemctl daemon-reload
```

Well, we are ready for the first execution of our service:

```
root:# systemctl start writing
```

No output here, but since this service is managed by `systemd`, we can ask the latter what is going on:

```
root:# systemctl status writing
writing.service - Write.sh Daemon
Loaded: loaded (/etc/systemd/system/writing.service; enabled)
Active: active (running) since Mon 2017-04-17 06:20:25 EDT; 57s ago
Main PID: 1582 (write.sh)
CGroup: /system.slice/writing.service
   └─1582 /bin/bash /root/write.sh
Apr 17 06:20:25 spoton systemd[1]: Started Write.sh Daemon.
```

The script is running; let's make some other checks:

```
root:# ls -lah /write.log
-rw-r--r-- 1 root root 469K Apr 17 06:23 /write.log
```

The `log` file is there, filling up; now let's check the terminal:

```
root:# ps -Heo user,tty,pid,ppid,pgid,args | grep write
root pts/0 1605 1048 1604 grep write
root ?     1582    1 1582 /bin/bash /root/write.sh
```

Here it is, without an associated controlling terminal. Last bit, we have to stop the daemon when we do not want it to run:

```
root:# systemctl stop writing
No output so let's verify:
root:# systemctl status writing
writing.service - Write.sh Daemon
Loaded: loaded (/etc/systemd/system/writing.service; enabled)
Active: inactive (dead) since Mon 2017-04-17 06:25:51 EDT; 3s ago
Process: 1582 ExecStart=/root/write.sh (code=killed, signal=TERM)
Main PID: 1582 (code=killed, signal=TERM)
Apr 17 06:20:25 spoton systemd[1]: Started Write.sh Daemon.
Apr 17 06:25:51 spoton systemd[1]: Stopping Write.sh Daemon...
Apr 17 06:25:51 spoton systemd[1]: Stopped Write.sh Daemon.
```

Finally, if we do not want our daemon to be managed by `systemd` anymore, we can just unlink it:

```
root:# systemctl disable writing.service
Removed symlink /etc/systemd/system/default.target.wants/writing.service.
```

Now, restart `systemd` daemon:

```
root:# systemctl daemon-reload
```

Summary

In this chapter, we had a look at how to set a process in the background and have it survive to our logouts and to most of the signal we could send to it. Next step was how to daemonize a process and how to make a system managed service out of it thanks to systemd. Is that all? Well, no. With a bit of creativity, we can assemble the bits and bricks we were given and create our own daemonized scripts and services, so this could be a nice homework during some rainy days.

We are now leaving daemons and moving onto something more related to system administration tasks, and we will see how to use some easy, powerful utilities and services to customize the environment we are working in and how to make it reasonably safe with little efforts.

12
Remote Connections over SSH

What is SSH?

The common answer to such questions is to use a secure shell and use SSH. The only drawback is that SSH is not a shell; it is actually a protocol often referred to SSH1 and SSH2: two different versions of the same protocol, incompatible with each other. Actually, nowadays, we are mostly dealing with SSH version 2 and OpenSSH server; it is the server program from the OpenBSD Project, which is available for a number of platforms.

What are the benefits of SSH and why should we use it? Short story long, SSH grants three main facilities:

- **Authentication**: This means it can make us sure of the identity of the other party. So, when someone tries to connect to our SSH server, the server will be able to obtain a digital proof of identity of the remote party prior to giving it access to the system.

- **Encryption**: Older protocols such as Telnet and FTP are nice and easy to use, but they have a huge drawback since they send data in clear, so if someone could not breach a server, they could always try to eavesdrop on the data to and from it. SSH addresses this issue by encrypting the data, so it cannot be read so easily.
- **Integrity**: It prevents tampering. If anyone intercepts the data and modifies it in transit, SSH will notice it.

A typical SSH connection goes through a series of steps involving establishing a session and authenticating:

- **Session**: The server listens to a port, usually port 22. The client contacts the server, which replies with the supported protocol versions. If any version is supported both by the client and the server, the connection continues. The server provides a host key, which is a proof of identity; and if it has been already recorded by the client on a previous session, it gets compared with the saved copy. The client and the server negotiate a session key, which will be used to encrypt the session (a symmetric key).

Once a secure channel has been established, the client authenticates to the server with a number of options such as Kerberos; it is host-based but usually uses one of the following methods:

- **Password**: The user must have a password-protected account on the remote server. This is probably the easiest way for the setup, but it holds some drawbacks such as we have to remember the username and password used on the remote host, and it makes it more difficult to automate logins into a script.
- **Public key**: Not to be confused with the encryption key, the public key method actually relies on a pair of SSH keys, one public and one private. One interesting thing is that the public key can be used to encrypt the data, which will be decrypted only by the private key. So, this is an asymmetric encryption since the two keys serve different purposes, and we cannot use the public key to decrypt data encrypted with the same public key. And there is no way to create a private key from a public one, so it becomes safe and easy to distribute the public key: whoever gets the public key can encrypt the data, but only those ones with the corresponding private key can decrypt it. So, it becomes safe to share the public key while the private one must be kept secret and unaccessible.

It is interesting to have a look at how the two different kinds of encryptions are used during an SSH session:

- **Symmetric encryption**: Used to encrypt all the data flowing through an SSH session, it relies on the Diffie-Hellman (or related) algorithm and relies on a large prime number, which works as follows:

    1. At the beginning of the session, both clients and servers chose a large prime number, which is used as a seed value. Then, the client and server chose one encryption generator such as AES and another prime number, which is not communicated to the other party.
    2. Now, we have a shared prime number, two private prime numbers, and an encryption generator, so each party derives a public key from its private prime number that it can share with the other side.
    3. Once shared, each party decrypts the other's public key, the algorithm, its private prime number, and the shared prime number to create a new master secret key that is the same for both, so it can be used to encrypt from both parts the subsequent traffic.
    In between, the process of establishing a master key involves the server using his host key to sign the data used in the transaction, and so it authenticates with the client, which now can trust the server.

- **Asymmetric encryption**: It is used in the authentication stage to authenticate the client onto the server. As we see, one of the the authentication methods is carried through a pair of keys, one public and one private:

    1. The client starts sending the ID of the pair of keys it wants to use for the authentication and a username.
    2. The server then checks whether the user account is available on the system and if inside there is a `.ssh` directory containing an `authorized_keys` file. If the file is available, it should contain the public keys stored by the server, so the ID sent by the client is matched against the IDs of the keys stored in this file.
    3. If the public key of the client is found, it is used to encrypt a random number that is then sent back to the client.
    4. The client, which generated the public key, holds its secret key, and so it can decrypt the packet sent by the server and obtain the secret random number.

5. On the client side, a random number is combined with the session key, and then hashed to obtain its MD5 hash value.
6. The MD5 hash value is then sent back to the server, which then uses the session key and the original random number to calculate the MD5 hash value on its own. If the two hash values match, it means that the client has the private key corresponding to the public key used to encrypt the random number and so the client is authenticated.

- **MD5 hashing**: We just hinted about MD5 hashing, so let's briefly explain what it is all about without drilling too much, since there are entire books on cryptographic and hashing algorithms. A hashing function is used to map a bunch of data with an arbitrary size to a fixed size. It is like creating a fingerprint of something but with a peculiar property: you can map the original data to a fixed size value using a hashing function, but you cannot map back from the fixed size value to the original data. Long story short, a hashing function is a one-way function. MD5 is an algorithm used by the hash function to produce a 128-bit hash value: whatever is the size of the hashed data, the MD5 hashed value produced will be 128 bits long--no more, no less. Although created as a cryptographic means, MD5 has proved itself vulnerable to different attacks, and so, it is used nowadays to check the integrity of the data, downloaded from a safe site and that has not been intentionally tampered.

SSH can give us a secure channel to work over the network, avoiding having the data being captured by third parties and having us securely authenticated. Most of the time, we are dealing with an OpenSSH server, but when it comes to clients, there are plenty of them for any operating systems: from command-line programs to graphical ones such as putty. It's just on us to choose whatever we find more ergonomic. Once we have chosen our preferred client, we can connect to the server; and since the most secure method is using public keys, we will see in the next chapter how to set up a passwordless connection to an SSH server.

Configuration files

Before playing with ssh and having a look at what it can do for us, let's take some time to see what are the most relevant files that are used to manage the ssh service and client. The configuration files for the SSHD daemon are usually stored in /etc/ssh where we can find some interesting files:

- `moduli`: This file contains the prime numbers and generators used by sshd in the Diffie-Hellman group exchange key exchange method, which is needed to create the shared session master encryption key.

- `sshd_config`: This is the configuration file for the ssh daemon. We will have a closer look at it later to see some interesting and useful directives, which alter the way we connect to a remote server.
- `ssh_config`: This is the system-wide SSH client configuration file that is used when no user-specific configuration file is found in the user home directory `~/.ssh/config`. We will see later on what we can do with it.
- `ssh_host_dsa_key`: This is the DSA private key used by the sshd daemon.
- `ssh_host_dsa_key_pub`: This is the DSA public key used by the sshd daemon.
- `ssh_host_rsa_key`: This is the RSA private key used by the sshd daemon.
- `ssh_host_rsa_key_pub`: This is the RSA public key used by the sshd daemon.
- `ssh_host_key`: This the RSA private key used by sshd for the SSH version 1 protocol.
- `ssh_host_key.pub`: This is the RSA public key used by sshd for the SSH version 1 protocol.
- `ssh_host_ecdsa_key`: This is the ECDSA private key used by the sshd daemon.
- `ssh_host_ecdsa_key.pub`: This is the ECDSA public key used by the sshd daemon.
- `ssh_host_ed25519_key`: This is the ED25519 private key used by the sshd daemon.
- `ssh_host_ed25519_key.pub`: This is the ED25519 public key used by the sshd daemon.

What are all these RSA, DSA, ECDSA, and ED25519 acronyms associated to the host keys? These acronyms refer to public key cryptosystems used for the authentication keys and open a world of holy wars: some say that **Digital Signature Algorithm (DSA)** is slower when encrypting but faster when decrypting compared to RSA (acronym from the name of the researchers behind this algorithm, Ron Rivest, Adi Shamir, and Leonard Adleman from MIT), which is deemed to be much more secure than DSA, while **Elliptic Curve Digital Signature Algorithm** (**ECDSA**) and **Edwards-curve Digital Signature Algorithm** (**ed25519**) are newcomers on the scene. All these are digital signature schemes that use different properties such as prime numbers or elliptic curves to ensure that the encryption itself is unbreakable, or more realistically, computationally unfeasible or not so likely. So, before proceeding, let's make a point: we cannot be sure that some encryption is really unbreakable, and we cannot be sure for how long some of them that nowadays look safe will be so in the future.

So, we can make an educated guess and chose an algorithm that is computationally expensive and allegedly without any backdoor from anyone. So, keeping in mind that we are never 100% safe, we can make our choice with some OpenSSH Project recommendations in mind:

- OpenSSH 7.0 deprecated DSA due to its weakness. So, we can safely discard this algorithm.
- Do not use keys smaller than 1024. This makes sense, since longer keys can be computationally heavier, but for everyday use, they do not give a relevant added hindrance.
- Do not use cyphers, such as Blowfish, CBC, RC4, MD5 based HMAC algorithms and RIPE-MD160 HMAC.
- Do not use SSH version 1, as it is deprecated and not supported.
- Use ECDA or ED25519, and if it not possible, we can create an RSA key of at least 2048 or 4096.

Quite complex, isn't it? Well, a rule of thumb to understand what NOT to use is to read the Release Notes page of the OpenSSH project we can find at `http://www.openssh.com/releasenotes.html` and have a look at the Future deprecation notice section.

Whatever we find here will be deprecated and eventually abandoned in the next releases, so even if we do not drill down into the details of the mathematics behind the encryption algorithms, we can trust the OpenSSH project and not use whatever is deprecated in any releases. When it comes to ciphers, these are algorithms that take chunks of plain data and create bits of obfuscated data. It suffices to say that even in this case, some holy wars are in play, with some major algorithms being considered weaker and some stronger:

- **Digital Encryption Standard (DES)**: Well regarded in the past, this is not really considered safe anymore due to the small keys used.
- **Triple DES**: This is based on DES and considered safer but not really efficient nowadays.
- **Advanced Encryption Standard (AES) or Rijndael**: This is a quite recent algorithm and well regarded. AES-256, for instance, is used in TLS/SSL, and it is considered safe.
- **IDEA**: This is a viable algorithm but due to patent use it is not so widespread.
- **Twofish**: Using blocks of 128 bits and a variable length key, it is one of the choices for our encryption needs.
- **Serpent**: If you do not have any ideas on what to choose, and cannot use AES, go with this, it has a block size of 128 bits and keys of 128, 192, and 256 bits. Slower than other options but safe: a block cipher with a block size of 128 bits.

After this short digression, we can proceed to having a look at another set of SSH config files that are optionally located on the user .ssh config directory:

- `authorized_keys`: In this file, we can find the list of the public keys that give access to the server. As we saw earlier, when a client tries to connect to the server, it looks for the account and if it exists, looks in the .ssh/authorized_keys file in the user home directory for the ID of the key pair provided by the client. If the ID is found, the client is authenticated with the user and key provided.
- `authorized_keys`: This file holds a list of authorized public keys for servers. When the client connects to a server, the server authenticates the client by checking its signed public key stored within this file.
- `known_hosts`: This file contains the host public keys of the server that the client had already accessed. When the server sends to the client their host public key, it has looked inside this file to see if it corresponds to the previously stored public key for the remote host.
- `config`: It holds the ssh client configuration for the user. It is really important in the passwordless connections since it helps to automate the connections. We will see more about it later.
- `id_dsa`: This holds the DSA private key for the user.
- `id_dsa.pub`: This holds the DSA public key for the user.
- `id_rsa`: This holds the RSA private key for the user.
- `id_rsa.pub`: This holds the RSA public key for the user.
- `Identity`: This contains the RSA private key of the user for SSH version 1.
- `Identity.pub`: This contains the RSA public key of the user for SSH version 1.

These are files we could find on a host, but probably we will not find all of them, for instance, not all the keys will be there; and we will have to create them taking the chance to give them some more meaningful names. Something we are sure to find on a remote host and interest us is the `sshd_config` file. Since this will help us to modify the way the daemon will offer the SSH server, let's have a look at it more in detail, covering some of the most interesting directives.

The sshd_config file

We will have a look at the directives that can be the most useful for our everyday service usage, but if we need to know all the details about all the configuration options, we can just invoke `man`:

```
man sshd_config
```

The main SSH daemon configuration file is located at the `/etc/ssh/sshd_config` event, though we can specify any file at the daemon startup using the `-f` option on the command line. That said, let's go through and have a look at the most interesting configuration bits:

- `AcceptEnv`: This allows the client to copy the environment variable into the session environment sent by the client. It can be useful, but it can also be dangerous, and the default is not to accept any client environment variable.
- `AllowGroups`: By default, the log in is only allowed for members from all groups available on the system, but with this directive, you can restrict it to only to the users whose primary or secondary groups matches the groups listed, even using a pattern, as we will see later. We can use group names only; no ID and the access directives are processed in this order: `DenyUsers`, `AllowUsers`, `DenyGroups`, `AllowGroups`.
- `AllowUsers`: By default, all users with a valid account are allowed to log in, but with this directive, we can restrict the access to only those members who match an account name or a patter. We can specify user names only and not IDs. We can also specify a member as `user@host` so that the restrictions will be applied not only to the account name but also to the origin host. This can be written in the CDIR/mask format. The access directives are processed in this order: `DenyUsers`, `AllowUsers`, `DenyGroups`, `AllowGroups`.

- `AuthenticationMethods`: We can specify the authentication methods that a user must successfully go through to be given access to the system. It defaults to *any* meaning that the user must successfully authenticate once to any of the available methods. If any authentication methods combination is listed, for instance, `password,publickey,keyboard-interactive,publickey`, the user will be forced to authenticate through all the authentication methods at least once and in the order they are listed. So, in the example show, the user has to successfully authenticate with the `publickey` method and then at least with a password. The `keyboad-interactive` method is a generic authentication, which relies on facilities such as PAM, RADIUS, and RSA Secure ID and can be limited by appending a column followed by the `bsdauth`, `pam`, or `skey` keywords. If the `publickey` method is used more than once, such as `publickey` and `publickey`, two different public keys will be required to successfully authenticate. Whatever method is listed, it then must be enabled in the configuration.
- `AuthorizedKeysFile`: Sometimes, we just put our client public authentication key in the `authorized_keys` file inside the `user ~./ssh` directory and nothing happens. Well, one of the issues could be originated by this directive, since it is here where the name of the file is defined. The default value is `.ssh/authorized_keys .ssh/authorized_keys2`, but we can also find some tokens such as `%h/.ssh/authorized_keys`, with `%h` standing for the home directory of the account autenticating; or we can also see `%%`, which stands for a simple `%` while a `%u` is replaced by the username. Once the tokens are expanded, the result is taken either as the full path to the file or the path relative to the user home directory.
- `Banner`: This is a nice option to show a message to the user before he authenticates. If `none` is supplied, no banner is shown. It is only available for SSH-2 and defaults to none.
- `ChallengeResponseAuthentication`: This allows the challenge-response authentication. It defaults to `yes`.
- `ChrootDirectory`: By specifying the full path to a directory, we can `chroot` a user into it after he successfully authenticates. It is not an easy task though since the directory must be owned by root and not writable by anyone else. In addition, we must provide some files required for a session, such as the shell, `/dev/null`, `/dev/zero`, `/dev/arandom`, `/dev/stdin`, `/dev/stdout`, `/dev/stderr`, and `/dev/ttyx`. We can also find some tokens such as `%h` standing for the home directory of the account authenticating; or we can also see `%%`, which stands for a simple `%` while a `%u` is replaced by the username.

- `Ciphers`: This allows us to specify the ciphers allowed for SSH-2. This is a good point to restrict the number and kind of ciphers we want to deal with. The default cipher list, comma separated, is `aes128-ctr`, `aes192-ctr`, `aes256-ctr`, `aes128cm@openssh.com`, `aes256-gcm@openssh.com`, and `chacha20-poly1305@openssh.com`
- `ClientAliveCountMax`: This is the number of the client alive messages that can be sent without the daemon receiving any reply from the client. When the max is hit, the daemon will disconnect the client. The default value is `3`; and this option is available only for SSH-2.
- `ClientAliveInterval`: This is the time interval, in seconds, after which if the client does not send any messages, the server will send itself a message through the encrypted channel to the client to push for a reply. The default is `0`. So, let's say that we set this option to `5` and the previous `ClientAliveCountMax` to `12`; the client will be disconnected after `60` seconds.
- `DenyGroups`: By default, members from all the groups are allowed to authenticate but with this directive, we can restrict them to a list of space-separated groups. So, the authentication is unavailable for those users whose primary or supplementary groups is listed in this directive or matched through a pattern.

We already mentioned the pattern available in `sshd config`, and this breaks down essentially to two characters:

- *** matches 0 or more characters**: Something like `192.168.*` will match all the IP addresses starting with `192.168`; or `*.foo.com` will match all the third-level domains for `foo.com` as well as the second-level domain called foo.com.
- **? matches exactly one character**: So, for instance, `192.16?.1` will match all the IPS from `192.160.1` to `192.168.9.1`.
- **Pattern list**: As the name states, this is a list of patterns delimited by commands. The single patterns can be negated by a leading exclamation mark; for example, `!*.noway.foo.com,*.foo.com` would allow the all the third-level domains for `foo.com` except those containing a noway right before `.foo.com`.

Groups must be specified by their name, not by their numeric ID; and the order in which this directive is processed is: `DenyUsers`, `AllowUsers`, `DenyGroups`, and `AllowGroups`.

- `DenyUsers`: Followed by a list of user name patterns separated by a space, this directive disallows the log in for those user accounts which match the listed patterns. As usual, only the names of the users and not their ID can be specified and by default all users are allowed to log in. We can also specify a member as `ser@host` so that the restrictions will be applied not only to the account name but also to the origin host; this can be written also in the CDIR/mask format. The access directives are processed in this order: `DenyUsers`, `AllowUsers`, `DenyGroups`, and `AllowGroups`.

- `DisableForwarding`: This directive disables all kinds of forwardings such as X11, TCP, ssh-agent, and `StreamLocal`. This is a nice directive to use if we want to trim down the service and make it safer.

- `ForceCommand`: This overrides any command sent by the client or listed in the `~/.ssh/rc` of the authenticating account; and it forces the execution of the command listed in this directive. The command is executed through the account shell with the `-c` option. This defaults to `no`.

- `HostbasedAuthentication`: This allows/denies the authentication based on `rhosts` or `hostS_equive` along with a successful public `jkey` client host authentication. The default is `no/`.

- `HostKey`: This directive specifies the file the private host key is kept in. By default, the locations are `/etc/ssh/ssh_host_rsa_key`, `/etc/ssh/ssh_host_ecdsa_key`, and `/etc/ssh/ssh_host_ed25519_key`. We can have multiple host keys defined for a single host. but it is important that the files holding them are not world or group accessible.

- `KbdInteractiveAuthentication`: This allows/denies the keyboard-interactive authentication. The default value is drawn from `ChallengeResponseAuthentication`, which is usually set to `yes`.

- `KerberosAuthentication`: This allows/denies the validation through a Kerberos server of the password provided by the client. The default value is `no`.

- `ListenAddress`: This lists the addresses SSH daemon will be listening on. We can use an IPv4/IPv6 address, a hostname, or a list of them and follow them with an optional port, such as following:

    ```
    Listen 192.168.0.10:6592
    ```

If no ports are specified, sshd will listen on those listed in the ports directive. The default configuration is to listen to all local addresses:

- `LoginGraceTime`: This is a timeout in seconds for the user to complete the log in process. It defaults to 120 seconds; with 0, we can disable the timeout.
- `LogLevel`: In case of any issues, we can modify the verbosity of the logs generated by sshd. The default level is `INFO`, but we can set it to any of `QUIET`, `FATAL`, `ERROR`, `INFO`, `VERBOSE`, `DEBUG`, `DEBUG1`, `DEBUG2`, `DEBUG3`. `DEBUG` and `DEBUG1` are equivalent while each `DEBUGx` enables a higher level of verbosity. `DEBUG` is not advised since it can disclose too many private informations related to the users.
- `Match`: With this directive, we can use conditional statements so that if they are satisfied, the following configuration lines will override the one in the main configuration block. If a keyword/configuration block appears in more than one match clause, only the first instance is taken in account. As a matching criteria, we can use the following directives: user, group, host, local address, local port, address, or all for all of them. We can match against a single value, a comma separated list and we can also use wildcards and negation operators.
- `MaxAuthTries`: This limits the maximum number or authentication attempts per single connection. Once half of the threshold is hit, the subsequent failed attempts are logged. It defaults to 6.
- `PasswordAuthentication`: This allows/denies password authentication. This defaults to yes.
- `PermitEmptyPasswords`: This allows/denies the use of empty passwords when password authentication is enabled. This is not safe to set to `yes` and defaults to no.
- `PermitRootLogin`: This lets a user log in as root. It can have the following values: yes, `prohibit-password`, `without-password`, `forced-commands-only`, and no. If set to `prohibit-password` or `without-password`, the `password` and `keyboard-interactive` authentications are not available for user root; if set to `forced-commands-only`, a log in with public key authentication is allowed but only if a command is specified.
- `PermitTTY`: This allows/denies the use of a `pty` (pseudo terminal) for the session. This defaults to `yes`.
- `PermitTunnel`: This allows/denies the *tun* device forwarding. It takes `yes`, `point-to-point`, `ethernet` or `no` as arguments. `Yes` enables both `point-to-point` and `ethernet` forwarding. This defaults to `no`.

- `PermitUserRC`: If set to `yes`, the commands inside `~/.ssh/rc` are executed. This defaults to `yes`.
- `Port`: This specifies the port number the SSH daemon will listen on. This defaults to `22`, but we should move this port to some higher number to avoid most of the script kiddies around trying to automatically deface the service.
- `PubkeyAuthentication`: This allows/denies public key authentication. This defaults to `yes`.
- `StrictModes`: This enables/disables file mode and ownership checks on the account's files and home directory before letting the log in process go through. If it is set to `yes`, it checks for a world-writable user `.ssh` directory or a world writable `home` directory, and if we leave our files or directories world-writable, the log in is denied. This does not apply to `ChrootDirectory`, whose permissions and ownership are always checked.
- `Subsystem`: This enables the execution of an external subsystem, usually an `sftp-server`. The syntax is a subsystem name followed by a command with an optional argument to be executed on a subsystem invocation. This defaults to the `no` subsystem configured.
- `SyslogFacility`: We can use any of these `syslog` facilities to log the messages from the SSH daemon: `DAEMON`, `USER`, `AUTH`, `LOCAL0`, `LOCAL1`, `LOCAL2`, `LOCAL3`, `LOCAL4`, `LOCAL5`, `LOCAL6`, and `LOCAL7`. This defaults to `AUTH`.
- `TCPKeepAlive`: This enables the server to send `TCP keepalive` to the client so that it will be able to detect any disconnection. This is not an easy choice: a temporary routing issue could lead to a forced disconnection from the server; but without a `keepalive`, a connection could hang indefinitely if the client disconnects or dies. This defaults to `yes`.
- `UseDNS`: This forces the SSH daemon to resolve, the host name through a DNS facility and check whether it resolves to the IP address of the client connecting. If this option is set to `no`, the usage of `from=` in `~/.ssh/authorized_keys` still does not support host names but IP addresses only; and the same is applicable for the Match Host directive. Setting this option to `yes` can cause delays in authentication due to the DNS resolution task. Defaults to `yes`.

- **UsePAM**: This enables/disables the Pluggable Authentication Module interface. Defaults to `no`. If set to `yes`, it will enable the authentication through PAM using `ChallengeResponseAuthentication` and `PasswordAuthentication`, along with the PAM account and session modules, so one of these must be disabled. Interestingly, enabling PAM will allow the SSH daemon to run as an unprivileged user. This defaults to `no`.
- **UsePrivilegeSeparation**: If this is enabled, after the user's log in, the SSH daemon will create a child process with the privileges of the authenticated user. It can take `yes`, `no`, or `sandbox` as arguments. If `sandbox` is selected, further mandatory restrictions are performed on the syscalls the child can perform so that it will be more difficult to use a compromised child to attack hosts or the local kernel. This defaults to sanbox.
- **X11Forwarding**: This allows/denies X11 forwarding. If set to `yes`, it can expost X11 to attacks, so this option must be taken with care. Defaults to `no`.

We just saw some of the configurations on the server side, but we can alter how we interact with the SSH daemon configuring the client too, so let's have a look at the most interesting options from the client side.

ssh_config

On the client side, we have a few ways to configure how a connection will be held:

- From the command line, passing options to the client while invoking it
- From the configuration file inside the user's home directory `~/.ssh/config`
- From the system-wide configuration file in `/etc/ssh/ssh_config`

For the configuration files, we must bear in mind that only the first value obtained for each directive will be used; so if we give the same directive multiple times, only the first one will be evaluated. So, we must keep the more specific options at the beginning of the configuration file while the broader one will be pushed toward the end.

As we will see in the next paragraph, where we will examine a practical use of the client configuration, the file is segmented into sections whose boundaries are delimited by the `Host` directive: whatever configuration directive is listed below the keyword will belong to the host specified, until the next Host declaration. Each line in the file contains a configuration directive and value, optionally enclosed in double quotes when containing spaces; lines starting with # or blank are considered comments. Multiple values can be separated by a whitespace or =. With these caveats in mind, let's have a look at the most interesting keywords in the client configuration file:

- `Host`: This directive can take a host name as an argument or a pattern, which can be negated with !. If * the following directives apply to all hosts. Whatever pattern or name is given here, it should match the host name we would give on the command line to connect to the remote host. All the directives following the `Host` keyword will be applied only to the host defined, up to the next `Host` or `Match` directive. If a host/pattern value is negated, all the directives for that host(s) are negated.
- `Match`: This limits the scope of the following directives, up to the next `Match` or `Host` declaration, to be applied only when the values specified are satisfied. The values can be `all`, which always matches or one or more among `canonical`, `exec`, `host`, `originalhost`, `user`, and `localuser`. The `all` value must appear alone or right after canonical, which are the only two options not requiring an argument. Values can be negated using !.
- `canonical`: This is matched when the configuration file is reparsed after the hostname canonicalization has taken place (we will see in a while what it means).
- `exec`: Executes a command using the account's shell; and if its `exit` status is zero then the condition is evaluated as `true`. If the command contains a whitespace then it must be quoted; it can accept tokens as arguments (we will see in a while what it means).
- `host`: This matches against the destination hostname, after any substitution operated by the `Hostname` or `CanonicalizeHostname` options. It can accept a comma-separated list, wildcards, and negation (!). For instance, take a look here:

    ```
    match host foo.com exec "test %p = 9999"
    IdentityFile foo.identity
    ```

    We will use the identity file called `foo.identity` only if the target host has the `foo.com` hostname and the the port equals to `9999`.

- `originalhost`: This is matched against the hostname specified on the client command line.
- `user`: This matches against the username used to log in on the remote host.
- `localuser`: This is matched against the local (client side) user running an SSH client.
- `BatchMode`: Useful for unattended log in from a script. If it is set to `yes`, no passphrases or passwords will be asked for and the `ServerAliveIntervall` will be set to `300` seconds in Debian. This defaults to `no`.
- `BindAddress`: Useful in client machines which have more than one IP address assigned; it specifies the source address for the connection. Does not work if `UsePrivilegedPort` is set to `yes`.
- `CanonicalDomains`: Used with `CanonicalizeHostname`; it sets a list of domain suffixes to search for the remote host to connect to.
- `CanonicalizeFallbackLocal`: If set to `yes`, the client will attemp to look up an unqualified hostname using the search rule of the client system. If set to `no` and `CanonicalizeHostname` is set to `yes` , it will fail immediately if the remote hostname cannot be found in any of the domains listed by `CanonicalDomains`. Defaults to `yes`.
- `CanonicalizeHostname`: Enables the canonicalization rewriting the hostname. If set to `no`, the local resolver will manage the hostname lookup; if set to `always`, it will rewrite the unqualified hostnames using the domains listed in `CanonicalDomains`. The `CanonicalizePermittedCNAMEs` rules will be applied. If set to `yes`, the canonicalization will be performed for those connections which do not use a `ProxyCommand` directive.
- `CanonicalizePermittedCNAMEs`: Lists the rules that must be followed during hostname canonicalization. The rules can have one of more of the following arguments:
    - `source_domains:target_domains`: The first being a list of patterns for domains that may follow the hostname in canonicalization; `target_domains` is a list of patterns of domains that the former domains may resolve to.
    - `CertificateFile`: Lists the file where to load the certificate file for the corresponding private key pointed to by the `IntentityFile` directive.

- `CheckHostIP`: Defines whether the client will check for the host IP in the `known_hosts` file for DNS spoofing prevention, adding the IP of the remote host to the `~/.ssh/known_hosts` file. Defaults to `yes`.
- `ConnectionAttempts`: The number of connection tries per second before exiting. Defaults to `1`.
- `ConnectTimeout`: Timeout in seconds for a connection try.
- `ForwardX11`: Enables X11 redirection over the connection and sets the DISPLAY value. Defaults to `no`.
- `GatewayPorts`: Allows/denies the connection of remote hosts to local forwarded ports. Defaults to `no`, meaning that the local forwarded ports bind to the loopback device address. If set to `yes`, they are bound to the `*` address.
- `GlobalKnownHostsFile`: Sets one or more file (separated by whitespaces) where the host keys are kept. Defaults to the default `/etc/ssh/ssh_known_hosts` and `/etc/ssh/ssh_known_hosts2`.
- `HostKeyAlias`: Sets an alias to be used instead of the hostname when searching or saving the host key in the `hostkey` file.
- `HostName`: Points to the real hostname of the remote host that we are going to log in. We can use this field to create a meaningful alias for the remote host, either using numeric IPS, tokens (we will see them later), or short names.
- `IdentityFile`: Defines the file the authentication identity is read from. Defaults to `~/.ssh/identity` for SSH-1, and `~/.ssh/id_dsa`, `~/.ssh/id_ecdsa`, `~/.ssh/id_ed25519` and `~/.ssh/id_rsa` for SSH-2. If no certificates have been associated using the `CertificateFile` directive, SSH will try to read a file whose name is crafted by adding `-cert.pub` to the name listed under `IdentityFile`. Tokens can be used as argument; and it is possible to repeatedly use this directive to add more identity files to the list of the ones tried.
- `Include`: Includes the configuration files listed. If a file is not pointed to by an absolute path, it is meant to be located under `~/.ssh` if included in a user configuration or under `/etc/ssh` if included in the system-wide configuration file. Wildcards can be used, and this directive can be listed as an argument for the `match` and `host` keywords for conditional includes.

- `LocalCommand`: We can write a command to be executed with the user shell once the local client has successfully connected to the remote host. It accepts the tokens, but it is ignored unless `PermitLocalCommand` is enabled.
- `LocalForward`: Enables the forwarding of a TCP local port over a secure connection to the remote host and port. It accepts two arguments: `[local_address:]port` and `remote_host:port`.

We can specify more than one forwarding but only a superuser can bind a local privileged port. The local port is bound to the address drawn from the `GatewayPorts` directive if not specified as an argument. If the localhost is given, the listening port will be accessible only from the local client machine; and an empty address means *, so the port will be accessible on all the interfaces.

- `NumberOfPasswordPrompts`: Defines how many times a password is asked for before declaring the login process as failed, the argument can be an integer which defaults to 3.
- `Port`: This is the port on the remote server that the client will try to connect to. Defaults to 22.
- `PreferredAuthentications`: Defines the order in which the client will try different authentication methods. Defaults to `gssapi-with-mic,hostbased,publickey`, `keyboard-interactive`, and `password`.
- `Protocol`: Defines the protocol supported by the client in order of preference. If more than one is listed, they must be separated by a command. If a preferred protocol fails, the next in the list will be tried. Defaults to 2.
- `ProxyCommand`: Defines the command used to connect to the remote server; and it is executed with the exec directive of the user's shell. Really useful used with `netcat` to proxy connections. Accepts tokens.
- `RemoteForward`: Enables the forwarding of a TCP port on the remote host on a secure connection to a port on the local machine. It accepts two arguments: `[local_address:]port` and `remote_host:port`.

We can specify more than one forwarding by only logging as a superuser on the remote host lets us bind a remote privileged port. If this is not specified, `local_address` is bound to the loop-back device. And if no remote host is specified, or * is used, then the forwarded port will be accessible on all interfaces on the remote host. To specify a remote address, we must enable the directive `GatewayPorts` in `sshd_config`.

- `ServerAliveCountMax`: Defines the maximum number of server alive messages without receiving a reply from the remote host. Once the threshold is hit, the session is disconnected. These kinds of messages are way different from the `TCPKeepAlive` messages: the first one is sent over the encrypted channel, and so is not spoofable, while the second is in clear and can be spoofed. Defaults to 3.
- `ServerAliveInterval`: Defines a timeout in seconds, after which the client will send a message through the secure channel. Defines a timeout in seconds after which if no data have been received the client will send a message to the server through the secure channel requesting a response. Defaults to 0, meaning that no messages will ever be sent.
- `StrictHostKeyChecking`: If this is set to yes, two things will happen:
    - The client will never automatically add a host key to the `~/.ssh/known_hosts` file.
    - The client will refuse to connect to a remote host whose key has changed from the one stored in the `known_hosts` file.

    If this is set to yes, the client will automatically add the new keys while if set to ask, which is the default value the client will ask the user to confirm the addition of the key to the `known_hosts` file.

- `TCPKeepAlive`: Enables/disables the keepalive messages sent by the client to the remote host. Defaults to yes ; and this will allow the client to detect network disconnections or remote host crashing. It is largely used in scripts for unattended disconnection detection.
- `Tunnel`: Enables forwarding between the client and the remote host for the tun device. Arguments can be yes, point-to-point, ethernet , or no. Defaults to yes , which enables the default point-to-point mode.
- `TunnelDevice`: Defines which tun devices to open both for the client and the remote host. The argument is specified as `client_tun:[host_tun]`.

    Devices can be addressed by their numerical ID or using any , which will force the usage of the next available tun device. If no `host_tun` is defined, it defaults to any. The default is any:any.

- `UsePrivilegedPort`: Enables/disables the usage of a privileged port of the outgoing connection. If it is set to yes, ssh must be `setuid root` since this is the only user who is able to use privileged ports. Defaults to no.
- `User`: Specifies the username of the remote account to log in.

- `UserKnownHostsFile`: Defines one or more files for the user's `host_key` database. If more than one file is specified, it must be separated by a whitespace. Defaults to `~/.ssh/known_hosts, ~/.ssh/known_hosts2`.
- `TOKENS`: We referred to them in some of the configuration directives, and these are special character combinations that can be expanded during the SSH session:
    - `%%`: This is expanded to a literal `%`
    - `%C`: Short for `%l%h%p%r`
    - `%d`: Expands to the home directory of the user on the client side
    - `%h`: This is the hostname of the remote host
    - `%i`: Expands to the local user ID
    - `%L`: Hostname of the client
    - `%l`: Hostname of the client, domain included, including the domain name
    - `%n`: Original hostname of the remote host as given on the command line
    - `%p`: Port on the remote host
    - `%r`: Username on the remote host
    - `%u`: Username on the client side

These tokens are accepted in a different extent as arguments to different configuration directives:

- `Match exec` makes use of `%%`, `%h`, `%L`, `%l`, `%n`, `%p`, `%r`, `%u`
- `CertificateFile` makes use of `%%`, `%d`, `%h`, `%l`, `%r`, and `%u`
- `ControlPath` makes use of `%%`, `%C`, `%h`, `%i`, `%L`, `%l`, `%n`, `%p`, `%r`, `%u`
- `HostName` makes use of `%%` and `%h`
- `IdentityAgent` and `IdentityFile` make use of `%%`, `%d`, `%h`, `%l`, `%r`, `%u`
- `LocalCommand` makes use of `%%`, `%C`, `%d`, `%h`, `%l`, `%n`, `%p`, `%r`, `%u`
- `ProxyCommand` makes use of `%%`, `%h`, `%p`, and `%r`

Some of the directives that we listed for `sshd_config`, which were also available on the `ssh_config` file, were omitted for brevity's sake. We tried to be as tidy as possible before going to the next paragraph, where you will learn how to create passwordless connections using some of the directives that we just examined so far.

Passwordless connections

One of the most useful features in the everyday life of a Linux user is the ability to connect to remote servers without the burden of remembering all the addresses, ports, users, and passwords. Well, if one resorts to using some kind of client such as Putty, it can store all these details in a connection snippet. We can recall when we need to log in to a remote host, but Linux offers a more *native* and practical way to reach this goal. We are talking about passwordless connections, which means we just ssh to a host alias and we are in, no questions asked, and nothing other than an alias to remember.

What do we need to set up such a nice connection method? We have a few actors in place: we have to check the server setup, generate some keys, and configure the client.

Configuring the server

Let's start from the server opening the /etc/ssh/ssd_config file and checking the following configuration directives:

```
Port 22
```

Let's start with the port. The standard port for the SSH service is 22, and it is at this value that most of the script kiddies around will probe your SSH daemon with some automated tools; so if you have a server publicly available, change the value to an unprivileged port such as 9527. Thus, a lot of these attacks will simply be ineffective:

```
#ListenAddress ::
#ListenAddress 0.0.0.0
```

If we need to bind the service to a specific address on our server, this is the directive we need to work on; we simply uncomment and fill in the appropriate value:

```
Protocol 2
```

We do not think to use version 1 of the protocol, not even as a second choice. We stay safe and go along protocol version 2:

```
# HostKeys for protocol version 2
HostKey /etc/ssh/ssh_host_rsa_key
HostKey /etc/ssh/ssh_host_dsa_key
HostKey /etc/ssh/ssh_host_ecdsa_key
HostKey /etc/ssh/ssh_host_ed25519_key
```

Ever wondered where the system-wide host keys are? Here, they are, and we can also decide to change names and path if we need to.

```
#Privilege Separation is turned on for security
UsePrivilegeSeparation yes
```

Definitely! We want to work with unprivileged processes so that no super user privileges can be exploited.

```
# Authentication:
LoginGraceTime 120
```

Just give us some time to log in.

```
#PermitRootLogin without-password
PermitRootLogin yes
```

One safe practice is to limit the log in to the root account on a remote host to key-based authentication. This way, an intruder will not able to break in by just guessing a password; he will need the client's secret key to enter, and the key is safely stored on our client, not on the server. Anyway, if we want to remotely set up a passwordless authentication for the root account, we must allow root logins with passwords. Once we are sure everything works, we will restrict without-password.

```
StrictModes yes
```

It is so easy to forget some world-writable permission on the home directory or on our ssh configuration files and keys, so better to enable this directive; and it will prevent us to log in if the home directory of the remote user we log in has some unsafe permissions set.

```
PubkeyAuthentication yes
```

Well, we are working on that so better to be sure this is set to `yes`.

```
AuthorizedKeysFile %h/.ssh/authorized_keys
```

Let's note down where our public key must be stored. The token tells us they are in the `.ssh` directory inside the home of the accounts the file `authorized_keys` is in the home directory of the account we used to login into the system.

```
HostbasedAuthentication no
```

Just for safety, let's ditch the host authentication:

`PermitEmptyPasswords no`

Let's check this. We must never switch this to yes unless we want logins without passwords. But who would want this?

`UsePAM yes`

There are a few reasons why we would like to set this to `yes`. One is that, with this on, the SSH daemon cannot be run as root; and this is a safe option.

Once we have the config bits in place, let's check that we also have the host keys that we need to proof the server identity to the client. As we can read from the configuration file, on the remote host, we should have a key for each algorithm supported in /etc/ssh:

```
root:# ls -lah /etc/ssh/
total 296K
drwxr-xr-x 2 root root 4.0K Apr 16 07:32 .
drwxr-xr-x 129 root root 12K Apr 17 04:00 ..
-rw-r--r-- 1 root root 237K Jul 22 2016 moduli
-rw-r--r-- 1 root root 1.7K Jul 22 2016 ssh_config
-rw-r--r-- 1 root root 2.6K Apr 16 07:32 sshd_config
-rw------- 1 root root 668 Apr 16 07:20 ssh_host_dsa_key
-rw-r--r-- 1 root root 601 Apr 16 07:20 ssh_host_dsa_key.pub
-rw------- 1 root root 227 Apr 16 07:20 ssh_host_ecdsa_key
-rw-r--r-- 1 root root 173 Apr 16 07:20 ssh_host_ecdsa_key.pub
-rw------- 1 root root 399 Apr 16 07:20 ssh_host_ed25519_key
-rw-r--r-- 1 root root 93 Apr 16 07:20 ssh_host_ed25519_key.pub
-rw------- 1 root root 1.7K Apr 16 07:20 ssh_host_rsa_key
-rw-r--r-- 1 root root 393 Apr 16 07:20 ssh_host_rsa_key.pub
```

There they are! So, we are fine. They usually get created when we install the OpenSSH server from our distribution packages, but we can also decide to create our very own host key. Let's see how. First, let's have a look at the fingerprint of one of the keys:

```
root:# ssh-keygen -f /etc/ssh/ssh_host_ecdsa_key.pub -l
256 fe:23:d3:9b:8a:80:30:ad:0d:ac:81:fa:ba:3f:6f:56
/etc/ssh/ssh_host_ecdsa_key.pub (ECDSA)
```

We used ssh-keygen, a utility which does a lot of things, from creating a key to modifying it or, as in this case, having a look at it. The first field of the resulting sting tells us the bit length of the key, the second sports the actual key, the third points to the file holding this key, and finally comes the encryption method.

```
root@spoton:~# ssh-keygen -f /etc/ssh/ssh_host_ecdsa_key.pub -lv
256 fe:23:d3:9b:8a:80:30:ad:0d:ac:81:fa:ba:3f:6f:56 /etc/ssh/ssh_host_ecdsa_key.pub (ECDSA)
+---[ECDSA 256]---+
|                 |
|                 |
|                 |
|o.               |
|*..         S    |
|oB .     E.      |
|+ o ..  ..       |
| .. o. .o.o.     |
|o+o=. . .++o     |
+-----------------+
root@spoton:~#
```

Using the -lv options will give you a nice ASCII fingerprint of the key

But let's say we do not trust the existing keys, and we want to create a new pair set of them:

```
root:# cd /etc/ssh
root:# ssh-keygen -A
ssh-keygen: generating new host keys: RSA1 RSA DSA ECDSA ED25519
```

Is this easy? Yes, it is:

```
root:# ls -lh ssh_h*
-rw------- 1 root root  668 Apr 24 06:13 ssh_host_dsa_key
-rw-r--r-- 1 root root  601 Apr 24 06:13 ssh_host_dsa_key.pub
-rw------- 1 root root  227 Apr 24 06:13 ssh_host_ecdsa_key
-rw-r--r-- 1 root root  173 Apr 24 06:13 ssh_host_ecdsa_key.pub
-rw------- 1 root root  399 Apr 24 06:13 ssh_host_ed25519_key
-rw-r--r-- 1 root root   93 Apr 24 06:13 ssh_host_ed25519_key.pub
-rw------- 1 root root  976 Apr 24 06:13 ssh_host_key
-rw-r--r-- 1 root root  641 Apr 24 06:13 ssh_host_key.pub
-rw------- 1 root root 1.7K Apr 24 06:13 ssh_host_rsa_key
-rw-r--r-- 1 root root  393 Apr 24 06:13 ssh_host_rsa_key.pub
```

Here are the new key files; let's check the same key again:

```
root:# ssh-keygen -f /etc/ssh/ssh_host_ecdsa_key.pub -l
256 24:4d:3e:6b:f4:0f:4b:bf:56:b9:b5:c4:b6:ab:c6:7b
/etc/ssh/ssh_host_ecdsa_key.pub (ECDSA)
```

The two keys are different:

```
24:4d:3e:6b:f4:0f:4b:bf:56:b9:b5:c4:b6:ab:c6:7b
fe:23:d3:9b:8a:80:30:ad:0d:ac:81:fa:ba:3f:6f:56
```

We took advantage of the -A option of ssh-keygen, which automatically creates a missing key for each type (`rsa1`, `rsa`, `dsa`, `ecdsa`, and `ed25519`). The keys are created with the default bit size, with no password, and with the default comments. Now, let's say again that we want to create our very own `ecdsa` host key pair:

```
root:# ssh-keygen -t ecdsa -a 1000 -b 521 -C "My hand crafted key" -f
/etc/ssh/ssh_host_crafted_ecdsa -o
Generating public/private ecdsa key pair.
Enter passphrase (empty for no passphrase):
Enter same passphrase again:
Your identification has been saved in /etc/ssh/ssh_host_crafted_ecdsa.
Your public key has been saved in /etc/ssh/ssh_host_crafted_ecdsa.pub.
The key fingerprint is:
28:74:b2:e6:a1:e5:6d:cd:ca:e7:f2:47:86:6d:39:d6 My hand crafted key
The key's randomart image is:
+---[ECDSA 521]---+
|                 |
|                 |
|     o .         |
|    . + .        |
|     * . So o    |
|     * + o. O E  |
|    . o o o= .   |
|     o... .      |
|      o=o.       |
+-----------------+
```

[413]

Our new ecdsa host key has been created

We created our new host key using some simple options:

- `-t`: This selects the type of the `keyboard-interactive`.
- `-a`: This option can be selected when saving a key in the ed25519 format or with any SSH-2 key when the `-o` option is selected. It specifies the number of **Key Derivation Function** (**KDF**) rounds to use to encrypt the private password. It makes the passphrase check slower and more resistant to a brute force attack. The higher the integer, the slower the check. It defaults to `64`, which is really good; we just got insane with `1000`.
- `-b`: Bit length of the key. Ecdsa can have a size of 256, 384, or 521 bit.
- `-C`: Is a comment you can associate to the key.
- `-f`: Is the path to the file that will hold the new key.
- `-o`: Saves the SSH-2 private key in the new OpenSSH format rather than the usual PEM format. The new format is more resistant to brute force attack, but it is not supported by OpenSSH versions lower than 6.5. The ed25519 keys are always saved in the new format, so they do not require this option on the command line.

Now, it is time to make the new key available to the server by adding it to the main sshd configuration file:

```
HostKey /etc/ssh/ssh_host_crafted_ecdsa
```

Let's restrict the permissions on the keys:

```
root:# chmod 600 *
```

So, no one other than root will be able to access the keys and configuration files:

```
root:# ls -lah | grep cra
-rw-------  1 root root 751 Apr 24 11:41 ssh_host_crafted_ecdsa
-rw-------  1 root root 225 Apr 24 11:39 ssh_host_crafted_ecdsa.pub
```

We notice two things:

- We created a private key whose name does not end with _key. We did this on purpose to differentiate it from the prebuilt keys. The key filename can be whatever we want, but better give it a meaningful value.
- ssh-keygen automatically added a trailing .pub to the private key file name and used the resulting name for the public key filename.

Safe permissions for ssh keys are:
700 for the .ssh directory, and
600 for the key files inside the .ssh directory.

Now, let's reload or restart the service to get the new key available for the SSH daemon:

```
root:# systemctl restart sshd ; systemctl status sshd
● ssh.service - OpenBSD Secure Shell server
Loaded: loaded (/lib/systemd/system/ssh.service; enabled)
Active: active (running) since Mon 2017-04-24 11:40:51 EDT; 5ms ago
Process: 30993 ExecReload=/bin/kill -HUP $MAINPID (code=exited,
status=0/SUCCESS)
Main PID: 31265 (sshd)
CGroup: /system.slice/ssh.service
    └─31265 /usr/sbin/sshd -D
```

Wow, it is working, let's see the logs:

```
root:# tail -f /var/log/syslog
Apr 24 11:40:51 spoton systemd[1]: Stopping OpenBSD Secure Shell server...
Apr 24 11:40:51 spoton systemd[1]: Starting OpenBSD Secure Shell server...
Apr 24 11:40:51 spoton systemd[1]: Started OpenBSD Secure Shell server.
Apr 24 11:40:51 spoton sshd[31265]: Could not load host key:
/etc/ssh/ssh_host_crafted_ecdsa
```

We are almost there. The daemon successfully started but refused to load the host key. What happened? Simply, we gave a passphrase during the key creation; and to load the key, a passphrase must be given but the daemon cannot interact and fill it in. We must remove the passphrase:

```
root:# ssh-keygen -p -f /etc/ssh/ssh_host_crafted_ecdsa
```

The program will ask for the old password, and when it comes to fill in a new one, let's just hit the *Enter* key twice so that no password will be added to the private key. Now, let's restart and check:

```
root:# systemctl restart ssh ; systemctl status ssh ; tail -n3 /var/log/syslog

● ssh.service - OpenBSD Secure Shell server
   Loaded: loaded (/lib/systemd/system/ssh.service; enabled)
   Active: active (running) since Mon 2017-04-24 11:59:32 EDT; 8ms ago
  Process: 30993 ExecReload=/bin/kill -HUP $MAINPID (code=exited,
status=0/SUCCESS)
 Main PID: 31517 (sshd)
   CGroup: /system.slice/ssh.service
           └─31517 /usr/sbin/sshd -D

Apr 24 11:59:32 spoton systemd[1]: Started OpenBSD Secure Shell server.
Apr 24 11:59:32 spoton systemd[1]: Stopping OpenBSD Secure Shell server...
Apr 24 11:59:32 spoton systemd[1]: Starting OpenBSD Secure Shell server...
Apr 24 11:59:32 spoton systemd[1]: Started OpenBSD Secure Shell server.
```

Now, it is really fine, the key has been loaded.

Preparing the remote account

Let's use a scenario where we will create a completely new user; whatever we will do here will be applicable to a preexisting user. First, let's create our new user test user on the remote host, and let's configure it so that it will be available through key authentication only:

```
root:# useradd -m test_user
```

So, we just created the `test_user` account and provided it with a `home` directory:

```
root:# ls -lah /home/test_user/
total 20K
drwxr-xr-x 2 test_user test_user 4.0K Apr 24 12:50 .
drwxr-xr-x 4 root      root      4.0K Apr 24 12:50 ..
-rw-r--r-- 1 test_user test_user  220 Nov  5 17:22 .bash_logout
-rw-r--r-- 1 test_user test_user 3.5K Nov  5 17:22 .bashrc
-rw-r--r-- 1 test_user test_user  675 Nov  5 17:22 .profile
```

Notice that there is no `.ssh` at the moment. Now, since we do want this account to be accessible only using a key, let's lock it:

```
root:# passwd -l test_user
```

The `-l` option in `passwd` locks the account using a nice trick. When we create an account, `passwd` asks for it; and then it encrypts the password and writes it into the `/etc/shadow` file, as we can see in a `shadow` file before locking:

```
root:# root@spoton:~# grep test_user /etc/shadow
test_user:$6$yTDup7NC$5eAg6QabTnMvwtqUfbmAcCy74zjHNj6RXafdIEBEmiVyz2DIVkdFg
zuuIFuscdAmIBp4B6lqh5tUNfDnK.8Q/1:17280:0:99999:7:::
```

The fields of the `shadow` file can be interpreted as follows:

```
login name
encrypted password
date of last password change
minimum password age
maximum password age
password warning period
password inactivity period
account expiration date
reserved field for future use
```

We will not go into the details of each field, a simple *man shadow* will give us all the information we need. What really matters is the second field holding the encrypted password. When a user tries to log in, the password they provide is encrypted and checked against the second field of the `/etc/shadow` file: if they match, the password is correct; if not, then the password is not correct and the user log in is refused. Have a look at the same string after the account has been locked:

```
root:# passwd -l test_user
test_user:!$6$yTDup7NC$5eAg6QabTnMvwtqUfbmAcCy74zjHNj6RXafdIEBEmiVyz2DIVkdF
gzuuIFuscdAmIBp4B6lqh5tUNfDnK.8Q/1:17280:0:99999:7:::
```

There is something new: the password field has ! at the beginning, actually changing its value. And here is the trick: a character such as ! or * can never be a result of the crypt(3) function used by passwd to encrypt the user password, so adding an exclamation mark makes the value unmatchable. Whatever value the user fills in, passwd will never be able to generate an exclamation mark; so, practically, the account is locked.

Just for the setup, let's enable the account again with a temporary password:

```
root:# passwd test_user
Enter new UNIX password:
Retype new UNIX password:
passwd: password updated successfully
```

We need to log in with a password to copy over our client public identity key. Once done, we will lock the account again.

So, now we have a username we can use and a port: 9999. We can jump back to the client and create our configuration.

Configuring the client

Back to our client; let's enter the home directory of the user we want to set up the connection for. Let's say that local_user wants to connect as test_user on the remote host called **spoton**.

Let's go to the local_user home directory, local_user:~$ cd /home/local_user, and have a look at what is inside it:

```
local_user:~$ ls -lah
total 20K
drwxr-xr-x 2 local_user local_user 4.0K Apr 24 18:34 .
drwxr-xr-x 4 root       root       4.0K Apr 24 18:34 ..
-rw-r--r-- 1 local_user local_user  220 Nov 15 18:49 .bash_logout
-rw-r--r-- 1 local_user local_user 3.5K Nov 15 18:49 .bashrc
-rw-r--r-- 1 local_user local_user  675 Nov 15 18:49 .profile
```

Well, the usual file for a new account, but there is a problem:

```
root:# egrep IdentityFile /etc/ssh/ssh_config
# IdentityFile ~/.ssh/identity
# IdentityFile ~/.ssh/id_rsa
# IdentityFile ~/.ssh/id_dsa
# IdentityFile ~/.ssh/id_ecdsa
# IdentityFile ~/.ssh/id_ed25519
```

We have no identity file set, so we need to uncomment one of those lines; and if we want, we can also change the file name. For now, we will just add this line to the `ssh_config` file:

`IdentityFile ~/.ssh/id_ecdsa_to_spoton`

We just modified the file name to make it clear that it will be used for the remote host named spoton. We could have different identity files for connecting to more than one remote server or as different users to the same server. So, it is better to find a meaningful name for the key file, one that will remind us what it is used for. Now that we have a reference in the client config file, we must create the `.ssh` directory:

`local_user:~$ mkdir .ssh`

Set the right access permissions:

`local_user:~$ chmod 700 .ssh`

Now, let's enter the `.ssh` directory and create our key; to keep things easy, we will not force a password on the private key:

```
local_user:~$ ssh-keygen -t ecdsa -a 64 -b 384 -C "Key for test_user on spoton" -f id_ecdsa_to_spoton -o
Generating public/private ecdsa key pair.
Enter passphrase (empty for no passphrase):
Enter same passphrase again:
Your identification has been saved in id_to_spoton.
Your public key has been saved in id_to_spoton.pub.
The key fingerprint is:
SHA256:ZhJMqQ19CpCIB3d9KEaVUhH5ngyOP8LDqGxxkvj967M Key for test_user on spoton
The key's randomart image is:
+---[ECDSA 384]---+
|ooo+o=*B         |
|o.o.*oB o        |
| . . Bo=         |
| . +..           |
|. . o.+S.        |
|.+ .. .++        |
| .+= .           |
|..o * +          |
|oo =E=           |
+----[SHA256]-----+
```

Remote Connections over SSH

We used a smaller key size of 384, since at 512, we can face some issues and the key can be refused with a message like this from the client when invoking it with the $-vvv$ option:

```
debug2: input_userauth_pk_ok: fp
SHA256:Y7KP6aAFrbzNYYMZLTAiFf71yiE8mzgfzZ6FnrDC964
debug3: sign_and_send_pubkey: ECDSA
SHA256:Y7KP6aAFrbzNYYMZLTAiFf71yiE8mzgfzZ6FnrDC964
Load key "/home/local_user/.ssh/id_ecdsa_to_spoton": invalid format
```

Now, we have a key pair, one public, and one private:

```
local_user:~$ ls -lah
total 16K
drw------- 2 root root 4.0K Apr 24 19:50 .
drwxr-xr-x 3 local_user local_user 4.0K Apr 24 18:52 ..
-rw------- 1 local_user local_user 634 Apr 24 19:44 id_ecdsa_to_spoton
-rw------- 1 local_user local_user 233 Apr 24 19:44 id_ecdsa_to_spoton.pub
```

The access rights are not good for the pub key, so better fix it to a safer 600:

```
local_user:~$ chmod 600 *
```

Now, as we already know, the private key must be kept safe on the client; but we must copy the public key over the remote host, and add it to `~/.ssh/authorized_keys` of `test_user`.

We have actually two ways to do it.

Manually, copy the public key over to the remote server; copy it into the authorized_keys file and fix the access rights. Or, you can use the `ssh-copy-id` utility.

Let's use this second method:

```
local_user:~$ ssh-copy-id -iid_ecdsa_to_spoton.pub -p 9999
test_user@192.168.0.5
/usr/bin/ssh-copy-id: INFO: Source of key(s) to be installed:
"id_ecdsa_to_spoton.pub"
The authenticity of host '[192.168.0.5]:9999 ([192.168.0.5]:9999)' can't be established.
ECDSA key fingerprint is
SHA256:LPSZkMIYkaMJXXnD6GvUGFMAjL6yM6pZwVRUojqmhGw.
Are you sure you want to continue connecting (yes/no)? yes
/usr/bin/ssh-copy-id: INFO: attempting to log in with the new key(s), to filter out any that are already installed
/usr/bin/ssh-copy-id: INFO: 1 key(s) remain to be installed -- if you are prompted now it is to install the new keys
test_user@192.168.0.5's password:
Number of key(s) added: 1
```

Now try logging in to the machine:

```
"ssh -p '9999' 'test_user@192.168.0.5'"
```

Check to make sure that only the key(s) you wanted were added.

Everything seems fine, so let's connect to the remote system as `test_user` using the password we set. Check that in the home directory inside the `.ssh` subdirectory, there is an `authorized_keys` file with our public key inside:

```
test_user@spoton:~/.ssh$ cd .ssh/
test_user@spoton:~/.ssh$ ls -lah
total 12K
drwx------ 2 test_user test_user 4.0K Apr 24 14:05 .
drwxr-xr-x 3 test_user test_user 4.0K Apr 24 14:05 ..
-rw------- 1 test_user test_user  281 Apr 24 14:05 authorized_keys
```

The file is actually there with the correct access settings. Let's have a look inside it:

```
test_user@spoton:~/.ssh$ cat authorized_keys
ecdsa-sha2-nistp384
AAAAE2VjZHNhLXNoYTItbmlzdHAzODQAAAAIbmlzdHAzODQAAABhBPlnKFqWXsCj47zKtrZzqj8
PUuAvFlpTPzTJ4faHF1Fb2YJkI4Ywc4gmRig/hz+0kAXtanla4pMQtE6NqwyNheqo5rru8czRM9
jRigqN8UwF7yZNf0LMxYV2aFCzrGcz6g== Key for test_user on spoton
```

It looks like the right key; let's log out and have a look at the `local_user` public identity key:

```
local_user:~$ cat id_ecdsa_to_spoton.pub
ecdsa-sha2-nistp384
AAAAE2VjZHNhLXNoYTItbmlzdHAzODQAAAAIbmlzdHAzODQAAABhBPlnKFqWXsCj47zKtrZzqj8
PUuAvFlpTPzTJ4faHF1Fb2YJkI4Ywc4gmRig/hz+0kAXtanla4pMQtE6NqwyNheqo5rru8czRM9
jRigqN8UwF7yZNf0LMxYV2aFCzrGcz6g== Key for test_user on spoton
```

So, we just have to try the connection to the remote host using the identity file we created; but first, we have to make sure we allowed the port called `9999` on the remote host. Once we are sure that nothing is in between, we can just issue on the client side:

```
local_user:~$ ssh -i /home/local_user/.ssh/id_ecdsa_to_spoton -p 9999
test_user@192.168.0.5
The programs included with the Debian GNU/Linux system are free software;
the exact distribution terms for each program are described in the
individual files in /usr/share/doc/*/copyright.
Debian GNU/Linux comes with ABSOLUTELY NO WARRANTY, to the extent permitted
by applicable law.
Last login: Mon Apr 24 14:54:43 2017 from moveaway.hereiam
test_user@spoton:~$
```

That's it! We just logged in without any passwords, but this is still cumbersome. You have to point to the identity file and remember the port and the address. Not really handy, but we can improve our experience by taking advantage of the local configuration file that the client expects inside the .ssh directory of the local account. So,
inside /home/local_user/.ssh, let's create a file called config and write the following directives:

```
Host *
UserKnownHostsFile /dev/null
StrictHostKeyChecking no
IdentitiesOnly yes
Host spoton
AddressFamily inet
ConnectionAttempts 10
ForwardAgent no
ForwardX11 no
ForwardX11Trusted no
GatewayPorts yes
HostBasedAuthentication no
HostKeyAlias spotalias
HostName 192.168.0.5
IdentityFile ~/.ssh/id_ecdsa_to_spoton
PasswordAuthentication no
Port 9999
Protocol 2
Compression yes
CompressionLevel 9
ServerAliveCountMax 3
ServerAliveInterval 15
TCPKeepAlive no
User test_user
```

We have two sections, one of which applies to any host and one more specific for the host - spoton. Any time we want to add another host, we just have to copy and paste the host specific section, change the Host, HostKeyAlias, Hostname, IdentityFile, User, and, if needed, Port and that is all. The config file will grow with specific sections and our connections will be simply as follows:

```
local_user:~$ ssh spoton
Warning: Permanently added 'spotalias,[192.168.0.5]:9999' (ECDSA) to the
list of known hosts.
The programs included with the Debian GNU/Linux system are free software;
the exact distribution terms for each program are described in the
individual files in /usr/share/doc/*/copyright.
Debian GNU/Linux comes with ABSOLUTELY NO WARRANTY, to the extent permitted
by applicable law.
```

```
Last login: Mon Apr 24 15:25:41 2017 from moveaway.hereiam
```

That's all, it is just matter to invoke SSH with the alias specified in `Host` and we connect, no passwords, ports, addresses, or identity files were requested. Last bit, let's lock the remote user:

```
root:# passwd -l test_user
passwd: password expiry information changed.
```

Now, let's check the account status:

```
root:# passwd -S test_user
test_user L 04/24/2017 0 99999 7 -1
```

The `L` shows us that the account is locked. So, we can go back to the client and try to connect again:

```
local_user:~$ ssh spoton
Warning: Permanently added 'spotalias,[192.168.0.5]:9999' (ECDSA) to the
list of known hosts.
The programs included with the Debian GNU/Linux system are free software;
the exact distribution terms for each program are described in the
individual files in /usr/share/doc/*/copyright.
Debian GNU/Linux comes with ABSOLUTELY NO WARRANTY, to the extent permitted
by applicable law.
Last login: Mon Apr 24 15:31:16 2017 from moveaway.hereiam
```

Here we are. The remote `test_user` account is locked, no one can use it locally or from a remote connection using a password. No one except the one who has the right private key; in this case, on our client called `local_user`.

We can play so many tricks with ssh that you could write an entire book on it, but we will limit our fun to a couple of nice functions offered by this tool. Proxying and tunneling we will see in the next paragraph.

Proxies and tunnels

Let's say we need a quick way to exit our network bypassing the firewall settings. Our machine cannot make any HTTP/HTTPS connection, but we can reach another remote host, which has a free access to the Internet. So, let's see a practical example. First, let's use `curl` to grab a remote page:

```
local_user:~$ curl www.packtpublishing.com
<!DOCTYPE html PUBLIC "-//W3C//DTD XHTML 1.0 Strict//EN"
"http://www.w3.org/TR/xhtml1/DTD/xhtml1-strict.dtd">
```

```
<html xmlns="http://www.w3.org/1999/xhtml" xml:lang="en">
<head>
<title>Best packtpublishing online</title>
<meta http-equiv="Content-Type" content="application/xhtml+xml;
charset=utf-8" />
<meta name="description" content="Free best online packtpublishing website"
/>
<meta name="keywords" content="online,packtpublishing,website" />
<link rel="stylesheet" type="text/css" href="online.css" media="screen" />
</head>
<body>
<div class="wrapper">
<div class="top"><p>packtpublishing info at packtpublishing.com</p></div>
<div class="header"><img src="header.png" alt="header"></div>
<div class="column" id="a">

<h1>Online packtpublishing top website</h1>
<br />
<a href="inc/online/packtpublishing.php"><img src="click2.png"
alt="login"></a>
<br />
<h1>deluxemanager+packtpublishing<img src="ctc.png" alt="@gmail.com"
style="float:right;"></h1>
<br />
www.packtpublishing.com 2014<br />
</div>
</body>
</html>
```

We just grabbed the `www.packtpub.com` home page; nice, isn't it? Now, just for fun, root let's use a simple firewall such as `ufw` to block any outgoing connection to port `80`:

```
root:# ufw deny out 80/tcp
Rule added
Rule added (v6)
```

Now, let's try to run the `curl` command once again; it will hang, since we denied any outgoing connections to any IP on port `80`. But now let's give the following command:

```
local_user:~$ ssh -f -N -D 8080 spoton
```

Warning: Permanently added `spoton, [192.168.0.5]:9999 (ECDSA)` to the list of known hosts.

And then:

```
local_user:~$ curl --proxy socks5h://localhost:8080 www.packtpublishing.com
<!DOCTYPE html PUBLIC "-//W3C//DTD XHTML 1.0 Strict//EN"
"http://www.w3.org/TR/xhtml1/DTD/xhtml1-strict.dtd">
<html xmlns="http://www.w3.org/1999/xhtml" xml:lang="en">
<head>
...
```

We omitted the rest of the HTML code, but it is the same as for the previous `curl` command, since we grabbed the same page. What happened? We invoked ssh with some options:

- `-f`: This forces ssh to the background just before the command execution.
- `-N`: This prevents ssh from executing any command on the remote host, since we are just proxying.
- `-D`: Followed by `[local_address]:port`, defines a local dynamic port forwarding and allocates a socket to listen for requests. When a connection is made to this port, this is forwarded over the secure connection to the remote host, while the application protocol is used to understand where to connect to from the remote machine. So, SSH will perform as a SOCKS server supporting the SOCKS4 and SOCKS5 protocols. If used frequently, port forwarding can be set into the account `ssh config` file. Just notice that only a superuser can forward a privileged port.

We then used `spoton` as the destination, since we have a config snippet saved for it so we do not need to specify addresses or password. But if we had no config, we would have written this:

```
local_user:~$ ssh -f -N -D 8080 test_user@192.168.0.5:9999
```

Fill in the user password when asked for. Once we have our SOCKS proxy on, we can then configure any applications such as curl, Chrome, and Firefox to make use of it.

We do not like a SOCKS proxy? So, why not simply tunnel everything into a secure connection?

```
local_user:~$ ssh -N -L 8888:www.anomali.com:443 spoton
```

Remote Connections over SSH

Now let's make a call:

```
local_user:~$ curl -k https://localhost:8888
<!DOCTYPE HTML PUBLIC "-//IETF//DTD HTML 2.0//EN">
<html><head>
<title>301 Moved Permanently</title>
</head><body>
<h1>Moved Permanently</h1>
<p>The document has moved <a
href="https://www.anomali.com/blog/">here</a>.</p>
</body></html>
```

What is interesting here is the `-L` option, which forces the connections to the given TCP port (`8888`) to be forwarded over the encrypted channel to the remote host (`spoton`); and port (`9999`) or Unix socket, which then connects to the final host (`www.anomali.com`) on the port designated (`443`). As for the proxy, if we use this feature frequently, we can set it up into the account ssh config file, while we can optionally specify a local address to bind the local port (in brackets if IPv6). The spoton can be replaced by the remote account name at the remote address and port, as shown in the previous example. Notice that we used a redirection on HTTP, but this is a tunnel, so we can use whatever protocol we want, not just HTTP.

But we can do even something fancier: we can let someone access a remote host through us. So, on the local machine, we just give the following command:

`local_user:~$ ssh -f -N -R 8181:www.anomali.com:443 spoton`

Then, on `spoton`, we will use, `curl` command:

```
test_user:~$ curl -k https://localhost:8181
<!DOCTYPE HTML PUBLIC "-//IETF//DTD HTML 2.0//EN">
<html><head>
<title>301 Moved Permanently</title>
</head><body>
<h1>Moved Permanently</h1>
<p>The document has moved <a
href="https://www.anomali.com/blog/">here</a>.</p>
</body></html>
```

That is, we access www.anomali.com from spoton through our local machine; and that is what -R allows us to do: forward the connections on the remote host (spoton) on the remote port (8181) to the local machine, and from there to the external site (www.anomali.com). We then had to use the -k option with curl to prevent it complaining about an insecure connection, since the mismatch from the apparent URL and the external site SSL certificate. As a last word, we must remember to re-enable the ports we closed with the firewall before moving on.

Nice, isn't it? Before leaving this chapter, let's indulge in some other tricks just to have fun. Let's go back to our public key stored in the test_user authorized_keys on spoton, and let's add something at the beginning of the key:

```
command="sudo ifconfig eth0",no-port-forwarding,no-X11-forwarding ecdsa-sha2-nistp384
AAAAE2VjZHNhLXNoYTItbm1zdHAzODQAAAAIbm1zdHAzODQAAABhBPlnKFqWXsCj47zKtrZzqj8
PUuAvFlpTPzTJ4faHF1Fb2YJkI4Ywc4gmRig/hz+0kAXtanla4pMQtE6NqwyNheqo5rru8czRM9
jRigqN8UwF7yZNf0LMxYV2aFCzrGcz6g== Key for test_user on spoton
```

We simply added a command to the key: each time we use this key to log in, the command will be executed. Since the user is unprivileged and the command requires to be run by root, we are using sudo, so let's add the following file to /etc/sudoers.d/:

```
root:# cat /etc/sudoers.d/test_user
test_user ALL = (root) NOPASSWD: /sbin/ifconfig eth0
```

The name of the file does not matter; it is the content that makes the difference, enabling test_user to run /sbin/ifconfig eth0 as root. This way, we will concede a small and restricted privilege. Now, from our local machine as local_user, let's connect to spoton using the public key that we created:

```
local_user:~$ ssh spoton
Warning: Permanently added 'spotalias,[192.168.0.5]:9999' (ECDSA) to the list of known hosts.
eth0 Link encap:Ethernet HWaddr 00:1d:ba:88:2a:e6
inet addr:192.168.0.5 Bcast:192.168.0.255 Mask:255.255.255.0
inet6 addr: redacted/64 Scope:Global
inet6 addr: redacted/64 Scope:Link
UP BROADCAST RUNNING MULTICAST MTU:1500 Metric:1
RX packets:614498 errors:0 dropped:0 overruns:0 frame:0
TX packets:29212 errors:0 dropped:0 overruns:0 carrier:0
collisions:0 txqueuelen:1000
RX bytes:119612772 (114.0 MiB) TX bytes:4249467 (4.0 MiB)
Interrupt:16
Connection to 192.168.0 5 closed.
```

We can create dedicated users/keys to restart services, check logs, execute whatever maintenance task, and we will just have to fire up the connection without bothering about permissions and commands.

Do we need to run a graphical application that we do not have installed and cannot install, but we know it is available on a remote host? We must be sure that the X11 forwarding is enabled in our user `ssh config` file:

```
ForwardX11 yes
ForwardX11Trusted yes
```

The forwarding is enabled on the remote server:

```
X11Forwarding yes
```

Obviously, on the remote server, there must be `Xorg` installed along with the `xauth` utility; and if we are using the same key, we have to clean it from the command snipped and revert to the original value. Once we are sure, we just type this:

```
test_user:~$ ssh -n -f -X spoton firefox
Warning: Permanently added 'spoton,[192.168.0.5]:9999' (ECDSA) to the list of known hosts.
zarrelli:~$ /usr/bin/xauth: file /root/.Xauthority does not exist
Xlib: extension "RANDR" missing on display "localhost:10.0".
```

In a few seconds, Firefox will be up and running on the remote host, but its window will be displayed on our local system.

Summary

We just scratched the surface of what we can actually do with SSH. There are so many things such as `ssh-agent`, `ssh-add`, and `ssh-keyring`, and so many complex and tricky things to do that a chapter cannot hold everything. Anyway, this is a starting point; and once we get familiar on the usage of both the server and the client, we can start a journey in the esoteric world of encrypted connections, jumphosts, proxies, and whatever we need or we want to know. As of now, we need to step further to another topic that will show us how to set up scheduled jobs to execute our script in a timely manner and how to properly log their execution so that we will be always able to understand what is going on with our creations. It's time for timed jobs, time to explore the at, cron and logging facilities.

13
It's Time for a Timer

Having had a peek into daemons and SSH tunnels, dealing with `cronjob` could look like a humble task, but let's think for a while about our daily routine: how many times do we need to schedule a job to be executed in a specific time frame, maybe late at night or while we are on vacation? How many times do we need a certain task to be executed every day at a precise hour, every single day? Do we really want to stay up late at night or give up our vacations, or more importantly, can we be sure we will always be available to run a task every day at the same hour? Simply, we can't be. So, a method to schedule jobs and have them executed when needed, everytime it is needed, can be humble, but it is what makes a system easier to manage and saves us a lot of headaches.

We have many tools and forked projects available, but we will focus on a couple of them. The most famous old tools around are **at** and **cron**. They do quite the same thing, but with a different spin and definitely with a different goal.

One shot at it

Sometimes, we need to fire a job at a specific hour without any need to repeat the action, so just a one off. What we can use in this case is a simple utility called `at` with its companion batch. What does it do? It simply reads from the input or a file on what to execute and when, and it will use `/bin/sh` to invoke whatever we want. There is a little twist though: batch will do it but not at a specific time. It will be done when the system load drops below 1.5 or any level specified at the `atd` runtime.

So, we introduced `atd`; what is this? This is the daemon that executes the one shot jobs defined and put in its queue by the `at` utility, and so, it is a daemon that usually runs under a dedicated daemon user:

```
root:# ps -fC atd
UID PID PPID C STIME TTY TIME CMD
daemon 722 1 0 Apr25 ? 00:00:00 /usr/sbin/atd -f
```

So, this is a daemon that is fired up as a system service, but we have some other options; we can pass it to modify how it deals with the scheduled jobs. Let's see what we can make use of:

- `-l`: Defines the load factor over which the scheduled jobs will not be run. If no limit is imposed, it defaults to 1.5; but, in systems with x CPUs, a good limit value could be higher than x-1.
- `-b`: This sets the minimum interval in seconds between two consecutive jobs being fired. This defaults to `60`.
- `-d`: Having issues here? This will enable a debug feature that will divert the error messages from `syslog` to `stderr`, usually the terminal. This option goes along with the `-f` option.
- `-f`: Good for debugging, this options forces `atd` to run in the foreground.
- `-s`: Forces the processing of the `at` and `batch` queue to only a single run. This is used for backward compatibility with older versions of `at`; and it is run as we ran the old `atrun` command.

Few files are involved in the `atd` running process:

- `/var/spool/cron/atjobs`: This is the directory where the jobs created by `at` are stored and `atd` will read the queue from. It must be owned by the same owner of the process (in our case, daemon) and have strict access rights of 700.
- `/var/spool/cron/atspool`: This is the directory that temporarily holds the output of the jobs. It is owned by a daemon user with an access mode of 700.
- `/etc/at.allow`, `/etc/at.deny`: In this file, we can set which account can submit jobs to `atd` and which are forbidden.

There is one limit in using `atd`; if it's spool directory is mounted with NFS, then whichever option you use for mounting, it will simply not work.

We saw a couple of interesting files:

```
/etc/at.allow
/etc/at.deny
```

This administrator who can submit jobs to the `atd` daemon can have a really simple syntax: it is a simple list of account names, one per line, with no whitespaces. There is a precedence order in which the files are parsed: `/etc/at.allow` is the first one to be read. If any account names are found in it, these will be the only accounts to be allowed to submit the jobs.

If `/etc/at.allow` does not exist, then `/etc/at.deny` is parsed and every account name found in it will be forbidden to send jobs to `atd`. If the file exists but it is empty, it is interpreted as that every account can submit jobs to `atd`.

If neither `/etc/at.allow` or `/etc/at.deny` exists, this means that only the superuser can submit jobs to `atd`.

In the systems, we use a sandbox. We have `/etc/at.deny` and its contents here:

```
root:# cat /etc/at.deny
alias
backup
bin
daemon
ftp
games
gnats
guest
irc
lp
mail
man
nobody
operator
proxy
qmaild
qmaill
qmailp
qmailq
qmailr
qmails
sync
sys
www-data
```

It's Time for a Timer

So for the rules we just saw, if `/etc/at.allow` is absent, all the accounts listed in `/etc/at.deny` are forbidden to submit jobs to `atd`. This makes sense as we can see that these are accounts related to services or a nobody user, and these are not supposed to have any need to submit a job.

This is all we need to know about the service part of the `at` facility; let's see what we can rely on to schedule a job. On the client side, we have the following utilities that we can use to submit jobs to `atd`.

The `at` and `batch read` commands from a standard input or a specified file, which are to be executed at a later time, using `/bin/sh`.

- `at`: This is the main utility we deal with, and its function is to submit jobs that are to be executed at a specific time. Time specification can be really smart and flexible.
- `HH:MM`: This specifies the time of the current day to run a command called by `at`. If the time has already passed, the command is intended to be run on the next day at the same hour.
- `midnight`: The job is meant to be run at midnight:

    ```
    root:# at midnight
    warning: commands will be executed using /bin/sh
    at> ls
    at> <EOT>
    job 6 at Fri Apr 28 00:00:00 2017
    ```

To submit a job, simply press *Ctrl+D* on a newline:

- `noon`: This job is meant to be run at noon
- `teatime`: This job will be run at 4 PM
- `AM-PM`: We can add a trailing AM or PM to have the job be executed at a certain hour in the morning or in the afternoon:

    ```
    root:# echo "systemctl restart ssh" | at 04:43 AM
    warning: commands will be executed using /bin/sh
    job 7 at Thu Apr 27 04:43:00 2017
    root:# echo "systemctl restart ssh" | at 04:43 PM
    warning: commands will be executed using /bin/sh
    job 8 at Thu Apr 27 16:43:00 2017
    ```

- `date month_name [year]`: We can also have a job running at a specific time on a precise day, month, and optionally, a year too; but, we have to keep in mind that whatever format we choose, the date must follow the time specification and not precede it:

  ```
  root:# echo "systemctl restart ssh" | at 11:45 Aug 28
  warning: commands will be executed using /bin/sh
  job 12 at Mon Aug 28 11:45:00 2017
  root:# echo "systemctl restart ssh" | at 11:45 Aug 28 2018
  warning: commands will be executed using /bin/sh
  job 13 at Tue Aug 28 11:45:00 2018
  ```

- `MMDD[CC]YY`: Date specification as month, day, optional century, and year without spaces:

  ```
  root:# echo "systemctl restart ssh" | at 11:45 070527
  warning: commands will be executed using /bin/sh
  job 14 at Mon Jul 5 11:45:00 2027
  ```

- `MM/DD/[CC]YY`: Date specification as month/day/optional century/year separated by a slash:

  ```
  root:# echo "systemctl restart ssh" | at 07:23 PM 08222017
  warning: commands will be executed using /bin/sh
  job 15 at Tue Aug 22 19:23:00 2017
  ```

- `DD.MM.[CC]YY`: Date specification as day.month.optional century.year separated by a dot:

  ```
  root:# echo "systemctl restart ssh" | at 18:05 15.09.29
  warning: commands will be executed using /bin/sh
  job 17 at Sat Sep 15 18:05:00 2029
  ```

- `[CC]YY-MM-DD`: Date specification as optional century year-month-day, separated by a dash:

  ```
  root:# echo "systemctl restart ssh" | at 18:15 17-09-15
  warning: commands will be executed using /bin/sh
  job 18 at Fri Sep 15 18:15:00 2017
  ```

- `now + minutes | hours | days | weeks`: We can also set the time in minutes, hours, days, or weeks from the time/date on the system at the moment of creating the job:

    ```
    root:# date ; echo "systemctl restart ssh" | at now + 1 minutes
    Thu Apr 27 05:22:11 EDT 2017
    warning: commands will be executed using /bin/sh
    job 20 at Thu Apr 27 05:23:00 2017
    root:# date ; echo "systemctl restart ssh" | at now + 1 days
    Thu Apr 27 05:22:59 EDT 2017
    warning: commands will be executed using /bin/sh
    job 21 at Fri Apr 28 05:22:00 2017
    root:# date ; echo "systemctl restart ssh" | at now + 2 weeks
    Thu Apr 27 05:23:05 EDT 2017
    warning: commands will be executed using /bin/sh
    job 22 at Thu May 11 05:23:00 2017
    ```

- `today`: We can set a job to be run at a specific hour relative to today; if we do not define an hour, it will be simply executed immediately:

    ```
    root:# date ; echo "systemctl restart ssh" | at today
    Thu Apr 27 05:25:06 EDT 2017
    warning: commands will be executed using /bin/sh
    job 23 at Thu Apr 27 05:25:00 2017
    root:# date ; echo "systemctl restart ssh" | at 14:28 today
    Thu Apr 27 05:25:19 EDT 2017
    warning: commands will be executed using /bin/sh
    job 24 at Thu Apr 27 14:28:00 2017
    ```

- `tomorrow`: We can set a job to be run at a specific hour the next day; if we do not define an hour, it will be simply executed at the same hour that the job has been created, but the next day:

    ```
    root:# date ; echo "systemctl restart ssh" | at tomorrow
    Thu Apr 27 05:27:34 EDT 2017
    warning: commands will be executed using /bin/sh
    job 25 at Fri Apr 28 05:27:00 2017
    root:# date ; echo "systemctl restart ssh" | at 14:28 tomorrow
    Thu Apr 27 05:27:41 EDT 2017
    warning: commands will be executed using /bin/sh
    job 26 at Fri Apr 28 14:28:00 2017
    ```

The complete reference for time specification is available at `/usr/share/doc/at/timespec`.

As we can see from the examples, the commands are read from stdin or from a file, if using the option -f filename:

```
root:# echo "systemctl restart ssh" > /root/atjob1
root:# at -f /root/atjob1 14:28 tomorrow
warning: commands will be executed using /bin/sh
job 27 at Fri Apr 28 14:28:00 2017
```

Once the job is put in the queue, it retains some bits from the moment it was created:

The environment variables except for BASH_VERSINFO, DISPLAY, EUID, GROUPS, SHELLOPTS, TERM, UID, _, and umask are retained from the time of invocation.

```
the working directory.
the umask.
```

What kind of environment libraries are exported to the job depends on the future developments; but, for instance, if we want to schedule a compile job for some program sources, we will have to set such libraries as LD_LIBRARY_PATH or LD_PRELOAD from inside the job itself since they are not inherited.

Once the job is executed, its results will be displayed to stdout and stderr and mailed to the user using /usr/sbin/sendmail, but, if it is executed from su and at and retains its original user id, the results will be mailed to the user who originally logged in to su.

Let's run a simple command that will generate some output, and then let's make sure an email is sent:

```
root:# echo "df" | at -m now
```

And now, let's check the mailbox for the default alias user for root (check /etc/aliases to know whom the emails to root will be delivered to):

```
From root@debian Thu Apr 27 07:56:28 2017
Return-path: <root@debian>
Envelope-to: root@debian
Delivery-date: Thu, 27 Apr 2017 07:56:28 -0400
Received: from root by spoton with local (Exim 4.84_2)
  (envelope-from <root@debian>)
  id 1d3i28-0002vS-Ep
  for root@debian; Thu, 27 Apr 2017 07:56:28 -0400
Subject: Output from your job 37
To: root@debian
Message-Id: <E1d3i28-0002vS-Ep@spoton>
From: root <root@debian>
Date: Thu, 27 Apr 2017 07:56:28 -0400
```

It's Time for a Timer

```
Filesystem 1K-blocks Used Available Use% Mounted on
/dev/sda1 117913932 12476420 99424792 12% /
udev 10240 0 10240 0% /dev
tmpfs 779256 9192 770064 2% /run
tmpfs 1948140 0 1948140 0% /dev/shm
tmpfs 5120 4 5116 1% /run/lock
tmpfs 1948140 0 1948140 0% /sys/fs/cgroup
tmpfs 389628 0 389628 0% /run/user/0
```

Now that we saw how to schedule a job, let's see what options it supports:

- `-q`: Force `at` to use the specified queue to place a job. Queues are designated with a single character, from a to z and from A to Z; the default queue is named after *a for at* and *b for batch*. Queues with higher letters have an increased niceness while there is a special queue named = , which is reserved for jobs that are actually running. If a job is submitted to a queue with a capital letter, it is treated as if it was submitted to batch; so, once the time specification is hit, the job is executed only if the load average of the system is below the threshold.
- `-V`: Just prints the version number of the utility to `stderr` and `exit` successfully.
- `-m`: Sends an email to the user once the job has been completed, even if the job itself has no output.
- `-M`: Never sends any emails to the user.
- `-f` filename: We already saw this option; it forces `at` to read from the specified file the commands to run within the job, rather than from the `stdin`.
- `-t [[CC]YY]MMDDhhmm[.ss]`: Defines the time to run the job named `at`/.
- `-l`: This is actually an alias for `atq`.
- `-r`: This is actually an alias for `atrm`.
- `-d`: This is actually an alias for `atrm`.
- `-b`: This is actually an alias for `batch`.
- `-v`: Shows when a job will be executed before reading it:

    ```
    root:# at -vf /root/atjob1 14:28 tomorrow
    Fri Apr 28 14:28:00 2017
    warning: commands will be executed using /bin/sh
    job 31 at Fri Apr 28 14:28:00 2017
    ```

- -c: Shows on the stdout the specified job:

```
root:# at -c 21
#!/bin/sh
# atrun uid=0 gid=0
# mail root 0
umask 22
XDG_SESSION_ID=68; export XDG_SESSION_ID
SSH_CLIENT=192.168.0.10\ 32994\ 9999; export SSH_CLIENT
SSH_TTY=/dev/pts/0; export SSH_TTY
USER=root; export USER
MAIL=/var/mail/root; export MAIL
PATH=/usr/local/sbin:/usr/local/bin:/usr/sbin:/usr/bin:/sbin:/bin;
export PATH
PWD=/root; export PWD
LANG=en_US.UTF-8; export LANG
SHLVL=1; export SHLVL
HOME=/root; export HOME
LOGNAME=root; export LOGNAME
SSH_CONNECTION=192.168.0.10\ 32994\ 192.168.0.5\ 9999; export
SSH_CONNECTION
XDG_RUNTIME_DIR=/run/user/0; export XDG_RUNTIME_DIR
cd /root || {
  echo 'Execution directory inaccessible' >&2
  exit 1
}
systemctl restart ssh
```

- batch: Runs a job when the average system load is under a specific threshold, the default threshold defaulting to 1.5. There is a major caveat though: in order to work correctly, batch depends on Linux on a proc filesystem mounted on /proc:

```
root:# echo "systemctl restart ssh" | batch
warning: commands will be executed using /bin/sh
job 33 at Thu Apr 27 07:08:00 2017
```

If a user is not logged on at the time at is invoked or when the file named /var/run/utmp is not readable, the email at the end of the job is sent to the account found as the value of the environment variable LOGNAME. If this variable is unavailable, the current user id will receive the email.

- `atq`: Shows a list of pending job, for the user. If run by superuser, it shows the list of all the scheduled jobs for all the accounts. The format of the list is here:

    ```
    job_id, date, hour, queue, account name
    ```

    Here, what the unprivileged users see is as follows:

    ```
    root:# atq
    3 Thu Apr 27 08:00:00 2017 a zarrelli
    ```

And this is what `root` sees at the same time on the same system:

```
root:# atq
2 Wed Apr 26 14:00:00 2017 a root
3 Thu Apr 27 08:00:00 2017 a zarrelli
```

As we can see from the list, the queue with the name of a, and `indeed` queues, are designated with a single character, from a to z and from A to Z, the default queue being named after *a for at* and *b for batch*. Queues with higher letters have an increased niceness, while there is a special queue named = , which is reserved for jobs actually running. If `atq` is given a specific queue as an argument, it will show only the jobs in that queue. Let's see what `atq` can show without arguments:

```
root:# atq
5 Wed Apr 26 05:46:00 2017 b root
2 Wed Apr 26 14:00:00 2017 a root
3 Thu Apr 27 08:00:00 2017 a zarrelli
```

Now, let's restrict the list to just the batch queue:

```
root:# atq -q b
5 Wed Apr 26 05:46:00 2017 b root
```

So, `atq` supports the following options:

- `-q`: It is the only option, along with V, accepted by `atq` and restricts its output to the specified queue content
- `-V`: Just prints the version number of the utility to the `stderr` and `exit` successfully
- `atrm`: Deletes jobs identified by the job id:

```
root:# atq
9 Wed Jan 31 11:45:00 2018 a root
3 Thu Apr 27 08:00:00 2017 a zarrelli
13 Tue Aug 28 11:45:00 2018 a root
29 Fri Apr 28 14:28:00 2017 a root
```

So, we have four jobs whose ids are 3, 9, 13, and 29; let's remove them:

```
root:# atrm 3 9 13 29
And check the queue again:
root:# atq
root:#
```

Nothing left, we are done. On a final note, `atrm` accepts only one option, that is -V.

What we saw so far is good for a one shot job, since `at` will not allow us to set some recurring task; so, if we want to execute some recurring jobs over time, we need to resort to a different kind of facility: the well-known cron service.

The cron scheduler

One of the most used facilities on a server is actually the scheduler, even if we do not realize how much we rely on it. Some of the services that run unattended on our systems are dealt with by a scheduler, which is in charge to run them at specific times over a span of days, weeks, and months. All those humble, repetitive tasks, which are so essential for the correct functioning of our environment, are hidden behind the curtains and do what we would not like to do, for instance, rotate all the system logs when it is needed. Would we do these jobs every day, at crazy hours, for all the services that require maintenance? No, we have better things to do. The cron scheduler does not have any better things to do; its purpose is to wake up every minute and check if something has to be done, and this makes it the best candidate to perform tedious repetitive tasks, at the same hour, maybe every day or every week. So, since one of the purposes of this book is to get the best we can from our system, we will have a look at this humble servant and learn how to configure and administer it so that it will side us in the necessary but not-so-funny task of administering our systems.

As with `at`, crontab relies on three different components: a utility, called `cron`; a set of configuration files, the most renowned being /etc/crontab; and a client/editor called crontab. Does it look a bit confusing? Let's go in an orderly manner and have a look at the cron service first.

cron

This service runs every minute, looks for jobs stored in its crontab files, and checks if it must be run in the current minute. If anything is found, it is executed; otherwise, cron will be rerun the next minute and so forth. Once the job has been executed, the output of the commands issued is mailed to the owner of the crontab or to the user specified in the MAILTO environment variable in the crontab, if any. Notably, every minute, cron not only reads the crontab files but also checks the modification file of its spool directory or if `/etc/crontab` has changed and, if so, it will analyze the modification time of all the crontab files and reload them to get any changes made to the job's specification. So, we do not worry about restarting cron if we changed anything. It will manage the changes by itself, but cron is also able to cope with clock changes: if the time has been changed by less than 3 hours backward, the already run jobs will not be rerun. Then, if the time shifts forward to less than 3 hours, the *skipped* jobs will be run as soon as the clock will hit the new time. This affects only those jobs that have been set with a specific execution time. So, those tasks, using keywords such as `@hourly`, and those who have the wildcard * in the hour or minute specification for the runtime will not be affected. If the clock is shifted by more than 3 hours, all the jobs will be run following the new time set.

Each distribution can implement a different kind of cron facility and have the configuration files in a slightly different location. If unsure, `man cron` and `man crontab` will show what is supported by the service and which locations the relevant files are kept at.

Then, there is one more surprise: there is no cron. Well, we can chuckle because actually we call cron the daemon part of the service, but what is actually used to provide that service can change according to the distribution that we are using. There are different schedulers available for our purposes. Here are some of them:

- `vixie-cron`: This is the father of all the modern crons: the venerable cron from Paul Vixie, coded in 1987.
- `bcron`: It is a cron replacement focused to provide a secure service.
- `cronie`: It is a Fedora-based form of vixie-cron.
- `dcron`: Dillon's cron is a stripped-down version of a cron; it is secure and simple.
- `fcron`: It could be a nice replacement to the classic vixie cron and it is designed for a system that is not continuously running. So, it has some interesting features like the ability to schedule jobs at startup.

These are just some cron implementations, and we are confident that somewhere there are some more, a fork or something original that addresses some precise requirement. For the purpose of this book, we will refer to vixie-cron as installed on a Debian system.

We do not have many options to interact with cron, but let's see what it supports:

- `-f`: It does not daemonize and will stay in the foreground. It is useful to debug what is going on with it.
- `-l`: It enables the Linux Standard Base compliant script names for files inside `/etc/cron.d` (http://lanana.org/lsbreg/cron/index.html). Only the files inside this directory will be affected; those under `/etc/cron.hourly`, `/etc/cron.daily`, `/etc/cron/weekly`, and `/etc/cron/monthly` will not be affected.
- `-n`: Includes the Fully Qualified Domain Name in the subject of the email sent after a job has been run; otherwise, only the hostname will be used.
- `-l`: Sets the log level. Errors are always logged; but, different levels unlock additional information that is recorded using the system log facility, usually syslog under the *cron* facility. The single level values can be summed and the resulting value will enable the collection of more than one kind of information:
  - `1`: It logs the start of all cron jobs
  - `2`: It logs the end of all cron jobs
  - `4`: It logs the end of all failed jobs, so all jobs with exit status are different from `0`
  - `8`: It logs the process identification number of all cron jobs
  - `15`: It will collect all the information (8+4+2+1) grabbed in the preceding levels
  - The default log level is 1, but we can specify 0 if we want to disable logging at all

There are a couple of things to keep in mind when using cron:

The cron daemons set up a number of environment variables when dealing with jobs, such as follows:

- `SHELL`: Set to `/bin/sh`
- `LOGNAME`: Set from the content of `/etc/passwd` line related to the crontab owner
- `HOME`: Set from the content of `/etc/passwd` line related to the crontab owner
- `PATH`: Set to `/usr/bin:/bin`

If any other environment variables must be set by the user, the easiest way to accomplish this is to set them into crontab definitions for vixie-cron; other implementations such as cronie do not allow this, so you can resort to prepend them on the crontab line entry before calling the script or program belonging to the job:

```
# m h dom mon dow command
export HTTP_PROXY=http://192.168.0.1:8080; env >> /var/log/proxy
```

If we take a look at the syslog file, we can see the crontab being installed:

```
Apr 28 16:57:35 moveaway crontab[27929]: (root) REPLACE (root)
Apr 28 16:57:35 moveaway crontab[27929]: (root) END EDIT (root)
Apr 28 16:58:01 moveaway cron[607]: (root) RELOAD (crontabs/root)
Apr 28 16:58:01 moveaway CRON[27977]: (root) CMD (export
HTTP_PROXY=http://192.168.0.1:8080; env >> /var/log/proxy)
```

So, if we did not make any mistakes, we should see the /var/log/proxy file being created and updated with the content of the environment the command named env has been invoked from:

```
root:# cat /var/log/proxy
LANGUAGE=en_GB:en
HOME=/root
LOGNAME=root
PATH=/usr/bin:/bin
LANG=en_GB.UTF-8
SHELL=/bin/sh
PWD=/root
HTTP_PROXY=http://192.168.0.1:8080
LANGUAGE=en_GB:en
HOME=/root
LOGNAME=root
PATH=/usr/bin:/bin
LANG=en_GB.UTF-8
SHELL=/bin/sh
PWD=/root
```

The HTTP_PROXY environment variable is set for the job, and we will see more and more of these lines growing into the file, so we will see in a while how to remove this crontab or the single job.

One environment is read instead of being set and this is called **MAILTO**. If it is defined, the output of the job will be sent to the name specified; if it is empty, no mail will be sent. MAILTO can also be set to send emails to a list of users separated by commas. If not, MAILTO is set so the outcome of a job will be sent to the owner of the crontab.

Some of the cron implementations support PAM, so if they happen to set up a new cron job for a user, and we face some authorization issues we have three files to look at:

- /etc/cron.allow
- /etc/cron.deny
- /etc/pam.d/cron

/etc/at.allow is the first file to be read if it exists. If any account names are found in it, these will be the only accounts to be allowed to submit jobs using the crontab utility. If /etc/cron.allow does not exist, then /etc/cron.deny is parsed and every account name found in it will be forbidden to send jobs to cron. If the file exists, but it is empty, only the superuser or those listed in /etc/cron.allow will be able to submit jobs. If neither /etc/cron.allow nor /etc/cron.deny are available, any user will be allowed to submit jobs to cron.

We talked about the crontab utility. What is this? It is actually the program that lets us write the crontab files, which instruct cron on which jobs to execute, when, and on behalf of whom. Indeed, each user can have his/her own crontab, which is stored in /var/spool/cron/crontabs; but we should not edit them manually. We must resort to the crontab utility, which will let us edit and install the crontab file in the correct way. So, how do we use crontab? Let's say we already have a file with our job specifications, and we will see later on how to write it; the only command we have to issue is here:

crontab filename

This will install a new crontab for the current user from the file specified, but we can also manually enter our job details by typing them on the command line with crontab.

As we can imply from the preceding command lines, if crontab is called without passing a username, it will work on the cron jobs of the user who invoked it. So, if we want to list or modify a user crontab, given that we have sufficient privileges, this is being superuser, we can issue the following:

root:# crontab -u zarrelli -l
no crontab for zarrelli

If we want to edit and install a new cron job, we can use the following syntax:

crontab -u user -e

Look at the following example:

```
root:# crontab -e -u zarrelli
no crontab for zarrelli - using an empty one

Select an editor.  To change later, run 'select-editor'.
  1. /bin/nano <---- easiest
  2. /usr/bin/mcedit
  3. /usr/bin/vim.gtk
  4. /usr/bin/vim.tiny

Choose 1-4 [1]:
```

Being the first time the `crontab` utility is invoked by the user, it could ask for the default editor to be used; if not, the visual or editor environment variable are instanced. If nothing is set, `/usr/bin/editor` will be used.

In the example shown, the Debian distribution triggered the configuration of `/etc/alternatives`, which provides the link to the default editor.

Once into the editor, each cron job must be specified on a line on its own, such as * * * * * ps.

We will see later what this sequence means; as of now, we just exit the editor and save the content:

```
crontab: installing new crontab
```

Once done, `crontab` informs us that the crontab has been installed, and it could be interesting to have it displayed on the `stdout`:

```
crontab -u zarrelli -l
```

As shown in the following example:

```
root:# crontab -u zarrelli -l
# Edit this file to introduce tasks to be run by cron.
#
# Each task to run has to be defined through a single line
# indicating with different fields when the task will be run
# and what command to run for the task
#
# To define the time you can provide concrete values for
# minute (m), hour (h), day of month (dom), month (mon),
# and day of week (dow) or use '*' in these fields (for 'any').#
# Notice that tasks will be started based on the cron's system
# daemon's notion of time and timezones.
```

```
#
# Output of the crontab jobs (including errors) is sent through
# email to the user the crontab file belongs to (unless redirected).
#
# For example, you can run a backup of all your user accounts
# at 5 a.m every week with:
# 0 5 * * 1 tar -zcf /var/backups/home.tgz /home/
#
# For more information see the manual pages of crontab(5) and cron(8)
#
# m h dom mon dow command
* * * * * ps
```

If we want to get rid of the crontab, there is a handy option that will remove it completely:

```
crontab -u zarrelli -r
```

But be careful-if you want to get rid of some jobs but retain the others, the best solution is to edit the crontab again, delete the lines related to the jobs we do not want, and then save it. The new crontab with the remaining jobs will be installed and will completely replace the old one.

If we are not confident in deleting a crontab, we could set an alias that points to crontab -i -r, which works with -r and prompts the user for a confirmation before deleting the crontab:

```
root:# crontab -ir
crontab: really delete root's crontab? (y/n)
```

We will not touch some distribution specific configurations, such as the support for /etc/cron.hourly, /etc/cron.daily, /etc/cron.weekly, and /etc/cron.monthly provided through the /etc/crontab file, since otherwise, we would end up drilling down all the bits and configurations of all possible cron implementations in all the main distributions.

What interests us here is to understand the underlying basic notions on how to deal with cron so that whatever different implementation we find, we will be able to deal with it and look into its idiosyncrasies. There are a couple of interesting things left to see now: one is the syntax we will use to define a job and the other is a quick glance to anacron: a utility we have often heard of.

It's Time for a Timer

Even if a `crontab` file can look a bit cryptic at first glance, it is not so difficult to understand what the sequence of the characters mean: the first field is for the minute when the job must be executed; the second for the hour; the third for the day of the month; the fourth for the month; the fifth for the day of the week; and the sixth for the command to execute. So, the `crontab` we just created a few lines ago can be read as laid out in the following table:

Fields	*	*	*	*	*	ps
Minutes	X					
Hours		X				
Day of the month			X			
Month				X		
Day of the week					X	
Command						X

What the fields mean

Okay, now we know what these fields mean, but what are those asterisks and what can we write into each field? Another table will make all this easier to understand:

Field	Allowed values	Metacharacters
Minutes	0-59	*, - /
Hours	0-23	*, - /
Day of the month	1-31	*, - /
Month	1-12 or Jan-Dec	*, - /
Day of the week	0-7 or Sun-Sat	*, - /

Which values can be used inside each field

We are almost there. Just a few things more to learn and we will be able to fully understand a crontab line; but first, what are those metacharacters and what do they mean?

> Keep in mind that Sunday can be specified both as 0 and 7 in the day of the week field.

- `*`: This stands for *every* and can be used in all the fields. So, inside a minute field it will tell cron to run the job every minute, inside the hour every hour, and so forth.
- `,`: The comma defines a list. For instance, 1, 5, and 15 in the day of the month will instruct cron to run the job on the first, the fifth, and on the fifteenth day.
- `-`: The hyphen defines an inclusive range. For instance, 4-7 in the day of the week field will force cron to execute the job from Thursday to Sunday.
- `/`: The forward slash is used to define steps, and it can be used with ranges so that it will skip the value of the number through the range. So, 1-59/2 in the minute field will give us all the odd minutes in one hour, since it will start from one and wait 2 minutes before the next execution; this can be specified as a list as well: 1, 3, 5, 7, 9, 11, 13, 15, 17, 19, 21, 23, 25, 27, 29, 31, 33, 35, 37, 39, 41, 43, 45, 47, 49, 51, 53, 55, 57, and 59.

As we can see, steps can be quite handy. The forward slash can also be combined with the asterisk: `*/2` in the hours field means *every 2 hours*, in the month field would be *every two months*, and so forth.

> Some implementations of cron support an extra field for the *year*, with values from 1970 to 2099 supporting the `*` and `-` metacharacters.

There is one set of special markers we have to see before analyzing a crontab line. We can define some recurrences using special keywords prefixed by an @, as shown in the next table:

Keyword	Execution	The same as
@yearly	Once a year, at midnight of Jan 1st	0 0 1 1 *
@annually	Equivalent to @yearly	0 0 1 1 *
@montly	Once a month, at midnight of the first day of the month	0 0 1 * *
@weekly	Once a week, at midnight between Sat and Sun	0 0 * * 0
@daily	Once a day, at midnight	0 0 * * *

It's Time for a Timer

`@midnight`	Equivalent to `@daily`	`0 0 * * *`
`@hourly`	Once an hour, at the tick of the hour	`0 * * * *`
`@reboot`	At cron daemon startup	`nothing`

Keywords with special meanings

`This` replaces all the first five fields altogether and can become handy if you do not have special constraints about hours or days, but you want something being executed in a generic time frame.

Before proceeding there are a few things to be aware of:

- Each line specifying a cron job must be ended by a newline.
- The percent sign `%` used in the command field is turned into a newline character, and all the data after the first `%` is sent to the `stdin` of the command to be executed. The percentage can be escaped by doubling it `%%` so that it will not be interpreted as a newline.
- Inside the crontab file, blank lines, leading spaces, and tabs are not parsed. If a line starts with `#` , it will be treated as a comment and not parsed.
- In the crontab file, we can either set some variables or define a cron job; nothing else is allowed.
- A variable can be assigned as `VARIABLE_NAME = value`.
- Spaces surrounding the equals sign are optional.
- No expansions or substitutions are performed on variables.
  So, `VARIABLE_NAME=$LOGNAME` will not instance `VARIABLE_NAME` since the value string is not even parsed for expansion or substitution.
- An empty value must be surrounded by quotes, and if the values contain blanks, quotes are required to preserve them.
- No per user time zones are available. The default system time zone is used instead.

So, with this in mind, let's have a look at a cron job specification:

35	1-24/4	*	*	Mon,Thu	/opt/scripts/script.sh
minutes	hours	Day of the month	month	Day of the week	command
Execute at minute 35 past every 4th hour, from 1 through 24 on Monday and Thursday					

A useful grid to make sense of a job specification line

Caged in a table, the job specification is easier to understand and becomes much easier if we use some keywords:

```
@weekly /opt/scripts/script.sh
```

That's all, the definition was shortened to two simple fields. But fiddling with the fields can lead us to something tricky:

```
1-59/2 * * * * /opt/scripts/script.sh
```

What does this do? Simply executes the script every odd minute, not even, odd.

But what if the system is rebooted or is a desktop, which can stay off for days or weeks? Using cron would lead to some jobs not being executed at all or just skipped, and this is not a desirable behavior. This is where anacron comes in handy: it will run a job even if we switch on the desktop after the scheduled time. How can it be? Simply, this utility keeps a log of all the jobs and when they were executed using a series of timestamped files held in `/var/spool/anacron`.

Let's proceed in an orderly manner and have a look at the file which drives anacron, whose name is `/etc/anacron`.

To better understand it, we must have a peek into its content:

```
root:# cat /etc/anacrontab
# /etc/anacrontab: configuration file for anacron
# See anacron(8) and anacrontab(5) for details.
SHELL=/bin/sh
PATH=/usr/local/sbin:/usr/local/bin:/sbin:/bin:/usr/sbin:/usr/bin
HOME=/root
LOGNAME=root
```

```
# These replace cron's entries
1 5 cron.daily run-parts --report /etc/cron.daily
7 10 cron.weekly run-parts --report /etc/cron.weekly
@monthly 15 cron.monthly run-parts --report /etc/cron.monthly
```

As we can notice, we can have variables with crontab, but the format of a job definition is slightly different and can have one of the following syntaxes:

period delay job_name command
@period_identifier delay job_name command

- `period`: Expressed in days specifying the frequency the job is run at. For instance, 10 is every 10 days.
- `@period`: Allows to use some keywords to specify the frequency: `@daily`, `@weekly`, and `@monthly` for once per day, week, and month.
- `delay`: Expressed in minutes, defines the delay after which anacron executes a scheduled job when the threshold is hit.
- `job-name`: We can give a job whatever identifier we want, but no slashes are allowed. It will be used by anacron as the name for the timestamp file of the job.
- `command`: Can be whatever command.

As we can see, the standard anacron file in the example will run the run-parts utility along with the directory argument. And, the exact job of run-parts is to run the scripts it finds in the directory it is being given as arguments. So, interpreting the anacron lines should be easy now, should't it? Editing it is easy as well: we can do it by hand, no special utilities are required or available.

The way anacron works is amazingly straightforward and effective: it checks each job specified in the `anacrontab` file and sees whether it has been executed in the last x specified in the period field. If it has not been run and the threshold is hit, it will execute the job after waiting for the delay set in the second field of the job definition. Once the task has been executed, anacron records the date in a timestamp file related to the job; so next time, it will just have to read it to know what to do:

```
root:# cat /var/spool/anacron/cron.weekly
20170424
```

Once all the jobs scheduled have been executed, anacron exits; but, we also send anacron a SIGUSR1 signal to kill it: it will wait for any running jobs to finish and then will cleanly exit.

But there is also another task performed by anacron once a job has been executed: if any output is created by the job, it is mailed to the user running anacron, usually root, or the one whose email is specified in the MAILTO environment variable from anacrontab. If a `LOGNAME` variable is instanced, it will be used as the sender of the email.

Finally, let's see which options are supported by anacron:

- `-f`: Forces anacron to execute all the defined jobs, regardless of the timestamps.
- `-u`: Just updates the timestamps of the jobs to the current date without executing them.
- `-s`: Serializes the execution of the jobs; meaning that, before starting the next job, anacron will wait for the current one to be completed.
- `-n`: Ignores the delay specification for each job and runs them as they hit the threshold. Implies the -s option.
- `-d`: Usually anacron goes in background, but this option will force it to the foreground. It is useful for debugging, since anacron will sendn the runtime messages to the stderr and to syslog. The output emails will be sent to the recipient anyway.
- `-q`: Does not print messages to the stderr and implies the `-d` option.
- `-t` file: Reads the jobs, definitions from the specified file instead of the default anacrontab.
- `-T`: Tests the validity of anacrontab. If there are any errors, they will be shown and anacron will return the value of 1; otherwise, it will return 0.
- `-S` directory: Uses the specified directory to store the timestamp files.
- `-V`: Prints anacron version and exits.
- `-h`: Prints the usage help and exits.

Summary

We now have two methods available to execute jobs: one is a daemon, which forks in the background and stays there working on some, hopefully, important tasks; the other is the schedulers, great for those jobs that must be executed with a recurring pattern. These tools can really help us to keep everything in order, and execute complex and boring tasks by easing the maintenance of a server or even a desktop. But Bash is not only made of commands, scripts, tasks, and services: it is the home we are working in on a daily basis. It is our playground, our workbench, something to get familiar with. So, the next chapter will deal with some utilities, configurations, and advice to make our Bash a cozy place to live our digital life.

14
Time for Safety

Safety is important, wherever we are. For example, in a construction site as in a newly built operating system, safety is a key factor to have things done the right way. Our shell is nothing different when it comes to safety: we spend most of our time inside our environment, trying to have things done, tasks running, and keep everything in order. This last chapter will give us some quick solutions and hints on how to strengthen it and preserve it from the most common issues using the shell. We will not use more advanced tools such as security or other kernel-level enhancement: such tools would require an entire book on their own, and they come after we clean up our shell. We will perform *housekeeping*, nothing really invasive, just a *finishing touch*, trying to find a balance between security, safety, and usability; and this is actually a hard goal: strengthen too much and even the easiest task will be almost impossible to be carried on. It will be be usable and probably our system will be too exposed or unsafe. We will try to hit the sweet spot, having a usable system, fairly safe and secure; but then it is up to the administrator of each system to decide what the balance should be: we can only advice a few tips and show what could be done.

The restricted shell

There are different ways to restrict what a user can do on a system and there are a lot of reasons why we would restrict a user's ability to interact with a system: maybe we want a user just to be able to copy a file to and from the system or to have a simple home where they can work on their tasks without peeking around the system. Anyway, whatever is our goal we can start working with a restrict shell.

Bash itself offers an additional layer of security using the following options:

- `rbash`
- `--restricted`
- `-r`

Time for Safety

Invoking `rbash` or simply `bash` with the `--restricted` or `-r` options spins a Bash instance that trims down what the users will be able to do on such an environment:

- The user cannot change the directory using the `cd` builtin. The user will be prevented to set or unset the values for the following environment variables:
    - BASH_ENV
    - ENV
    - SHELL
    - PATH
- The user will not be able to specify command names with slashes and this means no command names with absolute paths. No filenames containing a slash can be passed as an argument to the built-in command called .. So, the user will not be able to source (the `read and execute` command from) a file from outside his home directory.
- No filename containing a slash can be passed as an argument to the builtin command called `hash` using the `-p` option. Hash determines the full filename of a command specified as an argument by searching into the directories specified by the environmental variable: `$PATH`. If `-p filename` is given as an option, hash would use the filename as the full path to the command searched. So, no commands invoked outside the home directory.
- No functions definitions are imported at the start from the shell environment.
- No value is taken into account from the environment SHELLOPTS variable at startup and so no shell options are set for the shell.
- No redirections are allowed using the standard operators >, >|, <>, >&, &>, >>.
- No exec built-in is available to replace the shell with a different command.
- It is not possible to add or delete builtin commands using the `enable` builtin with `-d` or `-f` options.
- It is not possible to use the `enable` built-in to enable or disable the Bash built-ins.
- The option `-p` is not allowed for the built-in command, so no `$PATH` manipulation is possible.
- It is impossible to turn off a restricted mode using `set +r` or `set +o restricted`.

So, with all these limits, the user is caged in its home directory. But how do you set up an `rbash login` shell? The easiest method is to find the Bash link and redirect it to `rbash`:

```
root:# which bash
/bin/bash
root:# which rbash
```

```
/bin/rbash
root:# ls -lah /bin/rbash
lrwxrwxrwx 1 root root 4 Nov 5 2016 /bin/rbash -> bash
```

In this case, a link already exists between `rbash` and `bash`, but in this case there were not anyone of them, so we must create it:

```
root:# cd /bin
root:# ln -s bash rbash
```

Then, we have to check that `rbash` is listed in `/etc/shells`, which sports the full pathnames to valid login shells:

```
root:# cat /etc/shells
# /etc/shells: valid login shells
/bin/sh
/bin/dash
/bin/bash
/bin/rbash
```

Now, let's create a user with a restricted shell:

```
root:# adduser --shell /bin/rbash restricted
Adding user `restricted' ...
Adding new group `restricted' (1000) ...
Adding new user `restricted' (1000) with group `restricted' ...
Creating home directory `/home/restricted' ...
Copying files from `/etc/skel' ...
Enter new UNIX password:
Retype new UNIX password:
passwd: password updated successfully
Changing the user information for restricted
Enter the new value, or press ENTER for the default
 Full Name []:
 Room Number []:
 Work Phone []:
 Home Phone []:
 Other []:
Is the information correct? [Y/n] y
```

Once done, let's `su` to the user and test the `cd` command:

```
root:# cd /home/restricted
root:# su restricted
restricted:~$ cd
restricted:~$ cd: restricted
```

Here we are. The `cd` command is restricted as we expected it to be. Let's check some other restrictions:

```
restricted:~$ pwd
/home/restricted
restricted:~$ test "Redirection test"> redirected_file
rbash: redirected_file: restricted: cannot redirect output
```

Nice, no redirections, though the cage is not really isolated:

```
restricted:~$ ls -lah /sbin/c*
-rwxr-xr-x 1 root root 19K Mar 30 2015 /sbin/capsh
-rwxr-xr-x 1 root root 243K Mar 29 2015 /sbin/cfdisk
-rwxr-xr-x 1 root root 23K Mar 29 2015 /sbin/chcpu
-rwxr-xr-x 1 root root 9.4K Aug 23 2014 /sbin/crda
-rwxr-xr-x 1 root root 1.2K Jan 22 2015 /sbin/cryptdisks_start
-rwxr-xr-x 1 root root 1.2K Jan 22 2015 /sbin/cryptdisks_stop
-rwxr-xr-x 1 root root 58K Jan 22 2015 /sbin/cryptsetup
-rwxr-xr-x 1 root root 45K Jan 22 2015 /sbin/cryptsetup-reencrypt
-rwxr-xr-x 1 root root 11K Mar 29 2015 /sbin/ctrlaltdel
```

The restricted user can still do something outside its directory. Let's override this using a local profile:

```
root:# mkdir /home/restricted/bin
root:# ln -s /bin/df /home/restricted/bin/df
```

Now let's delete `.bash_profile` or `.profile` we find in the home directory and create it, if it does not exist, the file `.bashrc` whose only line should be:

```
PATH=$HOME/bin
```

Now, let's prevent the user from modifying it:

```
root:# chown root. /home/restricted/.bashrc
root:# chmod 755 /home/restricted/.bashrc
```

And now let's `su`:

```
root:# su restricted
```

And let's check what we can do:

```
restricted:~$ cd
rbash: cd: restricted
```

We are not allowed to do that, which we already know. Let's try to list some files:

```
restricted:~$ ls
rbash: ls: command not found
```

Great, no commands are available outside our `$HOME/bin`. Let's try again:

```
restricted:~$ ping
rbash: ping: command not found
```

As expected, there is another failure. Now let's try the `df` that command we linked inside our user's `$HOME/bin` directory:

```
restricted:~$ df
Filesystem 1K-blocks Used Available Use% Mounted on
/dev/sda1 117913932 12494776 99406436 12% /
udev 10240 0 10240 0% /dev
tmpfs 779256 9192 770064 2% /run
tmpfs 1948140 0 1948140 0% /dev/shm
tmpfs 5120 4 5116 1% /run/lock
tmpfs 1948140 0 1948140 0% /sys/fs/cgroup
tmpfs 389628 0 389628 0% /run/user/0
```

This works, we successfully limited the commands the user has access to and restricted it to his home directory. Great, looks like it has been contained, but there are some limitations:

The restricted user can escape this *cage* running a program, which has a shell function. A classical example is the `vi` editor:

```
restricted:~$ vi
:set shell=/bin/bash
:shell
restricted:~$ pwd
/home/restricted
restricted:~$ cd /
restricted:~$ ls -lah
total 11G
drwxr-xr-x 22 root root 4.0K Apr 17 06:32 .
drwxr-xr-x 22 root root 4.0K Apr 17 06:32 ..
drwxr-xr-x 2 root root 4.0K May 8 05:10 bin
drwxr-xr-x 3 root root 4.0K Apr 16 07:51 boot
drwxr-xr-x 19 root root 3.2K May 9 04:05 dev
drwxr-xr-x 131 root root 12K May 8 05:34 etc
drwxr-xr-x 4 root root 4.0K May 8 05:34 home
lrwxrwxrwx 1 root root 31 Apr 16 06:14 initrd.img ->
/boot/initrd.img-3.16.0-4-amd64
drwxr-xr-x 21 root root 4.0K Apr 17 03:59 lib
drwxr-xr-x 2 root root 4.0K Apr 16 06:13 lib64
```

```
drwx------  2 root root  16K Apr 16 06:13 lost+found
drwxr-xr-x  3 root root 4.0K Apr 16 06:13 media
drwxr-xr-x  2 root root 4.0K Apr 16 06:13 mnt
drwxr-xr-x  2 root root 4.0K Apr 16 06:13 opt
-rw-r--r--  1 root root  10G Apr 16 07:55 playground
dr-xr-xr-x 113 root root    0 May  9 04:05 proc
drwx------  9 root root 4.0K May  9 04:07 root
drwxr-xr-x 21 root root  840 May  9 04:10 run
drwxr-xr-x  2 root root 4.0K Apr 17 03:59 sbin
drwxr-xr-x  2 root root 4.0K Apr 16 06:13 srv
dr-xr-xr-x 13 root root    0 May  9 04:05 sys
drwxrwxrwt  8 root root 4.0K May  9 04:11 tmp
drwxr-xr-x 10 root root 4.0K Apr 16 06:13 usr
drwxr-xr-x 12 root root 4.0K Apr 16 06:32 var
lrwxrwxrwx  1 root root   27 Apr 16 06:14 vmlinuz -> boot/
vmlinuz-3.16.0-4-amd64
restricted:~$
```

Another method to escape a restricted shell is to invoke an unrestricted shell:

```
restricted:~$ cd
rbash: cd: restricted
restricted:~$ bash
restricted:~$ cd /
restricted:~$ pwd
/
restricted:~$
```

This also means that any script with a valid sha-bang will invoke a full-blown shell and escape any restrictions. All of these methods imply that the user has access either to Bash or to any programs featuring a shell function, otherwise jumping out from the cage would not be so easy. But we have to bear something important in mind: this is a method to cage some users in their working space, so it will separate them from each other, give them their own isolated home, and prevent them from inadvertently messing with other parts of the system. It is not a full-blown security layer hacker; for this kind of stuff, we should rely on something more at a kernel level, and it is outside the scope of this book, since it would require quite a long explanation about security, kernel compiling, third-party products, hardening, and so forth. Again, it is a book on its own.

So, we want to keep things clean, and what can we do to host remote connections in an orderly manner?

Restricted shells for OpenSSH

Even though the restricted shell for OpenSSH (http://www.pizzashack.org/rssh/) is not strictly a shell tool; its simplicity makes it a good candidate for helping to keep the house clean when some visitor knocks on wood. Rssh is available for a variety of distributions and platforms and offers a restricted shell allowing not only scp and ftp, but also csv, rdist, and rsync. So, we can create accounts available for file copy or synchronization without allowing a full shell access; and this can be handy to keep things on a low profile and lower the server exposure to attacks.

The first step consists in installing rssh from a package or from a source. In our example, we will rely on a package since the distribution used, Debian, has one; and also, using packages will ensure that the utility will be upgraded and patched by the maintainers whenever needed:

```
root:# apt-get install rssh
Reading package lists... Done
Building dependency tree
Reading state information... Done
Suggested packages:
  cvs rdist subversion makejail
The following NEW packages will be installed:
  rssh
0 upgraded, 1 newly installed, 0 to remove and 0 not upgraded.
Need to get 54.4 kB of archives.
After this operation, 119 kB of additional disk space will be used.
Get:1 http://ftp.us.debian.org/debian/ jessie/main rssh amd64 2.3.4-4+b1 [54.4 kB]
Fetched 54.4 kB in 0s (103 kB/s)
Preconfiguring packages ...
Selecting previously unselected package rssh.
(Reading database ... 62697 files and directories currently installed.)
Preparing to unpack .../rssh_2.3.4-4+b1_amd64.deb ...
Unpacking rssh (2.3.4-4+b1) ...
Processing triggers for man-db (2.7.0.2-5) ...
Setting up rssh (2.3.4-4+b1) ...
```

Once installed, we will have a new shell binary available:

```
root:# ls -lah /usr/bin/rssh
-rwxr-xr-x 1 root root 31K Nov 8 2014 /usr/bin/rssh
```

So, now let's use this new binary as the restricted user's shell:

```
root:# chsh -s `which rssh` restricted
```

Time for Safety

And let's verify directly on `/etc/passwd` that the shell has been assigned:

```
root:# egrep restricted /etc/passwd
restricted:x:1000:1000:,,,:/home/restricted:/usr/bin/rssh
```

It seems all OK, so let's connect from remote to the system where the restricted user resides:

```
zarrelli:~$ ssh -p 9999 restricted@192.168.0.5
Warning: Permanently added '[192.168.0.5]:9999' (ECDSA) to the list of
known hosts.
Restricted@192.168.0.5's password:
The programs included with the Debian GNU/Linux system are free software;
the exact distribution terms for each program are described in the
individual files in /usr/share/doc/*/copyright.
Debian GNU/Linux comes with ABSOLUTELY NO WARRANTY, to the extent
permitted by applicable law.
This account is restricted by rssh.
This user is locked out.
If you believe this is in error, please contact your system administrator.
Connection to 192.168.0.5 closed.
```

The account is locked out and this is the default behavior of `rssh` since we did not configure it yet. So, let's see the main configuration directives that we can use inside the `/etc/rssh.conf` file to enable some protocols and per user configurations:

- `allowsftp`: Allows sftp connections.
- `allowcvs`: Allows cvs connections.
- `allowrdist`: Allows rdist connections.
- `allowrsync`: Allows rsync connections.
- `allowsvnserve`: Allows svnserve connections.
- `umask`: Sets the umask for the files and directories created during a scp or sftp session. The umask is usually set by the shell upon user login, so to avoid this, rssh must set the umask itself.
- `logfacility`: Specifies which syslog facility or C macros to use for logging.
- `chrootpath`: A helper application for `rssh` (`rssh_chroot_helper`) calls the `chroot()` system call changing the root of the filesystem for the session. So, for example: `chrootpath=/opt/jails` will change the root of the virtual filesystem to `/opt/jails` for the users whose shell is `rssh`.

After the login, the `/var/caged/users` directory will appear to the user as the root directory of the filesystem, and it will not be able to get outside of it. If this directive is used, a `chroot` jail must be in place to provide the users a minimal environment. We will see later how to do it. If the user's home directory defined in `/etc/passwd` is inside the path specified by `chrootpath`, then the user will be `chdired` to his home directory, otherwise it will be `chdired` to the root of the `chroot` jail.

- user: With this directive, we can set a per user configuration that will override all others directives. The `user` keyword appears in a string separated in fields by colons (:) with the following structure:

  `user = "username:unask:access_digits:chroot_path"`

So, let's see what each fields represents:

- **username**: This is the account name we want to set the configuration for.
- **umask**: Is the umask expressed in octal for the user. It follows the same specification as if we were setting it for the Bash shell.
- **access_digits**: These are six binary digits that specify if the user is allowed to use `rsync`, `rdist`, `cvs`, `sftp`, `scp`, and `svnserve` in the order listed. `0` means the user is not allowed, a `1` means the user is allowed to use it.
- **path**: It specifies the path to the directory the user will be chrooted in.

Quotes are not mandatory except when there are spaces in the path field. In this case, we can user either single or double quotes. Spaces around = are fine. So, something like `user=restricted:022:100000:` means that the user restricted has a umask of `022` and has the `rsync` connections available. No `chroot` is specified:

`user = restricted:011:000110:"/usr/local/chroot jails"`

The previous statement means that the user restricted has an umask of `011`, `sftp`, and `scp` connections available, and it will be chrooted in `/usr/local/chroot jails`.

Knowing a bit more about configurations, let's enable just the `scp` connections for our restricted user by adding `user = restricted:277:000010` to `/etc/rssh.conf`.

Time for Safety

Time to check whether we finally can access the remote system:

```
zarrelli:~$ ssh -p 9999 restricted@192.168.0.5
Warning: Permanently added '[192.168.0.5]:9999' (ECDSA) to the list of
known hosts.
restricted@192.168.0.5's password:
The programs included with the Debian GNU/Linux system are free software;
the exact distribution terms for each program are described in the
individual files in /usr/share/doc/*/copyright.
Debian GNU/Linux comes with ABSOLUTELY NO WARRANTY, to the extent
permitted by applicable law.
Last login: Tue May 9 06:15:40 2017 from 192.168.0.10
This account is restricted by rssh.
Allowed commands: scp
If you believe this is in error, please contact your system administrator.
Connection to 192.168.0.5 closed.
```

This is interesting. The message is slightly different from the previous attempt: we are still prevented to log into the remote server using ssh, but it states that although the account is restricted by rssh, we can use `scp`. So, let's try it:

```
zarrelli:~$ scp -P 9999 test_file restricted@192.168.0.5:
Warning: Permanently added '[192.168.0.5]:9999' (ECDSA) to the list of
known hosts.
Restricted@192.168.0.5's password:
test_file
```

Well, it seems it worked. Let's have a look on the remote server:

```
root:# pwd
/home/restricted
root:# ls -lah test_file
-r-------- 1 restricted rssh_users 0 May 10 05:24 test_file
```

Here we go. In the home directory of the restricted user, we have our file with the access rights set to `400`, as expected. Nice and easy. But there is a small issue and we can see what it is about here:

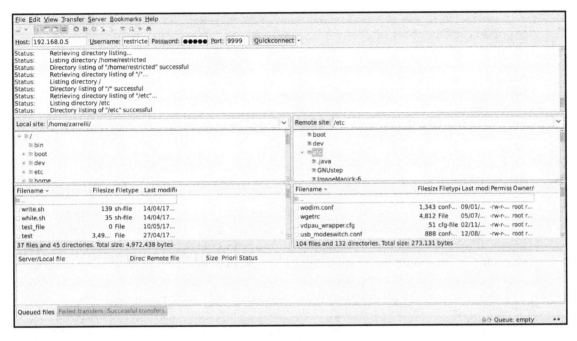

Using FileZilla we are able to browse the entire filesystem of the remote host

Even though the user is limited to a protocol, he can browse the remote filesystem without any restrictions other than the Unix/POSIX file permissions. In the example shown, we enabled the SFTP protocol and actually connected to the system as the restricted user browsing, having a look at the `/etc` directory. Can we prevent this? Yes, we can `chroot` the user into, ideally, a filesystem on its own, mounted with `nosuid` and possibly with a `noxec` options if supported. This way, even if a user uploads an executable, he will not be able to run it and/or exploit any `suid` rights. Is it easy to do? No, creating a `chroot` jail can be really hard since it requires copying the relevant binaries and libraries into the jail itself; versions and paths can change depending on the distribution used and also the release itself. Actually, the source tarball of rssh offers a script, which with some modifications can actually help copying all the necessary files to the jail. There are also some other scripts that we can easily find on the internet and that will help us in this sensible job. Anyway, there is a much easier way to provide a restricted sftp access to a server, and we do not have to look so far away from our environment since we can accomplish this task simply using the OpenSSH server.

Time for Safety

Restricted sftp sessions with OpenSSH

Using OpenSSH, everything can be easily done with five configuration lines and a few commands; let's see how. We are on the remote server.

First, let's open the OpenSSH file, which is usually found in `/etc/ssh/sshd_config` and add these few lines:

```
Match group sftp-only
ChrootDirectory /opt/jails/%u/exchange
X11Forwarding no
AllowTcpForwarding no
ForceCommand internal-sftp
```

We should already know what these directives are, but let's recall what we wrote in `Chapter 12`, *Remote Connections over SSH*, about remote connections over ssh:

- `Match`: With this directive, we can use conditional statements so that if they are satisfied the following configuration lines, we will override the ones in the main configuration block. If a keyword/configuration block appears in more than one match clause, only the first instance is taken in to account. As matching criteria, we can use the following directives: user, group, host, local address, l local port, address, or all for all of them. We can match a list, patterns an negation. In our example, we are going to match against a group that we are going to create in a moment: whatever account belongs to the group sftp-only will be subjected to the following configuration lines.
- `ChrootDirectory`: By specifying the full path to a directory, we can `chroot` a user into it after successful authentication. It is not an easy task since the directory must be owned by root and cannot be writable by anyone else. In addition, we must provide some files required for a session, like the shell, `/dev/null`, `/dev/zero`, `/dev/arandom`, `/dev/stdin`, `/dev/stdout`, `/dev/stderr`, and `/dev/ttyx`. We can also find some tokens such as `%h` standing for the home directory of the account authenticating, or we can also see `%%`, which stands for a simple `%`. `%u` is replaced by the username. In our case, we do not have to provide any binaries, because we will allow sftp connections only, since there is no shell, there is no chance of executing anything.
- `X11Forwarding`: This allows/denies the `X11` forwarding. If set to `yes`, it can expose `X11` to attacks; so this option must be taken with care. Defaults to `no`. We prevent the forwarding to `X11`: there is no need for it and it can expose the system.

- `AllowTcpForwarding`: This allow/denies TCP forwarding and can take as argument `yes`, `all`, `no`, or `local` and `remote`. The first two options allow the forwarding, the third denies it, and the `local` allows local forwarding only; `remote` enables remote forwarding only. There is no shell or TCP forwarding for our example.
- `ForceCommand`: Overrides any commands sent by the client or listed in the `~/.ssh/rc` of the authenticating account and forces the execution of the command listed in this directive. The command is executed through the account shell with the `-c` option. Defaults to `no`. In our case, we force the execution of the OpenSSH internal `sftp` subsystem.

    Talking about the subsystem, let's verify that in the same config file OpenSSH is configured to use the `internal-sftp` subsystem:

    Subsystem sftp internal-sftp

We may also want to add some more restrictions at the end of the configuration file:

PermitTunnel no
AllowAgentForwarding no

- `AllowAgentForwarding`: Defines whether ssh-agent forwarding is allowed or not. Defaults to `yes` to increase the security, and since it is not really needed for an `sftp` account, so we are going to disable it.
- `PermitTunnel`: This allows/denies the tunnel device forwarding. It takes yes, point-to-point, Ethernet, or no as arguments. Yes enables both point-to-point and Ethernet forwarding. Defaults to no, and we want to be sure it is disabled since we do not need a tunnel for an sftp account.

Now that we have all the service bits in place, let's restart the OpenSSH server, in our case, this:

root:# service ssh restart

Time to add our new group and move our restricted user there:

root:# addgroup sftp-only
root:# service ssh restart
root:# usermod -g sftp-only restricted
root:# usermod -s /bin/false restricted

Time for Safety

So, now we have our restricted user added to the `sftp-only` group without a valid shell to log in to the system:

```
restricted:x:1000:1003:,,,:/home/restricted:/bin/false
```

Now, let's make the user home directory owned by root so that the user would not be able to write into it:

```
root:# chown root. /home/restricted/
```

And let's create a new home owned by `root`:

```
root:# mkdir -p /opt/sftp-jails/restricted/exchange
root:# chown -R root. /opt/sftp-jails/
```

Also let a subdir owned by the restricted user who can write to it:

```
root:# chown restricted.root /opt/sftp-jails/restricted/exchange
root:# chmod 750 /opt/sftp-jails/restricted/exchange/
```

All fine now, let's try to log in:

```
zarrelli:~$ ssh -p 9999 restricted@192.168.0.5
Warning: Permanently added '[192.168.0.5]:9999' (ECDSA) to the list of known hosts.
restricted@192.168.0.5's password:
Could not chdir to home directory /home/restricted: No such file or directory
This service allows sftp connections only.
Connection to 192.168.0.5 closed.
```

That is fine: we do not want a full shell for the restricted user, so let's try sftp:

```
zarrelli:~$ sftp -P 9999 restricted@192.168.0.5
Warning: Permanently added '[192.168.0.5]:9999' (ECDSA) to the list of known hosts.
Restricted@192.168.0.5's password:
Connected to 192.168.0.5.
sftp>
```

Great, we are in, but let's check what we can actually do:

```
sftp> pwd
Remote working directory: /
sftp>
```

OK, we are in our remote root directory, but what is inside it?

```
sftp> ls -lah
drwxr-xr-x  0 0    0 4.0K May 11 14:56 .
drwxr-xr-x  0 0    0 4.0K May 11 14:56 ..
drwxr-x---  0 1000 0 4.0K May 11 15:00 exchange
```

This sounds familiar. It is the cage, so let's escape it:

```
sftp> cd /
sftp> pwd
Remote working directory: /
sftp> ls
exchange
sftp>
```

No, we actually cannot do so. At least, let's try to upload something:

```
sftp> put test_file
Uploading test_file to /test_file
remote open("/test_file"): Permission denied
sftp>
```

No way, the user's root directory is unwritable, so let's `cd` to the exchange directory and try the upload again:

```
sftp> cd exchange
sftp> put test_file
Uploading test_file to /exchange/test_file
test_file 100% 0 0.0KB/s 00:00
sftp>
```

It definitely works. Let's get the file back:

```
sftp> get test_file
Fetching /exchange/test_file to test_file
sftp> bye
```

Here we are, the account is ready for the customer to connect and share data. But what if we want to connect using a key for authentication?

Let's first modify `/etc/ssh/ssd_config` by adding the following line at the very end of the file:

```
AuthorizedKeysFile /opt/sftp-jails/authorized_keys/%u/authorized_keys
```

This will be under the match condition and will be triggered for all the users of the `sftp-only` group; but for this to be taken in to account, we have to reload the configuration:

```
root:# service ssh restart
```

So, since the new directive instructs OpenSSH to look for `authorized_keys` inside `/opt/sftp-jails/authorized_keys/{username}/authorized_keys` for all the users belonging to the `sftp-only` group, let's start creating the correct directories:

```
root:# mkdir -p /opt/sftp-jails/authorized_keys/restricted
```

This is the full path to the user directory holding the authentication key for the user that is restricted. We will have to create one of each user; and the name of the final directory must be the same as the username. Now, we have to trim ownership and access rights:

```
root:# cd /opt/sftp-jails
root:# chown -R root.sftp-only authorized_keys
root:# chown -R restricted.root authorized_keys/restricted
```

The `authorized_keys` directory belongs to user root and the group: `sftp-only`, while the subdirectory restricted belongs to user restricted and group root:

```
root:# chmod 750 /opt/sftp-jails/authorized_keys/
root:# chmod 500 /opt/sftp-jails/authorized_keys/restricted/
```

All the users from the `sftp-only` group can traverse the `authorized_keys` directory, but only the restricted user can traverse the directory restricted. Now, let's copy our key example to the final destination:

```
root:# cp id_ecdsa_to_spoton.pub /opt/sftp-jails/authorized_keys/restricted/authorized_keys
```

And now let's give it a correct ownership and access rights:

```
root:# chown restricted.root /opt/sftp-jails/authorized_keys/restricted/authorized_keys
root:#chmod 400 /opt/sftp-jails/authorized_keys/restricted/authorized_keys
```

So, we should end with such a configuration:

```
root:# cd /opt/
root:# tree -pug
.
└── [drwxr-xr-x root root ] sftp-jails
    ├── [drwxr-x--- root sftp-only] authorized_keys
    │   └── [dr-x------ restricted root ] restricted
    │       └── [-r-------- restricted root ] authorized_keys
```

```
        └── [drwxr-xr-x root sftp-only] restricted
            └── [drwxr-x--- restricted root ] exchange
                └── [-rw-r--r-- restricted sftp-only] test_file
```

Everything looks fine, so we just have to test what we have done so far. Let's go to the local server and try a connection on the remote server:

```
local_user:~$ sftp -i .ssh/id_ecdsa_to_spoton -P 9999
restricted@192.168.0.5
Warning: Permanently added '[192.168.0.5]:9999' (ECDSA) to the list of
known hosts.
Connected to 192.168.0.5.
sftp>
```

So, we are successfully connected using our identity key. We can then automate the connection adding the following snippet to the .ssh/config file of local_user:

```
Host spoton-sftp
AddressFamily inet
ConnectionAttempts 10
ForwardAgent no
ForwardX11 no
ForwardX11Trusted no
GatewayPorts no
HostBasedAuthentication no
HostKeyAlias sftp-alias
HostName 192.168.0.5
IdentityFile ~/.ssh/id_ecdsa_to_spoton
PasswordAuthentication no
Port 9999
Protocol 2
Compression yes
CompressionLevel 9
ServerAliveCountMax 3
ServerAliveInterval 15
TCPKeepAlive no
User restricted
```

Let's try a ssh connection:

```
local_user:~$ ssh spoton-sftp
Warning: Permanently added 'sftp-alias,[192.168.0.5]:9999' (ECDSA) to the
list of known hosts.
Could not chdir to home directory /home/restricted: No such file or
directory
This service allows sftp connections only.
Connection to 192.168.0.5 closed.
```

Time for Safety

This is correct, we should not be allowed to connect over `ssh` with shell or access a home directory.

Let's try an `sftp` connection:

```
local_user:~$ sftp spoton-sftp
Warning: Permanently added 'sftp-alias,[192.168.0.5]:9999' (ECDSA) to the
list of known hosts.
Connected to spoton-sftp.
```

Great, we are connected using our identity key and with no user or file or IP address specified. So, let's make some test:

```
sftp> pwd
Remote working directory: /
```

We are in our user root directory; let's try to climb up to the system root directory:

```
sftp> cd /
sftp> pwd
Remote working directory: /
sftp> ls
exchange
```

No way, we are caged into our root directory and cannot go to any upper levels. Let's look for a file to upload:

```
sftp> !ls
test_local
```

Let's try to upload it to the home directory:

```
sftp> put test_local
Uploading test_local to /test_local
remote open("/test_local"): Permission denied
```

We have no permission, as expected. We need to use the exchange subdirectory for our purposes:

```
sftp> cd exchange
sftp> put test_local
Uploading test_local to /exchange/test_local
test_local 100% 0 0.0KB/s 00:00
```

Successfully uploaded! Now, let's see what is inside the exchange directory:

```
sftp> ls
test_file  test_local
Ok, we have the old and the new file. Let's grab the old file:
sftp> get test_file
Fetching /exchange/test_file to test_file
sftp>
```

Done! Everything looks fine. Or something like that since we are blind on what happens during the connection. Since everything is in an isolated cage, there is no way to use a system facility such as `rsyslog` to actually record what the user is doing during an `sftp` session. Or, at least, the normal `rsyslog` configuration is not able to do this, but there are a few methods to work around this limitation. One that we are going to see involves the use of a pipe; it will make things really easy. First, let's modify a couple of directives in /etc/ssh/sshd_config.

The old `Subsystem` and `ForceCommand` now must be rewritten as:

```
Subsystem sftp internal-sftp -l INFO
ForceCommand internal-sftp -l INFO
```

Now the `internal-sftp` will log with a level of `INFO`, so we have to export this information to the main log using a socket. So, let's create a file:

```
root:# cat /etc/rsyslog.d/openssh-sftp.conf
module(load="imuxsock")
input(type="imuxsock" Socket="/opt/sftp-jails/restricted/dev/log"
CreatePath="on")
if $programname == 'internal-sftp' then /var/log/openssh-sftp.log
& stop
```

So, what we have done is instruct `rsyslog` to create a Unix socket in in the /dev directory of the restricted user; and the `sftp` subsystem will be able to send the log messages to `rsyslog` using that socket. Yes, but how are these messages written? They are written by simply accessing one of the properties of the message itself. In this case, if the name of the program that generated the messages is `internal-sftp`, then the message is written on /var/log/openssh-sftp.log. Once done, let's restart both `sshd` and `rsyslog`:

```
root:# service ssh restart
root:# service rsyslog restart
```

Time for Safety

 If you receive a message from `rsyslog` complaining about the `imuxsock` module already being loaded, just comment out the first line with `#`.

Now, we just have to make another connection and issue some commands in order to populate the log file:

```
root:# cat /var/log/openssh-sftp.log
May 11 14:28:25 spoton internal-sftp[16080]: session opened for local user restricted from [192.168.0.10]
May 11 14:28:26 spoton internal-sftp[16080]: opendir "/"
May 11 14:28:26 spoton internal-sftp[16080]: closedir "/"
May 11 14:28:35 spoton internal-sftp[16080]: opendir "/exchange"
May 11 14:28:35 spoton internal-sftp[16080]: closedir "/exchange"
May 11 14:28:39 spoton internal-sftp[16080]: open "/exchange/test_file" flags READ mode 0666
May 11 14:28:39 spoton internal-sftp[16080]: close "/exchange/test_file" bytes read 0 written 0
May 11 14:28:42 spoton internal-sftp[16080]: open "/exchange/test_file" flags WRITE,CREATE,TRUNCATE mode 0644
May 11 14:28:42 spoton internal-sftp[16080]: sent status Permission denied
May 11 14:29:00 spoton internal-sftp[16080]: opendir "/exchange"
May 11 14:29:00 spoton internal-sftp[16080]: closedir "/exchange"
May 11 14:29:05 spoton internal-sftp[16080]: remove name "/exchange/test_file"
May 11 14:29:06 spoton internal-sftp[16080]: opendir "/exchange"
May 11 14:29:06 spoton internal-sftp[16080]: closedir "/exchange"
May 11 14:29:09 spoton internal-sftp[16080]: open "/exchange/test_file" flags WRITE,CREATE,TRUNCATE mode 0644
May 11 14:29:09 spoton internal-sftp[16080]: close "/exchange/test_file" bytes read 0 written 0
May 11 14:29:10 spoton internal-sftp[16080]: opendir "/exchange"
May 11 14:29:10 spoton internal-sftp[16080]: closedir "/exchange"
May 11 14:30:45 spoton internal-sftp[16080]: session closed for local user restricted from [192.168.0.10]
```

That's it. Now we have a nice log showing us what the user has done during his `sftp` session; and the log itself is out of reach of any `sftp` users. In our example, we redirected the messages based on the name of the program, which created them; but we have other tags we can use to filter. So, let's see the more useful ones:

- `HOSTNAME`: The hostname as it appears in the message.
- `FROMHOST`: The hostname of the system the message was received from. In a chained configuration, this is the system next to the receiver, not necessarily the first sender.

- `syslogfacility`: The facility reported by the message in numerical form.
- `syslogfacility-text`: The facility reported by the message in text form.
- `syslogseverity`: The severity reported by the message in numerical form.
- `syslogseverity-text`: The severity reported by the message in text form.

By using these properties, we can do something interesting. Let's start creating another user with the same group and shell as restricted:

```
root:# adduser --shell /bin/false --gid 1003 casualuser
Adding user `casualuser' ...
Adding new user `casualuser' (1003) with group `sftp-only' ...
Creating home directory `/home/casualuser' ...
Copying files from `/etc/skel' ...
Enter new UNIX password:
Retype new UNIX password:
passwd: password updated successfully
Changing the user information for casualuser
Enter the new value, or press ENTER for the default
    Full Name []:
    Room Number []:
    Work Phone []:
    Home Phone []:
    Other []:
Is the information correct? [Y/n]
```

Now, let's change the home directory owner for the user's home directory:

```
root:# chown -R root. /home/casualuser/
```

Let's create the new jail copying the one we already have:

```
root:# cd /opt/sftp-jails
  root:# cp -ra restricted/ casualuser
```

We just have to fix the ownership now:

```
root:# cd casualuser
root:# chown -R casualuser.root exchange/
root:# cd exchange
root:# chown casualuser.sftp-only *
```

Time for copying the keys:

```
root:# cd /opt/sftp-jails/authorized_keys
root:# cp -ra restricted casualuser
root:# chown -R casualuser.root casualuser/
```

Time for Safety

In our example, for brevity, we are using the same key as the restricted user, but we can always create a new key and copy over the `authorized_keys` file to give each user their own key. Once done, let's try a connection:

```
local_user:~$ sftp -i .ssh/id_ecdsa_to_spoton -P 9999
casualuser@192.168.0.5
Warning: Permanently added '[192.168.0.5]:9999' (ECDSA) to the list of known hosts.
Connected to 192.168.0.5.
sftp> ls
dev exchange
sftp> !ls
test_file test_local
sftp> put test_file
Uploading test_file to /test_file
remote open("/test_file"): Permission denied
sftp> cd exchange
sftp> put test_file
Uploading test_file to /exchange/test_file
test_file
sftp>
```

OK, the user can access and has the right permissions, but what about logging? Nothing, we did not set up anything for logging, so let's modify `/etc/rsyslog.d/openssh-sftp.conf` by adding the following line:

```
input(type="imuxsock" Socket="/opt/sftp-jails/casualuser/dev/log" CreatePath="on")
```

Now, to get the new instructions taken in account, let's restart `rsyslog`:

```
service rsyslog restart
```

And let's connect again to generate some logging lines:

```
local_user:~$ sftp -i .ssh/id_ecdsa_to_spoton -P 9999
casualuser@192.168.0.5
Warning: Permanently added '[192.168.0.5]:9999' (ECDSA) to the list of known hosts.
Connected to 192.168.0.5.
sftp> ls
dev exchange
sftp> cd exchange
sftp> ls
test_file test_local
sftp> get test_local
Fetching /exchange/test_local to test_local
sftp> bye
```

Let's check the log file:

```
May 12 04:02:04 spoton internal-sftp[18573]: session opened for local user casualuser from [192.168.0.10]
May 12 04:02:06 spoton internal-sftp[18573]: opendir "/"
May 12 04:02:06 spoton internal-sftp[18573]: closedir "/"
May 12 04:02:11 spoton internal-sftp[18573]: opendir "/exchange"
May 12 04:02:11 spoton internal-sftp[18573]: closedir "/exchange"
May 12 04:02:15 spoton internal-sftp[18573]: open "/exchange/test_local" flags READ mode 0666
May 12 04:02:15 spoton internal-sftp[18573]: close "/exchange/test_local" bytes read 0 written 0
May 12 04:02:18 spoton internal-sftp[18573]: session closed for local user casualuser from [192.168.35.219]
May 12 04:06:45 spoton internal-sftp[18631]: session opened for local user casualuser from [192.168.0.10]
```

This is what is expected. We created a Unix socket in the new user's jail; and we are receiving the messages sent by the `internal-sftp` subsystem for the account session. Nice, but confusing. All the log messages from all the users will be contained in a single file, and since the command messages such as `May 12 04:02:11 spoton internal-sftp[18573]: closedir "/exchange"` are not identified by a user account name, but from a session ID [18631], it is feasible to follow all the actions performed during a session and trace them back to the user who made them. But overall, it is not so easy to read. What can we do? Well, as always we have to use a bit of imagination and creativity and bend the rules to take some advantages. Let's tinker with the `rsyslog` config file for `openssh-sftp`:

/etc/rsyslog.d/openssh-sftp.conf

Let's open it and replace its content with the following lines:

```
#module(load="imuxsock")
input(type="imuxsock" HOSTNAME="restricted" Socket="/opt/sftp-jails/restricted/dev/log" CreatePath="on")
input(type="imuxsock" HostName="casualuser" Socket="/opt/sftp-jails/casualuser/dev/log" CreatePath="on")
if $hostname == 'restricted' then /var/log/openssh-sftp/restricted-sftp.log
if $hostname == 'casualuser' then /var/log/openssh-sftp/casualuser-sftp.log
& stop
```

What did we do? We used a property manipulation string, which allowed us to associate a hostname property to the messages coming from a specific socket. Then, we added two rules to redirect the messages to a per user log file, based on the hostname property found in the messages themselves. We intentionally wrote the hostname property with different cases to show that the property name is case insensitive. Time to restart `rsyslogd`:

```
root:# service rsyslog restart
```

The logging facility is ready, let's connect again and make some *noise*:

```
local_user:~$ sftp -i .ssh/id_ecdsa_to_spoton -P 9999
casualuser@192.168.0.5
Warning: Permanently added '[192.168.0.5]:9999' (ECDSA) to the list of
known hosts.
Connected to 192.168.0.5.
sftp> ls
dev exchange
sftp> cd exchange
sftp> ls
test_file test_local
sftp> get test_local
Fetching /exchange/test_local to test_local
sftp> cd ..
sftp> put test_file
Uploading test_file to /test_file
remote open("/test_file"): Permission denied
sftp> cd /
sftp>
```

Now is the time to check:

```
root:# ls -lah /var/log/openssh-sftp/casualuser-sftp.log
-rw-r----- 1 root adm 757 May 12 05:14 /var/log/openssh-sftp/casualuser-
sftp.log
```

We connected as casualuser, and indeed we see a file named `casualuser-sftp.log` exactly where we expected to find it. Let's have a look at what is inside:

```
root:# cat /var/log/openssh-sftp/casualuser-sftp.log
May 12 05:13:48 casualuser internal-sftp[19004]: session opened for local
user casualuser from [192.168.0.10]
May 12 05:13:49 casualuser internal-sftp[19004]: opendir "/"
May 12 05:13:49 casualuser internal-sftp[19004]: closedir "/"
May 12 05:13:54 casualuser internal-sftp[19004]: opendir "/exchange"
May 12 05:13:54 casualuser internal-sftp[19004]: closedir "/exchange"
May 12 05:14:13 casualuser internal-sftp[19004]: open
"/exchange/test_local" flags READ mode 0666
May 12 05:14:13 casualuser internal-sftp[19004]: close
```

```
"/exchange/test_local" bytes read 0 written 0
May 12 05:14:23 casualuser internal-sftp[19004]: open "/test_file" flags
WRITE,CREATE,TRUNCATE mode 0644
May 12 05:14:23 casualuser internal-sftp[19004]: sent status Permission
denied
May 12 05:41:50 casualuser internal-sftp[19004]: session closed for local
user casualuser from [192.168.0.10]
```

That's it. Our sftp session has been fully logged and now if we want to know what the casual user did, we just have to open the log file and read it through. One interesting note, each line of message has now the name of the user it belongs to. Well, it would actually be the hostname, but we streched the rules to get what we wanted from the system. Is it really so? Let's make a final check connecting a restricted user to see if a new log file is being generated:

```
local_user:~$ sftp -i .ssh/id_ecdsa_to_spoton -P 9999
restricted@192.168.0.5
Warning: Permanently added '[192.168.0.5]:9999' (ECDSA) to the list of
known hosts.
Connected to 192.168.0.5.
sftp> mkdir test
Couldn't create directory: Permission denied
sftp> cd exchange
sftp> mkdir test
sftp> ls
test test_file test_local
sftp> dc test
Invalid command.
sftp> cd test
sftp> bye
```

Now that we have issued some commands as a restricted user, let's see if the file we want is really in place:

```
root:# ls -lah /var/log/openssh-sftp/restricted-sftp.log
-rw-r----- 1 root adm 607 May 12 05:47 /var/log/openssh-sftp/restricted-
sftp.log
```

The file is correctly in place, so let's have a look inside:

```
root:# cat /var/log/openssh-sftp/restricted-sftp.log
May 12 05:43:47 restricted internal-sftp[19147]: session opened for local
user restricted from [192.168.0.10]
May 12 05:47:04 restricted internal-sftp[19147]: mkdir name "/test" mode
0777
May 12 05:47:04 restricted internal-sftp[19147]: sent status Permission
denied
```

```
May 12 05:47:11 restricted internal-sftp[19147]: mkdir name
"/exchange/test" mode 0777
May 12 05:47:13 restricted internal-sftp[19147]: opendir "/exchange"
May 12 05:47:13 restricted internal-sftp[19147]: closedir "/exchange"
May 12 05:47:22 restricted internal-sftp[19147]: session closed for local
user restricted from [192.168.0.10]
```

The content is there; all the actions performed by the restricted user have been logged and are out of his reach. One last check here:

```
root:# grep restricted casualuser-sftp.log | wc -l
0
```

This confirms that no lines tagged as restricted are listed into the `casualuser-sftp.log`, so each user has his own log.

So, we now have a fully functional `sftp` server, along with individual jails and per user logging. There is just one nice touch left to give to our server, and this will bring us back to the old times: we are talking of a banner to display to our users. It can look like that is something not so useful or something that belongs to the past times but it is not that. When someone connects to our server must be notified that this is a private facility and no illegal action will be allowed. This is useful at least for two reasons:

- If an unauthorized user connects by mistake to our server, he has to know that he is not where he thinks he is; so we give him a chance to disconnect and no further actions will be taken.
- If an unknown user connects willfully to our server, he must be notified that he is not allowed to do so. In case he proceeds further, we will then be allowed in the future to show this as an evidence of his will to carry some illegal actions against our facility.

It can look quite simplistic, but with a banner in place, no one will be able to say *I did not know*. No, the user was notified and that matters. Since we do not want to scare our visitors, let's make a banner with a jazz using `figlet`, a utility that will apply some nice fonts to our messages ready to be displayed over a terminal. In our example, we are using Debian, so a simple `root:# apt-get install figlet` will install the utility. The default set of font is not so rich, but more can be downloaded from the site of this project at `http://www.figlet.org/fontdb.cgi`.

Let's first test what we have already installed on our system. For a Debian environment, the font files reside in `/usr/share/figlet/`, but this can differ based on the distribution used. So, to test all the fonts and see what we do like the most, a one line for loop is what we need:

```
root:# for i in $(ls -1 /usr/share/figlet/*.flf | awk -F "." '{print $1}') ; do figlet -f $i test ; echo $i ; done
```

A simple `for` loop will show us our message in all the fonts available. So, let's create a test file with our welcome banner:

```
Welcome
to our restricted
sftp server
```

Let's save it to a file named `header.txt` and pass it to `figlet stdin`:

```
root:# figlet -cf slant < header.txt > /opt/sftp/jails/sftp-banner
```

We will get something like what is shown in the following screenshot, which is nicely centered:

A simple `for` loop will show us our message in all the fonts available. Now, let's add some meaningful warning to a `footer.txt` file:

```
WARNING
This service is restricted to authorized users only. All activities on this
system are logged.
```

Let's pass this message through `figlet`:

```
root:# figlet -cf digital < footer.txt >> /opt/sftp-jails/sftp-banner
```

Since we have our banner, let's clean it up a bit:

```
root:# rm footer.txt header.txt
root:# chown root.root /opt/sftp-jails/sftp-banner
root:# chmod 500 /opt/sftp-jails/sftp-banner
```

That's all. So we try a new connection to the server, and we will get a nice welcome message like the one shown here:

Chapter 14

A nice welcome message will remind the visitors about the restriction of this sftp site.

Great, but let's say we saw a font that we like, but it is not installed. For the sake of this example, let's say we want to use the alligator font:

```
root:# figlet -cf alligator test
figlet: alligator: Unable to open font file
```

It is not installed so we cannot use it, but it is just a matter of downloading it and copying over the font directory:

```
root:# wget -P /usr/share/figlet/ http://www.figlet.org/fonts/alligator.flf
--2017-05-12 08:18:46--  http://www.figlet.org/fonts/alligator.flf
Resolving www.figlet.org (www.figlet.org)... 188.226.162.120
Connecting to www.figlet.org (www.figlet.org)|188.226.162.120|:80...
connected.
HTTP request sent, awaiting response... 200 OK
Length: 11285 (11K) [text/plain]
Saving to: '/usr/share/figlet/alligator.flf'

/usr/share/figlet/alligator.flf
```

```
100%[================================================================
====================================>] 11.02K  --.-KB/s   in 0s

2017-05-12 08:18:46 (44.3 MB/s) - '/usr/share/figlet/alligator.flf' saved
[11285/11285]
```

Now let's just give the previous command again:

```
root:# figlet -cf alligator test
```

The font is available to figlet, and so the result is what we can see in the following screenshot:

Installing a font is simply a matter of copying it in the fonts directory

So, let's have fun. Try to change and create your message in the style we prefer: a banner shall not be necessarily boring.

Summary

This is the last summary of this book and the last topic was figlet; and it was not just a coincidence. What we tried to make clear through all the chapters is that Bash is fun. Did we touch every possible topic and example? No, not at all, and this is the greatest thing of all: we have so many things to see, so many ways to bend Bash to do unthinkable tasks. Just think about something and then try the shell: in most cases a bit of imagination will find a creative way to overcome obstacles and to chuckle about what has been done. This book is named *Mastering Bash*, but no book can exhaust the massive amount of things that we can discover about this shell. So, this is not a landing point, this is just a step further, maybe higher than usual, but just a step in an ongoing journey in our favorite environment, in our beloved GNU/Linux operating system.

Index

/
/dev/tcp directory 355, 356
/dev/udp directory 355, 356

A
active checks 238
Advanced Encryption Standard (AES) 394
anonymous pipe 343
arithmetic operators
  % operator 63
  * operator 63
  ** operator 64
  + operator 62
  - operator 63
  / operator 63
  about 62
arrays 185, 186, 187, 188, 189, 190, 191, 192, 194, 195, 196, 197, 198, 199, 200
ASCII comparison operators 157
assignment operators
  %= operator 66
  *= operator 65
  ++ operators 67
  += operator 64
  -- operator 67
  -= operator 65
  /= operator 66
  about 64
associative array 187
at tool
  using 429, 430, 431, 433, 435, 438

B
background processes 328
backslash 165
Bash
  about 9, 12
  builtin commands 10
benefits, SSH
  asymmetric encryption 391
  authentication 389
  encryption 390
  integrity 390
  MD5 hashing 392
  password 390
  public key 390
  session 390
  symmetric encryption 391
bitwise operators
  about 68
  bitwise AND 71
  bitwise NOT (~) 72
  bitwise OR (|) 72
  bitwise XOR (^) 72
  left shift 68
  right shift 70
break command
  used, for exiting loop 216, 217

C
case statement
  about 169, 170, 171
  if else statements 169
  using 172, 173, 174, 175, 176, 177, 179, 180, 181, 182, 183, 184, 185
clause 170
code
  returning 241
command 243, 261
command line (CLI)
  arguments, passing 223, 225, 226, 228, 230, 232, 233, 235
command substitution 347, 348

configuration files 392
continue command
  used, for exiting loop 216, 217
coprocesses 352, 353
cron scheduler 439
cron
  about 429, 440, 441, 442
  reference link 441
crontab 443, 444, 446, 447, 449
cURLing 294

D

daemon
  about 367
  becoming 378
  trapping 378, 379, 381, 383
  using 384, 385, 386, 387
Digital Encryption Standard (DES) 394
Digital Signature Algorithm (DSA) 393
disown 374, 375
double fork 375, 376, 377

E

Elliptic Curve Digital Signature Algorithm (ECDSA) 393
emoji
  reference 304
end-of-file (eof) 373
environment variables 350, 352
escaping 165
exit codes 78

F

file
  output, redirecting 346
First In First Out (FIFO) 108, 327
flag 224
for loop 209, 210, 213
functions 200, 203, 205

G

Geopts 223
globbing 144
GNU license

reference 311

H

Hangup (HUP) 372
here document 155
here string 156

I

IDEA 394
if else statements 169
indirect referencing 205
inode numbers 102
Input/Output (I/O)
  redirecting 13, 16, 18
Inter-process Communication (IPC) 343

J

JavaScript Object Notation (JSON) 293
job controls 331, 333, 335

K

Key Derivation Function (KDF) 414
Korn 77

L

logical AND/OR operators
  using 184
logical operators
  about 74
  logical AND 75
  logical NOT (!) 74
  logical OR (||) 76
loop
  exiting, with break command 216, 217
  exiting, with continue command 216, 217

M

MAILTO 442
menu
  creating 218, 219, 221, 223
messages
  attachments 306, 310
  formatting 297, 298, 304
  formatting, reference 297

Multipurpose Internet Mail Extensions (MIME) 294

N

Nagios 237
Nagios plugin 261, 271, 275, 278
Nagios standard macros 244
named pipes 108
Netcat 357, 358, 359, 360, 363, 364, 365
nohup 368, 369, 370, 372, 373

O

OpenSSH
  reference 394, 459
  used, for restricted sftp sessions 464, 470, 479, 481
operators
  arithmetic operators 61
  assignment operators 64
  bitwise operators 68
  comma operator (,) 77
  evaluation order and precedence 78
  logical operators 74

P

parallel processing 336, 337, 340
passive checks 238
passwordless connections
  about 409
  client, configuring 418, 419, 421
  remote account, preparing 416, 418
  server, configuring 409, 410, 412, 414, 416
pipes 343, 344, 345, 346
Portable Operating System Interface (POSIX) 372
preprocessing 341
Process ID (PID) 150
process substitution 348, 349
proxies 423, 425, 427

Q

quoting 165

R

range 242
restricted sftp sessions

OpenSSH, using 464, 470, 480
restricted shell
  about 453, 456, 458
  for OpenSSH 459

S

script
  exiting 81, 83
Searchable Log of All Conversation and Knowledge (Slack)
  about 287, 288
  calls 288
  chat rooms 287
  clients 288
  direct messages 287
  integrated searches 287
  integration, with external services 288
  script, planning 310, 315, 319, 324
  teams 288
  URL 288
Self-Monitoring, Analysis, and Reporting Technology (S.M.A.R.T.) 261
Serpent 394
service definition 243, 261
Set Group ID (SGID) 27
Set User ID (SUID) 27
setsid 375, 376, 377
sha-bang
  about 21, 23
  issues, detecting 29, 31
  script, calling 23, 27
SIGnal due to TeleType INput (SIGTTIN) 328
SIGnal due to TTY OUtput (SIGTTOU) 328
Signal Hang Up (SIGHUP) 328
signals
  about 329, 331
  SIGCHILD 329
  SIGCONT 329
  SIGHUP 329
  SIGINT 329
  SIGKILL 329
  SIGQUIT 329
  SIGSEV 330
  SIGSTOP 329
  SIGTERM 329

SIGTRAP 329
SIGTSTP 329
SIGTTIN 329
SIGTTOU 330
Simple Network Monitoring Protocol (SNMP) 239
special characters
  , () case modificators 140
  ,, case modificators 140
  ^^ case modificator 140
  about 130
  array index ([]) 154
  asterisk (*) 144, 145
  backslash 142
  braces ({}) 153
  case modifiers 140
  case terminator (;&) 133
  case terminator (;;&) 133
  characters range ([]) 154
  colon character 142, 143
  comma character (,) 139
  commands, grouping 150, 151
  control characters 163
  dash character (-) 160
  delimiters 157
  dot character (.) 133, 135, 137
  double asterisk (**) 146
  double dash (--) 161
  double quotes 139, 166
  double semicolon character (;;) 132
  exclamation (!) 143
  exit status ($?) 150
  expression ([[]]) 154
  expression ([]) 154
  force redirection 158
  forward slash 142
  full path ({} ;) 153
  hash character (#) 130
  integer expression 155
  keywords 143
  logical AND 160
  logical OR (||) 159
  modulo operator 162
  operator 161
  parameter substitution (${}) 149
  pipe character (|) 157

  positional parameters ($* and $") 149
  Process ID (PID) ($$) 150
  quoted string expansion ($'...') 149
  semicolon character (;) 131
  single quotes (') 167
  single quotes ('...') 139
  substitution ($) 148
  test operators (?) 146, 148
special markers
  using, to define recurrences 447
SSH 389
ssh_config file 402, 406, 408
sshd_config file 396, 397, 399, 401
stderr 18, 21
stdin 18, 21
stdout 18, 21
subshells 328, 336, 337, 340, 341

T

test command
  about 93
  used, for testing files 94, 95, 99, 102, 105, 107, 109, 110
  used, for testing integers 112, 118
  used, for testing strings 119, 120, 123, 124
test
  conditions 125
thresholds
  about 242
  returning 241
triple DES 394
tunnels 423, 425, 427
Twofish 394

U

until loop 214, 215

V

variables
  about 32
  assigning 33
  environment variables 37, 39, 41, 44
  expansion 45, 47, 50
  name safety, maintaining 34
  pattern matching 50, 52, 54

special variables 55, 57
  substitution 33
  with limited scope 35, 37

W

Webhooks
  about 290
  incoming Webhook 290
  outgoing Webhook 290
  reference 290
What if...else 85, 90, 91, 92, 93
while loop 214, 215

Z

Zsh 77

CPSIA information can be obtained
at www.ICGtesting.com
Printed in the USA
LVHW101908101219
640063LV00008B/270/P